HIDDEN
OUT IN THE OPEN

HIDDEN OUT IN THE OPEN

SPANISH MIGRATION TO THE UNITED STATES (1875–1930)

EDITED BY
PHYLIS CANCILLA MARTINELLI
AND ANA VARELA-LAGO

UNIVERSITY PRESS OF COLORADO
Louisville

Published by University Press of Colorado
245 Century Circle, Suite 202
Louisville, Colorado 80027

 The University Press of Colorado is a proud member
of the Association of University Presses.

The University Press of Colorado is a cooperative publishing enterprise supported, in part,
by Adams State University, Colorado State University, Fort Lewis College, Metropolitan State
University of Denver, Regis University, University of Colorado, University of Northern Colorado,
University of Wyoming, Utah State University, and Western Colorado University.

∞ This paper meets the requirements of the ANSI / NISO Z39.48-1992 (Permanence of Paper).

ISBN: 978-1-60732-798-1 (cloth)
ISBN: 978-1-64642-043-8 (paper)
ISBN: 978-1-60732-799-8 (ebook)
DOI: https://doi.org/10.5876/9781607327998

Library of Congress Cataloging-in-Publication Data

Names: Martinelli, Phylis Cancilla, editor. | Varela-Lago, Ana (Ana Maria), editor.
Title: Hidden out in the open : Spanish migration to the United States (1875–1930) / edited by
  Phylis Cancilla Martinelli and Ana Varela-Lago.
Description: Boulder : University Press of Colorado, [2018] | Includes bibliographical references
  and index.
Identifiers: LCCN 2018021461 | ISBN 9781607327981 (cloth) | ISBN 9781646420438 (paper) |
  ISBN 9781607327998 (ebook)
Subjects: LCSH: Spaniards—United States—History—19th century. | Spaniards—United
  States—History—20th century. | Spaniards—United States—Ethnic identity. |
  Spaniards—Cultural assimilation—United States. | Spain—Emigration and immigration—19th
  century. | Spain—Emigration and immigration—20th century. | United States—Emigration
  and immigration—History—19th century. | United States—Emigration and
  immigration—History—20th century.
Classification: LCC E184.S7 H54 2018 | DDC 973/.0461—dc23
LC record available at https://lccn.loc.gov/2018021461

Chapter 2 is reprinted with permission and was originally published as "The Andalucía-Hawaii-
California Migration: A Study in Macrostructure and Microhistory," *Comparative Studies in Society
and History* 26, no. 2 (April 1984): 305–24. Chapter 3 is a revised version of an article originally published in *"Struggle a Hard Battle": Essays on Working-Class Immigrants*, ed. Dirk Hoerder (DeKalb:
Northern Illinois University Press, 1986), 170–98.

Cover illustrations. Top: The *Ateneo Español* in Beckley, West Virginia, photo courtesy of
Thomas Hidalgo. Bottom: Interior of a cigar factory in Tampa, Florida, photo courtesy of the
University of South Florida Library, Special Collections.

To Spanish immigrants and their descendants everywhere

CONTENTS

ILLUSTRATIONS

FIGURES

MAPS

TABLES

PREFACE AND ACKNOWLEDGMENTS

This book began as an outgrowth of previous research and out of the need to fill a gap in scholarship, but it was also shaped by the personal experiences of the editors. When Phylis C. Martinelli was writing her book *Undermining Race: Ethnic Identities in Arizona Copper Camps, 1880–1920*, she found that the growing literature on Italian and Mexican workers contrasted with the lack of research on Spanish immigrants, an important component of the workforce in the Arizona mining camps she studied. Her research led her to articles by Thomas Hidalgo and Luis Argeo on Spaniards in the coal and zinc mines of West Virginia. Social media, then in its infancy, opened the door to a thriving virtual community of Asturian Americans, descendants of immigrants from the Spanish region of Asturias in the United States.

During this time, Phylis also formed personal connections with Spain, as her son, who had traveled to Spain for language immersion studies, married a wonderful Spanish woman. Phylis's first trip to Spain was to attend the wedding, near Seville. Following the birth of her grandson, Victor, her visits to Andalusia became more regular. She also grew interested in the

Río Tinto Copper Mine in the neighboring province of Huelva, owned by a British-Australian company. Knowing of British copper interests in Arizona, she began to study the ties between the United States and Río Tinto. The result was a paper presented at the Western History Association Conference: "Spaniards: Racially In-Between Activists in Arizona Copper Towns 1900–1920," which in turn led to conversations with Darrin Pratt, of the University Press of Colorado, about the possibility of writing a book on the topic. The final product they envisioned was an edited volume on the experiences of Spanish immigrants in the United States, a subject about which there was a surprising gap in the ample and expanding scholarship on migration and ethnicity.

As Phylis approached possible contributors, she also found a coeditor. Ana Varela-Lago grew up in Galicia, a region where migration to the Americas touched most families, including hers. The legacy of this exodus still shapes the region, most visibly through a variety of public works (schools, fountains, roads) built with the support of migrants' remittances. Ana's interest in Spanish migration to the United States grew out of her personal experience when she moved to Tampa, Florida. There, she learned about the history of a Spanish immigrant community in the city dating back to the nineteenth century. One need only take a stroll through Ybor City and see the remnants of the cigar factories and the imposing clubhouses of the mutual aid societies, to appreciate the important role that the "Latin" (Cuban, Italian, Spanish) community played in the development of the city and of the state.

As a master's student in history at the University of South Florida, Ana conducted research on the history of Tampa's Spanish mutual aid societies, on the Galician immigrant community, and on the response of the Spanish community to the Spanish Civil War in Spain. She then moved to California to pursue a doctorate. At the University of California, San Diego, her research expanded to look at Spanish migration to the United States from a broader perspective. It culminated in her dissertation: "Conquerors, Immigrants, Exiles: The Spanish Diaspora in the United States (1848–1948)." Since then Ana has continued her research on the interplay of migration, imperialism, nationalism, and ethnic identity.

We have been fortunate to work with a wonderful group of scholars. We thank our contributors for their essays and for the enlightening exchanges over email that enriched our own thinking on this topic. We are grateful to

James D. Fernández, Montse Feu López, John Nieto-Phillips, and one anonymous reviewer for their close reading of the essays and for their valuable suggestions to improve the book. At the University Press of Colorado, we have enjoyed working with Darrin Pratt, Laura Furney, Charlotte Steinhardt, Beth Svinarich, and Dan Pratt. We thank them for their advice and assistance through the process. Special thanks go to Jessica d'Arbonne for her patience and encouragement as the project experienced delays due to unforeseen personal circumstances. Thank you also to Sonya Manes, whose expert copyediting has saved us from many an embarrassing mistake.

We appreciate the support of our home institutions: Saint Mary's College and Northern Arizona University. St. Mary's is a small college that encourages collaboration between faculty in different disciplines. This project allowed Phylis, a sociologist, to draw on the experience of her colleagues in the Departments of History and Modern Languages. A faculty development grant allowed her to participate in the Western History Association Conference. Ana's colleagues in the Department of History at Northern Arizona University have provided a welcoming and stimulating environment for both personal and professional growth. A summer grant from the College of Arts and Letters and funding from the Faculty Professional Development Office, the Department of History, and a CAL Dean's Research Grant have supported her research and the completion of this book.

Finally, we want to thank our families, and particularly our husbands, Philip Martinelli and James D'Emilio, for their continued love and support as we worked on this project.

HIDDEN
OUT IN THE OPEN

MAP 0.1. Map of Spain

INTRODUCTION

ANA VARELA-LAGO AND PHYLIS CANCILLA MARTINELLI

In his book *Our America: A Hispanic History of the United States*, historian Felipe Fernández-Armesto challenges the conventional narrative of American history. "Instead of looking at the making of the United States from the east," he explains, "we see what it looks like from the south, with Anglo-America injected or intruded into a Hispanic-accented account."[1] Echoing the title of Jose Martí's celebrated essay, Fernández-Armesto's volume represents an important addition to a growing body of literature that illuminates the rich and complex history of the United States, where the Anglo-Saxon heritage is one among many. As the director of the Spanish foundation that sponsored the project asserts in the foreword, this is also "a book on the presence of Spain in the history of America."[2]

Attention to the legacy of the Spanish past in the United States, building on the pioneering work of nineteenth-century scholars such as Herbert Howe Bancroft and Herbert Eugene Bolton, is not confined to the realm of academia. It also plays a significant role in the present-day interactions between the two nations, as a 2013 visit to the United States by Felipe

DOI: 10.5876/9781607327998.c000

de Borbón (then Crown Prince of Spain) and his wife illustrates. The royal tour included two of the states most associated with the Spanish presence in North America: California and Florida. In California, the delegation stopped at the Huntington Library to see the Junípero Serra exhibit, commemorating the tercentennial of the birth of the Spanish Franciscan and his role in the construction of the network of Catholic missions in California, two of which were also visited by the royal couple. In Florida, Prince Felipe observed the quincentennial of the landing of Juan Ponce de León in 1513, noting in his speech: "We cannot imagine today's United States without its Spanish legacy."[3] In 2015, a year after his proclamation as King of Spain, Felipe VI returned to Florida to commemorate the 450th anniversary of the founding of the city of Saint Augustine, the oldest European settlement in the United States, by the Asturian Pedro Menéndez de Avilés.

This book, too, examines the relations between Spain and the United States. The contributors, however, focus not on the *conquistadores* and *padres* of yore, but on more recent arrivals—Spanish immigrants who reached American shores in the late nineteenth and early twentieth centuries. Immigrants such as Salustiano Sánchez Blázquez, who as a teenager left his village in the province of Salamanca and went to Cuba to work cutting cane in the island's sugar fields. In 1920, he moved to the United States, toiling in the mines of Kentucky and Pennsylvania before settling at Niagara Falls in the early 1930s. Sánchez Blázquez's story received media attention because when he died, in 2013, he was believed to be the world's oldest living man.[4] Thousands of his compatriots followed a similar path, but their names seldom graced the pages of the newspapers.

Although research on Spanish migration to the United States has increased in recent decades, it remains in its infancy. In Spain, studies of emigration to the Americas have concentrated primarily on Latin American countries, which received the bulk of the Spanish exodus in the period of "mass migration" (1880–1930).[5] Still, in the past few years Spanish scholars have produced a number of regional studies, complementing the original work by Germán Rueda on the recent migration of Spaniards to the United States.[6] Bieito Alonso, Nancy Pérez Rey, Ana Varela-Lago, Juan Manuel Pérez, Carolina García Borrazás, and Francisco Sieiro Benedetto investigated the migration of Galicians to New York, Florida, Louisiana, and the Panama Canal.[7] Luis Argeo documented the migration of Asturians to the mines of West Virginia, and

Carlos Tarazona Grasa that of Aragonese shepherds to the American West.[8] María José García Hernandorena, Joan Frances Mira, Teresa Morell Moll, and Enric Morrió have studied the migration of Valencians to New York.[9]

In the United States, too, despite important contributions, the study of Spanish migration has lagged behind that of other communities. Basques have been the group more widely and systematically studied on both sides of the Atlantic, thanks in part to the formidable work of the Center for Basque Studies at the University of Nevada, Reno, and the support from the Basque government.[10] Yet, to Rosendo Adolfo Gómez's 1962 pathbreaking article "Spanish Immigration to the United States," we can now add a collection of journal articles, encyclopedia entries, master theses, doctoral dissertations, and video documentaries that enhance our understanding of this phenomenon.[11] The most recent addition to this list is an extraordinary collection of over 300 images of Spanish immigrants. The result of years of work and dedication by James D. Fernández and Luis Argeo, with the collaboration of local immigrant communities, this photographic archive is just one aspect of an ongoing project that seeks to recover and document the richness of the Spanish immigrant experience in the United States.[12]

Hidden Out in the Open is the first book-length study, in English, of the modern migration of Spaniards to the United States.[13] It represents an attempt to fill the gap in the research literature on this group, so intimately linked to the history of the Americas and of the United States. The essays cover a period (1875–1930) defined by the crucial transformations of the Progressive Era in the United States, and by similarly momentous changes in Spain following the Restoration of the Bourbon monarchy under Alfonso XII. These include the wars of independence in Cuba, the loss of the last remnants of the Spanish empire in 1898, and social and political mobilizations that culminated in the fall of the monarchy and the proclamation of the Second Spanish Republic in 1931. The defeat of the Republic, after the 1936 military coup that led to the Spanish Civil War and General Francisco Franco's victory in 1939, falls outside the scope of this collection. Readers interested in the response of Spanish immigrant communities in the United States to these events can consult a diverse and growing body of research on the subject.[14]

The chapters in this volume are geographically wide-ranging. They reflect the transnational nature of the Spanish diaspora in the Americas, encompassing networks that connected Spain, Cuba (and a number of Latin American countries), the United States, and American-controlled territories in Hawai'i and Panama. The diversity of locations also reveals the variety of jobs the immigrants engaged in, from construction gangs in the Panama Canal and the Florida Keys to mining crews in Arizona and West Virginia. In Hawai'i, Spaniards planted and cut cane in sugar plantations. Farming remained their main occupation as they moved from the islands to the fields and canneries of California at the turn of the twentieth century. In Brooklyn, and in Tampa, Florida, Spaniards toiled in a peculiar combination of craft and industry. In factories large and small, the sound of the *chavetas* (cigar knives) mixed with the voice of the *lectores* (readers) as workers, seated at their benches, hand-rolled high-quality Clear Havana cigars. The industry had its roots in Cuba but moved to the United States as a result of political unrest when the Cuban movement for independence gained strength during the nineteenth century.

Our selection of topics does not pretend to cover the full dimension of the Spanish immigrant experience in the United States. The very nature of this (unevenly developed) field would prevent that. As editors, our aim has been to showcase a diversity of approaches, even if all our contributors had a common focus. We also pay tribute to the pioneering work of scholars such as Beverly Lozano, Gary R. Mormino, and the late George E. Pozzetta, who in the 1980s were introducing the Spanish experience into the "mainstream" of American immigration history. While the book concentrates on a specific national group, its goal is to place the Spanish migrants in a broader context. In part, this reflects the importance of transcontinental connections rooted in the legacy of conquest and empire that defines the history of Spain in the Americas. But it also situates this migration at the intersection of worldwide trends (like the globalization of capital and labor, and technological develop-ments in transportation and communication) that shaped the period under study and that made this massive movement of population possible.

The collection opens with a chapter whose title captures the transnational nature of the Spanish migrant experience. The line "working in America and living in Spain" is based on a statement in *Windmills in Brooklyn*, Prudencio de Pereda's novel on Spanish migrants in New York.[15] It applied to the life of one of the protagonists, but also to those of many immigrants in the Spanish community in Brooklyn, where de Pereda grew up in the 1920s and 1930s. Varela-Lago's chapter explores the forging of a variety of transnational networks, from the 1870s to the 1920s. In the first section, she discusses the importance of the colonial wars in shaping the ethnic identity of Spanish communities in nineteenth-century America. While immigrants in the Spanish-speaking American republics established region-based mutual aid societies, similar attempts in the United States were perceived as divisive, not only because of the small size of the immigrant community, but also because of the challenge to Spanish unity posed by Cuban émigrés fighting for Cuban independence. Spanish immigrants favored national over regional identity in this period. They expressed this choice in the names of the clubs they established—La Nacional, Centro Español, Círculo Colón-Cervantes—as well as in a number of projects they participated in, such as the commemoration of Cervantes Day and of the Fourth Centennial of the Discovery of America, and the creation of Juntas Patrióticas (patriotic clubs) to support the Spanish Navy once war with the United States seemed imminent.

Following Spain's defeat in the Spanish-Cuban-American War, the migrants' activities to defend and vindicate the Spanish presence in the Americas continued by other means. Through the analysis of some of these initiatives—the translation to Spanish of Charles Lummis's *The Spanish Explorers*; the festivities honoring the founder of Saint Augustine; the promotion of the teaching of Spanish in the United States; and the commemoration of the Día de la Raza (Day of the [Hispanic] Race)—Varela-Lago examines the role played by Spanish migrants in the development of Hispanismo. This movement sought to promote the Spanish heritage in the United States and improve the image of Spain's imperial past, and it counted immigrants as participants and facilitators in developing the networks that brought together Hispanophiles in the United States and leaders of Americanism in Spain.

As the colonial struggles receded, and the number of Spanish migrants in the United States increased, there developed transregional and translocal networks characteristic of Spanish communities in Latin America and of a variety of immigrant groups in the United States. A fluid web of "parishes abroad" made it possible for the migrants to remain a vital presence in the life of their home communities and contributed to the preservation of strong local and regional identities. Newspaper articles, immigrant journals and memoirs, and consular reports illustrate the importance of these regional and local identities, often manifested in the names of mutual aid societies, restaurants, boardinghouses, and soccer teams, as well as in the foodways of these communities. These networks were also evident in the realm of political activism, particularly anarchism—a topic developed more fully in other chapters of the book.

Spanish anarchists were instrumental in the creation of Modern Schools (Escuelas Modernas), an enterprise that gained momentum following the execution of the founder of the movement, Francisco Ferrer, in Barcelona in 1909. In retaliation, a Spanish anarchist who had resided in Tampa assassinated the Spanish prime minister, José Canalejas—one more example of the global reach of the movement, and of the transnational networks in which most of the Spanish migrants in the United States operated. Varela-Lago also discusses a lesser-known aspect of the political webs that connected Spain and its diaspora: Spanish migrants' support of nationalist movements in their regions of origin (in particular, the Canary Islands, the Basque Country, and Catalonia). This political involvement, which, by the 1920s was increasingly critical of the monarchy of Alfonso XIII and the dictatorship of General Primo de Rivera (1923–1930), helps explain the migrants' jubilation at the news of the proclamation of the Spanish Republic in 1931, and their mobilization in its support during the Spanish Civil War.

Chapters 2 and 3, both published originally in the 1980s and since then a required point of reference for scholars of Spanish migration to the United States, illuminate important aspects of this exodus in different locales (Hawai'i, California, and Florida) and as part of different processes, which in the case of Hawai'i involved the recruitment of Spanish families to work on the islands' sugar plantations. Beverly Lozano expertly combines "macro" and "micro" perspectives as she analyzes the migration of Spaniards to Hawai'i and, later, California in the first decades of the twentieth century. While global, macro-structural trends were at work in this transfer of labor, as sugar cane planters in Hawai'i competed with other businesses in encouraging laborers to come to its shores, Lozano also pays attention to the agency of the migrants themselves, as they decided whether and how to participate in this exchange.

Reinforcing a theme that runs through this volume, Lozano's analysis highlights the importance of examining migration through a global lens that considers how conditions in the homeland contribute to and shape the experience of migrants in their host societies. One such example is the coexistence of patron-client relations and more impersonal laborer-employer relations in the Andalusian countryside. This experience, she argues, is key to understanding why most Spaniards left the plantations in Hawai'i for ranches in

California. On the surface, the agricultural tasks Spanish migrants engaged in were similar in both locales, but conditions in Hawai'i, Lozano asserts, "violated their cultural understanding of what tolerable working relations should involve."[16] In California, by contrast, the workers found a combination of free labor and the type of face-to-face interaction embodied in Spain's patron-client relationship. Wages, therefore, were not the only cause for the shift from Hawai'i to California. As Lozano explains, the migrants' agency opens a way for scholars to understand the intricacies of workers' responses to the global forces of capitalism.

The study of Spanish migration in Hawai'i also brings to light the complex interaction between capitalism, labor, ethnicity, and race. Like other immigrants, Spaniards became the "hands of America." But in the United States, they were frequently caught in a dynamic of "divide and conquer" that pitted ethnic groups against each other to the benefit of employers. As southern Europeans, Spaniards also participated in a hierarchical racial system that sometimes considered them "whites," but often placed them in between "whites" and "nonwhites." In the Panama Canal, the United States government institutionalized these racial differences through a number of practices, including a scale of wages that ranked Spaniards, as "semi-white" workers, between American citizens and (mostly black) West Indian laborers, the former being paid in the "gold" roll; the latter in the "silver" roll.[17] In Hawai'i, Lozano explains, American employers saw Spaniards as a positive counterweight to the increasingly militant Japanese workers. As "white" Europeans, they were also considered more desirable than Asians as a settler population, as they were understood to be more easily assimilable to American culture and values.

Chapter 3, by Gary R. Mormino and George E. Pozzetta, remains a classic within the literature on Spanish anarchism in the United States. It examines the transnational networks of labor militancy and anarchism that defined the identity of a good portion of the Spanish laboring classes at home and abroad. Paying close attention to the political and economic landscape in Spain and the conditions that shaped the migration of Spaniards to the Americas, the authors present an approach that was novel at the time, and a precursor of studies that challenge the definition of migration as a process of uprootedness (from home society) and assimilation (into host society), and advance a more holistic understanding of the immigrant experience.

Mormino and Pozzetta illustrate the benefits not only of a transnational approach (encompassing the networks that kept the migrants connected to communities in the homeland and in other locales), but also of a transethnic approach that emphasizes the importance of community and working-class solidarity across different ethnic and national groups. Tampa's significant role in the anti-imperial struggles in the Spanish Caribbean, and its rich multiracial and multiethnic topography (the "Latin" quarter included Italians, Cubans—white and black, and Spaniards, among others), made it an ideal setting for this innovative research.

As the authors indicate, this is a study of "group dynamics and organization."[18] The essay weaves the story of connections between Spaniards and Cubans, but also the tensions that shaped the debates over the Cuban question. While some Spanish anarchists, such as the famed Pedro Esteve, expressed little concern about Cuban independence, many did support José Martí's call to defend Cuba Libre. Immigrants' memoirs and oral histories complement the vivid narrative of the authors, as they describe the rhythm of work in Tampa's cigar factories and the role of institutions such as the reading (la lectura), a vital source of education and information for cigar workers, that helped forge a unique labor culture to which the anarchists contributed substantially. This thriving labor culture clashed not only with the American establishment, often willing to support vigilante methods to deal with "foreign radicals," but with more "mainstream" labor organizations such as Samuel Gompers's American Federation of Labor. The fear (and repression) of radicals only grew in the aftermath of World War I and the Russian Revolution. Mormino and Pozzetta use the reports from secret agents in the newly created Bureau of Investigation (precursor of the FBI) to illustrate the actions of the labor militants and of those who informed on them. The surveillance of anarchists, among others, did not prevent the assassination of the Spanish prime minister in 1912, but it did undermine the activities of the once-vibrant radical labor movement, whose last strike was, appropriately enough, to defend the lectura in the cigar factories. Later generations continued the struggle in their own way, fighting for social justice and against fascism during the Spanish Civil War.

Christopher Castañeda's chapter on the Spanish community in New York provides a valuable complement to the study of the anarchist movement in Florida and the webs that connected workers in Spain, Cuba, and the

United States in this period. As in Tampa, Spaniards in Brooklyn were also engaged primarily in the cigar industry. Castañeda describes the rich tapestry of ethnic groups involved in this industry in nineteenth-century America. He also details the difficult conditions these workers experienced, producing cigars in crowded tenement houses and falling victim to diseases such as tuberculosis. Cuban and Spanish cigar workers participated in the flowering labor movement that produced two important unions: the Cigarmakers' International Union (CMIU) and the American Federation of Labor (AFL), but, as Castañeda illustrates, they also created their own Spanish-speaking unions. Intermarriage between the two communities was relatively common, and both groups participated in the dynamic and radical labor culture reinforced by the lectura. But, as happened in Florida, the struggle for Cuban independence divided the community and contributed to the creation of separate, Cuban and *peninsular*, labor unions and ethnic associations.

Here too, an incipient anarchist movement, with links to the peninsula but also rooted in events in the United States, began to flourish. Critical of Spanish policies, many peninsular anarchists supported the Cuban movement for independence. Others joined Pedro Esteve in advocating a deeper transformation of society and politics, a belief that Esteve proclaimed in the immigrant enclaves he settled in (Brooklyn; Patterson, New Jersey; Ybor City, Tampa) and through his involvement with the Industrial Workers of the World. The execution of Spanish anarchist Francisco Ferrer in Spain contributed to the mobilization of Spanish anarchists and their supporters in the United States.

Castañeda's chapter shows the continuing relevance of the anarchist movement in the 1910s and 1920s, a period that also saw the rise of Spanish migration to the United States. While these years mark the end of an era for the craft cigar-making that had been the bedrock of Spanish anarchism in previous decades, they witness the transformation of Spanish migration to New York. Now, a high percentage of unionized dockworkers and merchant marine seamen were Spaniards. While addressing this constituency, the Spanish anarchist press and movement maintained its involvement with the broader Hispanic community in New York (including Mexicans, Cubans, and Puerto Ricans) and the larger anarchist movement. The response to the Sacco and Vanzetti case was only the best-known example of such connections.

Although the role of women in these immigrant communities tends to be less documented, it is clear from the articles by Castañeda and by Mormino and

Pozzetta that women were important participants in the anarchist movement they discuss. Both chapters highlight the work of Luisa Capetillo, a pioneering Puerto Rican lectora, activist, journalist, and feminist. Women were also crucial as sustainers of families, supporters of fundraisers, entertainers in festivals, and leaders in strikes, as illustrated by Pedro Esteve's daughter, Violetta.

The end point of Castañeda's chapter, 1925, marks the starting point of Brian Bunk's essay, chapter 5, as he introduces us to a different, if complementary, perspective on the Spanish immigrant community in New York. While chapter 4 focused primarily on immigrants as workers, and concentrated on men (reflecting the demographics of the initial wave of Spanish migration in the late nineteenth century), chapter 5 shifts our attention to a larger and more stable community in Greenwich Village, one of several Spanish enclaves in New York. Following the growth in Spanish migration in the first two decades of the twentieth century, a number of families had settled in the neighborhood by the 1920s. As Bunk illustrates, the socialization of the second generation, particularly of young Spanish American women, became an important aspect of the community's life.

Bunk's research combines attention to gender and to the performative aspects of ethnic identity. His analysis of two such performative events (a beauty pageant and a popularity contest) illuminates the intricate tapestry of identities developed by Spanish immigrants in the United States, as members of regions, nations, and a broader Hispanic community. The immigrants' social clubs, defined as "intermediate spaces" between the public and the private spheres, played a crucial role in this process of socialization, allowing young Spanish American women to experiment with certain freedoms, under the watchful eyes of the senior members of the community, in an effort to curb the ostensibly pernicious effects of Americanization. These attempts at control met with different levels of success. Bunk's essay shows that the social clubs were also arenas of contestation where women challenged the authority of the male leadership, as the dispute between the officers of the Casa de Galicia and the Spanish Ladies' Committee exemplifies.

Bunk also examines the complex cultural dynamics that defined the relations between Spanish immigrants and American society at large. Thus, he explains how young Spanish Americans' views of a Spain they had never seen may have been shaped as much by their socialization within the family and the community as by the Orientalizing images of Spain prevalent in

American popular culture in the 1920s. Likewise, he shows how concerns about the perceived isolation of the immigrant community led American reformers to carry out research to ascertain the level of assimilation among Spanish American youth, and particularly among young women. This illuminating essay provides an essential lens through which to examine important, but often neglected, aspects of the immigrant experience, such as the acculturation of the young and the enforcement of proper gender roles in the community.

Like Castañeda, Bunk concludes his chapter with a reference to the dismantling of these immigrant settlements. Urban renewal projects and the anti-immigrant legislation that reduced Spanish immigration to a trickle after 1924 contributed to the disintegration of these enclaves, replaced by more ethnically mixed neighborhoods. As Phylis Cancilla Martinelli indicates in chapter 6, this process of disintegration was not limited to urban centers. Research on the Spanish immigrant experience in Arizona is particularly challenging, as traces of some of these Spanish communities have vanished. Some, like the bustling community of Barcelona, which housed 1,000 families in the first decades of the twentieth century, were physically eliminated by open-pit mining.

Martinelli explains that Spaniards' interest in mining in the American Southwest dates back to the sixteenth century, and some of the mining and metallurgy techniques they developed were still in use in the United States until new technologies were introduced in the Progressive Era. Despite the long legacy of Spanish presence in the area, and the Spanish immigrant presence in the twentieth century, few studies have investigated their experiences. Like other chapters in this volume, this essay contributes, in Martinelli's words, to "diversify immigration history." It also engages with the historiography of this particular region, as it seeks to "'re-envision' Western history."[19]

Perhaps even more than was the case in Spanish immigrant communities in Florida, New York, Hawai'i, and California, Spaniards in Arizona were hidden under broader categories (Hispanic, Latino) that do not differentiate by national origin. Martinelli favors the terms Latin and EuroLatin to examine the interaction of Mexicans and southern Europeans (Italians and Spaniards) in this environment. The story of mining provides a fascinating narrative of the interrelationship of local, regional, national, and global labor markets. Miners from northern Spain, displaced by the success of Welsh coal, moved to southern Spain to work on Huelva's copper mines. These mines, in turn, were being developed and financed by British companies and supervised by American managers. The companies' expansion into mining areas in the American Southwest opened paths for Spanish miners to migrate to states such as Arizona. There they joined an international labor force and established connections that integrated them into new local and regional labor networks.

In this multiethnic environment, racial designations prevalent in nineteenth-century America situated Spaniards as members of an in-between group, not quite "White" but members of a "Spanish" or "Latin" race. Racial characterization had important economic consequences, as it often determined who had access to high-paying jobs. Martinelli's chapter teases out the intricate ethnic landscape of Arizona's mining towns. Racial categories were fluid and changed from place to place and even across time in one place. Immigrant groups, too, maintained their own racial and cultural preferences. Mexicans and Spaniards usually preferred to live apart but were also willing to self-identify as "Latins" when conditions called for unity. This was particularly the case at times of labor unrest, which often included workers' demands for equal pay. But, as Lozano explained in the case of Hawai'i, wages were not the only matter of contention. Martinelli states that some strikes were caused by what Latin miners perceived as lack of "respect from their Anglo supervisors."[20]

Spaniards in West Virginia also experienced the ethnic segregation and racial prejudice described by Martinelli in the Arizona camps and were derided as poor and foreign. As a scholar, and the grandson of Spaniards, Thomas Hidalgo has a privileged view of this migration. Both his maternal and paternal grandfathers migrated as young men from the same town in Andalusia in the 1920s, helped by friends who had lived in the United States for years. Their Spanish wives would later join them. The dearth of information on this community led Hidalgo to undertake his own investigation. In his chapter, he uses a sample of citizenship and immigration records together with oral histories of the children of these migrants to recover the experiences of the members of this once-vibrant immigrant community.

Hidalgo's methodical analysis of the documents of 163 Spanish immigrants to Raleigh and Fayette Counties in West Virginia shows that more than half of them hailed from the region of Andalusia, with another

30 percent coming from the northern regions of Galicia and Asturias. The reasons remembered by their descendants for this migration combined economic hardship with political discontent, whether due to the oppressive role of the Catholic Church in rural Spain, the fear of being drafted for Spain's colonial wars in Morocco, or the consequences of labor activism and mobilization. While some migrants traveled directly from Spain to the United States, most of those who eventually settled in West Virginia arrived after stays in other (primarily Latin American) countries and other states in the Union. Coal mining was not, for the most part, the original trade of these immigrants, but the expansion of the coal-mining industry, the relatively high wages it offered, and the fact that the job did not require training or the ability to speak English, contributed to its appeal. Frugal immigrants, such as Hidalgo's maternal grandfather, could save enough money to return to Spain or to provide for their families to join them in the United States. Unfortunately, labor conditions in the mines were such that accidents, resulting in serious injuries and death, were commonplace. When unions began to organize in the coal mines in the 1930s, many Spanish immigrants joined, and some took leadership positions.

Hidalgo's oral histories bring to life the process of identity formation within the community, through the maintenance of the Spanish language (of obligatory use at home) and foodways, as well as the traditions associated with wine making and the *matanza* (butchering of hogs to make ham and sausages). In an interesting syncretism of the American and European festival calendar, Spaniards used Thanksgiving to do the matanza, a festival associated in many European countries with the feast of Saint Martin, also in November. These cultural traditions, the connections to Spain through the networks of return migration, and the creation of mutual aid societies such as the Ateneo Español, strengthened this ethnic identity. But, as Hidalgo indicated, World War II would contribute to the decline of the tight-knit community. The history of its past, however, still comes alive in the reminiscences of the immigrants' children and grandchildren. Hidalgo's work represents a valuable strand in migration studies, as it both contributes to the recovery of these memories and to its dissemination. As an educator, he used his research on the Spanish community as a model to design a multicultural curriculum that would illuminate the complex networks that linked together the people of West Virginia, of the United States, and of the world.

The last chapter in the collection shifts the lenses and focuses on what the migration of Spaniards meant to the Spanish state. In chapter 8, Ana Varela-Lago studies the response of the Spanish state to the recruitment of Spaniards to work in territories that were becoming outposts of an emerging American empire in the years following Spain's defeat in the Spanish-Cuban-American war. Cuban independence did not curtail Spanish migration to the island. In fact, Spanish workers contributed to building Cuba's infrastructure as the United States military government embarked on a campaign of economic development that included considerable investment in transportation and public works. It was in Cuba where American agents first appreciated the quality of Spanish labor. That realization drove the systematic efforts to recruit Spaniards to work in the Panama Canal and the sugar plantations in Hawai'i. This recruitment, in turn, fueled the debates over emigration in Spain at the time.

Spaniards had migrated to the Americas for generations, but this exodus had often been couched in the familiar language of the Spanish conquest. In this narrative, the migrants were heirs to the intrepid spirit of the original *conquistadores*. The deliberate recruitment of Spaniards by American companies as instruments of American expansion in the aftermath of 1898 had a sobering effect on the Spanish psyche. Coming on the heels of the loss of its last Caribbean colonies, it highlighted the country's difficulties as it struggled to compete in the modern world. It also underlined the subservience of Spain to its former foe. As the Spanish prime minister aptly put it, using a physical metaphor, Spain was now the hands to the American head.

The harsh conditions that prevailed in this labor recruitment prompted the Spanish Parliament to adopt legislation to protect the migrants and, sometimes, ban the recruitment altogether. More challenging perhaps was the task of protecting the thousands of Spaniards who migrated to the United States in the 1910s and 1920s. As Varela-Lago shows, the consular system was ill suited to face the challenges of a population dispersed across such a vast territory. Lack of embassies and consulates, poor preparation of consular officials (who could not always speak English), lack of resources to furnish consular offices, and low salaries defined the unenviable position of the consuls and did not contribute to fostering a good relationship between them and the migrants they were supposed to serve. World War I added to the difficulty of the situation, as an overstretched embassy had to defend Spanish citizens from being illegally drafted to serve in the American army (in violation of Spain's neutrality and the 1902 Treaty of Friendship between the two countries).

The anti-immigrant legislation that followed World War I practically stopped the migration of Spaniards to the United States. While the Spanish state did not lament this, the outcome did affect the Spanish communities already established in the country, as their numbers rapidly dwindled. For those who remained, the 1930s would offer a different set of challenges. Franco's victory in the Spanish Civil War persuaded many migrants to cut ties with their homeland. Some determined not to return until democracy was restored in Spain—it turned out to be a very long wait.

As we mentioned before, this selection of chapters does not (and could not) exhaust the possible range of topics. We do hope that with its varied themes and approaches this volume begins to fill the gap in our knowledge of the Spanish immigrant experience in the United States and encourages further research on the diversity and complexity of this experience.

NOTES

1. Felipe Fernández-Armesto, *Our America: A Hispanic History of the United States* (New York: W. W. Norton and Company, 2013), xxviii.

2. Fernández-Armesto, *Our America*, xiv.

3. "Spanish royalty in Miami to celebrate 500-year link to Florida," *Miami Herald*, November 18, 2013; "No podemos imaginar el Estados Unidos de hoy sin el legado español," *El País*, November 19, 2013. The visit was covered by the press in both countries. See, for example, "Los príncipes de Asturias visitan California y Florida," *El País*, November 13, 2013; "Prince Felipe, Princess Letizia of Spain visit the Huntington," *Pasadena Star-News*, November 17, 2013. When Spanish prime minister Mariano Rajoy visited the White House in January 2014, he offered President Barack Obama three facsimiles of documents from the sixteenth century that highlighted the Spanish connection to the Americas and another important quincentennial: a *mapamundi*, the biography of Vasco Núñez de Balboa, and his letter to King Ferdinand relating the discovery of the Pacific Ocean.

4. "Salustiano Sánchez, el hombre más viejo del mundo," *El País*, September 16, 2013; "World's Oldest Man Dies at 112," *Buffalo News*, September 14, 2013.

5. See, for example, Nicolás Sánchez-Albornoz, ed. *Españoles hacia América: La emigración en masa, 1880–1930* (Madrid: Alianza Editorial, 1988).

6. Germán Rueda, *La emigración contemporánea de españoles a Estados Unidos, 1820–1950: De "Dons" a "Místers"* (Madrid: Mapfre, 1993); Germán Rueda Hernánz, "Vida y desventuras de ocho mil españoles en Hawai durante las primeras décadas del siglo XX," *Revista de Historia Contemporánea* 3 (Diciembre 1984): 125–42.

7. Bieito Alonso, *Obreiros alén mar: Mariñeiros, fogoneiros e anarquistas galegos en New York* (Vigo: A Nosa Terra, 2006); Nancy Pérez Rey, "Unha achega á emigración galega a Nova York," *Estudos Migratorios* 1, no. 2 (2008): 31–61; Ana Varela-Lago, "La emigración gallega a los Estados Unidos: La colonia gallega de Tampa, Florida," in *Proceedings of the 4th International Conference on Galician Studies*, ed. Benigno Fernández Salgado (Oxford: Centre for Galician Studies, 1997), 431–49; Ana Varela-Lago, "A emigración galega aos Estados Unidos: Galegos en Louisiana, Florida e Nova York (1870–1940)," *Estudos Migratorios* 1, no. 2 (2008): 63–84; Juan Manuel Pérez, *Pro Mundi Beneficio: Los trabajadores gallegos en la construcción del canal de Panamá, 1904–1914* (A Coruña: Fundación Pedro Barrié de la Maza, 2007); Carolina García Borrazás and Francisco Sieiro Benedetto, *Galicia en Panamá: Historia de una emigración* (Santiago de Compostela: C. García, 2011); see also Germán Rueda Hernánz and Carmen González López-Briones, "Los gallegos entre los españoles de Estados Unidos," in *VIII Xornadas de Historia de Galicia: Cuestións de Historia Galega*, ed. Jesús de Juana and Xavier Castro (Ourense: Servicio de Publicacións da Deputación Provincial de Ourense, 1995), 103–76.

8. Luis Argeo, "Asturian West Virginia," *Goldenseal* 35, no. 3 (Fall 2009): 14–18. See also his documentary *AsturianUS* (n.p.: Neutral Density Films, 2006); *Borregueros, Aragoneses en el Oeste Americano*, directed by Carlos Tarazona Grasa, DVD (n.p.: 2008); Carlos Tarazona Grasa, *Borregueros: Desde Aragón al Oeste Americano* (Barbastro: Gráficas Barbastro, 2017).

9. María José García Hernandorena, "Una aventura americana: Carletins als Estats Units d'Amèrica," *Carletins* 1 (2013): 50–55; Pepa García Hernandorena, "Recovered Memory: The Use of Biographic Stories in the Second and Third Generation of Valencian Emigrants to the United States of America in the Early 20th Century," *Catalan Social Sciences Review* 6 (2016): 65–78; Joan Frances Mira, "La migración valenciana al área de Nueva York," in *Los valencianos en América: Jornadas sobre la emigración*, ed. Torcuato Pérez de Guzmán (Valencia: Generalitat Valenciana, 1993), 109–14; Teresa Morell Moll, *Valencians a Nova York: El cas de la marina Alta (1912–1920)* (La Pobla Llarga: Edicions 96, 2012); Enric Morrió, "Binillobers als Estats Units d'Amèrica," *Alberri* 24 (2014): 213–61. Juli Esteve has also written several documentaries on this migration in a series entitled *Del Montgó a Manhattan: Valencians a Nova York*.

10. A complete catalogue of the publications on Basque migration produced by the Center for Basque Studies at the University of Nevada, Reno, can be found

at the William A. Douglas Center for Basque Studies, last accessed May 6, 2016, https://www.unr.edu/basque-studies/cbs-press.

11. R. A. Gómez, "Spanish Immigration to the United States," *Americas* 19 (July 1962): 59–78. See, for example, Brian Bunk, "When the Bounding Basque Met the Brown Bomber: Race and Ethnicity in World Boxing before the Second World War," *Sport in Society* 11, no. 6 (2008): 643–56; Brian Bunk, "Boxer in New York: Spaniards, Puerto Ricans, and Attempts to Construct a Hispano Race," *Journal of American Ethnic History* 35, no. 4 (2016): 32–58; Christopher J. Castañeda, "Times of Propaganda and Struggle: *El Despertar* and Brooklyn's Spanish Anarchists (1890–1905)," in *Radical Gotham. Anarchism in New York City from Schwab's Saloon to Occupy Wall Street*, ed. Tom Goyens (Urbana: University of Illinois Press, 2017), 77–99; James D. Fernández, "The Discovery of Spain in New York, circa 1930," in *Nueva York, 1613–1945*, ed. Edward Sullivan (New York: New York Historical Society, 2010), 216–33; Suronda González, "Talking Like My Grandmothers: Spanish Immigrant Women in Spelter, West Virginia" (master's thesis, West Virginia University, 1991); Suronda González, "Forging Their Place in Appalachia: Spanish Immigrants in Spelter, West Virginia," *Journal of Appalachian Studies* 5, no. 2 (1999): 197–206; Julie Greene, "Spaniards on the Silver Roll: Labor Troubles and Liminality in the Panama Canal Zone," *International Labor and Working-Class History* 66 (Fall 2004): 78–98; Thomas G. Hidalgo, "Reconstructing a History of Spanish Immigrants in West Virginia: Implications for Multicultural Education" (PhD diss., University of Massachusetts, Amherst, 1999); Thomas Hidalgo, "*En las Montañas*: Spaniards in Southern West Virginia," *Goldenseal* 27, no. 4 (Winter 2001): 52–59; *Weaving with Spanish Threads*, directed by Eve A. Ma, DVD (Berkeley, CA: Palomino Productions, 2006); Phylis Cancilla Martinelli, *Undermining Race: Ethnic Identities in Arizona Copper Camps, 1880–1920* (Tucson: University of Arizona Press, 2009); Gary R. Mormino and George E. Pozzetta, *The Immigrant World of Ybor City: Italians and Their Latin Neighbors in Tampa, 1885–1985* (Urbana: University of Illinois Press, 1987); Carol L. Schmid, "Spanish and Spanish Americans, 1870–1940," in *Immigrants in American History: Arrival, Adaption, and Integration*, ed. Elliott R. Barkan (Santa Barbara, CA: ABC-CLIO, 2013), 2: 623–27; Ana Varela-Lago, "From Patriotism to Mutualism: The Early Years of the Centro Español de Tampa, 1891–1903," *Tampa Bay History* 15, no. 2 (1993): 5–23; Ana Varela-Lago, "Conquerors, Immigrants, Exiles: The Spanish Diaspora in the United States (1848–1948)" (PhD diss., University of California, San Diego, 2008).

12. James D. Fernández and Luis Argeo, *Invisible Immigrants: Spaniards in the US (1868–1945)* (New York: White Stone Ridge, 2014). For more information on this project, see "Spanish Immigrants in the United States," accessed April 16, 2018, https://tracesofspainintheus.org.

13. As mentioned in note 10, this statement does not include research on the Basque diaspora, which has its own long and distinguished bibliography.

14. A selection of these titles includes James D. Fernández, "Nueva York: The Spanish-Speaking Community Responds," in *Facing Fascism: New York & The Spanish Civil War*, ed. Peter N. Carroll and James D. Fernández (New York: New York University Press, 2007), 84–91; Montserrat Feu-López, "*España Libre* (1939–1977) and the Spanish Exile Community in New York" (PhD diss., University of Houston, 2011); Emilio González López (with Amado Ricón), *Castelao, Propagandista da República en Norteamérica* (A Coruña: Ediciós do Castro, 2000); Marta Rey García, *Stars for Spain: La guerra civil española en los Estados Unidos* (A Coruña: Ediciós do Castro, 1997); Marta Rey García, "Los españoles de los Estados Unidos y la Guerra Civil (1936–1939)," *REDEN* 7 (1994): 107–20; Lisa Tignor, "*La Colonia Latina*: The Response of Tampa's Immigrant Community to the Spanish Civil War," *Tampa Bay History* 12, no. 1 (1990): 19–28; Ana Varela-Lago, "¡No Pasarán! The Spanish Civil War's Impact on Tampa's Latin Community, 1936–1939," *Tampa Bay History* 19, no. 2 (1997): 5–35 (the Spanish Civil War Oral History Project, at the Library of the University of South Florida, Tampa, documents the response of the Tampa Spanish community to the conflict: http://www.lib.usf.edu/special-collections/florida-studies/ybor-city-west-tampa); Ana Varela-Lago, "From Migrants to Exiles: The Spanish Civil War and the Spanish Immigrant Communities in the United States," *Camino Real* 7, no. 10 (2015): 111–28.

15. Prudencio de Pereda, *Windmills in Brooklyn* (New York: Atheneum, 1960), 49.

16. See Beverly Lozano, "The Andalucía-Hawaii-California Migration: A Study in Macrostructure and Microhistory," *Comparative Studies in Society and History* 26, no. 2 (April 1984): 305–24 (chapter 2 in this volume), 81.

17. For a discussion of this system, see Julie Greene, "Spaniards on the Silver Roll: Labor Troubles and Liminality in the Panama Canal Zone," *International Labor and Working-Class History* 66 (Fall 2004): 78–98.

18. See Gary R. Mormino and George E. Pozzetta, "Spanish Anarchism in Tampa, Florida, 1886–1931" (chapter 3 in this volume), 91.

19. See Phylis Cancilla Martinelli, "Miners from Spain to Arizona Copper Camps, 1880–1930" (chapter 6 in this volume), 207.

20. See Martinelli, "Miners from Spain" (chapter 6 in this volume), 235.

1

WORKING IN AMERICA AND LIVING IN SPAIN

The Making of Transnational Communities among Spanish Immigrants in the United States

ANA VARELA-LAGO

In *Windmills in Brooklyn*, a novel about Spanish immigrants in New York, Prudencio de Pereda writes of one of his protagonists: "Agapito was a Spaniard and he lived in Spain. America was the place he worked in."[1] Agapito López had left his native Galicia in the early twentieth century drawn by the tales of the Americanos (wealthy returnees from America). On the ship to New York, he heard about the Spanish mutual aid society in Brooklyn. With the help of this society he found a room in a Spanish boardinghouse in Brooklyn Heights and began his training as a cigar salesman. Two years later, he had saved enough money to return to his village and marry his sweetheart, who remained in Spain. He would repeat the journey several times to visit his wife and attend the birth of his five children. But, his dream of retiring in Galicia was shattered by the Spanish Civil War. When the conflict started, he moved his family to the United States, never to return to Spain.

While Agapito is a fictional character, his life illustrates a path familiar to many Spanish immigrants in the United States. Like Agapito, thousands of these migrants came from Galicia, the northwestern corner of Spain, for centuries a

DOI: 10.5876/9781607327998.c001

leading area of emigration to the Americas.[2] Whether they eventually returned to Spain or settled in the United States, these migrants contributed to building a range of transnational networks that kept these worlds connected and that were, in turn, transformed by the military coup that started the Spanish Civil War in 1936. This chapter examines the development of a number of such networks. It begins in the late nineteenth century, as colonial wars in Cuba and American expansionism contributed to a heightened sense of *españolismo* (Spanishness) among Spanish immigrants. The defense of Spain and its role in the colonization of the Americas that this españolismo entailed would continue in the twentieth century, in more favorable conditions, under the mantle of Hispanismo.[3] The first two decades of the twentieth century, the period of "mass" migration of Spaniards to the United States, saw the blooming of a number of networks based not only on national identities, but on regional and local identities as well. These will be discussed in the second part of the chapter. The third part will focus more specifically on transnational political networks, such as those established by the anarchist movement and the nationalist movements in Catalonia and the Basque Country. While not exhaustive in its coverage of transnational networks and identities among these immigrants, the chapter seeks to illustrate their richness and variety, and to integrate the study of these communities within the scholarship of migration both in the United States and Spain, as well as the broader study of diasporas and transnationalism worldwide.

"TO AVOID AN EXHIBITION OF PROVINCIALISM IN A FOREIGN LAND": SPANISH IMMIGRANTS AND THE COLONIAL WARS IN CUBA

The statement quoted above appeared in the April 1879 issue of *La Llumanera de Nova York,* a Catalan monthly magazine that began publication in New York in 1874. It was inserted in an article titled "Societat Coral Espanyola de Nova York" (Spanish Choral Society of New York), which recorded the meeting of the newly created Catalan Choral Society of New York. The report stated that the first action of the society's governing body, following the approval of the bylaws, had been to change the name from "Catalan" to "Spanish." The reason for this modification was to more accurately reflect the membership of the organization, since not all of its members hailed from Catalonia, but also, and perhaps more important, "to avoid an exhibition of provincialism in a foreign land."[4]

While Spanish immigrants in the United States shunned "provincialism," those in Spanish-speaking America embraced it. The 1870s and 1880s witnessed the emergence of a number of region-based mutual aid societies created by Spanish immigrants. These included the Laurak Bat (Basque Club) in Buenos Aires (1878), Centros Gallegos (Galician Clubs) in Buenos Aires and Montevideo (both founded in 1879), and the Centre Català (Catalan Club) in Buenos Aires (1886), besides several similar organizations in Cuba, at the time a Spanish overseas province.[5]

Demographics may help explain this different approach to region-based associations in North and South America, as the Spanish immigrant population in the former Spanish colonies was significantly larger than that in the United States. In 1869, for example, the census of the city of Buenos Aires recorded 14,609 Spaniards. This was three times the number of Spaniards residing in the entire United States according to the 1880 census (5,121).[6] Besides the smaller size of the immigrant community, another important factor contributed to the appeal of "national" versus region-based associations in the United States: the colonial wars in Cuba. The Pact of Zanjón ended the Ten Years' War (1868–78) on the island, but some Cuban leaders, such as Calixto García, rejected the treaty and pledged to continue the fight. García found support among the Cuban émigré community of New York to organize the Comité Revolucionario Cubano (Cuban Revolutionary Committee) and launch another offensive, La Guerra Chiquita (The Little War), in 1879. Although the insurrection failed, the nationalist movement gained strength in the 1880s and 1890s under the leadership of José Martí with the support of Cuban cigar workers in New York and Florida.[7]

The activities of Cuban patriots, and American support for the cause of Free Cuba, were crucial to the decision of Spanish immigrants in the United States to downplay regional identities in favor of a national one, as was the case of the Spanish Choral Society of New York. In 1868, Spanish immigrants in Brooklyn named their mutual aid society La Nacional. In Tampa, Florida, in 1891, they established the Centro Español.[8] Articles in *Las Novedades*, New York's preeminent Spanish newspaper at the time, hailed the Centro's clubhouse as a monument to the unity and patriotism of the Spaniards, as well as a valuable tool "to counteract the negative propaganda of those who want to see us hated by the North Americans."[9] The clubhouse's inauguration, in 1892, the fourth centennial of the "discovery" of America, offered an ideal opportunity for Spanish immigrants to highlight Spain's long-standing history in the continent. As one Tampa correspondent put it: "in this year of glorious commemorations for our beloved fatherland, it seems as if her children stand up like giants to show that the descendants of those heroes, that after four hundred years remain the admiration of the world, have not degenerated."[10]

In the last decades of the nineteenth century, Spanish immigrant elites, particularly in New York, led and participated in a number of patriotic initiatives that celebrated Spain's imperial past and defended her rightful place as a colonial power among modern nations. *La Llumanera* and *Las Novedades* exemplify the nature of this participation. Supported by immigrant commercial elites, these publications were established in the mid-1870s, as the United States prepared to celebrate its Centennial. The editors of both periodicals, Arturo Cuyás and José G. García respectively, embraced the 1876 Philadelphia Centennial Exhibition as an opportunity to strengthen commercial relations between Spain and the Americas and to showcase Spain to the world.[11] Cuyás and García also helped organize the festivities of Cervantes Day, honoring the famed author of *Don Quixote* (figure 1.1), in New York in the 1870s.[12] In fact, the United States was the first country, outside of Spain, where the idea of building a monument to Cervantes took hold (figure 1.2). Although the projected statue to Cervantes in Central Park never materialized, the funds collected by Spanish immigrants in New York in the 1870s ended up in Spain four decades later, when Cuyás donated them to the committee in charge of building a monument to the writer in Madrid's Plaza de España.[13]

The United States was also the first country outside of Spain to have an Ibero-American club, a project launched in Madrid by the Unión Iberoamericana (Ibero-American Union) to strengthen the relations between Spain and the American Republics and coordinate the commemoration of the Columbian voyages in 1892. Arturo Baldasano, the Spanish consul in New Orleans and a member of the Unión, was the force behind the founding of the Centro Español e Hispanoamericano (Spanish and Hispanic-American Club) in the city in 1884. In 1885, the Centro hosted the first meeting in the United States to plan the Columbian Centennial. As consul general in New York, Baldasano was also instrumental in the establishment of the Círculo Colón-Cervantes (Columbus-Cervantes Club) there in 1891. The club's name emphasized the connection between the "discovery" and the colonization

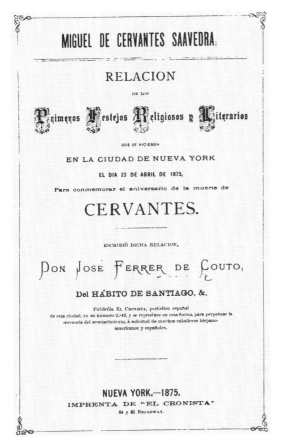

FIGURE 1.1. Booklet commemorating the anniversary of the death of Miguel de Cervantes in New York in 1875. Spanish immigrant elites in the United States sought to emphasize the unity of the Hispanic family in the midst of colonial wars for Cuban independence.

of the Americas by Spain. Through the Círculo, the Spanish elites took an active role in the celebration of the Columbian Centennial in New York and in the World's Columbian Exposition in Chicago the following year. The Chicago celebrations included the visit of Columbus's Spanish descendant, the Duke of Veragua, and of the Infanta Eulalia, representing the Spanish royal house. Eulalia, the aunt of the Spanish monarch, was the first member of the Spanish royal family ever to visit the American continent.[14]

These performances of Hispanismo did not deter Cuban patriots from continuing their fight for a free Cuba. As a new war for independence started on the island in 1895, Spanish immigrants followed events and supported their country in a variety of ways. In Tampa, where Cuban cigar workers

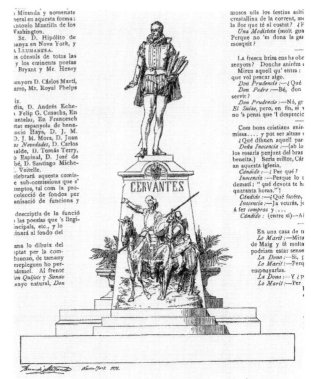

FIGURE I.2. Model of the statue honoring Cervantes that Spanish immigrants planned to donate to the city of New York to place in Central Park. Source: *La Llumanera de Nova York*, June 1878.

contributed thousands of dollars weekly to the war effort, the Centro Español sponsored a collection to aid wounded Spanish soldiers returning to the peninsula from Cuba and the Philippines. In August 1896, the Centro called on the Spanish community to support a Comité Patriótico (Patriotic Committee) whose purpose was to collect funds to finance the construction of warships for the Spanish Navy.[15] This initiative originated in the Spanish community in Mexico, but it soon found echo among Spanish communities across the Americas. José García and Arturo Cuyás joined New York's Comité Patriótico. While García used the pages of *Las Novedades* to rally support for Spain, Cuyás, author of a popular English-Spanish dictionary, put his linguistic skills to the service of the Spanish government. He published a laudatory historical study of Spanish colonialism in America and translated to English the most recent Spanish legislation granting autonomy to Cuba and Puerto Rico to make it available to the American public and legislators.[16] As head of the Associated Spanish and Cuban Press, Cuyás also penned letters to American newspapers taking issue with their interpretation of events in Cuba and offering the Spanish perspective.[17] In 1897, Spaniards in Tampa and New York organized funeral masses in honor of Antonio Cánovas del Castillo, the Spanish prime minister assassinated by an anarchist.[18] Their support for the motherland, however, became more problematic once the United States declared war on Spain in 1898, in the aftermath of the explosion of the battleship *Maine* in Havana harbor. When the two countries broke diplomatic relations, hundreds of Spaniards left the United States. Cuyás and García fled to Canada, fearing persecution in the United States as Spanish spies.[19]

"SPAIN, MOTHER OF AMERICA": THE TRANSNATIONAL NETWORKS OF HISPANISMO

José García returned to New York after the war, resuming publication of *Las Novedades* in 1899. As he explained to his readers, the paper was to shed the "exclusivist character" that had characterized it in the previous years, as it aimed to become an organ of Hispanismo, "applauding and encouraging the progress of all nations of Spanish origin."[20] Arturo Cuyás returned to Spain, eventually settling in Madrid, where he also participated in the transnational networks of Hispanismo that developed in the aftermath of the Spanish-Cuban-American War. As editor of *El Hogar Español* (The Spanish Home), the monthly publication of the housing cooperative of the same name, he often wrote (and often in laudatory terms) of developments in the United States.[21] Cuyás also wrote an advice column for adolescents and reported on the activities of the Exploradores Españoles (Spanish explorers), the Spanish branch of the Boy Scouts, which he helped found in Madrid in 1912.[22]

His best-known work, *Hace falta un muchacho*, published in 1913, was inspired by the book of the same title (*Boy Wanted*) by American author Nixon Waterman. In fact, Cuyás was one of the pioneers in Spain of the self-improvement literature for adolescents already popular in the United States.[23] The book illustrates Cuyás's complex relationship with the United States. In the introduction, he speaks of his "deep love for the Fatherland, proven with actions as well as with words, in defense of her interests, in enemy country, and under critical circumstances," a reference to his activities in the United States during the Spanish-Cuban-American War.[24] At the same time, he praises American patriotism and tells his young Spanish readers about the pledge of allegiance that started the day in New York's public schools.

Since Spain lacked a written national anthem that children could memorize, Cuyás composed his own "greeting to the flag." The five-verse poem was meant to remind Spanish youth of the golden age of Spain's imperial past. One of the stanzas read: "You [the Spanish flag] traveled triumphantly the entire globe / . . . / and under your shadow grew the fruitful seed / of the Spanish presence in half the world." The final verse connected the imperial legacy to the present and future generations: "We eagerly turn our eyes to you / searching for the lighthouse that points to the harbor / because as long as your red flashes continue to shine / the ship will not lose the course / that leads us to a glorious future / even greater than our glorious past."[25]

It was in this book that Cuyás first introduced young Spaniards to the work of another American author, Charles Lummis, an ardent Hispanist. Cuyás had read Lummis's *The Spanish Pioneers* (figure 1.3) soon after its publication in 1893, and he had used the book's positive portrayal of Spanish colonization in America as supporting evidence in his own 1897 publication defending Spanish rule in Cuba.[26] In 1916, with the backing of fellow Spanish emigrants, Eusebio Molera and Juan Cebrián, Cuyás translated Lummis's book into Spanish.

Like Cuyás, Molera and Cebrián, Spanish engineers who had settled in California in 1870, not only embraced but actively participated in the wave of Hispanophilia that swept the United States at the turn of the twentieth century. Historians have analyzed this American discovery of Spain, and the cultural appropriation of the Spanish past that it entailed, as important elements in the refashioning of the United States as an imperial power.[27] Here I argue that they also played an important role in the refashioning of Spain's national identity in the aftermath of 1898, and that Spanish immigrant elites were instrumental in this process.

Eusebio Molera, a Catalan, was one of the leading organizers of the 1909 Portolá Festival, commemorating the discovery of San Francisco Bay by Gaspar de Portolá in 1769. He also translated the log of the *San Carlos*, the first ship to enter the bay of San Francisco, and contributed to the erection of a statue of Fray Junípero Serra in Golden Gate Park.[28] In his visits to Spain, Molera would lecture on the California Missions; he was also involved in a number of cultural initiatives in his native Vic, in central Catalonia.[29] It was in one of these trips, as emissary of the San Francisco committee to invite

LOS

EXPLORADORES ESPAÑOLES

DEL SIGLO XVI

VINDICACIÓN DE LA ACCIÓN COLO-
NIZADORA ESPAÑOLA EN AMÉRICA

OBRA ESCRITA EN INGLÉS POR
CHARLES F. LUMMIS
VERSIÓN CASTELLANA CON DATOS
BIOGRÁFICOS DEL AUTOR POR
ARTURO CUYÁS
PRÓLOGO DE
RAFAEL ALTAMIRA
CATEDRÁTICO DE HISTORIA DE LAS INSTITUCIONES DE AMÉRICA
EN LA UNIVERSIDAD DE MADRID

Editado por Ramón de S. N. ARALUCE
CALLE DE CORTES, NÚM. 392 :: BARCELONA
1916

FIGURE 1.3. First
Spanish edition of
Charles Lummis's
Spanish Pioneers.

the Spanish government to participate in the Panama-Pacific International
Exposition, that he presented Lummis's *The Spanish Pioneers* as a gift to king
Alfonso XIII. It was probably then that arrangements were made with Cuyás
to publish a Spanish translation.

The first edition of *Los exploradores españoles del siglo XVI* (The Spanish
Explorers of the Sixteenth Century), as the volume was titled, appeared in
Barcelona in 1916.[30] Its subtitle, *Vindicación de la acción colonizadora española
en América* (Vindication of the Spanish colonization of America) announced
its positive portrayal of Spain's imperial past. A prologue by Spanish historian Rafael Altamira, a renowned *Americanista,* elaborated on the address

Altamira had delivered at the meeting of the American Historical Association in San Francisco, where he had compared the Spanish exploration and colonization of America to the American conquest of the West. "A common fund of moral qualities . . . endurance in suffering, serenity in danger, energy in strife, force in struggle, and valor in difficulties," he explained to his American audience, "made possible among you the epic of the West . . . and shone with remarkable luster among our discoverers and conquerors."[31]

Like Lummis, Altamira saw *Los exploradores españoles* as a much-needed addition to the dearth of textbooks dealing with this period both in Spain and in the United States. It served also as an excellent complement to the recent book written by Spanish author Julián Juderías, a defense of Spain against the *leyenda negra* (black legend).[32] Juan Cebrián agreed. He funded the publication of a new edition of Juderías's book (25,000 copies), and he offered 500 copies, free of charge, to the first government in Spanish-speaking America that would establish these two books as textbooks in the country's schools.[33] Cebrián also financed the distribution and publication of Lummis's book in Spain, and distributed more than 40,000 copies of the English version in the United States, Canada, and England.[34] In 1928, already on his deathbed, Lummis worked on a new edition of the *Spanish Pioneers*, to which he added a section on the California missions. Cebrián funded the printing of this edition as well (figure 1.4).[35] In Spain, a "National Edition" of *Los exploradores españoles* appeared in 1930, with a prologue by General Primo de Rivera, the Spanish ruler who had made Hispanismo one of the cornerstones of his dictatorship.[36]

In Florida, too, Anglo-Americans and Spanish immigrant elites collaborated in the celebration of a shared past. One of the first projects of the Florida State Historical Society, founded in 1921, was to send experts to the Archivo de Indias (Archive of the Indies) in Seville to obtain copies of all the documents pertaining to Spanish Florida. The state also held annual lavish parades and festivals commemorating an array of Spanish explorers: Ponce de León, Hernando de Soto, and Pedro Menéndez de Avilés, the founder of Saint Augustine. In 1924, the Asturian city of Avilés honored its most illustrious son by transferring his remains from a humble niche in the church of San Nicolás, where they had lain since 1591, to a sumptuous funeral monument in the same church. A delegation from Florida attended the ceremony. It included Angel L. Cuesta, a prominent Spanish cigar manufacturer from Tampa, and Miguel de Zárraga, the editor of *La Tribuna*, a Spanish weekly

FIGURE 1.4. Juan C. Cebrián donated copies of Lummis's book to a number of institutions, including the University of California.

published in New York, and a correspondent for several Spanish newspapers, including the conservative Madrid daily *ABC*. In one of his reports on the festivities, Zárraga proudly stated that America was "a prolongation of Spain" and the American delegates "the direct and legitimate descendants of the glorious Spanish explorers of the sixteenth century."[37] The city of Avilés donated Menéndez's old coffin to Saint Augustine. After many vicissitudes, it now rests at the Mission Nombre de Dios Museum.[38]

Language, together with history, formed another important pillar of the Hispanista movement that fueled these transatlantic connections. Spanish, already a popular language in parts of the United States, experienced a boom following the outbreak of war in Europe in 1914.[39] In 1916, the tercentenary of the death of Miguel de Cervantes, Eusebio Molera and Juan Cebrián donated a monument to the Spanish author to the city of San Francisco.[40] Cebrián also gifted a bust of Cervantes to the library of the University of California at Berkeley, the repository of an extensive collection of books on Spain and Spanish America, many of which had been donated by Cebrián himself.[41] Together with American Hispanist Archer Huntington, the founder of the Hispanic Society of America, Cebrián was instrumental in the establishment of the American Association of Teachers of Spanish in October 1916. A year later, the association published the first issue of its journal, *Hispania*, whose editor was the renowned folklorist and Stanford professor Aurelio M. Espinosa.[42] In 1918, Cebrián contributed to the foundation of the *Hispanic American Historical Review*.[43] The journal counted among its collaborators prestigious Spanish scholars, such as Ramón Menéndez Pidal, Américo Castro, Tomás Navarro Tomás, and Federico de Onís. The latter, hired by Columbia University in 1916 to teach Spanish literature and philology, helped establish the Hispanic Institute (Instituto de las Españas) there in 1920.[44] At the same time, American teachers and students of Spanish visited Spain through the popular *cursos de verano para extranjeros* (summer courses for foreigners), organized by the Spanish government.

Trade and commerce also contributed to strengthening the connections between Spain and America in the initial decades of the twentieth century. In 1919, the first issue of the monthly *Los Estados Unidos* (The United States) was published in Barcelona. A project of the Casa de América de Barcelona, a powerful center of Hispanismo in Catalonia, the magazine sought "to promote relations of all kinds between Spain and the United States."[45] Articles by Rafael Altamira and Charles Lummis graced its pages, as did contributions by American and Spanish consuls, and others, including Antonio Cuyás (Arturo's brother), the chief of the commercial delegation in the Spanish Embassy in Washington. The Casa de América de Barcelona established a network of delegates in the American continent, several of them in the United States.[46] As happened in Latin America, the rise in Spanish migration to the United States in the early twentieth century contributed to the increasing demand for Spanish products in the country. The pages of Spanish immigrant periodical publications are dotted with advertisements for Spanish food products, Spanish literature and newspapers, and Spanish music.

Spanish immigrants participated in and benefitted from the growing appeal of Hispanismo in America. Some found work as translators and teachers of Spanish.[47] Advertisements for Spanish academies, private tutors, and self-teaching courses such as the Galeno method appeared regularly in *La Prensa*, the New York Spanish daily. In 1920, *La Prensa* started running an educational page, *"El eco de las aulas"* (The Echo of the Classrooms) for students of Spanish, and it established prizes for the best Spanish compositions by American high school and college students. In 1917, Spanish immigrant societies in the United States joined the growing Hispanista movement in both sides of the Atlantic in celebrating Columbus's voyages with a *fiesta de la raza* (Day of the [Hispanic] race) (figure 1.5).[48]

The festivities, however, developed according to local conditions. In San Francisco, for example, the program included a visit to the Cervantes monument in Golden Gate; in New York, it involved a civic parade to the Columbus statue in Central Park.[49] In Tampa, in 1925, Spaniards planned to commemorate not only Columbus's landing but also the "Landing of the Spanish Conquerors in Florida" with lavish celebrations that included an automobile parade representing the Hispanic American Republics, Italy, the United States, and a variety of Spanish regions; dance and costume contests; and fireworks, all recorded in film by Pathé News.[50]

"THE OVERSEAS PARISH": BUILDING TRANSREGIONAL AND TRANSLOCAL NETWORKS IN THE SPANISH DIASPORA IN THE UNITED STATES

Participation in the development of a transnational Hispanic identity did not mean that Spanish migrants abandoned their characteristic localism. The very figure of Christopher Columbus illustrates the power of this distinctive exaltation of the *patria chica* (little fatherland), as debates arose in Spain as to whether Galicia or Catalonia could claim the honor of being the birthplace of the Admiral.[51] The *Harvard Encyclopedia of American Ethnic Groups* acknowledged the strength of this diverse cultural heritage. The entry for "Spaniards" states that "immigrants from Spain [have] not functioned as a traditional ethnic group." "The expression of ethnic heritage," it explains, "takes the form established in Spain—the expression of one of Spain's several, not always harmonious, constituent cultures."[52] As one reader of *La Prensa* put it, in a letter to the editor in the midst of a debate over the need for Spaniards in New York to unite, "We [Spaniards] can't tolerate each other for

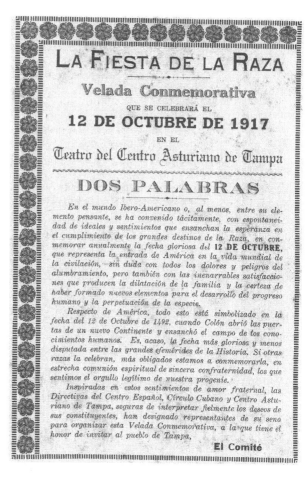

FIGURE 1.5.
Commemoration of
the Fiesta de la Raza
in Tampa in 1917.
(Author's collection.)

too long. There is as much difference between the character of an Asturian
and an Andalusian as there is between that of a Latin and an Anglo Saxon."[53]

The region remains a powerful source of identity in Spain. In the late nineteenth century, this sentiment fueled the growth of regionalist movements
in Catalonia, Galicia, the Basque Country, and the Canary Islands. Spanish
immigrants in the Americas played a crucial role in the rise of these movements. Key elements of the Galician identity, such as the Galician anthem,
emanated from the Galician community in Cuba, which also led to the creation of a Galician Academy to further the study of the Galician culture
and language.[54] In the United States, *La Llumanera de Nova York* participated

in and supported the activities of the Renaixença, the Catalan cultural Renaissance, which also included the establishment of an Academy of the Catalan Language.[55]

As we will see later in the chapter, Spanish immigrants in the United States contributed to movements for national independence in their home regions in the twentieth century. These activities exemplify the importance of what historian James Clifford has termed "the lateral axes of diaspora," networks that connect the same diasporic community not only between home and host societies but across different territories as well.[56] The "imagined community" created by readers of *La Llumanera* brought together Catalans in Spain, the United States, and a variety of other locations in the Americas.[57]

If the members of the Catalan Choral Society mentioned in the opening of this chapter had been careful to avoid a display of provincialism in the United States, the Spanish immigrants that arrived at American shores in the decades following the Spanish-Cuban-American War had fewer qualms about expressing their regional identity. Conditions, of course, had changed. The number of Spanish immigrants had increased considerably by then, and the anti-Spanish sentiment prevalent in the previous decades had dissipated significantly. Some Spanish societies did not manage this transition successfully. In Tampa, for example, the Centro Español's dawdling to offer health benefits to its growing immigrant membership prompted a number of its members to break away and establish a delegation of the Centro Asturiano de la Habana in 1902.[58]

The expansion of the American economy in the aftermath of the War of 1898 contributed to the rise of Spanish migration to Tampa. The American occupation of Cuba consolidated a trend toward the monopolization of the Clear Havana cigar industry. In the summer of 1899, cigar manufacturers from Tampa, Key West, New Orleans, and Havana created a trust: the Havana-American Company. Tampa became the headquarters of the organization. It was estimated that 90 percent of the Clear Havana cigars consumed in the United States would be produced there. This output, in turn, meant an increase in the labor force, almost doubling the number of cigar workers, from 6,000 to 11,000.[59] The transnational networks established by Spanish immigrants in the nineteenth century supplied thousands of Asturian and Galician workers for this expansion. Among them was fourteen-year-old José González, who left Asturias for Tampa in 1905 with an older cousin who had settled in the city a few years earlier. Upon arrival, José started as an apprentice in the same factory where his cousin worked, owned by a fellow Asturian. His earnings would later help to fund the migration to Tampa of two siblings, Luisa, in 1913, and Víctor in 1916.[60] The father of Tampa author José Yglesias followed a similar path, leaving his native Galicia with a young cousin (both aged thirteen) to join the thriving Galician community there.[61]

While Spanish migration to the United States never rose to the levels reached by other immigrant groups, it experienced a significant increase in the first decade of the twentieth century. When the Dillingham Commission issued its report on immigration in 1911, only North Dakota lacked a Spanish immigrant presence. As we mention elsewhere, over half (55%) of the Spanish immigrants in the country resided in three states (New York, Florida, and California); another 23 percent lived in Texas and the western states. Spaniards worked primarily as cigar makers, sheepherders, fruit pickers, seamen, and miners.[62] World War I intensified this migration, and it opened up new opportunities for employment, as Spanish immigrants were actively recruited to work in the war industries. In 1919, an article in *The Literary Digest* stated that "from 30 to 40 percent of the unskilled workers in munition plants, shipyards, mines, and other industries were Spaniards."[63]

The recruitment of Spanish workers took place both in the United States and in Spain. New York's Spanish daily *La Prensa* ran ads, in Spanish, from labor agencies offering jobs in a variety of industries, mines, and public works. Spanish women, too, were sought for "patriotic labor," making candy for American servicemen in Europe.[64] American companies also sent agents to Spain. In January 1916, the Bulletin of the Spanish Consejo Superior de Emigración (High Council on Emigration; *BCSE*) denounced that a company based in New York was recruiting workers in Galicia and neighboring León to work in shipyards. Warnings to prospective emigrants that they would face "tough work at sea or in naval factories" did not deter 200 Spanish seamen who left for the United States the following month.[65] This emigration continued in the coming years. In 1918, the inspector of emigration from the city of La Coruña, in northern Galicia, reported that emigrants leaving from that port to the United States were almost exclusively Galician seamen and stokers, lured by the high wages offered in America. The inspector in Vigo (southern Galicia) anticipated that the migratory wave would only increase, as these workers would write back to relatives and neighbors encouraging them to leave as well.[66] A decade later, the *BCSE* reported that the wages earned by Galician seamen and stokers in the American merchant marine allowed Galician coastal communities to benefit from "the periodical remittance of copious savings."[67]

From Southern Spain too came reports of high rates of emigration to the United States. In 1916, an article in the *BCSE* revealed that in the month of April alone 200 farmers had left the Andalusian province of Almería to work picking fruit in the orchards of California. The workers came from a handful of villages, and their goal was to "return two or three years later with good savings."[68] In 1918, similar reports stated that the migration from Almería to California continued, and was "well organized." Farmers left for "San Francisco, Los Angeles and other places in the same region, where they get good wages and they live together in the ranches in groups of 10 or 12, which allows them to save quite a bit of money."[69]

By 1920, the United States ranked third in the statistics of Spanish emigration to the Americas, after Cuba and Argentina. An average of 4,000 Spaniards left for the United States every month.[70] Spanish immigrant enclaves expanded beyond New York, the West, and the Southeast and into states such as New Jersey, Michigan, Pennsylvania, and Ohio. As the reports from the *BCSE* indicate, the majority of these immigrants maintained close connection with their home communities in Spain, through tight-knit migration networks and remittances. In 1913, Angel Cuesta, the prominent Spanish cigar manufacturer, estimated that the immigrant community in Tampa sent over $250,000 annually to Spain in remittances.[71] When José González, one of Tampa's cigar workers, returned to Spain for a visit in 1917, he recorded in his journal that the Basque migrants on the ship carried an average of $5,000 to $6,000 each to the Basque Country.[72]

These transnational networks kept alive the connections between what some historians of Galician emigration have described as the "parish over here" (in Spain) and the "parish over there" the "overseas parish."[73] Indeed, while we speak of the nation and the region, it is important to note that these migratory networks were often very localized in nature—translocal. Among Basque immigrants to the West, for example, Navarrese were more prominent in California, Arizona, and western Nevada; while Biscayans settled in northern Nevada, southern Idaho, and eastern Oregon. Furthermore, most

Biscayans came from a handful of villages near the coast in the northeast corner of the province.[74] In West Virginia, Galicians and Andalusians lived in the coal-mining communities in the south of the state, while Asturians worked in the zinc-smelting plants in the north.[75] One scholar wrote, "entire families from the town of Salinas . . . in Asturias . . . migrated to Harrison County to work in the metal and glass industries there."[76] The majority of Galicians in Tampa came from a small number of parishes in the provinces of Lugo and Coruña.[77] In New York, too, Galician migration originated in a scattering of coastal parishes in the province of Coruña. Immigrants from the interior province of Orense were more likely to settle in New Jersey.[78]

These settlements, in turn, offered opportunities for other immigrants to open establishments that catered to the workers' needs, such as boardinghouses and restaurants. Spanish hotels and restaurants had been a common presence in New York already in the mid-nineteenth century, serving a population composed primarily of travelers, merchants, and clerical workers from Spain and Spanish-speaking America. Arturo Cuyás's father, Antonio, owned the Hotel Barcelona in Manhattan (later to become the Hotel del Recreo). *La Llumanera de Nova York* and *Las Novedades* ran advertisements for these and other establishments, such as the Restaurant Español, and the Hotel Español e Hispanoamericano. The latter announced itself to be a "Casa Española" (Spanish house) where meals were served "Spanish style."[79]

By the 1920s, a growing number of Spanish boardinghouses, restaurants, and grocery stores offered immigrants a "home away from home." Reflecting the community's geographic diversity, these establishments catered to a variety of regional tastes. Grocery stores would sell Spanish olive oil and cheese, but also "Galician sardines," while restaurants' menus offered customers regional specialties such as *paella valenciana, bacalao a la Vizcaína, patas de ternera a la Andaluza,* and *olla a la Catalana.* Among the most successful entrepreneurs in 1920s New York was the Basque Valentín Aguirre, whose restaurant Jai-Alai, decorated with murals of *pelota* players (a traditional Basque sport), advertised "platos típicos regionales" (typical regional dishes).[80]

A native of Biscay, Aguirre had migrated to the United States in 1895. After a stint working in the dockyards of New York, he and his wife opened a boardinghouse, Casa Vizcaína (Biscayan House), in the Spanish section of Manhattan. In 1910, they moved to Greenwich Village, where they operated the Santa Lucía Hotel as well as a travel agency. For most of the Basques arriving in New York in the first decades of the twentieth century, Aguirre's hotel was a necessary and welcome stop in their journey west. Aguirre's business was part of an extensive network of Basque hotels that dotted the American West, often placed near train stations, for easy access to newly arrived immigrants.[81] Boardinghouses were also common in Tampa's Spanish enclave, Ybor City. In 1900, 33 percent of Spanish immigrants there lived in these establishments, reflecting the demographics of this mobile workforce, made up primarily of single men, or married men with families in Spain.[82] Boarders were also found in private homes, as a way for housewives to supplement the family income. A high percentage of the Galician immigrants interviewed in Caroline Ware's study of Greenwich Village in the 1920s lived in boardinghouses.[83]

Social clubs and mutual aid societies were an indispensable complement to the boardinghouses in the immigrant enclaves. As the report of the Dillingham Commission stated of Tampa Spaniards, "to avoid the monotony of their boardinghouses [they] must have clubs. In case of sickness they must have sanatoria."[84] These mutual aid societies had been modeled after the *centros* created by Spanish immigrants, often along regional lines, in Latin American countries. Their membership, in some cases reaching the tens of thousands, surpassed in size the population of most of the towns in the immigrants' provinces of origin.

The centros offered a wide range of services to their members. Their impressive clubhouses included classrooms, well-stocked libraries, and cantinas, where the immigrants could attend night classes, or relax reading the Spanish press or playing cards or dominoes with friends. In the centros' theaters and ballrooms members could enjoy Spanish plays and *zarzuelas* (Spanish operetta), attend conferences, and have a good time at a variety of dances and festivals. The centros also provided much-needed medical care, for a moderate monthly fee, which also covered burial in their cemeteries.[85] This was the model adopted in Tampa by the two main Spanish mutual aid societies: the Centro Español and the Centro Asturiano. In New York, where the immigrant community was more diverse and the union more elusive, the efforts of the Unión Benéfica Española (Spanish Benevolent Union), a mutual aid society founded in 1914, to build a Spanish Hospital came to naught.[86] Galician and Asturian immigrants in the United States, as elsewhere, did contribute funds to build two hospitals in Spain, one in Cesuras

(Galicia); the other, sponsored by the Centro Asturiano de la Habana, near Oviedo (Asturias).[87]

By the 1920s, Spaniards in the United States sustained a number of ethnic associations. Some of them were based on the immigrants' region of origin. In Tampa, for example, besides the Centro Español and Centro Asturiano, there was a Galician society, Acción Gallega (Galician Action), and a society of immigrants from the Canary Islands (Agrupación Canaria). In New York, there existed organizations of immigrants from Galicia (Casa Galicia), Andalusia (Centro Andaluz), Aragon (Centro Aragonés), Asturias (Centro Asturiano), the Balearic Islands (Centro Balear), Catalonia (Centre Nacionalista Català), the Basque Country (Centro Vasco Americano), and Valencia (Círculo Valenciano).

Some immigrants, particularly Galicians and Asturians, also participated in a network of locally based associations. Like the Jewish *landsmanschaften*, membership in these organizations included natives of a particular village or municipality. Most of these clubs took the form of *sociedades de instrucción* (societies of instruction), whose goal was to fund the construction of primary schools in the homeland. Some of these societies, of which there were close to 400 in the Americas, had branches in several countries, as the "homeland parish" expanded its geography to encompass a transnational network of "overseas" parishes. In Tampa, for example, there existed several delegations of Galician societies of instruction headquartered in Havana. They included Hijos de San Miguel y Reinante, the Círculo Habanero de la Devesa, La Unión Mañonesa, and La Devesana. In New York, Galician immigrants from coastal communities in the province of Coruña created the Sociedad de Naturales de Sada (with branches in Havana and Buenos Aires), Socorros Mutuos de Muros y sus Contornos, Bueu, Beluso y sus contornos, Hijos de Palmeira, and El Anzuelo (from the municipality of Mugardos). Many of the primary schools built by these societies of instruction are still in use today.[88]

The school building was just one of the many ways the migrants established their presence in their home villages. Besides periodic remittances to their families, migrants often contributed generously to a variety of initiatives. In 1924, the natives of Sada (Coruña) in New York, organized a collection to aid the victims of severe storms in their town, while immigrants from Pego (Alicante) sent funds for a charity hospital in their village.[89] The Centro Aragonés of New York contributed to the erection of a monument to Joaquín Costa, a prominent intellectual and political figure, in Zaragoza. They also established a prize for the best biography of Costa written by schoolchildren in Aragon.[90] Sometimes, the migrants themselves were celebrated and memorialized in monuments in their home villages. Such was the case with Angel Cuesta, the Tampa cigar manufacturer who had underwritten a number of projects in his native Panes (Asturias), including the building of a school, roads, water system, and a public market. In 1935, his neighbors honored Cuesta with a monument in the village's public square. A few months later, his serialized memoirs were published in the local newspaper, *El Eco de los Valles*.[91]

The press played a crucial role in nourishing the "imagined community" created by these transnational networks. Much like *La Llumanera de Nova York* had done for the Catalan diaspora in the nineteenth century, newspapers such as *El Eco de los Valles* illuminate the web of connections that linked small Asturian villages to Asturian diasporas in the Americas. An article in 1903, reporting on the efforts by the municipal government to build a road to the hamlet of Ruenes, listed the committees in charge of collecting money to fund the project. These included representatives of migrants from the area residing in Cuba, Mexico, and the United States.[92] In Galicia, magazines such as *Vida Gallega* (Galician Life; figure 1.6), partially financed by and directed to the Galician diaspora in the Americas, highlighted the achievements of Galicians inside and outside of the region's geographic borders. One of its regular columns was titled "Los Gallegos en Nueva York" (Galicians in New York).[93]

Spanish immigrants' celebrations in the United States remained rooted in regional and local customs emanating from Spain's rich repository of popular traditions. The publication of the first issue of *La Llumanera* in 1874 was celebrated by Catalans in New York with a "Catalan lunch" at the home of Emilio Puig, the businessman who funded the paper. The decorations of the dining room included a floral arrangement representing the seal of Catalonia, and "a small chapel of the Virgin of Montserrat made with stones picked up in those mountains."[94] The feast of Montserrat, patron saint of Catalonia, received special mention on the pages of the magazine. In 1880, *La Llumanera* sent a correspondent to Montserrat, near Barcelona, to report on the millennial celebrations of the medieval abbey.[95] In his memoirs, Gavín W. González, son of Asturian immigrants who settled in West Virginia, writes evocatively

FIGURE 1.6. Galician magazines, such as *Vida Gallega*, connected Galicia to its diaspora in America. This page informs its readers about Galician immigrants in New York and Buenos Aires. The young children, born in New York, are dressed in the traditional Galician regional costume.

of Spanish immigrants enjoying the Romería de San Juan (an open-air picnic in honor of Saint John): people "sang and danced to the music of bagpipes or an accordion . . . the men snapped their fingers and the ladies clickity-clacked the castanets as they danced 'La Jota Aragonesa' with reckless abandon."[96] In the fall, Spanish immigrants would gather to make wine and carry out the *matanza* (butchering of pigs) to make *chorizos* and *morcillas* (sausages) and *filloas* (a Galician delicacy, made with pig's blood).[97] Wine making and matanza were also popular activities among Spanish immigrants in California.[98]

News and advertisements of festivals and other social events in the Spanish immigrant press suggest that as time passed and a generation of children born in the United States reached adulthood, these gatherings often combined traditional Spanish customs with American popular culture and an American festive calendar. Thus, Spanish immigrants organized *romerías, fiestas, verbenas, and bailes* to celebrate Independence Day, Labor Day, Halloween, and Thanksgiving. At these events the sounds of the traditional *gaitas* (bagpipes) would alternate with those of the music bands, and the dance of the *jotas* and *muiñeiras* (regional Spanish dances) with those of the American foxtrot.

Sporting events offered another important venue for the performance of this Spanish identity. *Pelota* and *jai alai* were played in the many *frontones* (ball courts) dotting the western states where Basque immigrants settled. In New York and the east coast, however, soccer was the most popular sport within the Spanish community. In 1929, around 5,000 people attended the game of the Galicia Sporting Club. The club provided buses to drive Spanish immigrants from communities across New York and New Jersey. Although soccer crossed national boundaries (as membership was open to non-Spaniards), the names of the clubs attest to the importance of regional (Galicia, Vasco Americano) and local (Barcelona, Coruña, Goyán, Calpe American) identities within the immigrant community.[99]

The growth of this flourishing network of immigrant societies in the first two decades of the twentieth century came to an end by the 1930s, when the combined effects of the Great Depression and of the quota legislation curtailing Spanish immigration to the United States began to be felt.[100] Attempts to unite the community under one big Spanish society failed. In 1929, the Unión Benéfica Española and the Centro Hispano Americano (established in 1903) did take the first steps to merge. La Nacional and La Cosmopolita, both located in Brooklyn, did the same, but other associations (Casa Galicia, Centro Vasco Americano, and Centro Asturiano) declined to join.[101] Casa Galicia and Centro Asturiano (itself a delegation of the Centro Asturiano of Havana) had a number of subdelegations in other states. Casa Galicia's goal was not to join with other Spanish societies, but to unite "all Galicians in the United States." "Let's do 'our' work in the United States," the association stated in a flyer, "and let the sons of other regions do 'theirs'. That way, we will continue to be very 'Galician,' but no less 'Spanish.'"[102]

A set of unforeseen events was to bring together this diverse community. In the 1930s, the fall of Alfonso XIII and the Bourbon monarchy, the proclamation of a Republic, and the civil war that followed the military coup of 1936 acted as catalysts that mobilized the Spanish immigrant communities in the Americas in an unprecedented fashion. These events shed light on another important network of transnational connections, based primarily on political ideologies. Two of the more relevant in the Spanish case were the internationalist movement of anarchism and the nationalist movements in Catalonia and the Basque Country.

TRANSNATIONAL POLITICS AND THE SPANISH
DIASPORA IN THE UNITED STATES

Spaniards in the United States followed political developments in Spain closely. In the last decades of the nineteenth century, when the colonial wars in Cuba contributed to heightening Spanish patriotism, the Spanish immigrant press in New York offered a variety of positions across the political spectrum, from the ultraconservative José Ferrer de Couto, the editor of *La Crónica* (later *El Cronista*), to the more liberal-minded Arturo Cuyás (*La Llumanera de Nova York*) and José García (*Las Novedades*), to the progressive and self-proclaimed free-thinker Ramón Verea, editor of *El Progreso*.[103] The anarchist press, however, represented the most militant of the transnational political networks established by Spaniards in the United States.[104]

As historian Carlos Serrano has pointed out, Spanish anarchists were particularly peripatetic, the outcome of state repression as well as anarchists' prominence in areas of emigration with easy access to ports, such as Catalonia and Galicia.[105] In summer 1901, in the midst of violent strikes by anarchist-led unions in Spain, manifestos of solidarity published by anarchists in Tampa singled out the violence in Barcelona and Coruña, and called on Tampa cigar workers to protest against the "mass shootings and cruel and systematic persecution of our brothers by the barbarous Spanish government." The signatories hoped that Spanish workers could soon "get rid of the tyranny of the government, the priests, and the bourgeoisie!"[106] The solidarity of the Spanish anarchists in America contributed to the survival of the movement in Spain. Besides collecting money for strikers, Spaniards in the United States helped anarchist publications when they faced financial difficulties. Perhaps more important, as Serrano explains, was the practice of "relay" (*relevo*): when censorship or outright closure threatened anarchist publications in the peninsula, their leaders used the Spanish anarchist press in America to express their views.[107]

In the late nineteenth century, Tampa was one of the most important centers of anarchism in America. Pedro Esteve, a native of Barcelona and the most prominent Spanish anarchist in the United States at the time, was instrumental in developing this radical environment. In 1892, Esteve left Spain for New York, where he became the editor of the anarchist newspaper *El Despertar* (The Awakening). Later, he would move to Paterson, New Jersey, to publish *La Questione Sociale* (The Social Question) with Italian anarchist Errico Malatesta. In 1905, Esteve participated in the foundational convention of the Industrial Workers of the World Union in Chicago. Escaping police persecution, he moved to Tampa in 1906 invited by anarchist groups who pooled their money to provide him with a printing press, *La Políglota* (The Polyglot).[108] Anarchist newspapers and literature reached a wide audience as they were discussed in anarchist cultural centers and read by the *lectores* (readers) in the cigar factories while cigar makers worked at their tables, a tradition imported from Cuba. Maximiliano Olay, another prominent Spanish anarchist, claimed that he turned to anarchism after hearing a lector read the anarchist newspaper *Tierra y Libertad* (Land and Liberty) in a Tampa cigar factory.[109]

When Francisco Ferrer, the founder of the Escuela moderna (Modern school) movement in Spain was executed in Barcelona in 1909, Pedro Esteve called a meeting in Tampa to protest the "infamous assassination" and vowed to continue Ferrer's legacy by building several modern schools in the city. According to the official bulletin of the *Institución Francisco Ferrer*, which started publication in March 1910, the Tampa society had 250 members and over $200 in funds. While there is no evidence that these schools came to fruition, we do know that at least one of the members of the Institución managed to avenge Ferrer's death.[110] In 1912, Manuel Pardiñas traveled from Tampa to Spain, where he assassinated Spanish premier José Canalejas. By then, Esteve had moved to New York, where he published the weekly *Cultura Obrera* (Workers' Culture) and worked with the Industrial Workers of the World to unionize Spanish maritime workers in the east coast.[111] Maximiliano Olay moved to New York too. He worked as a lector in cigar factories, and attended the Centro Ferrer in Harlem and the Modern School at Stelton, in New Jersey. In 1919, Olay settled in Chicago, where he worked as a translator, and continued to organize anarchist groups such as the Free Society and to write for the anarchist press in Cuba, Spain, and the United States.[112]

The activities of Spanish anarchists in the United States remained a concern for both governments through most of the decade. In 1913, after the failed attempt to capture Pardiñas before he assassinated Canalejas, Spanish ambassador Juan Riaño requested the aid of the State Department to investigate an alleged anarchist plot to kill the Spanish monarch, Alfonso XIII.[113] In 1919, it was President Woodrow Wilson who was feared to be the possible target of anarchist violence. In February of that year, acting on tips that Spanish anarchists were planning to assassinate Wilson upon his return from Europe, the police raided the offices of two Spanish radical clubs. Fourteen Spaniards were arrested in New York and ten more in Philadelphia. Among them was the organizer of the Spanish branch of the Industrial Workers of the World and editor of the Spanish anarchist weekly *El Corsario* (The Corsair). Charged with violating Wilson's proclamation against the publication of seditious literature, they were deported.[114]

The United States had advocated the exclusion and deportation of immigrant anarchists since the turn of the twentieth century, in the aftermath of President William McKinley's assassination by an anarchist in 1901. In 1903 and 1907 anarchists were added to the list of undesirables banned from entering the country. After World War I, fears of Bolshevism led to the deportation of thousands of foreign "radicals" in the notorious Palmer raids. At the same time, Congress discussed measures to drastically cut the immigration from "radical" countries. Harold Knutson, the Republican congressman from Minnesota, singled out Spain as a particular culprit. "Before the war, immigration from Spain was practically unknown," Knutson stated, as he explained that in a recent visit to Ellis Island in December 1920, he had found that 2,000 immigrants from Spain had arrived in one day. He believed that this increase was due to Spanish government policies. "Spain is a seething mass of anarchy," Knutson declared, "and the [Spanish] Government is gathering these anarchists up and dumping them on us."[115] The deportations and the legislation that resulted in the National Origins Quota Acts of the 1920s reduced the Spanish immigrant presence in the United States considerably, but they did not eliminate the anarchist threat. In 1923, news of the bombing of the Spanish and Italian consulates in Philadelphia set off a search for Spanish radicals presumed to have set the bombs to protest the alliance between Mussolini's Italy and Spain, now ruled by General Primo de Rivera.[116]

During the dictatorship of Primo de Rivera (1923–30) a new set of transnational networks gained strength among Spanish immigrants in the United States, including those that supported nationalist movements for independence in Catalonia and the Basque Country. While these movements developed in the context of the national struggles for self-determination that defined the "Wilsonian Moment" in the aftermath of World War I, their roots can be traced back to the nineteenth century—one of the outcomes of Spain's defeat in the Spanish-Cuban-American War.[117] Secundino Delgado, an immigrant from the Canary Islands, hailed as the "father of Canarian nationalism," illustrates a singular combination of anticolonial, ethnonationalist, and anarchist thought inspired by the wars of independence in Cuba.[118]

Born in 1867 in the island of Tenerife, Delgado migrated to Cuba as a teenager in the 1880s, and later to the United States. After a short stay in New York, Delgado moved to Tampa, where, together with fellow Spaniard Luis Barcia, he began publishing the anarchist weekly *El Esclavo* (The Slave) in 1894. When the war started in Cuba a year later, Delgado moved to Havana to work for the cause of Cuban independence. Persecuted by Spanish authorities on the island, he eventually settled in Venezuela. There, in 1897, he published the Canarian nationalist paper *El Guanche* and called for the independence of the Canary Islands from Spain. Expelled from Venezuela under diplomatic pressure from Spain, he returned to Tenerife in 1900. There, he worked with the Asociación Obrera Canaria (Canarian Workers' Association) and contributed to its organ *El Obrero* (The Worker). A year later, he founded the Partido Popular Autonomista (Autonomist Popular Party) seeking home rule for the archipelago, and edited the newspaper *Vacaguaré*. Charged with participating in an attack against the General Captaincy in Havana in 1896, he was imprisoned in Madrid by General Weyler in 1902. In 1904, he wrote the autobiographic *¡Vacaguaré! (Via Crucis)*, which was published in Mexico while he was traveling again in the Americas. He returned to Tenerife in 1910, where he died in 1912.[119] Although he did not live to see the independence of his homeland, Delgado's activities set the stage for the foundation of the Partido Nacionalista Canario (Canarian Nationalist Party) in Havana in 1924.

Catalan and Basque nationalist groups made their official appearance in the United States also in the 1920s. From its foundation in New York, in January 1920, the Centre Nacionalista Català (Catalan Nationalist Center) faced the blistering criticism of the Spanish immigrant elites. The weekly *La Tribuna* (co-owned by Castilian Miguel de Zárraga and Galician Jaime V. Lago) took issue with the term "nationalist." Using the United States as a model, Zárraga explained that he supported regional autonomy or something akin to a federal state in the peninsula (the United States of Spain, or United States of Iberia), but one where all regions would contribute to the unity of the nation, the "greater Spain." He was adamantly opposed, therefore, to what he called Catalan separatism.[120] "The seed of *separatismo* must be stamped out," he wrote. And in a language that anticipated the nationalist discourse of the Primo de Rivera dictatorship, he divided the community between "Spanish" and "anti-Spanish." One was "either with Spain or against it."[121] Juan Cebrián, the ardent hispanista from California, also used the pages of *La Tribuna* to characterize Catalan nationalism as "an obfuscation," particularly at a time when things Spanish were becoming so popular in America.[122] Antinationalist Catalans such as Antonio Cuyás, Arturo Cuyás's brother, joined the chorus of critical voices. Cuyás repeated the phrase uttered by Alfonso XIII in a recent visit to Barcelona: "Spain, one and indivisible." He reminded Catalans that even the American immigrant commission considered the Spanish race one of the most remarkably homogeneous ethnic groups in Europe.[123]

The activities of the Centre Nacionalista Català were also closely monitored by the Spanish government. A few months after the founding of the *centre*, Ambassador Juan Riaño wrote to the Spanish consul in New York and asked him to determine whether the club "pursued political ends contrary to the established institutions." Riaño suggested that the consul use his influence in the colony to "prevent and thwart the pursuit of goals against legality."[124] Consul Alejandro Berea assured the ambassador that the centre was a cultural and artistic association, but Riaño confronted him with the centre's publication, *Catalonia*, and its defense of "Catalonia's national freedom." He urged Berea to inform him of "the best means to counter this campaign."[125]

The clash between the leaders of the Spanish community and supporters of the centre came to a head in September 1920, when the battleship *Alfonso XIII* visited New York. As representatives of the Spanish colony entertained the naval officers and sang the praises of the Spanish Navy, they were met by a flyer signed by three Catalan Separatist groups. Titled, "From Catalonia to the people of the United States," the leaflet was an indictment of Spain's history, particularly its imperial history, and a denunciation of her colonial wars in Morocco.[126] To add insult to injury, it called on the United States to do for

Catalonia what they had done for Cuba in 1898; that is, to help it achieve its independence from Spain.

In *La Tribuna*, Miguel de Zárraga described the Catalanist manifesto as a "shameful insult to Spain," and asked that its authors renounce Spanish citizenship or go to Africa to fight for Morocco.[127] Ambassador Riaño wrote the US Department of State and requested that they carry out an investigation on the matter. The bureau's agents, however, did not find any information on the Separatist Clubs. Consul Berea reported to Riaño that the New York centre had nothing to do with the manifesto, and that its members believed it had been printed precisely to damage their reputation before the Spanish colony in New York.[128]

In 1921, an article published in New York's *Globe* by the vice-president of the Centre Nacionalista Català again ignited controversy, and was discussed in the Spanish Senate. The piece, which dealt with the Spanish military defeat at Annual (Morocco), declared the "total and definitive failure of the Spanish army" and called for the "restoration of the Iberian nationalities" to counter the "fatal artificial unity imposed by the Spanish influence," while blaming the Madrid government for the social violence then rampant in Catalonia.[129] Senator Antonio Royo Villanova asked the minister of foreign affairs whether there was any juridical or political tool available to Spain to punish such declarations. Royo stated that, as a liberal, he did not have a problem with Spaniards being critical of their government, but he believed that they "should wash their dirty linen at home" and not use the foreign press to do so.[130] The minister, who had discussed the matter with Ambassador Riaño, understood that any action on the part of the Spanish government on this matter would fail against American laws on freedom of the press. In fact, a lawyer consulted by the embassy explained that there was nothing punishable in the article.

Things only got worse in 1923, when General Primo de Rivera came to power, through a military coup, in the aftermath of the Annual disaster. Through the pages of *Catalonia*, the Centre Nacionalista Català denounced the new regime and called on Spaniards to take citizenship papers in the United States. Ambassador Riaño's efforts to stop this "anti-Spanish" campaign by appealing to the State Department were unsuccessful.[131] This criticism of the dictatorship was not confined to leaflets or the Catalan press, however. In an unprecedented move within the Spanish colony in New York, supporters of Catalan independence brought the "dirty laundry" into the open on the pages of the *New York Times*. There, a "Catalonian" denounced Primo de Rivera for the restrictions on the use of the Catalan flag and language and "the imprisonment and banishment of Catalonian patriots," while an "Asturian" praised the regime for its pacification of Catalonia and the fact that the "'patriots' of Deputy Francisco Macia's pattern are no longer free to cry, even in the Cortes [Spanish Parliament], 'Death to Spain!'"[132]

Francesc Macià, the founder of the independentist party Estat Català, was exiled in France, but his party was supported by the Catalan diaspora in the Americas, which had established a network of Catalan Separatist Clubs in Argentina, Chile, Cuba, and the United States. Following the example of Sinn Fein in Ireland, Estat Català sought to train armed groups to rise against the Spanish state in Catalonia. In June 1925, a group associated with the party planned an unsuccessful assassination attempt against Alfonso XIII. In 1926, the party raised a small army to invade Catalonia from France, but the plan was discovered and aborted by the French *gendarmerie*. According to Josep Carner-Ribalta, a veteran of these struggles, the resources for these actions came from Catalans abroad. A call from Macià to the Catalan Clubs in America in 1926 produced close to one million francs. Of these, 164,000 came from the New York Club, a significant amount considering the small size of the community, only surpassed by the funds collected in Cuba, but ahead of those collected in Buenos Aires.[133] The failed invasion of Catalonia led to Macià's departure from France to Belgium, and later to a tour of the Americas where the party was reorganized.

It was in Havana in 1928 that the leaders of the movement organized the Partit Separatista Revolucionari de Catalunya (Revolutionary Separatist Party of Catalonia) inspired by the Cuban Revolutionary Party founded by José Martí in the 1890s. The independentist Cuban-Catalan connection was also evident in the flag adopted by the party to represent the Catalan Republic, which combined the yellow and red bars of the Catalan flag with the lone star (white over blue) of the Cuban flag. After Cuba, Francesc Macià stopped in New York, where he met with Catalan supporters before heading back to Europe.

The activities of the Centre Nacionalista Català exemplify the transnationalism of the Catalan diaspora in the United States. One of the centre's members, Josep Gibernau, a Catalan author who came to the United States in his teens, remembered the excitement he felt at his college graduation in 1929. "We were becoming great admirers of America and its institutions," Gibernau wrote, "and it in turn, reinforced our Catalan Nationalism. Our rebellion against the militaristic Centralism of Madrid was enhanced when we saw American freedom and respect for the rights of its citizens and the efforts toward establishing a truly democratic society."[134]

Basques too had a long tradition of political organization in the diaspora, as many had fled to America in the aftermath of the nineteenth-century Carlist wars.[135] In 1877, Basque immigrants in Buenos Aires organized the Laurac Bat to protest the abolition of the historic Basque *fueros* (rights) by the Spanish liberal government.[136] Several Basque nationalist newspapers saw the light in Latin America. In 1907, the editors of one such publication, *Euzkotarra*, were expelled from Mexico upon pressure from the Spanish Embassy. They moved to the United States and continued to publish the paper, in New Orleans, until 1909. It was also through Mexico that the Basque nationalist movement developed in New York in the 1920s.

As had happened in Catalonia, the dictatorship of Primo de Rivera forced some of the leaders of the Basque nationalist movement into exile. Elías Gallastegui was one of them. Gallastegui had split with the traditional line of Basque nationalism and espoused a more radical view, advocating independence. In Mexico, he helped organize supporters of the Partido Nacionalista Vasco (Basque Nationalist Party). Attempts to do the same in New York with the members of the Centro Vasco Americano failed, but one group broke away from the centro to create a nationalist club called Aberria (Homeland).[137] The club also published a newspaper, *Aberi*.[138] Articles in *Aberi* praised the work of the Irish diaspora in America that had created patriotic clubs to support independence in the homeland, and they encouraged Basque immigrants to do the same.[139] The transnational connection between homeland and diaspora was also expressed in the paper's advice to its readers to mail the publication to their friends and relatives in Euzkadi once they had finished reading it.[140]

Basque and Catalan nationalists were not the only critical voices against the dictatorship of Primo de Rivera. In January 1924, three months after the military coup, a representative of the Grupo Cultura of Detroit wrote a letter to the editor of *La Prensa* complaining of the paper's bias, as it often published reports by English author F. Britten Austin favorable to the regime and critical of the Spanish workers. The writer asked *La Prensa* to allow for an alternative presentation of the Spanish reality in its pages.[141] In Tampa, a Christmas collection for Spanish conscripts fighting in Morocco sparked a debate over the political implications of such an act (it is worth noting that many emigrants had left Spain precisely to avoid military conscription and the war in Morocco). "Do not contribute for patriotism," wrote Victoriano Manteiga, the editor of the Spanish daily *La Gaceta*, "but to help, to show your love for the young who fight and die." Republican supporters in Tampa protested this contribution; others chose to subvert the collection of cigars to be sent to the front by inserting in them "revolutionary proclamations."[142] Juan González, a merchant from Asturias, took a different tack. For several years he wrote letters to President Calvin Coolidge requesting American support and protection to establish a republic in Spain.[143]

By 1929, the calls, both in Spain and abroad, to end the dictatorship had grown louder. "Is Primo de Rivera in power as a result of the popular will?" asked a Spaniard from West Virginia in a letter to *La Prensa*, "No," he replied, "We need a bit of freedom—we are surrounded by bayonets."[144] The lack of individual freedoms, the strict censorship of the press, and the regime's hostility toward regional nationalists and anarchists were the main focus of criticism by Spaniards in the United States. As historian Alejandro Quiroga argues, the regime's national-Catholic crusade was part of a strategy of "negative integration," which sought "the assimilation of the lower and middle classes through nationalist ideas that emphasized foreign and domestic foes."[145] This strategy contributed to the radicalization of important sectors of the Spanish diaspora in America. The appeal of regional nationalisms and international anarchism, the immigrants' anticlericalism, and their rejection of the colonial enterprise in Morocco ran against the dictatorship's version of Spanish national identity, which emphasized the imperial tradition, the monarchy, and the church. In this context, we can better understand the enthusiasm felt by many Spaniards in the United States in 1931, when the dictatorship, and the Bourbon monarchy, fell and Spain became a republic. We can also understand the immigrants' overwhelming support for the Republic during the Spanish Civil War (1936–39).

Much had changed in the decades that separated the colonial wars in Cuba from the beginning of the Spanish Civil War. In the late nineteenth century, Spaniards in the United States were among the staunchest defenders of Spain's colonial rule in the Americas; by the 1930s, they overwhelmingly rejected the imperial aspirations of General Francisco Franco's self-proclaimed crusade. In Tampa, anticipating Franco's victory, the officers of the Centro Español voted to strike from its bylaws the article that conferred honorary membership on the Spanish consul, and to declare the stars and stripes their only official flag. This was a remarkable vote for an institution that had been founded to defend Spaniards and Spanishness in the heart of one of the most active strongholds of Cuban insurgency in the United States.[146] In fact, that very movement was now appropriated by the Spanish diaspora. As one of the Spanish Republican leaders wrote about his visit to the Cuban Club in Tampa in 1937, "the Cuban Club brought me memories of the Cuban war for independence, where [José] Martí found his death at the hands of Spaniards of the same ilk as those who launched the war against this Spain of 1936, which, like the Cuba of 1898, wants to be free."[147]

In 1939, as General Franco celebrated his victory in the Spanish Civil War, the editor of the New York pro-Republican Spanish daily *La Voz* reminded its readers of their country's long diasporic tradition: "the path opened by the Discovery and the Conquest has been followed many times by the emigrants." This path, he continued, referring to the Spanish republican refugees, was now open to the "Spanish patriots penned in concentration camps in France."[148] Like Agapito, the character in *Windmills in Brooklyn*, many Spaniards never returned to Spain after the war. Franco's victory, and the forty-year dictatorship that ensued, would open a new phase in the relationship between Spain and the Spanish immigrant communities in the United States.

NOTES

1. Prudencio de Pereda, *Windmills in Brooklyn* (New York: Atheneum, 1960), 49. On the novel, see also Carmen González López-Briones, "Windmills in Brooklyn, A Story of the Spanish Immigrants in New York," *Revista de Estudios Norteamericanos* 5 (1997): 119–32.

2. For general studies of Spanish migration to the United States in the past two centuries, see R. A. Gómez, "Spanish Immigration to the United States," *Americas* 19 (July 1962): 59–78; and Germán Rueda, *La emigración contemporánea de españoles a los Estados Unidos, 1820–1950: De "Dons" a "Místers"* (Madrid: Mapfre, 1993). For the specific case of Galicians, see Bieito Alonso, *Obreiros alén mar: Mariñeiros, fogoneiros e anarquistas galegos en New York* (Vigo: A Nosa Terra, 2006); Germán Rueda Hernánz

and Carmen González López-Briones, "Los gallegos entre los españoles de Estados Unidos," in *VIII Xornadas de Historia de Galicia: Cuestións de Historia Galega*, ed. Jesús de Juana and Xavier Castro (Ourense, Spain: Servicio de Publicacións da Deputación Provincial de Ourense, 1995), 103–76; Nancy Pérez Rey, "Unha achega á emigración galega a Nova York," *Estudos Migratorios* 1, no. 2 (2008): 31–61; Ana M. Varela-Lago, "La emigración gallega a los Estados Unidos: La colonia gallega de Tampa, Florida," in *Proceedings of the 4th International Conference on Galician Studies*, ed. Benigno Fernández Salgado (Oxford: Centre for Galician Studies, 1997): 431–49; and Ana Varela-Lago, "A emigración galega aos Estados Unidos: Galegos en Louisiana, Florida e Nova York (1870–1940)," *Estudos Migratorios* 1, no. 2 (2008): 63–84.

3. The connection between Hispanismo and Spanish national politics in this period has been analyzed in the classic study by Fredrick B. Pike, *Hispanismo, 1898–1936. Spanish Conservatives and Liberals and Their Relations with Spanish America* (Notre Dame: University of Notre Dame Press, 1971). Recent studies of this topic include Isidro Sepúlveda, *El sueño de la Madre Patria: Hispanoamericanismo y nacionalismo* (Madrid: Marcial Pons, 2005) and David Marcilhacy, *Raza hispana: Hispanoamericanismo e imaginario nacional en la España de la Restauración* (Madrid: Instituto de Estudios Políticos y Constitucionales, 2010).

4. "Societat Coral Espanyola de Nova York," *La Llumanera de Nova York*, April 1879, 6 (Unless otherwise stated, all translations are by the author).

5. Among them were the Sociedad de Beneficencia de Naturales de Galicia en la Habana (1871), the Sociedad Vasco-Navarra de Beneficencia, and the Sociedad Asturiana de Beneficencia (both founded in Havana in 1877), the Centro Gallego de la Habana (1879), the Sociedad de Beneficencia de Naturales de Andalucía (1881), the Sociedad Montañesa de Beneficencia (1883), and the Centro Asturiano de la Habana (1886).

6. Jose C. Moya, *Cousins and Strangers: Spanish Immigrants in Buenos Aires, 1850–1930* (Berkeley: University of California Press, 1998), 149; Rueda, *La emigración contemporánea de españoles*, 283.

7. Gerald E. Poyo, *"With All, and for the Good of All": The Emergence of Popular Nationalism in the Cuban Communities of the United States, 1848–1898* (Durham, NC: Duke University Press, 1989), 62–69.

8. The Centro Español's bylaws reflected the growing tension between Cubans and peninsulares (Spaniards born in Spain) in one of the most important centers of Cuban nationalism in the United States. The club offered to protect its members "against any contingency they may face due to their national origin." On the founding and evolution of the Centro Español, see Ana M. Varela-Lago, "From Patriotism to Mutualism: The Early Years of the Centro Español de Tampa, 1891–1903," *Tampa Bay History* 15, no. 2 (1993): 5–23.

9. "El Centro Español de Tampa," *Las Novedades*, June 23, 1892.

10. "Carta de Tampa," *Las Novedades*, July 7, 1892.

11. "Lo Centenari de la República," *La Llumanera*, November 1874, 2; "Reforma indispensable," *Las Novedades*, November 28, 1877, 1.

12. José Ferrer de Couto, *Miguel de Cervantes Saavedra: Relación de los Primeros Festejos Religiosos y Literarios que se hicieron en la ciudad de Nueva York el día 23 de abril de 1875 para conmemorar el aniversario de la muerte de CERVANTES* (Nueva York: El Cronista, 1875).

13. "Donativo," *La Vanguardia*, April 5, 1914, 18. The collection was added to the national subscription for the monument honoring Cervantes on the third centennial of his death. On the Cervantes festivities in New York, see Ana Varela-Lago, "Conquerors, Immigrants, Exiles: The Spanish Diaspora in the United States (1848–1948)" (PhD diss., University of California, San Diego, 2008), 57–64.

14. For a fuller discussion and analysis of these celebrations, and of their contested nature, particularly between Spanish and Italian immigrants, see Varela-Lago, "Conquerors, Immigrants, Exiles," 65–89.

15. Varela-Lago, "From Patriotism to Mutualism," 11–12.

16. Arturo Cuyás, *The New Constitutional Laws for Cuba* (New York: Associated Spanish and Cuban Press, 1897).

17. See, for example, "Object to Tammany's Gift," *New York Times*, November 21, 1897.

18. "In Honor of Canovas," *New York Times*, August 15, 1897; "Tributo de los españoles de Nueva York," *Las Novedades*, August 19, 1897.

19. "Spanish Spies Disappear," *New York Times*, May 29, 1898; "The Alleged Spanish Spies," *New York Times*, May 30, 1898; "Spanish Spies in Danger," *New York Times*, May 30, 1898; "Señor Carranza's Letter," *New York Times*, June 5, 1898.

20. "A nuestros lectores," *Las Novedades*, February 9, 1898.

21. See, for example, his columns under the heading "El Progreso Mundial," in *El Hogar Español*, October 1911 and March 1912.

22. The column appeared under the heading "Pláticas con los muchachos."

23. Arturo Cuyás Armengol, *Hace falta un muchacho: Libro de orientación en la vida, para los adolescentes* (Madrid: Julián Palacios, 1913).

24. Cuyás Armengol, *Hace falta un muchacho*, xii.

25. Cuyás Armengol, *Hace falta un muchacho*, 91.

26. See note 16.

27. See, for example, Richard Kagan, "The Spanish *Craze* in the United States: Cultural Entitlement and the Appropriation of Spain's Cultural Patrimony, ca. 1890–ca. 1930," *Revista Complutense de Historia de América* 36 (2010): 37–58; Richard Kagan et al., *When Spain Fascinated America* (Madrid: Fundación Zuloaga, 2010); and

Christopher Schmidt-Nowara, "Spanish Origins of American Empire: Hispanism, History, and Commemoration, 1898–1915," *International History Review* 30 (March 2008): 32–51.

28. Although Serra had been born in the island of Majorca, in the Balearic Islands, he was often honored as a son of Catalonia. Molera's obituary mentioned that he "was proud of his ancestry and spoke the Catalan language even more fluently than Spanish." D. Q. Troy, "In Memoriam: Eusebius Joseph Molera," *California Historical Society Quarterly* 11, no. 1 (March 1932): 95. Molera had also been president of the Academy of Sciences in California and of the Pacific Astronomical Society.

29. On Molera's links to Catalonia, see Miquel S. Ylla-Català I Genís, "Un vigatà a Califòrnia: Aproximació a la figura d'Eusebi Molera I Bros (1847–1932)," *Ausa* (Publicació del Patronat d'Estudis Osonencs) 15, no. 130 (1993): 237–46, and Santi Ponce I Vivet, "Eusebi Molera i Bros: Aproximació a la figura d'un vigatà inquiet," *Lliçó inaugural: Universitat de Vic* (1996–97): 223–32.

30. Charles Lummis, *Los exploradores españoles del siglo XVI: Vindicación de la acción colonizadora en América* (Barcelona: Araluce, 1916). Lummis was awarded the cross of the order of Isabel la Católica for this book and for his work preserving the Spanish heritage in the United States.

31. Rafael Altamira, "The Share of Spain in the History of the Pacific Ocean," in *The Pacific Ocean in History*, ed. H. Morse Stephens and Herbert E. Bolton (New York: Macmillan, 1917), 52.

32. The term "black legend" (*leyenda negra*) was coined by Julián Juderías in 1913. He defined it as "the legend of the inquisitorial Spain, ignorant, fanatical, incapable, now as before, of figuring among the cultivated nations, always open to violent repression, enemy of progress and of innovations." Julián Juderías, *La Leyenda negra y la verdad histórica* (Madrid: Tipografía de la Revista de Archivos, Bibliotecas y Museos, 1914), 15. On how the black legend shaped US relations with the Hispanic world see, Angel del Río, *The Clash and Attraction of Two Cultures: The Hispanic and Anglo-Saxon Worlds in America* (Baton Rouge: Louisiana State University Press, 1965); and Philip Wayne Powell, *Tree of Hate: Propaganda and Prejudices Affecting United States Relations with the Hispanic World* (New York: Basic Books, 1971).

33. "A los gobiernos hispanoparlantes," *La Prensa*, January 27, 1917.

34. "Biografía leída por don M. López Otero en la Academia de Bellas Artes de San Fernando con motivo del homenaje a D. Juan C. Cebrián," *Arquitectura* 15, no. 168 (April 1933): 100.

35. Charles F. Lummis, *The Spanish Pioneers and the California Missions* (Chicago: A. C. McClurg, 1929).

36. Charles F. Lummis, *Los exploradores españoles del siglo XVI* (Barcelona: Araluce, 1930). Cebrián underwrote the printing of 50,000 copies. The title page

read: "homage of a thankful Spain to the memory of Carlos F. Lummis, the generous and dauntless writer who, since 1890, dared to proclaim the highly civilizing work of Spain in America, against the centuries-old calumnies piled upon the Hispanic race."

37. "Homenaje al adelantado de la Florida," *ABC*, August 9, 1924. On the festivities, see also "Spain Hails Americans at Avilés Celebration," *New York Times*, August 11, 1924; "New Tie with Spain is Made at Tomb," *New York Times*, August 31, 1924.

38. The unity between the two countries was further memorialized in a commemorative bronze plaque made to accompany the restored coffin of Menéndez in Saint Augustine. A copy of the plaque was sent to Avilés in 1928 to be placed near Menéndez's remains in the church of San Nicolás. It acknowledged, "the debt owed by the New World to Spain, for the Civilization, Culture and Progress contributed to Florida and to the Republic of the United States of America." "Es honrado el fundador de St. Augustine, Florida," *La Prensa*, September 13, 1928.

39. Spanish filled the linguistic gap created by the ban on teaching German, in the aftermath of the Great War. The increase in trade between the United States and Latin America, another outcome of the war in Europe, also contributed to the rising popularity of Spanish. James D. Fernández has argued that American Hispanophilia was a manifestation of "Longfellow's law," which states that "U.S. interest in Spain is and always has been largely mediated by U.S. interest in Latin America." James D. Fernández, "'Longfellow's Law': The Place of Latin America and Spain in U. S. Hispanism, circa 1915," in *Spain in America: The Origins of Hispanism in the United States*, ed. Richard Kagan (Urbana: University of Illinois Press, 2002), 124.

40. The monument, which still stands in Golden Gate Park, was designed by Spanish architect José Mora.

41. In 1925, Cebrián shared with the University of California the expense of compiling and publishing a catalogue of such collections, *Spain and Spanish America in the Libraries of the University of California: A Catalogue of Books* (Berkeley: California University, 1928–30; repr., New York: Burt Franklin, 1969).

42. Fernández, "'Longfellow's Law,'" 125–34.

43. Charles E. Chapman, "The Founding of the Review," *Hispanic American Historical Review* 1, no. 1 (February 1918): 17. The idea for such a journal had been suggested by Rafael Altamira when he attended the Pacific Historical Congress in San Francisco.

44. On Federico de Onís's work in the United States, see Matilde Albert Robatto, "Federico de Onís entre España y Estados Unidos," in *Los lazos de la cultura: El Centro de Estudios Históricos de Madrid y la Universidad de Puerto Rico, 1916–1939*, ed. Consuelo

Naranjo, María Dolores Luque, and Miguel Angel Puig-Samper (Madrid: CSIC, 2002), 238–66.

45. *Los Estados Unidos*, May 1, 1919.

46. Fundació Casa Amèrica Catalunya, *Casa Amèrica Catalunya: Un trajecte centenari* (Barcelona: Fundació Casa Amèrica Catalunya, 2007), 55–57.

47. In his novel on Spanish life in New York, Luis de Oteyza dramatizes this situation when a destitute Asturian immigrant was saved from deportation by the sudden demand for Spanish speakers to teach in American schools and colleges. Luis de Oteyza, *Anticípolis* (Madrid: Renacimiento, 1931), 33.

48. The Fiesta de la Raza became a National holiday in most Spanish-speaking American Republics in the 1910s and 1920s. It was declared a National Holiday in Spain in 1918. On the concept of race in Spain, see Joshua Goode, *Impurity of Blood: Defining Race in Spain, 1870–1930* (Baton Rouge: Louisiana State University Press, 2009). On the concept of Hispanic race in the Hispanic world, see David Marcilhacy, *Raza hispana: Hispanoamericanismo e imaginario nacional en la España de la Restauración* (Madrid: Centro de Estudios Políticos y Constitucionales, 2010).

49. "Se celebrará la Fiesta de la Raza," *Hispano America*, August 24, 1918; "La Fiesta de la Raza se celebró con un esplendor sin precedentes en el gran Banquete del Commodore," *La Prensa*, October 13, 1924.

50. Flyer, Centro Español Papers, University of South Florida Library, Special Collections.

51. Celso García de la Riega defended the Galician thesis, while Luis Ulloa Cisneros argued that Columbus was Catalan. Celso García de la Riega, *Colón, español: Su origen y patria* (Madrid: Sucesores de Rivadeneira, 1914); Luis Ulloa, *Cristòfor Colom fou català: La veritable gènesi del descobriment* (Barcelona: Llibreria Catalònia, 1927). On this polemic, see also David Marcilhacy, "Cristóbal Colón, un héroe hispanizado: Controversia en torno a su patria de origen y homenajes monumentales," in *Construir España: Nacionalismo español y procesos de nacionalización*, ed. Javier Moreno Luzón (Madrid: Centro de Estudios Políticos y Constitucionales, 2007), 153–81.

52. "SPANIARDS," in *The Harvard Encyclopedia of American Ethnic Groups*, ed. Stephan Thernston, Ann Orlov, and Oscar Handlin (Cambridge, MA: Harvard University Press, 1980), 950.

53. "De nuestros lectores," *La Prensa*, March 25, 1929.

54. Xosé-Manoel Núñez, "The Region as Essence of the Fatherland: Regionalist Variants of Spanish Nationalism (1840–1936)," *European History Quarterly* 31, no. 4 (2001): 483–518; Xosé M. Núñez Seixas, "Inmigración y Galleguismo en Cuba (1879–1936)," *Revista de Indias* 53, no. 197 (1993): 53–95.

55. "La Academia de la Llengua Catalana," "Lo Primer Congrés Catalanista," *La Llumanera*, January 1881, 2–3. Lluís Costa, *La Llumanera de Nova York: Un periòdic*

entre Catalunya i Amèrica (Barcelona: Llibres de l'Index, 2012): 68–77. See also Emmy Smith Ready, "La Renaixença in New/Nueva/Nova York: An Exploration of Catalan Immigrant Print Culture" (PhD diss., New York University, 2016).

56. James Clifford, "Diasporas," *Cultural Anthropology* 9, no. 3 (1994): 302–38.

57. I borrow the term from Benedict Anderson, *Imagined Communities: Reflections on the Origin and Spread of Nationalism*, 2nd. ed. (London: Verso, 1991). *La Llumanera* had agencies in Brazil, Colombia, Cuba, France, England, Guatemala, Mexico, Peru, Puerto Rico, the United States, and Venezuela. Costa, *La Llumanera de Nova York*, 51–54.

58. Varela-Lago, "From Patriotism to Mutualism," 16–18.

59. "Importante transacción," *Las Novedades*, August 17, 1899; "Sobre Tabaco," *Las Novedades*, September 21, 1899.

60. José González Fernández Papers, University of South Florida Library, Special Collections.

61. José Yglesias, *The Goodbye Land* (New York: Pantheon Books, 1967), 3.

62. See Ana Varela-Lago, "'Spanish Hands for the American Head?': Spanish Migration to the United States and the Spanish State" (chapter 8 in this volume).

63. "Spaniards in the United States," *Literary Digest* 60, no. 2 (March 22, 1919): 40.

64. "Muchachas y Señoras, Trabajo patriótico y esencial," *La Prensa*, October 23, 1918. See, for example, *La Prensa*, June 23, 1917, 8.

65. "Guía de emigrantes," *Boletín del Consejo Superior de Emigración* (henceforth BCSE) (January–February 1916): 165–66.

66. "Emigración por puertos: Coruña," *BCSE* (1918): 436; "Emigración por puertos: Vigo," *BCSE* (1918): 470.

67. "Vigo," *BCSE* (1927): 501.

68. "Migración española transoceánica en Abril de 1916," *BCSE* (1916): 352; "Almería," *BCSE* (1917): 921.

69. "Emigración por puertos: Málaga," *BCSE* (1918): 448.

70. "Resumen de la emigración española en 1920," *BCSE* (1922): 503–4. This increase was also reported in American newspapers. See, for example, "More Spaniards Coming," *New York Times*, October 19, 1920.

71. Angel Cuesta to Ambassador Juan Riaño, February 21, 1913, Archivo General de la Administración–Ministerio de Asuntos Exteriores (Henceforth AGA-MAE), Caja 8121.

72. José González Fernández Papers, University of South Florida Library, Special Collections.

73. José Antonio Durán, "La Parroquia de acá y de acolá en la Galicia tradicional," in *Indianos: Monografías de Los Cuadernos del Norte* (Oviedo, Spain: Caja de Ahorros de Asturias, 1984), 63–68.

74. William A. Douglass and Jon Bilbao, *Amerikanuak: Basques in the New World* (Reno: University of Nevada Press, 1975), 302, 330–31, 335–36.

75. Thomas G. Hidalgo, "Reconstructing a History of Spanish Immigrants in West Virginia: Implications for Multicultural Education" (PhD diss., University of Massachusetts, Amherst, 1999), 75–76. See also Thomas G. Hidalgo, "From the Mountains and Plains of Spain to the Hills and Hollers of West Virginia: Spanish Immigration into Southern West Virginia in the Early Twentieth Century" (chapter 7 in this volume).

76. Dorothy Davis, *History of Harrison County* (Clarksburg: American Association of University Women, 1970), cited in Hidalgo, "Reconstructing a History," 19.

77. Varela-Lago, "La Emigración gallega a los Estados Unidos," 435–40.

78. Pérez Rey, "Unha achega á emigración galega a Nova York," 36–42.

79. See, for example, *La Llumanera*, January 1875, 7.

80. See also Pérez Rey, "Unha achega á emigración galega a Nova York," 52.

81. In her comprehensive study of these establishments, Jerónima Echevarria has painstakingly gathered information on close to 300 Basque hotels functioning between 1856 and 1939 in twelve states. Jerónima Echeverria, *Home Away from Home: A History of Basque Boardinghouses* (Reno: University of Nevada Press, 1999).

82. Less than 50 percent of Spanish immigrants in Tampa were married, compared to 66 percent of Cubans and 72 percent of Italians. Gary R. Mormino and George E. Pozzetta, *The Immigrant World of Ybor City: Italians and Their Latin Neighbors in Tampa, 1885–1985* (Urbana: University of Illinois Press, 1987), 75. By 1910 there were 810 Spanish boarders, compared to 352 Cubans and 45 Italians. These figures correlated with those on marital status. Spaniards in Tampa had the lowest marriage rate among males over twenty.

83. Caroline F. Ware, *Greenwich Village, 1920–1930: A Comment on American Civilization in the Post-War Years* (Boston: Houghton Mifflin Co., 1935; repr., New York: Octagon Books, 1977), 227–31. See also *Spaniards in Caroline Ware's classic* (New York University, 2011), https://espanyu.files.wordpress.com/2012/02/caroline-ware.pdf.

84. US Congress, Senate, Immigration Commission Report, *Immigrants in Industries*, 14; "Cigar and Tobacco Manufacturing" (Washington: Government Printing Office, 1911), 228.

85. Other services offered by the centros included saving banks and gyms. They also sponsored a variety of sporting events. For a study of these regional centros in Cuba, see Elwood Warren Shomo Jr., "The Centros Regionales of Havana, Cuba, with Special Emphasis on the History and Services of the Centro Asturiano" (master's thesis, University of Miami, 1959).

86. Jesús Tato, "Cómo se originó la idea y para qué es el Sanatorio Español," *La Prensa*, September 29, 1919; "De nuestros lectores," *La Prensa*, January 9, 1929.

87. "Para el Sanatorio de Cesuras: Un donativo de los gallegos de Tampa," *La Voz de Galicia*, January 15, 1928; "El Centro Asturiano manda las primeras 500,000 pesetas para Asturias," *La Prensa*, April 29, 1929.

88. For Tampa, see Varela-Lago, "La emigración gallega a los Estados Unidos," 440–44. For New York, see Pérez Rey, "Unha achega á emigración galega a Nova York," 53–56. According to historian Vicente Peña, these societies of instruction built 225 primary schools in Galicia alone. Vicente Peña Saavedra, *Éxodo, organización comunitaria e intervención escolar: La impronta educativa de la emigración transoceánica en Galicia*, 2 vols. (A Coruña, Spain: Xunta de Galicia, 1991).

89. "La colecta por las víctimas de Sada aumenta," *La Prensa*, April 23, 1924; "Colectan los de Pego para su hospital," *La Prensa*, May 2, 1924.

90. "Contribúyese para el monumento en honor de Costa," *La Prensa*, October 2, 1928; "La estatua a Joaquín Costa," *Plus Ultra*, December 1928; "El Centro Aragonés impulsa sus actividades," *La Prensa*, January 18, 1929.

91. "Grandes Fiestas de San Cipriano en Panes: Inauguración del Parque y Monumento del Excmo. Señor don Angel L. Cuesta," *El Eco de los Valles*, September 25, 1935; "Auto-Semblanza del Hombre: Memorias del Excmo. Sr. D. Angel L. Cuesta," *El Eco de los Valles*, January 10, 1936.

92. "Carretera de Ruenes," *El Eco de los Valles*, November 17, 1903.

93. See, for example, "Los Gallegos en New York," *Vida Gallega*, April 10, 1910.

94. "La Exposició de Filadelfia," *La Llumanera*, December 1874.

95. "A Montserrat," *La Llumanera*, September 1875. See also the illustrations on the pilgrimage to Montserrat in *La Llumanera*, August 1875; "Las festas de Montserrat," May 1880.

96. Gavín W. González, *Pinnick Kinnick Hill: An American Story* (Morgantown: West Virginia University Press, 2003), 3.

97. Hidalgo, "Reconstructing a History," 144–49. See also his chapter in this volume.

98. See, for example, Anne Aguilar Santucci, *Memories of Spain* (Rocklin, CA: Club Español, 1994), 230–36; Anne Aguilar Santucci, "Spanish Settlers Changed Rocklin," *Placer Herald*, November 1, 2006; Manuela Rodríguez, *Memories of a Spaniard*, 56–57 (typescript in author's possession). I thank Aaron Olivas for bringing these sources to my attention.

99. See also Brian Bunk, "Pageants, Popularity Contests, and Spanish Identities in 1920s New York" (chapter 5 in this volume).

100. The Immigration Act of 1921 set the annual national quotas for immigrants of the Eastern Hemisphere at 3 percent of the foreign-born population of each nationality residing in the United States in 1910. The Immigration Act of 1924 set the quotas at 2 percent of each nationality residing in the country in 1890. The

Spanish quota went from 912 in 1921 to 131 in 1924. In 1929, the total quota for all countries was set at 150,000. National quotas were based on the proportion of the population of each nationality (both native-born and foreign-born) residing in the country in 1920. This raised the Spanish quota to 252.

101. "La Unión Benéfica Española y el Centro Hispano Americano . . . ," *La Prensa*, January 25, 1929; "El Centro Hispano Americano aprueba fusión . . . ," *La Prensa*, July 4, 1929. "De nuestros lectores," *La Prensa*, November 29, 1929.

102. "A los Gallegos de los Estados Unidos," *La Prensa*, May 13, 1929. In 1930, the Galician centers of New York and Newark were finalizing their union. "Por la Unión," *Plus Ultra* (February–May 1930).

103. Varela-Lago, "Conquerors, Immigrants, Exiles," 32–53.

104. For specific examples of this involvement, see chapters 3 and 4 in this volume, by Gary R. Mormino and George E. Pozzetta, and by Christopher Castañeda, on the Spanish communities in Tampa and New York respectively.

105. Carlos Serrano, *El turno del pueblo: Crisis nacional, movimientos populares y populismo en España (1890–1910)*, 2nd. ed. (Barcelona: Península, 2000), 125–26.

106. *Manifiesto*, Trabajadores, Tampa, July 5, 1901. Microfilmed copy in University of South Florida Library, "El Internacional . . . Assorted Manifestos and other newspapers."

107. Serrano, *El turno del pueblo*, 136–37.

108. On Pedro Esteve and his links with the Tampa immigrant community, see Joan Casanovas i Codina, "Pedro Esteve: A Catalan Anarchist in the United States," *Catalan Review* 5, no. 1 (July 1991): 57–77; Serrano, *El turno del pueblo*, 125–68; and Gary R. Mormino and Geroge E. Pozzetta, "Spanish Anarchism in Tampa, Florida, 1886–1931" (chapter 3 in this volume).

109. Maximiliano Olay, *Mirando al mundo* (n.p.: Impresos Americalee, 1941?), 15. Readers were paid by the cigar workers to read daily to them in the cigar factories. Gary Mormino and George Pozzetta, "The Reader Lights the Candle: Cuban and Florida Cigar Workers' Oral Tradition," *Labor's Heritage* 5 (Spring 1993): 4–27; Araceli Tinajero, *El Lector de tabaquería: Historia de una tradición cubana* (Madrid: Verbum, 2007).

110. "Nuestro origen," *Institución Francisco Ferrer: Boletín Oficial*, March 26, 1910, 1.

111. Alonso, *Obreiros alén mar*, 113. On the activities of Spanish anarchists and Wobblies in New York, see also Bieito Alonso, "Migración y sindicalismo: Marineros y anarquistas españoles en Nueva York (1902–1930)," *Historia Social*, 54 (2006): 113–35.

112. Olay, *Mirando al mundo*, 24–25.

113. The king suffered an attempt against his life in April 1913, by José Sánchez Alegre, a Catalan anarchist.

114. "Bomb Planned for Wilson," *New York Times*, February 24, 1919. According to the press account, *El Corsario* had a circulation of 1,400.

115. "House Cuts to Year Bar on Immigration," *New York Times*, December 11, 1920.

116. "Consulates Bombed in Philadelphia," *New York Times*, November 24, 1923; "Nation Joins Hunt for Bomb Plotters," *New York Times*, November 26, 1923.

117. I borrow the term from Erez Manela, *The Wilsonian Moment: Self-Determination and the International Origins of Anticolonial Nationalism* (New York: Oxford University Press, 2007). On the rise of nationalisms in Spain, see, for example, Enric Ucelay Da Cal, "The Restoration Monarchy and the Competition of Nationalisms," in *Spanish History Since 1808*, ed. José Alvarez Junco and Adrian Shubert (London: Arnold, 2000), 121–36.

118. Manuel de Paz Sánchez, "Identidades lejanas: El proyecto nacionalista canario en América (1895–1933)," *Catharum* 10 (2009): 43–70. On the connections between Cuban and Canarian nationalism in the late nineteenth century, see Manuel Hernández González, "Martí y Canarias: Relaciones entre los nacionalismos canario y cubano en la segunda mitad del siglo XIX," *Anuario de Estudios Atlánticos* 54-I (2008): 291–320.

119. On Secundino Delgado, see Manuel Suárez Rosales, *Secundino Delgado: Apuntes para una biografía del padre de la nacionalidad canaria* (Islas Canarias: C. Hernández García, 1980); Manuel de Paz Sánchez, "Secundino Delgado y la emancipación cubana," in *El 98 Canario-Americano: Estudios y documentos*, ed. Manuel de Paz Sánchez (La Laguna: Ayuntamiento de San Cristóbal de La Laguna, 1999), 147–59.

120. "Dentro de España," *La Tribuna*, March 27, 1920; "Los Catalanistas de Cuba," *La Tribuna*, May 29, 1920.

121. "¿Separatistas?" *La Tribuna*, March 20, 1920.

122. Juan Cebrián, "Ante el separatismo," *La Tribuna*, April 10, 1920.

123. Antonio Cuyás, "Una frase de Alfonso XIII," *La Tribuna*, July 31, 1920.

124. Juan Riaño to Alejandro Berea, April 12, 1920, AGA-MAE, Caja 8208.

125. Juan Riaño to Alejandro Berea, July 15, 1920, AGA-MAE, Caja 8208.

126. The manifesto, dated September 7, 1920, was signed by the Separatist Catalan Clubs of New Orleans, New York, and Washington, DC, AGA-MAE, Caja 8208.

127. "Estridencias," *La Tribuna*, September 18, 1920.

128. Correspondence in AGA-MAE, Caja 8208. Similar manifestos appeared in New York in 1924, see José Canals Ginesta, "Separatismo catalán en Nueva York," *La Prensa*, April 29, 1924.

129. *Diario de Sesiones*, Senado, n. 95, p. 1941. The senate session took place on November 18, 1921.

130. This argument was shared by members of the Spanish immigrant elite in New York. In a letter to the Centre Nacionalista Català, A. B. Caragol, a Catalan businessman, wrote that as far as politics was concerned, Spaniards abroad should show absolute support for the government, whatever its form. It was for those in the peninsula to debate internal political matters. A. B. Caragol to Centre Nacionalista Català, April 7, 1920, AGA-MAE, Caja 8208.

131. As he wrote to his superiors in Spain, his work was hindered by "the absolute freedom of propaganda that exists in this country, where the press attacks with all impunity the highest representation of the State." Juan Riaño to president of the Directorio Militar, June 9, 1924, AGA-MAE, Caja 8208.

132. Catalonian, "News from Spain," *New York Times*, December 14, 1923; Asturian, "Spain under the Directorate," *New York Times*, December 23, 1923. A number of these exchanges appeared on the letters to the editor page of the *New York Times* during the dictatorship of Primo de Rivera (1923–30).

133. Josep Carner-Ribalta, *De Balaguer a Nova York passant per Moscou I Prats de Molló* (Paris: Edicions Catalanes de París, 1972), 94.

134. J. A. Gibernau, *Triumphs and Failures of American Foreign Policy from Roosevelt to Reagan, 1936–1986* (Phoenix: Phoenix Books, 1986), 14.

135. These were a series of dynastic civil wars, following the death of King Ferdinand VII in 1833, between supporters of Ferdinand's daughter Isabella (Isabelinos) and those of his brother Carlos (Carlists). There were three Carlist wars in the nineteenth century: 1833–39, 1846–49, and 1872–76.

136. Gloria P. Totoricagueña, *Identity, Culture, and Politics in the Basque Diaspora* (Reno: University of Nevada Press, 2004), 68.

137. Koldo San Sebastián, *The Basque Archives: Vascos en Estados Unidos (1938–1943)* (Donostia, Spain: Editorial Txertoa, 1991), 15–16.

138. According to an anonymous "patriot" who denounced the paper to the Spanish consul in New York, *Aberi* portrayed Spain "as an illiterate, semi-savage nation, ruled by a bunch of hangmen and murderers." "Un patriota" to Alejandro Berea, April 24, 1926, AGA-MAE, Caja 8266.

139. See, for example, the article "Nuestra Labor," *Aberi*, May 9, 1926, AGA-MAE, Caja 8266.

140. "No romped este periódico, ni usarlo como envoltura. Después de leerlo, remitídlo a vuestros familiares y amigos que dejásteis en Euzkadi." *Aberi*, May 9, 1926, AGA-MAE, Caja 8266.

141. "Vida obrera," *La Prensa*, January 21, 1924. The author argued that F. Britten Austin's analysis was based on erroneous information, as he did not know the reality of the working class in Spain and wrote about it based on reports given to him by the police and the employers (*patronal*).

142. "Chungas y no chungas," *La Gaceta*, October 24 and November 24, 1925.

143. Juan González to president of the United States, December 3, 1926, National Archives, Record Group 59, M1369, File 852.01/13.

144. "De nuestros lectores," *La Prensa*, March 2, 1929.

145. Alejandro Quiroga, *Making Spaniards: Primo de Rivera and the Nationalization of the Masses, 1923–30* (New York: Palgrave Macmillan, 2007), 183.

146. "El Centro Español acordó eliminar los privilegios que a los cónsules se concedían," *La Gaceta*, May 20, 1939. Centro Asturiano de Tampa, Junta General, April 24, 1939, Centro Asturiano Papers, University of South Florida Library, Special Collections.

147. Marcelino Domingo, *El mundo ante España: México ejemplo* (Paris: La Technique du Livre, 1938), 394–95.

148. "España en América," *La Voz*, April 1, 1939.

2

THE ANDALUCÍA-HAWAII-CALIFORNIA MIGRATION

A Study in Macrostructure and Microhistory

BEVERLY LOZANO

The development of world-systems theory enables us to explain human migration without resorting to the theoretically barren lists of "push-pull" factors and personal motivations that characterize previous studies. Although individuals still make private decisions to move, the patterned movement of groups is better understood as an essential component in a global economic order with shifting demands for labor.[1] National migration policies can also be interpreted within this global context. Since migration plays a central role in moving workers to regions where their labor is needed, governmental legislation regulating these movements has reflected capitalists' needs for a free labor force. It is with this in mind that Aristide Zolberg summarizes the behavior of one nation-state in the world-system as "an element in the interest-calculus of others."[2]

However, when we concentrate exclusively on the significance of global economic factors in structuring migration, our attention tends to remain

DOI: 10.5876/9781607327998.c002

fixed on the ways in which capital realizes its interests at the macrostructural level. The marketplace is raised to the status of an independent causal variable, and labor, cast in the role of capital's exploited object, is quietly obliterated as an active force in shaping the world system. The cultural understandings regarding work that migrant groups carry with them are not accounted for, and we overlook their impact as intervening variables that explain the actual consequences of migration for both workers and their employers.[3] This oversight leads to generalizations such as Zolberg's that "all classes in the countries of the core become as one bourgeoisie in relation to all classes elsewhere, which become as one proletariat."[4] Class relations thus simplified, the dominant class appears to possess uncontested power to orchestrate the movements of workers in its inexorable search for profits. At this level of abstraction, it is impossible for us to see how the strategies of the migrants themselves shape the conditions under which their labor is used, much less the conditions under which profits may be threatened.

The members of the Hawaiian Sugar Planters Association, however, were men who dealt with practical matters, and in 1921 they struggled with the same problem they had faced since the 1850s. Despite the fact that in a period of over seventy years they had spent nearly $18 million inducing laborers to migrate to the Hawaiian cane fields,[5] they were now confronted with a shortage of 6,000 workers and the loss of crops worth $5 million. Claiming on behalf of the sugar planters that there was practically no country in the world to which they had not gone for a labor supply, Walter Dillingham, chairman of the Hawaiian Emergency Labor Commission, described the dimensions of the labor problem to the United States Senate Committee on Immigration in the following way: "As a result of this shortage and the restless, independent attitude of the field laborer, a lack of business control has developed, and a shifting of laborers from place to place has directly followed efforts on the part of planters to urge the laborers to greater efficiency. . . . It is obvious that the possibility of conducting the business efficiently is destroyed."[6]

Perhaps Dillingham exaggerated the consequences that resulted from the tendencies of these restless and independent workers to shift from place to place. But as he went on to enumerate the planters' impressions of each successive wave of workers, it seemed that none could satisfy the need for a stable force of fieldworkers. The Japanese, for example, constituting 60 percent of the workforce, had "ceased to appreciate the opportunities given them as individuals," and aimed "collectively to revolutionize the control of agricultural industries" by becoming planters themselves.[7] The Chinese coolies were "not so kind and tractable as it was anticipated they would be."[8] Even the few Siberians who came to Hawaii turned out to have "socialist tendencies."[9] And above all, the laborers were "restless," constantly shifting in a way that threatened a loss of business control.

According to Dillingham, competition for labor with capitalists located in the eastern United States, Latin America—indeed, in places as far-flung as the prospective workers themselves—required Hawaiian planters to offer wages, bonuses, and other subsidies so substantial relative to other opportunities that laborers were not only attracted to Hawaii but, paradoxically, could afford to leave after several years.[10] For instance, in 1920 workers earned a large bonus above their regular wages. "Finding themselves with money sufficient to the purpose," Dillingham explained, "laborers have availed themselves of the opportunity to leave the less attractive field occupations."[11]

It is likely that many did so. However, just as it is empirically risky to generalize about the effectiveness and results of the strategies of the bourgeoisie, so it is with respect to the proletariat that worked for them. In this article, I will present the turn-of-the-century journey made by one group of agricultural workers who answered the call to Hawaii, the Spaniards from Andalucía. Because all but 1,200 of the original 7,735 moved on to California following a brief stay in the islands, they appear to fall into that category of "restless worker" that left the fields for pursuits the planters might consider more attractive. But as we shall see, this was not to be their strategy at all, and in discovering what these people actually did, we may better understand the causes of the disturbing lack of business control complained of by the Hawaii sugar planters.

THE METHODOLOGICAL TASK

What we wish to discover is an explanation of the causes and consequences of migration that neither reifies macrostructural factors nor trivializes individual motivations. In order to do so, we must reconcile (1) the historical-comparative perspective that locates the migration within the context of the broad structural developments leading up to it with (2) migrants' accounts of how they incorporated these developments into their own migration strategies. By identifying the group's shared understandings of the migration as revealed in the personal accounts of the members, we can then cast these understandings against the historical backdrop in which structural elements come into play. Migration is then interpreted as a complex social process involving factors at *each* level of analysis, rather than as the inevitable workings of disembodied structures such as "the market" or "the system," or the mere agglomeration of infinitely varied private reasons.

Furthermore, this approach addresses the basic theoretical issue of temporality in the analysis of social action. Structural factors such as changes in patterns of land tenure or demand for labor transform the conditions of social life over time. The historical period in which these changes exercise their effects may coincide with the life span of the migrants acting in response to them. When this is so, individuals can take conscious account of these structural factors as they articulate their reasons for migrating and their plans for achieving their goals. On the other hand, the structural forces encouraging migration may have developed and converged over a long historical period extending back to a time inaccessible to the migrants' memories or awareness. In this case, individuals are likely to explain their movements in terms of highly varied private factors that bear no obvious relationship to the structural context in which the theorist locates the migration. This apparent discontinuity between structural and individual data is stressed by Anthony Giddens: "The micro- versus macro-sociological distinction puts an emphasis upon contrasting small groups with larger collectivities or communities; but a more profound difference is between *face-to-face interaction and interaction with others who are physically absent (and often temporally absent also)*."[12]

In other words, because the structural framework that shapes options and constraints is only partially visible to any generational cohort, it becomes impossible to get at the most determining level of analysis with a method that depends solely upon the articulated responses of immigrants. However, when such responses are placed in their historical context, that is, when the "absent" actors are given a voice in the analysis, their significance can be inferred in such a way as to breach the apparent discontinuity between the individual and structural levels of analysis.

In this chapter, I introduce both macro- and microhistorical data to explain the ways in which structural forces shaped the decisions of Andalucian agricultural day laborers as they migrated to Hawaii and, subsequently, to California. In discussing this movement, I present the social and economic conditions in southern Spain at the time of migration in the context of their historical development. Historical factors related to the pattern of recruitment and to the region of final settlement are also examined. Finally, information based on thirteen oral histories related to me by members of the group will provide the microhistorical context that locates the group within the macrostructural framework. The histories will be supplemented with case studies obtained by another investigator in 1940. By comparing similarities and differences between settings, I show the ways in which the group's movements are indeed grounded in macrostructural factors, but in a distinctive manner, conditioned by the group's own cultural perspective on work, and with consequences that acted back upon the macrostructure.

HISTORICAL DEVELOPMENT OF ANDALUCIAN RURAL SOCIETY

Agriculture has long been a primary productive base of the Spanish economy. During the first sixty years of the twentieth century, it represented the largest single source of the Spanish national income. Accounting for 43 percent of the nation's economic base in 1900, agricultural production engaged more than half of Spain's total population in forty-six of the fifty provinces. In the southern region of Andalucía, where the migration discussed here originated, from 70 to 80 percent of the population was engaged in agricultural labor.[13] However, an analysis of the development of this activity reveals the establishment of distinct systems of land tenure that resulted in differing class structures between the northern and southern regions of the country.

In northern Spain, small peasant proprietors emerged as the dominant rural class, whereas in the south, holdings were much larger and their value much greater. Here, medium-sized holdings that would support but not enrich a peasant family were rare: 33 percent of the estates in Andalucía were larger than 125 acres, and 22 percent of all estates larger than 250 acres were located there.[14] Moreover, while these large-sized holdings occupied two to three times as much land as in the agricultural central region, they earned from three to four times the income.[15]

Although the immigrants interviewed in this study referred to the lands they had worked in Spain in a variety of ways—cortijo, hacienda, vega—depending on what area they were from, the term most frequently employed in the literature on rural Spain to discuss the large estates is *latifundio*.[16] Their prevalence in the southern provinces has historical roots that go back to the time of the reconquest of this region at the end of the fifteenth century. When the land was taken back from the Moorish invaders, attempts were made to colonize the area, which had become depopulated during the Moorish occupation. The Spanish Crown offered small holdings as inducements to prospective settlers, but early in the colonization process, the recipients of these grants began to subdivide or to concentrate the plots, depending on the need of poorer farmers to sell what they had for cash and the capacity of wealthier farmers to buy up such holdings. This resulted in a pattern of land distribution that even then foreshadowed the social and economic inequalities that prompted the Andalucía-Hawaii-California migration of the early 1900s.

By the eighteenth century, the Council of Castile had denounced the tyranny of the upper classes and suggested expropriation of the lands, but it was not until the establishment of a constitutional monarchy at the beginning of the nineteenth century that liberal reformers managed to legislate new agrarian measures in the form of disentailment. Not only did this land reform promise to help amortize Spain's national debt by providing a broader base of taxable property, but it instituted the possession of property as an individual right and made property subject to exchange on the market rather than through patrimonial arrangements.[17] Furthermore, reformers reasoned, disentailment "would at the same time [serve] to tear down the whole defective privileged social structure, which was based on an unjust distribution of landed property."[18]

According to Jaime Vicens Vives in his *Economic History of Spain*, the national economy did in fact recover as lands went into economic circulation.[19] However, the "unjust distribution of landed property" was not so easily remedied. Whether one believes accounts claiming the land to have been bought up by "una burguesía especuladora," or by a bourgeoisie consisting of "merchants, speculators and financiers," or by a combination of "aristocrats and capitalists," redistribution of the land to the poor was not to occur.[20] Not only did the resulting organization of a *neolatifundio* system frustrate the hopes of peasants who had expected to gain from the land reforms, but it left many who had labored for the old feudal owners unemployed. Finally, the mid-1800s saw substantial growth in population. These factors combined to

create a rural society in which a few large landowners dominated an agricultural region inhabited by a growing pool of landless day laborers. The traditional arrangements of the displaced feudal system that had defined rights
and obligations between peasant and lord did not exist for the day laborers,
and their increasing numbers operated to depress the wages on which they
now depended for a living.

It is tempting to characterize the social and economic relations that
resulted from this transition in labor and land tenure as modern and capi-
talistic, that is, as impersonal and rationalized. Indeed, Juan Díaz del Moral
refers to the mid-nineteenth-century workers in this region as a rural proletariat.[21] However, a more careful examination of the social relations of production must be undertaken in order to appreciate the specific understandings
brought by such laborers to their work situations.[22]

The Andalucian latifundios were owned by individuals rather than corporations. This rural oligarchy included members of the nobility, but was
primarily made up of untitled persons, many of them related by blood or
by marriage. Absenteeism was common, and large estates not managed by
owners were usually leased intact to a single large tenant, the *arrendador*, or
labrador, who might sublease it in small plots to tenants, but who tended
more often to cultivate it with hired labor.[23]

Because of the incentives resulting from such a pattern of management,
agriculture was often inefficient and unproductive. Where farming was
conducted by an administrator producing profits for a distant owner, min-
imizing wages by leaving certain tasks unperformed might work as well
as maximizing production by applying more labor. Resident owners could
prefer to farm their lands extensively rather than intensively where heavier
capital investment and labor costs would minimize the attractiveness of
the extra margin of profit.[24] And the minority of small tenants had little
incentive and fewer means to improve production when their rents were
subject to frequent negotiation and capital was supplied at usurious rates
by the owners themselves. As summarized by Edward Malefakis: "The latifundio system did not bring the optimal production that both the capitalist and socialist worlds associate with large-scale operations. Rather than
stimulating him to farm them well, the size of the latifundista's properties
merely provided him sufficient reserves so that he could afford the luxury
of farming them badly."[25]

The working class in such a system of agrarian production was varied, and its segments tended to overlap. At the bottom of the social hierarchy were those who worked the land for others, and members of this group can be differentiated on the basis of whether or not they were permanently employed by an owner. Such an arrangement was highly desired, for it minimized the insecurity faced by the worker and his family, and among the day-laboring class there were many individuals who sought to accommodate themselves to the field bosses and owners who might help them get permanent jobs.[26] At the same time, tenant farmers might engage in occasional wage labor to supplement their income in bad years. In 1902, the average income for all employed individuals in Spain was four pesetas a day, but in Andalucía, the average income that year was 1.75 pesetas a day.[27] At these low rates, collective family labor in which all family members searched for work was the rule, and a permanent position for one family member increased the likelihood that others would find work in the same enterprise through the personal contacts thus generated.

Despite the complexity of the class structure that existed, it is not uncommon to see the traditional patron-client model of social relations applied to this region when interactions between the classes are discussed. For example, J. A. Pitt-Rivers characterizes contacts between workers and owners as belonging to a patron-client system based on cordial and reciprocal face-to-face encounters.[28] In emphasizing the strength of patron-client bonds, Michael Kenny too comments with reference to the Spaniards: "Its potency is more understandable among a people whose stoic consideration of this transient life comes perilously close to fatalism, whose traditional class structure of the many poor and few rich is changing but slowly, and whose dependence on moral and material support in this largely barren land of the mystics is an almost instinctive 'just-in-case' type of insurance."[29]

While a traditional system of reciprocal relations between the landowner and those who worked the land may have existed at one time, David Gilmore's study of this area asserts that "historical data show that the modern class system (wage labor employed within an 'impersonal bourgeois latifundism') took form at the turn of the last century."[30] In fact, insurrections and strikes of agricultural workers were recorded for the years 1861, 1871, 1881, and 1903, because laborers were not guaranteed any special rights to traditionally held privileges, but rather were faced with high unemployment rates and low wages.

Nonetheless, while historical analysis points to a socioeconomic system in which the impersonal sale of labor power predominated, it is still necessary to refer to patron-client relations in a discussion of turn-of-the-century Andalucía. From 1903 to 1905, two years before the migration studied here began, agricultural workers engaged in slowdowns, sabotage, and crop burnings in their struggle for higher wages in the face of severe unemployment. But the 1905 drought which ruined that year's crop and resulted in famine dashed their hopes of gaining concessions from the landowners. In his account of the strikes and subsequent disaster, Díaz del Moral tells us: "The enthusiasm of the masses had been slowly declining since the failure of the general strikes. Nevertheless, they maintained a strong solidarity until 1905. Then, when overcome by the crisis, they began to desert. Deceitfully, *they renewed some of the broken ties of the patron-client relationship with the master* to save themselves from the terrible calamity: the large majority confessed that they had been mistaken"[31] (emphasis added).

Whether they did so in deceit or in despair, the point is that for some of the laborers, a familiarity with the old patron-client ties remained. While day labor for wages was the rule, the social system was still sufficiently flexible that some people could take advantage of the personal acquaintance with their landlords in order to survive. Always, in the towns where the laborers lived, there had been some workers related to or familiar with the more privileged permanent workers of the employer. Some of these patron-client ties went back through several generations of a family, and while not all in the town could benefit from them, certainly all were familiar with the social norms and etiquette that governed them.

In other words, the rural society abandoned by the Andalucian immigrants at the turn of the century would be most accurately characterized as one based primarily on the impersonal social relations of production between wage laborers and employers, but one with which an understanding of patron-client relations coexisted and was sometimes preferred.

HAWAIIAN AGRICULTURE AND THE SEARCH FOR LABORERS

By the mid-nineteenth century, the effects of a declining whaling industry were being reflected in the falling profits of Hawaiian Island mercantilists, principally Americans and Europeans, whose trade depended on the outfitting of ships sailing from Honolulu. At the same time, important changes were taking place in the Hawaiian landholding system. Both Crown and public lands comprising more than half of the islands were declared inalienable in 1865, and Hawaii's monarchs derived income by offering these lands for use under long-term lease.[32] This, coupled with the increased demand for staple tropical crops such as sugar and coffee presented by growing communities along North America's Pacific coast, provided the incentive for businessmen to transfer their investments to agricultural production. Between the years 1860 and 1866, sugar exports advanced from less than a million and a half pounds to more than 17 million pounds, a trend that was to continue for many years.[33]

The industry was highly organized. Plantation owners formed associations through which they lobbied for favorable treaties, tariffs, and finally, in 1898, annexation to the United States. Another important feature was the agency system in which business houses in Honolulu furnished capital and served as agents both for marketing the product and for recruiting labor.

In this island society whose native population had been declining, the question of labor recruitment among the planters was one that went hand in hand with the issue of racial balance in the population as a whole. In a process that began as early as 1851 with the importation of 195 Chinese workers, the Hawaiian Sugar Planters Association brought workers from places as diverse as Micronesia and Norway to labor in the fields. However, it was the Japanese who provided the bulk of the workforce: by 1900, Japanese made up one half of the adult male population of the islands, and American planters, who dominated the growing industry, were concerned about the apparent tendencies of this group toward collective action.[34] The Planters' Labor and Supply Company had encouraged immigration from Japan in 1889, claiming that "the Japanese make good house, farm and plantation servants."[35] However, by 1900, striking Japanese workers were described as "taking up a very independent attitude."[36] From then on, a sharp distinction was to be made between immigration for labor supply and immigration for population upbuilding.[37]

Walter Dillingham, speaking two decades later, summarizes the difference: "The solution of these two problems . . . must be founded on a frank differentiation between labor intended to relieve the present crisis and labor intended for permanent population. For the former, Hawaii needs the most efficient labor available, regardless of race or color; for the latter she needs a carefully selected agricultural people who can continue her industries, be assimilated into her population, and constitute the base on which to build a body politic essentially American."[38]

As early as 1899, special inducements such as sharecropping and racial wage differentials had been considered by planters, who looked to Europe for white labor from among those they termed "Latin peasants."[39] In addition to published reports regarding "the state of labor . . . in European countries," favorable reports had been received "concerning the success in Cuba of Spanish laborers as cane planters," and in 1907, planters impelled their agents to "investigate the possibilities in the district of Malaga, South Spain, where sugar planting is conducted."[40]

THE MIGRATION TO HAWAII

In 1907, agents for the Hawaiian Sugar Planters Association posted handbills around the Andalucian countryside announcing a migration with one-way passage paid to "the State of Hawaii, United States of America."[41] Following a description of the islands filled with appealing adjectives extolling the climate and scenery, conditions of eligibility were detailed. First, immigrants had to be certified agricultural workers with families. The men could be no older than forty-five years of age, the women no older than forty. Families with male offspring older than seventeen were specifically recruited, and the salaries ranged from $20 gold per month for the head of the household to $12 gold per month for the wives and $10 for female children over age fifteen. Upon signing up to work in the cane fields, they were promised, in addition to their wages, a house worth $500, water, wood, free schooling for the children, and a garden plot. There was no contract required, contract labor having been forbidden once Hawaii became a US territory.

The first migration included 2,269 Andalucians. In 1911, 1912, and 1913, five more groups sailed to Hawaii, bringing the total number of immigrants to 7,735. In 1914, World War I broke out, and no additional passages were made thereafter.[42] Who were the laborers that answered the planters' advertisements? At this point, we will turn to the microhistorical accounts in which the immigrants describe themselves.

I personally obtained thirteen oral histories from members of the Andalucía-Hawaii-California migration. Five had been born in Spain, six in

Hawaii, and two following their family's arrival in California. Four of the interviews were conducted in Spanish, and the rest in some mixture of Spanish and English. At the time of this study, all the subjects were living in California; the interviews were tape-recorded in their homes and lasted a minimum of an hour and a half.

Those from whom the histories were obtained had indeed been, or were descended from, landless day laborers. When asked what they and their families had done for a living in Spain, they responded with comments such as the following: "We lived in a little town and walked to work in the countryside. We'd work two days here, three days there, wherever we could find something."

All described large landholdings as predominating in the area they came from—cortijos, haciendas, *ranchos*, etc. "The men would go out and talk with the rich. If they had work for a day or so, you'd get paid. If not, what could you do?"

To supplement earnings gained in this way, family members would engage in various activities they referred to with the phrase, *buscarse la vida*. Literally translated, this means "to seek out a living," and according to those interviewed, it implies to live by one's wits. Such activities included gleaning the fields by the women and children, with the owner's permission, after male family members had harvested the crop for wages. One woman explained, "One wouldn't be paid to do that, because the owner of the land would just give it outright, to help out." Other things mentioned were wood collecting and the gathering of dung. The former could be used or sold as kindling, the latter as fertilizer.

When asked to describe their employers and their relations with them, most claimed that they worked for the *señorito*, a term meaning "little lord" and conveying a somewhat negative connotation. (The use of the term persists in the area to this day and refers to owners of large estates.) Other frequently used terms included *los ricos* (the rich), *los dueños* (the owners), or *los patrones* (the bosses or owners). Some whose families had maintained close relations with their employers—the women working as servants or wet-nurses in the house, the men as permanent laborers—spoke about them in mixed terms. For example: "We worked for the rich—people we knew. They were rich people, good people. My mother was raised in the house of the señoritos, who were my godparents. They were good to me, but when they had no work, there was nothing we could do about it. We would have to work for other families."

At such times, the family would rely solely on day wages for labor on other owners' lands. While referring to the family she worked for as "good people," this woman also described the requirements as being harsh. "It's not like here. There, you work like a panting dog until your tongue hangs out. There, you don't sit down!" When asked why she and her family left Spain, despite the fact that more than many in their town, they were in a position to enjoy some of the benefits of the patron-client relationship, she stated: "Life in Spain was very bad. The one who had didn't help the one who didn't have. If he had something, it was for himself and not for anybody else."

A number of respondents mentioned that at one time their families had owned a small plot of land, but that as times worsened they had had to sell it and rely on day labor: "My father's family had owned a little farm. But in later years, they had to sell it and go out to work. Things got tougher economically." Others had never owned any property: "You're born and raised on a cortijo. That's where my parents stayed. The people who worked it lived there, and the owners came up on the weekends."

It is clear from the responses that the Andalucian immigrants indeed displayed knowledge of both the wage labor system and the system of patron-client relations. While the latter offered a modicum of security, it could not always be relied upon. One can see their attitudes about the patrones, as well as their primary orientation toward wages, in the reasons given for deciding to migrate. Both a resentment toward the element of social control exercised by the señoritos and the promise of higher wages elsewhere figure into the responses. When asked why the family left Spain, respondents made statements like the following:

One of the worst conditions for them was religion. The big ranches had churches and if you didn't go to church, they'd fire you.

The church thing. When they told my father he had to go, it made him angry. The dueño would be at the door and he would eye who was coming in and who wasn't. If you weren't there, you'd have to have a good excuse or he'd reprimand you.

It is important to note the relationship between the church and the landowners at this time, for the connection between religion and the local economy is not immediately apparent in the individual responses of these immigrants. At the turn of the century, the church hierarchy organized, under the auspices of the landowners, Catholic worker associations. Members were taxed to provide funds for the poorest laborers in the area in the hope of pacifying those elements of the agricultural labor force who were striking for higher wages or asking outright for land redistribution.[43] It is at this political juncture that the church and the señoritos come together in the immigrants' stated reasons for leaving. Enforced church attendance was one of the means that landowners employed in attempting to control the workforce and to collect tribute.

Another reason occasionally mentioned as a motive to migrate was the military draft—*la quinta*. Spain was at war with Morocco and to families whose sons were eligible for military service, migration provided a sometimes clandestine means of escape. Several respondents indicated that they smuggled themselves onto the ships waiting to depart from Malaga or Gibraltar, saying that they migrated *de contrabando*—as contraband.[44] It is ironic that the young men the families concealed from the port authorities were an asset to them on this migration, for the sugar planters offered these sons a wage just below that of the fathers and slightly above that of the mothers'—$15 gold per month. But in every case, the promise of higher wages was given in addition to the other factors mentioned as reasons for migrating.

Having addressed the questions of who the immigrants were and why they left Spain, we may now observe their activities in the setting they found on the first leg of the migration, Hawaii. Here was the promise of higher wages, guaranteed employment, and what they hoped would be an alternative to a life in which "things were very bad."

The migration to Hawaii was to have been a permanent one. The agricultural workers recruited by the sugar planters were indeed provided with the benefits promised in the advertisements. Initially, they went to work in the fields cutting cane. When asked in general terms to describe their lives in Hawaii, however, an interesting pattern of response developed, both among those who relied on their parents' memories and among those who had given elaborate first-hand accounts of life in Spain. Very little could be recalled about Hawaii. Responses might include descriptions of the scenery or the climate, but as to their lives as workers there, they had little spontaneous comment. They were asked specific questions focusing on the same details that they had reported unprompted in their accounts of life in Spain: for example, where did you work, whom did you work for and what were they like, how did you go about finding work?

Their brief answers revealed that in Hawaii, as in Spain, they worked on large landholdings, the plantations, and were paid a wage. However, rather than working for landowners who were visible, if socially distant, in Hawaii they worked for sugar companies under the supervision of a *luna*, or foreman. Impressions about the persons who directed their work seemed to be neutral and, at the time of my study, memories of their contacts with them almost nonexistent.

George Schnack complained of a similar pattern of response to a survey he conducted in 1940 among Andalucian immigrants in California.[45] When asked to rate the lunas' treatment of them as workers, two of his respondents claimed to have liked it and two to have disliked it, and thirteen respondents rated the treatment they received as neither good nor bad. From his survey results, Schnack concluded that conditions on the plantations were not a factor in the Andalucians' decision to migrate again to California.

However, in addition to the survey, Schnack conducted open-ended interviews with these and six other respondents. A close examination of his twenty-three case studies reveals that in over one-third of their *spontaneous* accounts, certain features characteristic of the plantation system of agriculture were mentioned in a negative light—particularly the lunas. The incomes of the lunas were calculated according to how much labor they could extract from gangs of workers, and the effect of this arrangement was reflected in these more detailed interviews. Field bosses were described as "inconsiderate" and "rough and mean" people who had to learn that "they could not treat the Spanish in that manner." These "slave drivers" prodded their workers and instigated antagonisms among them so that "each group worked feverishly and even fought to keep another from getting ahead." One of Schnack's respondents actually rose to the position of luna for a time. According to him, his job was to "see that laborers did the proper amount of work," even if he had to be "tough." Because he could not stand "mistreating other human beings," he quit the job and left Hawaii. In addition to the system of labor management, several of those interviewed in 1940 recalled their dealings with the company stores. One person pointed out that the stores "managed to keep [the workers] always in debt so that they couldn't leave the plantation."

Although the Andalucians had known little but agricultural work, and would continue as day laborers for years following their arrival in California, the plantation system of Hawaii violated their cultural understanding of what tolerable working relations should involve. By the time of my study, the most common response to questions about why they left Hawaii was a shrug and the comment "I don't know—we just didn't like it there." As with their responses about leaving Spain, they nearly all mentioned that they had heard they could earn higher wages in California; with this information only, it might seem that the prospect of economic gain was the most consistent driving force behind their extensive movements. And, yet, Hawaii was not without opportunities for earning better wages, for some of the workers had already found jobs away from the fields at even higher rates of pay.[46] Thus, while wages were given as a reason for migration both from Spain to Hawaii and from Hawaii to California, where the respondents finally established permanent settlements, we must look at what the Andalucians did once they reached California to understand the social structural elements that enabled them to fashion those settlements.

THE MIGRATION TO CALIFORNIA

It is not clear how the first members of the group found their way to the West Coast of the United States. However, by 1909, several hundred families who had gone to Hawaii in 1907 were reported to be working in the fruit orchards of the Vaca, Suisun, and Santa Clara Valleys of California.[47] Word reached subsequent immigrants to Hawaii that wages on the California ranches were good and that employment was plentiful enough to support families. Most of the Andalucians working in Hawaii chose to move on, again with the understanding that they would be employed as agricultural laborers. It should be noted that a couple of those interviewed mentioned that they and others spent a brief time working in factories in San Francisco and Seattle, two debarkation points on the West Coast. Nonetheless, they too kept moving until at last they found themselves living and working in conditions strikingly similar to, and yet in some respects critically different from, those they had left behind in Spain. Although, over the years, the children were to move into new occupations and lifestyles, the people of the Andalucía-Hawaii-California migration settled into communities from which they did not move again. It is the process of that final settlement that will be discussed in the following pages.

As noted, the Andalucians in Hawaii heard from the first few who had preceded them to the mainland of the United States that there was work in the northern California fruit orchards. This time, as in their accounts of life in Spain, their answers to my questions were spontaneous and detailed.

> We knew some people in Fairfield. They let us stay with them a few days, and my father and brother went out to the ranches. Wherever they saw a ranch and a house, they'd go up to the door and ask for the owner of the land. If he had work, they'd stay. If not, they'd try at the next place.

> My dad went to San Francisco. The *compadre* said, "Things aren't so good here—it's all factories." My dad said he didn't want any part of San Francisco, except to visit. He came back to Vacaville and the next day, he went out to the ranches with my brother. That's how he found a job.

I interviewed people who had settled in Vacaville, Stockton, Fairfield, and the Santa Clara area, and all gave reports similar to these. Moreover, many claimed to have lived on the ranch itself at one time or another. After the rancher became acquainted with the workers, he might offer them a permanent position. At this point, the family would occupy a small house near the main ranch house, and while the laborer worked in the orchards, his wife might help in the care of the rancher's children.

At first glance, one sees in these accounts an establishment of ties similar to the ones that in Spain had provided the laborer and his family with a desirable security, desirable at least in comparison to the lot of those who did not have it. But at the same time, the Andalucians did not necessarily stay on any one ranch if it seemed they could earn more on another. In fact, most families were able to save enough from the collective family earnings to buy a house in a nearby town and, in time, restricted their relations with their employers to the economic sphere.

When asked how life in California compared with that in Spain, the people interviewed found the new life preferable for the following reasons. While one could, as in Spain, go out and find seasonal work on a permanent basis from year to year with the patrones with whom they had become acquainted, the social monitoring of employee behavior was absent in California. In a sense, these loosely structured patron-client ties could be drawn upon in the early days by the new arrivals as a means of establishing a secure work position within a modern wage system. While close face-to-face interaction and personal acquaintance provided the initial basis of security, when the laborer wanted to move on, there were no socially or politically institutionalized bonds of loyalty that bound him to any one rancher. In fact, most of the Andalucian immigrants spent most of their lives as day laborers, living entirely from their wages, rather than as permanent clients of any particular patron. However, they did tend to work for the same three or four ranchers each year.

People were asked to compare their social and economic relations with their new employers to those they'd left behind in Spain.

> We still worked for the rich. For us, it was the same, because you had to work for this one and that one. But because they were good to us, we were satisfied. Also, in Spain, you'd only work a day or two in one place—not like here, where you go to a ranch and stay until the work is done.

> It was the same as in Spain. We still worked for the same people. And if you complied, they paid you. If not, you got fired—same thing. But here, all they looked at was your work. They treated everyone the same. If you worked, you ate. No one had to beg. And there was enough work.

In every case, while the respondent recalled working for the same employers over a period of years, and perhaps had even lived for a time on the ranch, the quality of the relationship was expressed in terms that encompassed both a social and an economic assessment: an honest day's work for a just employer at a fair day's wage. This, coupled with the fact that fruit culture in California used more modern techniques of cultivation than in Spain (frequent pruning, spraying, irrigation, etc.), which generated more tasks for longer periods of time, made agricultural work a means to family survival in a way that the Andalucian latifundio system did not. And yet, until the 1940s, they found themselves still working as day laborers in a seasonal agricultural economy in which they were paid wages by people with whom, in some ways, they had secured some of the guarantees associated with patron-client relations.

In later years, when the canneries and war industries offered more attractive wages and opportunities, the children of these immigrants would leave ranch work altogether. But for nearly forty years following their induced exodus from Andalucía, they continued to apply their knowledge and skills to the structural constraints they encountered, moving until they established themselves in situations congenial enough to allow them to approximate their own conceptions of life and work. While the Hawaiian sugar planters perceived the disruptive loss of their laborers as due to some restlessness inherent among those who worked in the fields, we can better understand the workers' movements and final settlement in terms of a persistent struggle to restructure constraining economic realities in ways that allowed for the formation of improved social realities. These improvements were judged in terms of what had been considered desirable, but difficult to establish, in Spain. It was this, and not the restlessness of the worker, that the sugar planters did not account for when they saw the failure of their generous financial inducements to the immigrants.

SIMILARITIES AND DIFFERENCES IN SETTINGS COMPARED

In both Hawaii and southern Spain, the agricultural economy was based on landholdings large relative to the size associated with peasant family farming—in Spain the latifundios; in Hawaii the plantations. In neither instance did the Andalucians work their own lands. In Hawaii, however, as in Spain, the setting did allow for the establishment of a household economy in which vegetables could be grown, a few animals and fowl kept, and the countryside scoured for wild-growing foodstuffs or fuel that could be traded or used at home.

What differences might account for the fact that the Andalucians did not make this a permanent home, despite the fact that their original desire for higher wages seems to have been substantially met? A few people claimed that adjustment to the climate proved difficult, but an equal number recalled vividly how much they enjoyed the natural beauties of Hawaii and stated that the climate did not affect them adversely. Again, some professed dislike for the Hawaiian ethnic mixture, which included many Asians; but in California, they also found themselves in contact with ethnic groups they had not met in Spain. In fact, many of them were the same groups they had worked with in the fields of Hawaii—Japanese, Filipinos, and Chinese. And yet, the Andalucians did not leave California.

A structural difference which the Andalucians do not dwell upon, but which is suggestive when one considers their pattern of final settlement, has to do with the system of management on the large plantations compared with that of the latifundios. As mentioned above, in Spain, the laborers knew the señoritos, and were often supervised directly by them. Certainly, the personal nature of these contacts caused frequent resentment toward the Spanish employers, and this resentment was sometimes given as one of the reasons for leaving. But on the other hand, the Andalucians knew how to manage this type of relationship to their advantage if the opportunity presented itself. Probably the greatest advantage represented by these ties was the fact that a relatively permanent position minimized the need to travel from place to place in order to earn a living.

In Hawaii, however, none of the laborers knew the owners, who were, in fact, bureaucratically organized corporations. The workers were supervised by overseers about whom, if they remember them at all, their attitudes remain largely neutral. While the wages were better than they had been in Spain, the work involved considerable relocation from plantation to plantation. There was no opportunity to stabilize a family life in one area or village since the placement of labor was dictated solely by the needs of the plantations as assessed by the sugar companies and implemented by the overseers. Although this factor was not specifically mentioned by the people interviewed as a reason for leaving Hawaii, when we compare the structural similarities and differences between Spain and California, it appears to be one of the important features besides acceptable wages the latter setting offered that Hawaii did not.

First, it has often been remarked that the climate and topography of Spain and California are strikingly similar. Interestingly, however, this was not mentioned by any of those interviewed as a reason for staying in California. Second, both the Spanish latifundios and the California orchards represented relatively large landholdings and though, in the latter case, there was probably a greater proportion of small plots than in the former, holding out to the Andalucians the possibility of someday owning land, the majority did not become ranchers themselves.

The pattern of California landholding did, however, lend itself to a kind of social arrangement that in southern Spain had ensured a greater security of job tenure, but which had become ever more difficult to establish. In California, the Andalucians were successful in developing contacts that enabled them to work for one or two ranchers on a fairly permanent, if still seasonal, basis. Here, they could maximize both their wages and their security within a geographical range that allowed them to settle in small towns like the ones they had known in Spain. That this factor, missing in Hawaii, is significant is attested to in the comment of one woman, who said, when asked why she liked it in California, "Because, if they treat you well here—well, here you stay! Why go looking around here and there?" (In other words, contradicting Walter Dillingham, why shift restlessly from place to place?).

If the setting was similar in some essential respects to that of southern Spain, it also differed in several ways that made it a more desirable home to the Andalucians. The system of agriculture was modernized, and for a time at least, the techniques of intensive cultivation ensured a greater degree of more regular employment. The orchard industry was well linked by the railroad, with its refrigerated cars, to an expanding eastern market.[48] It was also linked with a growing local canning industry. These combined structural features made for a vital agricultural system in which the Andalucians could both earn satisfactory wages and establish the stable form of community and family life that neither Spain nor Hawaii could provide them.

IMPLICATIONS FOR THEORY

To focus exclusively on the macrostructural level of analysis is to miss important and determining aspects of social action. A theoretical approach that explains migration solely in terms of the migrants' reactions to wages and policies set by others powerful enough to maximize their own "interest calculus" fails to capture the ways in which migration strategies may represent significant undercurrents running counter to dominant structures of exploitation.[49] As Alejandro Portes and John Walton point out: "Contrary to the usual image, the response of the exploited to conditions created for them by the capitalist system is seldom passive acquiescence. Their effort to manipulate, in turn, these conditions is based on the two resources left in the absence of capital: one's own labor and social bonds of solidarity and mutual support within the working class. [Migration] is a way through which the exploited contribute to ever expanding structures of economic domination and, simultaneously, the form in which they react to their constraints."[50]

World-systems theorists have revealed to us a global economic structure in which exploitation and inequality are dominant features subject to modification only through class struggle and active resistance by the working class. While the most dramatic instance of such struggle may well be proletarian revolution, we must be cautious not to overlook other aspects of class and cultural life that through their persistence and development make problematic the final and complete domination of capital.

NOTES

I am deeply grateful to Gary Hamilton for his generous comments on an earlier version of this chapter. My thanks also go to John Walton, who provided several critical insights.

1. Michael Burawoy, "The Functions and Reproduction of Migrant Labor: Comparative Material from South Africa and the United States," *American Journal of Sociology* 81, no. 5 (1976): 1050–88.

2. Aristide Zolberg, "Migration Policies in a World System," in *Human Migration: Patterns and Policies*, ed. William H. McNeill and Ruth S. Adams (Bloomington, IN: Indiana University Press, 1978), 241–86.

3. See Barrington Moore Jr., *Social Origins of Dictatorship and Democracy: Lord and Peasant in the Making of the Modern World* (Boston: Beacon Press, 1966), 485, for a discussion of this issue.

4. Zolberg, "Migration Policies," 280.

5. Edward Johannessen, *The Hawaiian Labor Movement: A Brief History* (Boston: Bruce Humphries Inc., 1956), 27.

6. US Congress, Senate, Committee on Immigration, *Hearings on Immigration into Hawaii before Committee on Immigration*, 67th Cong., 1st sess. (Washington, DC: Government Printing Office, 1921), 6.

7. US Congress, *Hearings*, 5.

8. US Congress, *Hearings*, 36.

9. US Congress, *Hearings*, 34.

10. As Alejandro Portes and John Walton point out, "for immigrants to be useful to an expanding capitalist economy, the situation had to be arranged so that the means they initially received would *not* be sufficient for their survival." *Labor, Class and the International System* (New York: Academic Press, 1981), 52.

11. US Congress, *Hearings*, 4.

12. See Anthony Giddens, *Central Problems in Social Theory: Action, Structure and Contradiction in Social Analysis* (Berkeley: University of California Press, 1979), 203.

13. Edward Malefakis, *Agrarian Reform and Peasant Revolution in Spain: Origins of the Civil War* (New Haven: Yale University Press, 1970), 96.

14. Spanish Institute for Agrarian Reform, *Agrarian Reform in Spain* (London: United Editorial Ltd., 1937), 38–40.

15. Malefakis, *Agrarian Reform*, 22.

16. For example, see Pascual Carrión, *Los latifundios en España: Su importancia, origen, consecuencias y solución* (Madrid: Gráficas Reunidas, 1932); Malefakis, *Agrarian Reform*; Juan Martínez Alier, *Labourers and Landowners in Southern Spain* (London: George Allen and Unwind, 1971); and Jaime Vicens Vives, *An Economic History of Spain* (Princeton, NJ: Princeton University Press, 1969)

17. Miguel Artola, *La burguesía revolucionaria (1808–1874)* (Madrid: Alianza Editorial, 1974), 149.

18. Spanish Institute for Agrarian Reform, *Agrarian Reform*, 17.

19. Vicens Vives, *Economic History*, 613

20. First quotation: J. A. Oddone, *La emigración europea al Río de la Plata: motivaciones y proceso de incorporación* (Montevideo: Ediciones de la Banda Oriental, 1966), 39; second quotation: Artola, *La burguesía revolucionaria*, 165; third quotation: Vicens Vives, *Economic History*, 637. Last quotation: Carrión, *Los latifundios en España*, 16.

21. Juan Díaz del Moral, *Historia de las agitaciones campesinas andaluzas-Córdoba: Antecedentes para una reforma agraria* (Madrid: Alianza Editorial, 1969).

22. In a comparative study suggesting how one should go about investigating agrarian class societies, Juan Martínez Alier cautions that "a proper theory of the [various] social formations will include an industrial sociology or a sociology of work in the different rural settings." "Peasants and Labourers: Spain, Cuba and Highland Peru," *Journal of Peasant Studies* 1, no. 2 (1974), 154. In other words, theory about rural class relations must be grounded not on typologies based on feudal-capitalistic or traditional-modern dichotomies, but on a firm understanding of peasant or laborer attitudes toward work and systems of remuneration and on accurate investigations of the specific social milieux in which these operate. See also A. Stinchcombe, "Agricultural Enterprise and Rural Class Relations," *American Journal of Sociology* 67, no. 2 (1961): 165–76.

23. Malefakis, *Agrarian Reform*, ch. 5.

24. Carrión, *Los latifundios en España*, 343.

25. Malefakis, *Agrarian Reform*, 91.

26. Malefakis, *Agrarian Reform*, 98.

27. Malefakis, *Agrarian Reform*, 100.

28. J. A. Pitt-Rivers, "Introduction," in *Mediterranean Countrymen: Essays in the Social Anthropology of the Mediterranean* (Paris: Mouton, 1963), 21.

29. Michael Kenny, "Patterns of Patronage in Spain," in *Friends, Followers and Factions: A Reader in Political Clientelism*, ed. Steffen W. Schmidt, James C. Scott, Carl Lande, and Laura Guasti (Berkeley: University of California Press, 1977), 356.

30. David Gilmore, "Patronage and Class Conflict in Southern Spain," *Man* 12, no. 3/4 (1977): 446–58.

31. Díaz del Moral, *Historia*, 217.

32. Legislative Reference Bureau, *Public Land Policy in Hawaii: An Historical Analysis*, Report no. 5 (Honolulu, 1959). 4. Under such a system of long-term leasing in which agriculturalists didn't actually have to purchase the land they farmed, capital obtained through the use of the same leases as collateral could be employed for other purposes such as plantation development and improvement.

33. Ralph S. Kuykendall, *The Hawaiian Kingdom 1854–1874: Twenty Critical Years* (Honolulu: University of Hawaii Press, 1953), 143.

34. John Reinecke, *Feigned Necessity: Hawaii's Attempt to Obtain Chinese Contract Labor, 1921–23* (San Francisco: Chinese Materials Center, 1979), 20.

35. "Japanese Immigrants," *Planters Monthly* 8, no. 4 (1889): 149.

36. "Report of Committee on Labor to the President and Members of the Hawaii Sugar Planters Association," *Planters Monthly* 19, no. 11 (1900): 515.

37. Kuykendall, *Hawaiian Kingdom*, 181.

38. US Congress, *Hearings*, 17.

39. "State of Labor on the Hawaiian Islands," *Planters Monthly* 18, no. 12 (1899): 562; "President's Address," *Hawaiian Planters Record* 2, no. 1 (1910): 4.

40. First quotation: "State of Labor," 562.; second and third quotations: US Congress, *Hearings*, 43.

41. "*Emigración con pasaje gratuito al estado de Hawaii*," reproduced in *Winters Express* [Winters, California], Centennial Edition (1975), 76.

42. George Schnack, "Subjective Factors in the Migration of Spanish from Hawaii to California" (MA thesis, Stanford University, 1940). One cannot help but note the small size of this migration, given the fact that other regions of Spain had emigration rates as high as 20.6 per thousand, mostly bound for Latin America. The highest rate from the latifundio region was found in Granada, and only amounted to 8.0 per thousand. Malefakis suggests that this may result from the southern farm laborer's preference to "combat the injustice of his situation rather than flee from it." Malefakis, *Agrarian Reform*, 105. See also I. S. MacDonald, "Agricultural Organization, Migration and Militancy in Rural Italy," *Economic History Review* 16, no. l (August 1963), 61–75, on this point.

43. Díaz del Moral, *Historia*, 145.

44. It has been reported that the Andalucía-Hawaii-California migration was a clandestine migration, since apparently it is not recorded anywhere in the Spanish records. See Rosendo A. Gómez, "Spanish Immigration to the United States," *Americas* 19, no. 1 (1962): 59–78. A number of people I interviewed confirmed that, indeed,

they came without knowledge of the authorities, but it is doubtful that this was the case for all of them.

45. Schnack, "Subjective Factors," 35.

46. In 1910, there were 1,990 Andalucians in Hawaii, of whom 515 worked on plantations. Even allowing for a number of women and children who might not be employed, this still suggests that a considerable number of workers from the 1907 passage had already made their way off the plantations and into other occupations. Schnack, "Subjective Factors," 52.

47. Ronald H. Limbaugh and Walter A. Payne, *Vacaville: The Heritage of a California Community* (Vacaville: Vacaville City Council, 1978).

48. Limbaugh and Payne, *Vacaville,* 127.

49. See Alejandro Portes for his discussion of what he terms the "microstructures of migration." "Migration and Underdevelopment," in *Latin American Immigration Project. Occasional Papers* (Durham, North Carolina, 1978), 53.

50. Portes and Walton, *Labor, Class,* 64.

3

SPANISH ANARCHISM IN TAMPA, FLORIDA, 1886–1931

GARY R. MORMINO AND GEORGE E. POZZETTA[†]

One hundred and twenty-five years ago, revolutionaries driven by a messianic faith threatened to paralyze world governments through apocalyptic acts of terror. Motivated by anarchist dreams of brotherhood and nihilist rejection of authority, waves of violence terrified the public, outraged the ruling classes, and canonized a handful of true believers who fulfilled "propaganda by deed."

Tampa, Florida, seemed an unlikely setting for such melodrama. But city leaders waged a dedicated campaign to combat real and imagined threats to the establishment by radicals in general, anarchists in particular, and most especially *los lectores*, the readers of the cigar factories, who, critics argued, fomented subversive thoughts from their tribunes. This essay will examine the origins, development, and nature of Spanish anarchism in Tampa, Florida, in the period from 1886 to 1931, a study not of radical violence—of which there was little—but of group dynamics and organization—of which there was much.[1]

DOI: 10.5876/9781607327998.c003

To understand Spanish anarchism, one must appreciate the contours of anarchism and emigration on the peninsula. Emigration has played a significant role in Spanish society for 500 years. The major points of origin for Tampa's Spaniards were the northwestern provinces of Asturias and Galicia, which have been called the nursery of Spanish emigrants.[2] "The Asturians do not leave Spain for money," an elderly Spanish immigrant recalled, "but for the sheer adventure of it." He added that sheer misery characterized the lives of Asturians he knew as a youth in the 1890s.[3]

Small farmers and peasants in rural Asturias and Galicia struggled to earn a living on a very hard land. An observer described Galicia in 1581 as a barren region, where the coarse rye bread seemed unfit for human consumption.[4] Landholding patterns aggravated the plight of the agrarian workers. The disentailment of church lands beginning in the later eighteenth century, which in France helped ameliorate the land-hungry peasants, only increased the misery of the lower classes. Unlike southern Spain, dominated by the *latifundio*, northern Spain was characterized by hopelessly small family plots. In part because of the primitive roads and isolation, in part because of the burdensome laws of tenancy, much of northwestern Spain was governed by the antiquated system of *foros* (hereditary quitrents). The rural classes, pressed by the landowner, exercised little control over their own lives, since lawyers, bankers, and priests generally ruled the villages. In the later nineteenth century, the church, having lost its lands and rural roots, shifted attention to other domains and in the process lost its most fervent supporters, the agrarian masses. "Pray to God and the saints," suggested a Spanish proverb, "but put fertilizer on the crops." To many, the church, in its defense of the established order, symbolized the inequities of Spain.[5]

Declining agricultural prices, the result of worldwide glut in the late nineteenth century, cruelly coincided with a spiraling birthrate. Between 1768 and 1900, Spain's population doubled to 18.6 million persons. Moreover, the population density of northern Spain figured among the highest in Europe. Spaniards reacted to the social and economic upheaval through a variety of responses. Between the 1880s and 1920, 820,000 Spaniards migrated to America. Historian Charles J. Esdaile maintains that between 1882 and 1914 over 2 million Spaniards migrated to Cuba or Latin America, while another million sought new lives in France, Italy, or Algeria. "The new immigrants were from the north, mostly from Asturias and Galicia," writes Louis A.

Pérez, "many destitute, and often desperate, but strong-willed, self-possessed, and, most of all, determined to make it."[6]

In Spain, anarchism possessed a passionate fascination with *los miserables*—landless laborers, tenant farmers, peasants, and failing artisans who felt the sting of class hatred and saw the chasm of inequality more sharply than anyone. "Where law is an open fraud, public life a chimera, and politics the personification of corruption," noted a Spanish observer, "the organization of 'No Law!' is a logical and natural answer."[7] Temma Kaplan maintains that anarchism also appealed to small-scale producers and independent agrarians.[8]

An outgrowth of nineteenth-century social and economic conditions, the anarchist movement quickly shifted from the cafes and doctrinal stage into action, capturing the imagination of the rural and urban proletariat. Anarchist doctrines had circulated in Spain from the 1840s, thanks largely to the efforts of disciples of Pierre-Joseph Proudhon, Ramón de la Sagra, and Francisco Pi y Margall. Yet it was not until 1868, following the First International and the liberal revolution that led to the overthrow of Queen Isabella II, that ideas and activists from Russia, France, and Italy came to Spain, most notably Giuseppe Fanelli.[9]

Mikhail Bakunin's writings enjoyed an immediate and lasting influence in Spain. His philosophy—drawn from millenarian Christianity, the Enlightenment, and Proudhon—emphasized at its core the inherent good of humankind and the repressive nature of institutions and hierarchies. Whereas Rousseau argued the perfectibility of life through the proper balance of institutions, Bakunin insisted on removing the political yoke of the state. "The urge to destroy is a creative urge," he exhorted the masses.[10]

Bakunin and Karl Marx passionately quarreled over the means and ends of the revolution. Marx's admiration for the disciplined and centralized German proletariat differed from Bakunin's mistrust of institutionalized classes and his faith in the precapitalist masses of Russia, Spain, and Italy. He believed in the spontaneity of the rural masses and an atavistic desire to restore community as the basic unit of social life. The dichotomies of the Spanish labor movement stand as a testimonial to the loggerhead between Marx and Bakunin: socialism versus anarchism, institutions versus spontaneity, political action versus propaganda by deed, authority versus freedom.[11]

Bakunin's message electrified the dispossessed Spanish rural masses, promising communal control in a world long dominated by reactionary clergy, corrupt bureaucrats, and the dreaded Guardia Civil. Bakunin's appeal to direct action also found a receptive audience among a people who venerated the social bandit and the promise of freedom. "Anarchism in Spain is not a national disease nor the outward manifestation of working-class insanity," wrote G. H. B. Ward. "It is the industrial workers' indictment of a government which has signally failed to accomplish social betterment by political means."[12]

In 1881, five years after Bakunin's death, anarchists organized the Federación de Trabajadores de la Región Española. The movement, soon declared illegal, spread to the countryside and industrial cities. In the largely rural provinces of Asturias and Galicia the countryside convulsed with rent strikes and cattle maiming, assassinations and arson. The Spanish establishment trembled, for threats came not only in the form of peasant uprisings but, more chilling, from a solitary actor. Marcelino García and Manuel Rey y García exemplified the Spanish anarchists of this era. "I was born in 1893 in San Martín (Oviedo) in the Asturias region of northern Spain, where all the rebels come from," García recollected. He added, "I was born an anarchist . . . At seven or eight years old I already had great admiration for the anarchists. I saw in them men who were willing to fight for the poor." "My father was a socialist." Manuel Rey y García reminisced, "I was born on October 26, 1888, in Castofoya, a village in Galicia, Spain . . . 'Feed the hungry, give shelter to the poor'—I believed in that but the church never practiced it. The priest had fancy glasses and drank expensive wine."[13]

Bakunin's greatest legacy lay in the convincing strength of his propaganda by deed. In the quarter-century following his death, anarchism leaped from the salons of Madrid to the front page. Manifestos soon flooded the countryside, pronouncing "Peace to Men, War to Institutions." Although terrorism was never more than a minority doctrine—running counter to other anarchist sentiments such as self-improvement and rationalist education—apocalyptic and infectious acts of violence, designed to remove symbols of social and political order, riveted Spain. In November 1893, an anarchist hurled a bomb inside the Barcelona Opera House, killing twenty-nine. In August 1897, Michele Angiolillo assassinated Spanish prime minister Antonio Cánovas del Castillo. In 1912, Spain's premier José Canalejas y Méndez died at the hands of Manuel Pardiñas, a Spanish anarchist who had lived in Tampa, Florida.[14]

EMIGRATION

While students of Spanish anarchism have largely devoted their energies to examining the long lasting and significant influence this ideology has had on the development of peninsular Spain, only recently have they examined the diffusion of radicals and radicalism to the various parts of the colonial empire. Indeed, the collective tissues joining the motherland and its outposts acquired a durability and strength that allowed them to survive until well into the twentieth century.

Cuba was the pearl of the Spanish colonial world, and as such the island served as a lodestar for both disaffected radicals and conservative elites. The end of the Ten Years' War in 1878 brought peace, but also social dislocation. Spain encouraged and subsidized migration to Cuba in the 1880s, precisely at the moment the island's factories and cities were flooded with emancipated slaves and rural migrants.[15] For Spain, it was hoped, migration would serve as a social safety valve and at the same time increase the loyalist population abroad. But the full spectrum of political ideologies present in Spain re-formed in Cuba, and the doctrines of anarchism occupied a conspicuous place in this ferment.[16]

Enrique Roig San Martín and Enrique Messonier helped disseminate anarchist ideas in Cuba beginning in the 1870s.[17] Roig San Martín had worked in his early career as a lector in the tobacco industry and had received his "training" at the hands of militant *tabaqueros* (cigar makers). By the early 1880s San Martín had participated in the founding of a variety of workers' groups, and in 1887 he and Messonier began publishing the island's first anarcho-syndicalist newspaper, *El Productor*.[18] His leadership also contributed to the formation of a broadly based workers' movement. Its reform agenda included evening schools for workers, day-care centers, an orphanage, and other social welfare institutions for the working class. Messonier founded the newspaper *El Obrero*, and established an education center in Santiago. In the years surrounding the turn of the century, the island witnessed a remarkable growth of anarchist groups in small towns, particularly in Havana and Santa Clara Provinces.[19]

Catalans seemed to dominate the ranks of Spanish anarchists in Cuba, influenced by the ardent workers' movement in Barcelona. Catalan publications spread across the Americas, eventually finding their way to the libraries of the Spanish, Cuban, and Italian mutual aid societies and anarchist ranks.[20]

The work of Spanish anarchists in Cuba can be most clearly seen in labor organization and in the independence movement. In the years before the outbreak of the Cuban War for Independence, 1895–98, anarchists played important roles in the movement. This was especially true in the case of the cigar makers, artisans who occupied a vanguard position in the struggle to organize Cuban workers. The increased radicalization of the cigar work force spiraled upward as seen in labor agitation after 1880.[21] So disruptive did labor militancy become that increasing numbers of cigar manufacturers sought locations away from the island. As radicals achieved greater success and greater disruption of the industry, the colonial government adopted increasingly stringent measures against them, thus pressuring many to leave the island. Large numbers of these men found their way to such expatriate centers of Spanish-Cuban cigar manufacturing in Key West, Tampa, and New York. Ironically, the cigar outposts in Key West and Tampa had been founded largely to escape the radicals' influence, only to be populated by political exiles and radicals from the Ten Years' War (1868–78).[22]

On a wider level, the 1892 Congreso Obrero in Havana proved to be an important step in the developing relationship between the workers' movement in Cuba and anarchism. Guided by the principle of "revolutionary socialism," the congress proclaimed a vigorous proletarian ideology, urging the adoption of the general strike and declaring unequivocally that "los obreros formamos una sola clase."[23] The pursuit of working-class goals constantly clashed with the struggle for Cuba Libre and independence. To understand the combustible mixture of worker militancy, radical ideology, and patriotic fervor requires an understanding of the cigar-making outposts that were founded by Spanish cigar manufacturers in the United States.

Perhaps the most remarkable of these outposts was begun by a gifted *patrón*, Vicente Martínez Ybor. Born in Valencia in 1818, Martínez Ybor arrived in Cuba in 1832 to avoid compulsory military service. There, his successes came quickly, ascending from apprentice to broker to manufacturer. Displaying a deft touch and an entrepreneurial instinct, he helped modernize a primitive tobacco economy. He seized what was upon his arrival essentially a cottage industry, erecting factories in Havana, creating new markets, concentrating capital, and expanding operations to meet a near-insatiable demand for hand-rolled Cuban cigars.[24]

The gathering storm of Cuban independence swept Martínez Ybor into its vortex. His public support for the separatists and insurgents stemmed principally from economic motivation: a free Cuba would save cigar manufacturers from paying burdensome taxes to Spain. But he also displayed a genuine sympathy for the Cuban cause. In 1868, the fierce rebellion forced Martínez Ybor into exile in Key West, Florida. Key West quickly emerged as a Cuban sanctuary, burgeoning with more than a thousand Cuban exiles by 1870. Soon, Cubans dominated the island as cigar factories appeared. By 1873, Key West tabaqueros produced 25 million cigars. Labor unrest flowed from Cuba to Key West.[25]

Martínez Ybor was not alone. A number of like-minded countrymen rivaled him in stature. Born in the post-Napoleonic era and sensing diminishing economic opportunities and an empire in disintegration, Spaniards such as Ignacio Haya, Enrique Pendás, Peregrino Rey, and Angel Cuesta followed and perfected the example set by Martínez Ybor. Conscious of their dependence upon a Cuban workforce, these patrones favored Spaniards for the upper echelon positions in the industry, thus stimulating emigration from Iberia and Cuba.[26] The site of Key West increasingly troubled the new owners. In addition to issues of fresh water and transportation, Spanish American owners expressed increasing concerns over the nascent labor movement, which contained anarchist elements. A search for a new cigar capital began.

In 1884, Gavino Gutiérrez, a talented Spanish engineer, had visited Tampa, Florida, and stopped in Key West on his return to New York. There, he consulted with Martínez Ybor about the possibilities of the location. Tampa's climate was suitable for rolling cigars, land was inexpensive, and a new railroad hub had just been constructed. Perhaps most important, city officials assured vigilant protection from labor agitators. The Tampa Board of Trade agreed to sell Martínez Ybor land on which to create a separate company town northeast of the city. An industrial community plotted by Gutiérrez, financed by Martínez Ybor and Haya, and vitalized by Cuban and Spanish workers showed signs of life in the spring of 1886.[27]

The emergent Spanish community manifested a remarkable vitality and cohesiveness. Quite naturally, it was shaped in its initial years by Spaniards who had worked in Cuba and Key West. The great majority of Tampa's Spaniards spent time in Cuba, many working in the cigar trade centered in

Havana. They followed a familiar pattern of migration characterized by a flow of skilled labor and mercantile activity and long periods of sojourner status. Most Spanish males came as single men, living in boardinghouses. Many also came with designs of accumulating enough money to purchase land and eventually return to the *patria chica* (Spanish villages).[28]

Asturian and Galician villages such as Ferrera de los Gavitos, Pintueles, Las Villas, Candamo, Moutas, and Infiesto sent steady streams of Spaniards to Cuba and later to Florida. Spaniards left the Old World in chain migrations, assisted by a complex and well-organized network of kinfolk, compatriots, and agents. Typical was the life story of Fermín Souto. "I was born in the little village of Ferrol de Galicia in June of 1858," Souto told an interviewer in 1935. "My father was a stone cutter . . . my mother was born and raised in the country. I am, therefore, a plebian. My parents were poor people, and in those days a poor man could only look forward to a very meager education. On October 30, 1870, a friend took me to Havana, Cuba."[29] A half-century later, María Ordieres followed Souto's path. "I was born and raised in Candamo, Asturias," she explained. "My father heard that in Tampa, Florida, the cigar industry was in need of workers. So in 1923 he left for Tampa. My brother and I followed since we were the oldest and could work."[30]

LIFE IN TAMPA'S LATIN COMMUNITY

The size of the "Latin" (a local term incorporating Spaniards, Cubans, and Italians—the term "Hispanic" was not used until after the 1960s) community grew rapidly after 1890. The Spanish community, although small during the first fifteen years, exercised a powerful influence. In 1890, the United States Census, a notoriously poor indicator of the true count of immigrants, registered 233 Spaniards and 1,313 Cubans in Tampa. By 1900, almost a thousand Spaniards had clustered in Ybor City, as well as 3,533 Cubans and 1,315 Italians. In 1910, Tampa's Latin immigrants had grown to 2,337 Spanish-born residents, 3,859 Cubans, and 2,519 Italians. Many Cuban-born settlers were the children of Spanish immigrants to the island.[31]

Held together by a vibrant Latin culture, infused with a set of distinctive work rhythms, and pulsating with a heightened political consciousness, Ybor City offered its Spanish *compañeros* contrasting values and alternatives: immigrant solidarity buffered by American individualism, a comfortable lifestyle set off by strident demands for reform and revolution, an elite work force challenged by threats of technology and Cuban independence.

Ybor City may have been touted as a planned industrial town, but the enclave's first decade reflected the rawness of a mining camp and the dangers of a frontier presidio.[32] Small, inexpensive, wooden-framed houses soon clustered alongside brick factories, testimonials to the business acumen of Haya and Martínez Ybor. The businessmen typically offered cigar manufacturers factories rent-free for several years, knowing that they would be making profits selling homes to immigrants. Moreover, homeownership helped domesticate the rawness of the new community and, they hoped, tame labor militancy.

Customs, however, did not easily surrender to new economies. Cubans, buffeted by escalating tensions in the homeland, proved reluctant homeowners. Their peripatetic lifestyle permitted—and at times forced—them to move from factory to factory, from Tampa to Key West to Havana. Testifying to Congress in an 1892 committee hearing on immigration, Ramón Williams, consul-general to Cuba, remarked, "I should say that there is no emigration from the island of Cuba in the European sense of the word; that is, there is no emigrant class. There is steerage, but they go as regular passengers. Between Key West and Havana people go as between Albany and New York . . . they go back and forward as French laborers go from Canada to New England . . . The people here look upon Florida as so much a part of their own country."[33]

Spaniards maintained a very distinctive demographic profile. Persistently high ratios of males to females characterized the Spanish presence. The boardinghouse served as an important institution for single Spanish men, as well as a hothouse for radical politics. In 1900, fully one-third of Tampa's Spaniards lived in boardinghouses, a percentage unchanged a decade later. In 1910, census takers counted 810 Spanish boarders, as compared to only 352 Cubans and 45 Italians. Whereas the patrones interacted comfortably with Tampa's Anglo elites, Spanish workers—of whom only 19 percent spoke English in 1910—turned inward for support. The result was a creative and resourceful outpouring of organizational energies.[34]

Traditions of immigrant mutual aid run deep in the history of the Americas. Immigrants, in order to protect themselves from a real or imagined hostile world, and to reinforce their Old World value systems, created cooperative institutions. In Ybor City, voluntary associations played roles far beyond that of the usual burial societies and folk fairs.

To understand the sway of these ethnic societies, one must appreciate the milieu from which these institutions evolved. Ybor City was an instant town, a community emerging from Tampa, a city that as late as 1880 numbered fewer than a thousand inhabitants. Consequently, there existed few institutions to minister to the immigrants and, given Deep South attitudes toward immigrants, Catholics, and radicals, little promise of assistance.

In July 1887, Guillermo Machado, a Spanish physician, founded La Igual, the first cooperative healthcare endeavor. A number of cooperative medical programs followed, based on the concept of "The Equal," offering cigar makers, families, and boarders cradle-to-grave protection and care. Tampa's medical fraternity railed against Ybor City's "socialist doctors," threatening to bar them from medical practice. Mutual aid societies and cooperatives contracted with physicians to care for their members. The American Medical Association and its Florida affiliates confronted physicians such as Francesco Adamo with a choice: practice with the cooperatives and face expulsion from the AMA.[35]

The history and legacy of the Centro Español (organized in 1891) and Centro Asturiano (1902) serve as the standard for cooperative care. Modeled after Havana's renowned namesakes, the Centro Español and Centro Asturiano (figure 3.1) embarked on campaigns to facilitate programs of mutual relief and promote a vibrant cultural life. Remarkably, the institutions housed a diverse collection of personalities: cigar manufacturers and workers, anarchists and nationalists, Asturians and Galicians. The organizations also chartered a course for the future, allowing second-generation sons born in Cuba and Tampa to become members, a practice not observed at the Havana *centros*.[36]

Tampa's Spanish societies embarked on a building frenzy to offer their membership modern and inexpensive health care. In 1904, Centro Español constructed a $90,000 hospital for members and their families, an institution far superior to any public facility in Tampa and perhaps the state. Asturians completed Sanatorio Covadonga in 1905, a modern hospital with rooms for sixty patients and a pharmacy.[37]

ANARCHIST CLUBS

Spanish anarchists arriving in Tampa found a community that possessed a wide spectrum of radical ideologies. Angelo Massari moved to Ybor City in

FIGURE 3.1. Clubhouse of the Centro Asturiano in Tampa. The mutual aid society, founded in 1902 as a branch of the Centro Asturiano in Havana, Cuba, is still in existence today. Courtesy of University of South Florida Library, Special Collections.

1902. Sixty years later, he wrote a memoir, a Horatio Alger story of how an impoverished emigrant from Sicily became a bank owner. Describing the community in 1902, he observed, "In our community, socialism and anarchism were in vogue . . . I associated with a group of friends who had organized a club for social studies. At the club I read pamphlets, newspapers, books, and all kinds of sociological literature. I also attended all the lectures and debates that the two groups, socialist and anarchist, organized, inviting to Tampa the greatest exponents of the two theories who were living in the North." While few American bankers shared Massari's flirtation with anarchism, many Spanish immigrants in Tampa did. The proliferation of speaking clubs and debating societies revealed the diverse nature of Tampa's radical community.[38]

Although records are scanty, it appears that anarchist groups were the most numerous. This was almost certainly true of the years prior to 1898, when expatriate Cuban anarchist groups in support of independence swelled the numbers. Yet, throughout the period under review, those groups organized and attended by Spaniards formed the majority. Judging by the dispatches from Spanish consuls in Key West, the Spanish government was deeply concerned with the free flow of nihilists, anarchists, and socialists, as well as their dangerous ideas. "These anarchist and socialist ideas," writes Gerald Poyo, "also gained widespread support in Key West and Tampa during the final half of the 1880s from veteran organizers such as [Carlos] Baliño, [Guillermo] Sorondo, Oscar Martín, Eduardo Pajarín, and Mateo Leal."[39]

Most of these groups were small entities organized for the purpose of self-education and debate. Typically, such groups had a secretary, who was responsible for maintaining correspondence with like-minded individuals elsewhere and for supplying a club library (usually featuring pamphlets and anarchist newspapers). More often than not, meetings were held at the homes of members, although some of the larger groups rented meeting space in union halls or ethnic club buildings. The Italian and Spanish-language press in Tampa is filled with announcements of anarchist group meetings for the years preceding World War I.[40]

Not all organizations restricted membership to specific nationalities or income. The celebrated Spanish anarchist Pedro Esteve, for instance, guided the fortunes of Antorcha (Torch), a cultural center open to freethinkers of all nationalities. Antorcha offered free classes on myriad subjects, musical recitals, literary gatherings, and a gymnasium for exercise and sport. When not engaged in activities of the mind, members could take fencing lessons under the tutelage of a young Italian socialist named Arturo Massolo. Radicals also infused Tampeños with a vibrant Spanish-language theater. In 1918, El Internacional announced that Aurora (Dawn), "a Socialist drama of the first order," would be performed at the Centro Asturiano.[41] While Italian, Spanish, and English blended freely at Antorcha, Spanish was recognized as the lingua franca.

Pedro Esteve led a dashing life. Born in Barcelona in 1866, he played a significant role in the Catalan anarchist movement. While on a lecture tour with the Italian anarchist Errico Malatesta, Pedro met Maria Roda in Milan. She was born in nearby Como, the daughter of an anarchist laborer. Pedro and Maria became one of the first couples of anarchism. One of their ten children died in a bomb blast that was intended for Pedro. Roda became a fiery leader in America. Her childhood schoolmate Sante Caserio assassinated

Marie François Sadi Carnot, the president of France, in 1894. Marcelino García remembered, "The greatest influence in my life was Pedro Esteve. Look at his picture and you will see why. He was a great moral influence."[42] Esteve worked for the most important and longest-lasting anarchist paper of Barcelona, *El Productor,* and there learned the trade that defined his working career. Following a series of attacks and uprisings in the 1890s, the Spanish government resolved to crush the anarchists. Esteve and other prominent anarchists escaped. Esteve immigrated to Brooklyn, where he became active in the publication of *El Despertar* (The Awakening). He then moved to Paterson, New Jersey, a well-known center of anarchist activity, where Italians and Spanish were especially prominent among the radical ranks.[43] Shortly after the turn of the century, Spanish anarchists in Tampa invited Esteve to move southward and take up residence in the city synonymous with cigars. With funds collected from various groups, supporters supplied Esteve with a residence and his own printing shop, named appropriately La Políglota (The Polyglot).[44]

In bursts of creativity, Esteve advanced the anarchist movement in Tampa. When not reading to fellow cigar makers in the local factories, he established free evening schools for workers and made books available to the growing cadre of followers. Publicly, he spoke and fraternized frequently at the major immigrant clubs, debating socialists and radicals. When anarchist luminaries visited Tampa, a public debate with Esteve became the capstone of their stay. Among others, he crossed swords and broke bread with Emma Goldman and Elizabeth Gurley Flynn, the fiery Italian anarchists Luigi Galleani and Carlo Tresca, and Italian socialists Giuseppe Bertelli and Arturo Caroti.[45]

Esteve had landed in one of America's most politically charged communities. His message exhorting workers to resist capitalist oppression found sympathetic ears. His press printed union newspapers, including *El Internacional.* Meanwhile, he continued to write articles for various anarchist journals, including *Il Martello* and *La Questione Sociale* of Paterson, New Jersey, and *El Despertar* of New York. In 1911, a close friend, the Italian anarchist Alfonso Coniglio, collected and published a series of Esteve's essays under the title of *La Legge* (The Law). Earlier Esteve had written *Memoria,* a tract on the 1893 International Anarchist Conference held in Chicago.[46]

Esteve was hardly alone writing and publishing in this creative era. Prior to 1900, *El Esclavo* (The Slave) was the most influential newspaper. Most of

the journals were short lived, barely surviving on the subscriptions and donations of a small membership. Their fugitive publications can be traced by
the scattered handfuls of surviving issues. Anarchist newspapers printed in
New York City and Paterson, for example, carried columns that occasionally
reported on events in Tampa.[47]

Anarchist groups strove to meet the social and cultural needs of their
members as well as to provide for their political education. To accomplish
these goals, they collected small monthly dues, from ten to twenty-five cents
per member. A portion of these funds went toward the purchase of books
and materials for the club libraries. Whether it was a single shelf of books
in a member's home or a collection numbering into the hundreds, each
group supplied some access to literary material.[48] The collections typically
featured a wide assortment of reading items, ranging from simple spelling
and grammar texts to Spanish-language editions of the great radical masters. The works of Karl Marx, Mikhail Bakunin, Peter Kropotkin, and Errico
Malatesta were to be found on nearly all shelves. Most volumes in these holdings were small, inexpensive pamphlets offering polemical essays on various
topics or excerpts from larger studies. Some were printed in Tampa (usually at Esteve's La Políglota) and featured the writings of local literati. More
numerous, however, were the publications contained in several educational
series sponsored by leftist cooperatives. Most popular in Tampa were three
series: *Biblioteca Socialista-Anarchia*, *Biblioteca Popolare Educativa*, and *Liberia
Sociologica*, distributed from several northeast locations.[49]

Spanish residents also enjoyed access to anarchist thoughts through other
channels. The various unions representing cigar workers all subsidized newspapers that invariably featured excerpts from leftist tracts and not infrequently
carried extensive debates among socialists, anarchists, and syndicalists. Printed
in Spanish and distributed widely throughout Tampa, these journals provided
important sources of information for the wider community (figure 3.2). Among
the labor papers that followed these practices (in order of appearance) were
La Federación, *El Federal*, *Boletín Obrero*, and *El Internacional*. "The organization
of labor that is not planted squarely on the class struggle," urged *La Federación*
on December 14, 1900, "can develop only in one direction—the direction of a
buffer for the capitalist class, run by Labor Lieutenants of Capital."[50]

The anarchists maintained a withering assault upon the Catholic Church,
blunting its influence in places such as Tampa. To outside observers, the

FIGURE 3.2. Mastheads of anarchist periodicals published by Spanish immigrants in Tampa.

church, enlisting the aid of Jesuit, Franciscan, and Scalabrinian missions, figured to be the key institution to soften the impact of industrialization and broker the lives of vulnerable immigrants in Tampa and the harsh outside world. But the church, vilified in the Old World and rejected in the New World, contributed to Ybor City's social world. Anarchists continued to attack religion as vehemently in Florida as they had in Spain, and the condemnations struck responsive chords among Cubans, Italians, and Spaniards. Cubans despised the church because of its support of Spanish colonialism; Spanish radicals never forgave the church for ignoring the common people; Sicilians remembered indolent, wealthy priests amidst a starving peasantry. The Catholic Church, thundered Néstor Carbonell, a staunch supporter of Cuban independence, "stands as the enemy of scientific truth, justice, and liberty." Jesuit father W. J. Tyrell confessed to his superiors in a 1911 report that not 3 percent of Ybor City's population came to church and, more to the point, that community members "have no respect for religion or priest."[51]

CUBA

The impassioned battle over Cuba set the terms for debate in Ybor City between 1886 and 1898. The cause of Cuba Libre deeply divided *peninsulares* between anarchist critics of colonial policy and fervent nationalists. The issue, of course, ruptured relationships within Ybor City.

Cubans dominated Ybor City's workforce. For the city's 1,313 Cubans in 1890, a figure which tripled during the decade, the struggle for revolution transcended all other issues. Cubans in Ybor City defined themselves as exiles, not immigrants, whose sharpened sense of class consciousness and political awareness infused the cigar industry with their ethos.[52]

In Tampa, the appearance of José Martí (figure 3.3) in 1891 electrified the Cuban community. But Martí did not singlehandedly forge the tools of revolution; rather, he found in Tampa the resources necessary to temper a movement. If Martí embodied the movement, the proletariat of Ybor City was its soul. The most tangible result of Martí's visit was the creation of the Cuban Revolutionary Party, organized in 1892. "El Día de la Patria" became the theme song of Ybor City: one day's salary for the homeland. Spanish agents shadowed Martí's movements and came perilously close to poisoning the Apostle of Cuban Liberty.[53]

Caught in a vicious crossfire between defenders of empire and torchbearers of revolution were the Spanish anarchists; some Cuban radicals perceived anarchism as a Trojan horse, designed to confuse the patriots over the immediate aim of the rebellion. Martí worked assiduously to enlist the support of anarchists on the side of the independence movement. In this effort he was remarkably successful, particularly after the 1892 Congreso Obrero, which contained a heavy anarchist element. Martí was careful to praise effusively the actions of the anarchist leaders who had expressed sympathies for the revolution, but he challenged the anarchists on the necessity of political action.[54]

Support for the Cuban revolution posed several ideological and personal problems for Spanish anarchists. Indeed, not all rallied to the cause of Cuba Libre, as some were pulled more strongly by nationalist sentiments. Yet, many believed, as Pedro Esteve claimed, "It is good to love 'la patria' but it is better to love liberty and justice."[55] Martí and the Cuban anarchist Carlos Baliño were able to win over what was probably a majority of Spanish anarchists in Tampa to the revolutionary cause. Baliño in particular argued that it would be absurd to endorse individual liberty and oppose collective liberty.

FIGURE 3.3. The leader of Cuban independence, José Martí, with cigar workers in Ybor City (Tampa) in 1891. Contributions from cigar makers were crucial to support the activities of the Partido Revolucionario Cubano (Cuban Revolutionary Party). Courtesy of University of South Florida Library, Special Collections.

For his part, Martí readily pledged guarantees of freedom to anarchists in the new republic to come. Baliño visited Ybor City often in the 1890s. In October 1892, he spoke at a celebration of the Grito de Yara, stressing the need for anarchists, socialists, and patriots to work together for a free Cuba.[56]

The sinking of the *USS Maine* in February 1898 ominously redefined the precarious presence of Spaniards in Tampa. Historian Ana Varela-Lago suggests that a more accurate name for the conflict is "the Spanish-Cuban-American War of 1898." Whereas natives earlier suspected Spaniards of un-American traits; they now existed as dangerous enemy aliens, to be feared. Cubans, to win sympathy with American elements, attacked the Spanish anarchists. Furthermore, the fact that 50,000 American soldiers were destined to disembark from Tampa seriously brought into focus the Spanish problem: a potential fifth column. "Dark scowls lurk upon the faces of American men as Spanish is heard spoken," observed a correspondent from the *New York Times*.

In a preemptive strike, the army seized control of Centro Español in April 1898, commandeering the building until August. Scores of Spaniards fled Tampa.[57] For the Cuban community, the era of exile ended. Emigrés became immigrants. Cubans shifted the struggle for justice from Havana and Madrid to Tampa, as a new era of labor militancy dawned.

Beleaguered by the crises of the 1890s, bewildered by the non-English "ghettos" in their backyard, and befuddled by an inability to control the aliens, Tampans lashed out at Latins in a series of virulent confrontations. The war and the concomitant events in the 1890s encapsulated the three value clusters most nervously contemplated by nativists: fears of Catholicism, alien hordes, and foreign radicalism.[58] The last-named characteristic was the one natives most feared. The sinister image of the Spanish anarchist threatened Tampa for a half century. Bred in the fields of Asturias and Galicia, incubated in the coffee houses of Key West and Havana, and fought over in the factories of Ybor City and West Tampa, anarchism and radicalism set the terms of debate for labor relations between 1886 and 1931.

LABOR

"The cigar industry is to this city what the iron industry is to Pittsburgh," rejoiced the *Tampa Morning Tribune* in 1896.[59] Fully aware of the vulnerability of a one-industry town, Tampa city fathers resolved to protect the factory owners and cigar industry at all cost. "Tampa can afford to lose cigarmakers," editorialized one paper, "Tampa cannot afford to lose cigar factories."[60] The city's economic fortunes rose and fell with the public's demand for and the industry's supply of premium, hand-rolled cigars. By 1895, the city boasted 130 cigar factories, which accounted for 75 percent of the city's payroll. Nearly 10,000 first- and second-generation immigrants and children labored in the city's factories by 1910.[61] Cigars defined Tampa, making the city the most important industrial city in Florida. City leaders resolved to keep it that way, but were troubled by the customs and culture of an industry and workforce they neither approved nor understood.

Tampa's cigar industry was characterized by skilled workers possessing a special work ethos. Dominated by a premodern craft mentality with a complement of artisan work styles and outlooks, it created an industrial environment governed by the rhythms of the individual. There existed within factories a clear occupational hierarchy, somewhat organized along ethnic lines during the early decades. The first major division existed between salaried and piecework employees. The former category included foremen, managers, skilled clerical staff, salesmen, and accountants, most of whom were Spaniards. The salaried staff also included *selectors* (graders and selectors of tobacco), positions also dominated by Spaniards. They also commanded most of the higher-paying positions of the next hierarchy, which included banders, packers, and box makers. The coveted position of *chavatero* (knife sharpener) was generally held by a Gallego. Cubans, and later Italians, filled the most plentiful positions, such as rollers, bunchers, and strippers.

Cigar makers maintained distinctive work customs. They exercised, above all, a fierce independence. Coming and going as they pleased, pocketing free cigars as they left, and hiring a *cafetero* to bring gallons of hot milk and strong Cuban coffee to the work benches. While Ybor City was a one-industry town, it was not a one-company town (figure 3.4). Numerous small factories and enterprises proliferated, allowing for diversity within the ranks of owners and making control more difficult.

No institution dramatized Ybor City's *ambiente* more than *la lectura*, the practice of reading in the cigar factories (figure 3.5). Reading to assembled cigar makers from a *tribuna* (a raised platform) had begun in Cuba in the 1850s and spread to Puerto Rico, Key West, Tampa, and New York City. Prototypes of los lectores could be found in Spanish villages, where the *obreros conscientes*—local, self-educated activists for education and workers' rights—served as teachers, propagandists, and apostles of the oral tradition. "You know what Victor Hugo say?" asked ninety-five-year-old cigar maker José Vega Díaz. "In all towns, in every place, they have a schoolteacher. And in every town, the schoolteacher is the light. He lights the candle. But in every town they try to blow away the light. The preachers, the priests. That's why they [the church, the owner] don't want the reader. The reader lights the candle. It was a good thing."[62]

The procedures surrounding the selection of the reader and the readings reveal much. "You know when we read in the factories," began Wilfredo Rodríguez, the last Tampa reader still alive in 1982, "we were employed by the cigarmakers, not the owners." Selection of the reader followed a strict protocol. Each candidate—generally male and Cuban or Spanish, although there was one Italian, an Afro-Cuban, Facundo Acción, and several

FIGURE 3.4. The cigar factory of Cuesta-Rey was one of many such constructions that dotted Tampa's urban landscape. Courtesy of the University of South Florida Library, Special Collections.

women—auditioned in front of workers, demonstrating clarity of voice, conviction, and dramatic talents.[63]

The career of Luisa Capetillo reveals the combustibility of la lectura and la lectora. Luisa Capetillo was born in 1879 in Arecibo, Puerto Rico, a place described by Araceli Tinajero as a "hub of radical labor culture." The daughter of a Basque father and a Corsican mother who never married, Luisa was raised to be a free thinker and to challenge authority. Well educated, Capetillo embraced anarchism and became a reader in 1906 at a local cigar factory. "I am irresistibly drawn to literature," she proclaimed, part of a remarkable body of letters and creative writing. In 1911, she published the first edition of her writings, *Mi Opinión*. From the factory tribune and the newspaper, she fought for workers' reforms, stressing the importance of education in the uplift of laborers. She was one of Puerto Rico's pioneering suffragists. In 1913, Capetillo arrived in Ybor City. Fellow workers chose her as a lectora.

FIGURE 3.5. The interior of a cigar factory. Workers rolled cigars at their tables while listening to the *lector* reading from a newspaper. Courtesy of the University of South Florida Library, Special Collections.

While in Tampa, she wrote a play, *Influencias de las ideas modernas*. The theatrical work introduces the character of Angelina, the daughter of a cigar manufacturer. Through her reading of the works of Victor Hugo, Leo Tolstoy, and Émile Zola, Angelina beseeches her father to share his wealth with the workers. In Tampa she published the second edition of *Mi Opinión*. By 1915, Capetillo had moved to Havana, Cuba, where she was arrested for crossdressing! Capetillo would have appreciated the words from the *Mujeres Libres'* Anthem (1937), "Fists upraised, women of Iberia . . . We want to write anew, the word WOMAN . . . onward, onward, toward the light."[64]

Readings tended to reinforce the proletariat themes of the class struggle. "We had four daily shifts (*turnos*)," explained Abelardo Gutiérrez Díaz, a Spanish-born reader. The first hour was a reading of the news, and the reading was always in Spanish. This fact helps explain why virtually all of the Italian immigrants in Ybor City spoke Spanish. The second hour was the most popular, and cigar workers recalled listening to serialized novels with fondness. Favorite novelists included Émile Zola, Victor Hugo, Miguel de Cervantes, Alexander Dumas, Armando Palacio Valdés, Benito Pérez Galdós, Vicente Blasco Ibáñez, and Pedro Mata. The third hour featured readings from political works, including the writings of Maxim Gorky, Karl Marx, Errico Malatesta, Peter Kropotkin, Mikhail Bakunin, and Leo Tolstoy. Readings from Spanish and American anarchist and socialist papers became regular features. "These were partisan newspapers," a veteran reader recalled. "Some were anarchist and communist papers. All were read." The cigarmakers' literary favorites reflected a healthy distrust of the established church and a heightened sense of international brotherhood.[65]

The reader served as a lightning rod for the persistent clashes between workers and management. Factory owners and city officials frequently blamed readers for fomenting labor unrest. "They [the manufacturers] say we became too radical, reading the news from labor organizations and political groups," explained Honorato Henry Domínguez, a former lector. "We read those things, it is true," he confessed. But, he added, "We read only what the cigarmakers wanted us to read."[66] The reader served as disseminator, not originator of class-conscious literature. "The reader enlightened the worker," remembered Emanuel LaRosa, who was born in 1891. This was certainly true of the young men who turned to anarchism. Pedro Esteve's close friend, Alfonso Coniglio, amplified the readers' image. "But it was at La Rosa Española that I first heard a reader. I cannot tell you how important they were, how much they taught us. Especially an illiterate like me. To them we owe particularly our sense of the class struggle." The moment Maximiliano Olay heard a Tampa lector read the newspaper *Tierra y Libertad* (Land and Liberty) was the moment he chose to become an anarchist.[67]

A crazy-quilt pattern of radical ideologies, ethnic rivalries, establishment terror, and truculent strikes characterized labor relations in Tampa. "People date their lives from various strikes in Tampa," recalled José Yglesias, the son of Spanish and Cuban immigrants and perhaps Tampa's greatest author.[68] From the beginning, labor unrest wracked Ybor City, ironic in view of the fact that Martínez Ybor chose Tampa because of its promise of labor peace. In January 1887, Ramón Rubiera, a fiery Cuban labor organizer, called a strike because Martínez Ybor imported Spanish foremen for his factory. A series of strikes resulting in the death of a Cuban worker disrupted the manufacture of cigars.

Throughout the trouble, Tampa newspapers reported polemical debates between anarchist and socialist factions within the labor movement. The *Tampa Journal* blamed anarchists for the strike, labeling them "evil men, agitators, revolutionists" who sought to "gratify their morbid ideas of distinction, heroism and fame by imposing upon the ignorant prejudices of the masses."[69]

Native Tampans reacted to the new wave of labor and ethnic turbulence with measured tones. Calling an emergency meeting, the Tampa Board of Trade pledged full police powers to protect property. Authorities identified the "troublemakers" and warned them to leave Tampa or suffer the consequences. The *Tampa Tribune* supported the actions, predicting that the aggressive posture "will no doubt have a most salutary effect upon . . . citizens of anarchist tendencies who still may be lurking in our midst." Ultimately, the organizers of the strike and seventy-five workers left Tampa under police escort.[70] The first May Day parade in Ybor City—in memory of the Haymarket massacre—added an interesting footnote to the event. According to Cuban historian José Rivero Muñiz, "the greater part of the demonstrators were Spanish anarchists."[71] The *Tampa Tribune* explained to its readers the sinister role of anarchists in our midst. "Left to himself, the cigarmaker is a fairly good citizen. But unfortunately, there is another class which takes evident delight in meddling between the employer and the employed. It is this class of mischief-breeding, anarchist agitators that causes the differences which result in frequent strikes. It would be entirely correct for the people of Tampa to force this undesirable element to abandon their abode in this city." Tampa's leaders frequently took action.[72]

Between 1887 and 1894 alone, twenty-three strikes occurred, revealing the volatile nature of cigar work and the near impossibility of unifying the disparate demands and goals of craft unions, a multiethnic workforce, and radical leaders.[73] Anarchists performed an instrumental role in shaping the character of the early Ybor City labor movement. A variety of aggravating circumstances, from brittle tobacco to tepid drinking water to ethnic slurs or contract violations, could empty a factory with the simple command: "¡Para las calles!" (To the streets!). To the business community, such behavior pointed to the nefarious role of anarchists and agitators. In reality, cigar makers grasped at the opportunity to control their lives and assert their independence. Given the individualized factory structure within Ybor City, control—for an hour or day—was easily realized. Keeping power meant something else.

The anarcho-syndicalist model—with its strong emphasis upon education, local control, and nonpolitical direct action—found a receptive audience among the Latin workforce. Ybor City offered an ideal environment in which to test anarcho-syndicalist methods, such as sabotage, obstruction, and the general strike. Just as anarchism appealed to the village-oriented peasants of Spain, so too did syndicalism promise a reservoir of strength at the factory level. Cigar workers easily imagined their place in a world absent the pillars of the church, the state, and military.

Tampans, however, imagined a city that now resembled Paris or the Haymarket. The *Tribune* explained that Latins "when subjected to the devilish influences of even one unprincipled socialist, communist, or anarchist . . . are transformed into little less than madmen, and there is no peace, no order, until the cause is removed."[74] In 1892, officials acted swiftly to remove such cancerous influences. A vigilance committee, composed of 100 of the city's leaders, including past and future mayors, hung a banner across Ybor City's Bijou Theatre. The manifesto, written in Spanish and signed by Herman Glogowski, Tampa's Jewish immigrant mayor, read:

> TAMPA VIGILANCE COMMITTEE . . .
> hereby give warning to all—
> Cubans, Spaniards, and all others—
> That lawlessness in Ybor City
> must cease.

Tenaciously, the Spanish radicals slung together and persisted. In April 1893, the local paper hinted that within Ybor City, "there is in full blast to-day a club of Nihilists numbering more than 100 members with sympathizers on the outside." Rumors circulated that the nihilist cell clubhouse featured pictures of August Spies (the Haymarket martyr) and his comrades.[75]

La Huelga de la Pesa, the Weight Strike of 1899, marked an important watershed in Ybor City labor relations. Cigar makers met stiffening resistance to their growing independence. The introduction of weight scales at the Martínez Ybor factory symbolized a new order. Ostensibly, the scales were designed to weigh an allotted amount of tobacco, a measure of efficiency. In reality, principles were at stake: power, honor, and custom. To weigh the tobacco on a heartless machine affronted a Spaniard's dignity. Many of the pioneer patrones were dead; a new era had arrived, personified by Yankee efficiency and corporate rationality.[76]

Management enforced a lockout at all factories in June 1899. By July, 4,000 workers were shut out. Thousands returned to Cuba. "A complaint so trivial as to be almost ludicrous has caused the wholesale paralysis of an industry," railed the *Tribune*. "Tampa is afflicted with one of the most dangerous and obnoxious classes of people that ever has been tolerated by any civilized community. It is the professional agitator . . . These people are regular anarchists."[77]

The resolution to the Weight Strike came with surprising swiftness. In August, management conceded to every demand. The strike is significant for several reasons. First, it was the only strike workers ever won. Second, it led to the formation of a militant union, La Sociedad de Torcedores de Tampa, commonly called La Resistencia (for its call to resist capital). The real victory, however, came not on the picket lines but in corporate boardrooms. In September 1899, industry journals announced the creation of the Cigar Trust, succeeded two years later by the American Tobacco Company.

The Weight Strike set the stage for Tampa's first great labor struggle of the new century. In 1901, La Resistencia called for workers to join one central union and "to resist the exploitation of labor by capital." A protracted, tumultuous four-month strike ensured, marked by mass evictions, violence, and suffering.[78] La Resistencia succeeded in organizing Ybor City's first panethnic union, claiming a membership of 1,558 Cubans, 550 Spaniards, and 310 Italians. A newspaper, *La Federación,* articulated the workers' goals.[79]

In July 1901, La Resistencia called for a general strike. Only a handful of factories remained open as Ybor City fell silent, save for the *cocinas económicas* (soup kitchens operated by the union) and demonstrations. A citizens committee composed of business leaders abducted thirteen strike and union leaders on the evening of August 5, 1901. Hired thugs shanghaied the Latins to Honduras and warned them never to set foot in Tampa again. Since the deportees included the president and treasurer of the union, strike funds conveniently froze. America's most famous cigar maker and former reader (in Yiddish), Samuel Gompers, refused to aid Ybor City strikers, claiming La Resistencia failed to conform to American trade union means and goals. Manufacturers appealed to cigar workers in Key West and Cuba to come to Tampa. The federal government assisted in a boat lift, facilitating the transportation and quelling riots in Key West and Havana. "The striking cigar makers are keeping very quiet," noted the *United States Tobacco Journal* in August

1901. The trade journal added, "That exception is a woman named Luise [*sic*] Herrera, who is the secretary of the Resistencia Strippers' Union. Whenever and wherever she can secure an audience, she delivers herself of the most vituperative language against the manufacturers, and especially the committee of citizens who rid Tampa of her brother Anarchists." By late November 1901, the strike had been broken. By 1902, La Resistencia was dissolved.[80]

The decade between 1901 and 1910 witnessed economic prosperity in the cigar industry, accompanied by surging numbers of Latin immigrants and the modernization of Ybor City's infrastructure. In 1910, the Cigar Makers International Union (CMIU) had grown to 6,000 members. But 1910 marked the longest and most violent strike in the city's history. Cigar workers charged that owners precipitated the strike as a means of testing their open shop demands and squelching the union's growing strength. In June 1910, manufacturers dismissed union selectors. By August 1910, 12,000 cigar makers were out of work. A reporter covering a mass union meeting observed, "It was a demonstration such as reared its head within the gates of old Barcelona, that hot-bed of Latin civic disturbance."[81]

As economic dislocations resulting from the strike shattered the area's economy, Tampa leaders reacted with customary anger. The killing of an American bookkeeper employed at the Bustillo and Díaz Company electrified the city. Authorities arrested two Italians on suspicion of complicity, but before they could be brought to trial, a mob seized and lynched them. Soon thereafter, arsonists burned a cigar factory and the Tribune building barely missed the same fate. The leaders of the strike, including Spaniard José de la Campa, were arrested for "inciting a riot and being accessories [to murder]." The renowned Spanish anarchist, Pedro Esteve was living in Ybor City in 1910. His son Sirio recalled his father's ordeal. "He . . . was forced to flee Tampa during labor disturbances there. Vigilantes broke up his printing shop, where he had been editing an anarchist newspaper, and beat a worker with a big belt from the linotype machine. . . . He [my father] cut his beard and mustache and fled Tampa for his life."[82]

Cigar factories reopened in October 1910, protected by citizens' armed patrols. Arbitrary arrests, illegal searches, the destruction of printing presses characterized the era. Again, large numbers of strikebreakers arrived in Tampa, and again, Tampa's second general strike in a decade ended badly for cigar makers.[83]

Prosperity returned to Ybor City as factories reopened and sales of cigars surged. On the eve of World War I, the radical movements across America crested. The war, with its accompanying values of 100 percent Americanization, the Espionage and Sedition Acts, and the Red Scare profoundly impacted radicals and the radical movements.[84]

One would assume that Ybor City radicals, with their notoriety, would have been hounded by local and federal agents throughout the Great War. Careful readings of Tampa newspapers reveal little such repression. However, a scanning of the Spanish-language press and interviews with survivors convey a very different story. Fortunately, the Federal Bureau of Investigation's opening of previously closed files allowed a more comprehensive appraisal of the war years. Documents compiled by the special Bureau of Investigation indicate a systematic pattern of government espionage, establishment violence, and local/federal paranoia over radicals in Ybor City. Literally hundreds of pages of testimonials and reports substantiate a policy of federal and local interventionism.[85]

In November 1919, Bureau of Investigation agent A.V. French wrote to his Washington superiors: "I can state that the Italian-Spanish colonies of West Tampa and Ybor City, are the most advanced toward the 'Social Revolution.' I would say that they have established here a Soviet on the small scale. They do what they like and if they wouldn't be a little frightened by the action taken by the US government in the north against the reds, I would have the impression here of being in Russia."[86] A letter from a prominent Tampa family decried "an intolerable and unbearable situation . . . there is a bunch of anarchists, IWWs and radical Socialists."[87] Agents lamented their failed efforts to infiltrate the radical infrastructure, especially the Spanish-language press. Undercover spies posed as Red Cross Employment Bureau officials to obtain desired information. A vast network of agencies and individuals—including Tampa City Hall, the Spanish consul, the police department, the American Legion, and local newspapers—supplied information to the Bureau of Investigation.

Authorities were especially interested in exposing "los lectores." A March 1919 report dispatch indicated that "every reader in the factories in Tampa was reading Bolsheviki literature." The agent regretted his inability to translate the extensive materials.[88] Dossiers cataloged alleged radicals. José Millares was "a reader and a socialist"; Agustín Sánchez was "an admitted anarchist and reader"; and Abelardo Hernández was "a reader at Cuesta Rey," "a Spaniard," and a "radical." A tobacco trade journal echoed the sentiments of federal investigators. "It has been ascertained that the favorite mental pabulum dispensed by the factory reader is Bolsheviki literature," admitted the spokesman.[89]

If the readers agitated the Latin workforce and created instability, the solitary terrorist threatened the very foundation of law and order. In 1920, a young Latin brazenly admitted to a disguised agent that he had "in his veins the same blood of Brescia [sic]." Gaetano Bresci, an Italian anarchist from Paterson, New Jersey, had assassinated King Umberto I of Italy in 1900.[90] In 1913, the Mexican consul warned that anarchists in Tampa plotted to kill President Victoriano Huerta of Mexico, then involved in a test of wills with the United States. Agents quickly arrested and deported Marcelo Salinas, a Cuban who was editor of El Obrero Industrial, and Maximiliano Olay, an Asturian anarchist who worked as a reader. Salinas and Olay had befriended Manuel Pardiñas, the man who assassinated the Spanish prime minister in November 1912. In 1919, authorities fearful of anarchist threats on the life of President Woodrow Wilson, arrested twenty-four Spaniards in New York and Philadelphia.[91]

While seriously weakened, Ybor City radicals arose occasionally after 1919 to rage at the establishment. The cause célèbre of Sacco and Vanzetti was especially resonant in Tampa. On August 5, 1927, 15,000 cigar makers went out on strike in protest of the anarchists' treatment. A few days later, stores closed in Ybor City and West Tampa in solidarity to the cigar workers' strike. More than 5,000 Latins attended a rally at the Labor Temple to hear speeches in English, Italian, and Spanish. In the 1930s, the tragedy of the Spanish Civil War aroused the Spanish community, bringing out the passion of anarchists and the generosity of ordinary immigrants and their children.[92]

But the deportations, seizures, and intimidations that occurred during the era 1886–1920 seriously weakened the Tampa anarchist community. The 1920–21 strike revealed the toll of the Red Scare. Radicals surrendered their role to traditional union leaders, who fought for closed shops. By the 1920s, the radical edge of Ybor City had been dulled and blunted. The labor wars of attrition, the end of mass immigration, and intimidation wrought a real loss. The last great strike occurred in 1931, appropriately over the reader. The workers lost and readers' voices silenced.[93] The diminishing presence of young immigrants was noticeable. In the 1890s, most of Ybor City's workforce was young; by the 1930s, Ybor City's immigrants were aging. Their children, however, were less enraptured by novels read in factories or the presence of Old World anarchists. Their heroes increasingly tended to be baseball players and boxers, *boliteros* (numbers runners) and bootleggers, doctors and lawyers. Most ironically, the successes of capitalism convinced many Spanish immigrants that while Tampa may never become a workers' utopia, it offered them and their children a slice of the American dream. Compared to Spain, many Latins became convinced that the rewards to be won at a cigar bench, grocery store, or university were more realistic than dreams of a classless society. Anarchism was an ideology borne of Old World scarcity. Ybor City was rooted in New World abundance.

The bankruptcy of American capitalism may have aroused anarchist dreams during the Great Depression, but World War II reconfirmed the American dream. Pearl Harbor electrified Ybor City, and the sons and daughters of Spanish immigrants rallied, enlisting in the military, volunteering for the Red Cross, and buying war bonds. When the war began, many second-generation Spaniards who felt the sting of discrimination thought that they had not been fully accepted into the American mainstream. A 1942 George Gallup poll confirmed their suspicion. Americans ranked Spaniards, Italians, and Mexicans near the bottom of a list when asked how they would rate the peoples or races of the world. Only the Japanese ranked lower. Braulio Alonso, the son of Spanish immigrants, enlisted in the armed forces, becoming a captain. In the 1930s, he had marched in parades and sung "¡No Pasarán!" Alonso, who went on to become a revered educator, harbored no memories of the glory of battle. "War is unpleasant, vicious, bloody and sacrificial," he recollected. He and others felt that the war was just and had resulted in a more egalitarian society.[94]

The study of anarchism in the United States will benefit greatly from fresh perspectives and new generations of scholars; indeed, the literature from the last decade signifies the attention paid to this topic.[95]

NOTES

This essay was originally published in 1986 by Northern Illinois University Press. It seems like a lifetime ago, because so much has happened since that year. George Pozzetta, a dear colleague since our graduate school days at the University of North

Carolina, cowrote *The Immigrant World of Ybor City*, which came out a year later, in 1987. Sadly, George died in 1994, a great personal loss, but an even greater loss to students of immigration history. Were George alive, this revised essay would be better. I am especially delighted to revisit this topic, in part because a former student, Ana Varela-Lago, is coediting the volume; in part because of the fascination of the topic. When I take students on an Ybor City class tour, I muse what the Italian and Spanish anarchists might think of the tattoo parlors and the crass merchandizing.

1. The topic of Spanish anarchism has benefited from many first-rate studies, among them: Martha A. Ackelsberg, *Free Women of Spain: Anarchism and the Struggle for the Emancipation of Women* (Bloomington: Indiana University Press, 1991); Paul Avrich, *Anarchist Portraits* (Princeton, NJ: Princeton University Press, 1990); Avrich, *Anarchist Voices: An Oral History of Anarchism in America* (Princeton, NJ: Princeton University Press, 1995); Murray Bookchin, *The Spanish Anarchists: The Heroic Years, 1886–1936* (New York: Free Life Editions, 1977); Gerald Brenan, *The Spanish Labyrinth: An Account of the Social and Political Background of the Civil War* (Cambridge: Cambridge University Press, 1964); George Richard Esenwein, *Anarchist Ideology and the Working-Class Movement in Spain, 1868–1898* (Berkeley: University of California Press, 1989); Eric J. Hobsbawm, *Primitive Rebels: Studies in Archaic Forms of Social Movements in the Nineteenth Century* (New York: W.W. Norton, 1959); Robert Kerr, *Red Years / Black Years: A Political History of Spanish Anarchism, 1911–37* (Philadelphia: Institute for the Study of Human Issues, 1978); Temma Kaplan, *Anarchists of Andalusia* (Princeton, NJ: Princeton University Press, 1978); Joan Connelly Ullman, *La semana trágica: Estudio sobre las causas socioeconómicas del anticlericalismo en España* (Barcelona: Ediciones Síntesis, 1972).

2. R. A. Gómez, "Spanish Immigration to the United States," *Americas* 19 (July 1962): 59–77; Salvador de Madariaga, *Spain: A Modern History* (New York: Praeger, 1958), 136.

3. Julio Cuevas, interview with authors, July 29, 1983, Tampa, Florida. Many of the interviews cited may be accessed at the University of South Florida Library, Special Collections, Tampa, Florida.

4. Fernand Braudel, *The Mediterranean and the Mediterranean World in the Age of Philip II*, 2 vols. (New York: Harper and Row, 1972), 1:588.

5. Enrique Alvarez Suárez, *Asturias* (n.p.: Maten Artes Gráficas, 1924), 92–104; Richard Herr, *Spain*, Modern Nations in Historical Perspective Series (Englewood Cliffs, NJ: Prentice-Hall, 1971), 115–22; Brenan, *The Spanish Labyrinth*, 93; Kerr, *Red Years / Black Years*, 10; Madariaga, *Spain*, 133; Raymond Carr, *Spain, 1808–1939* (Oxford: Clarendon Press, 1966).

6. Ann M. Pescatello, *Power and Pawn: The Female in Iberian Societies and Cultures* (Westport, CT: Greenwood Press, 1976), 30; Madariaga, *Spain*, 133; Louis A.

Pérez, *Cuba: Between Reform and Revolution* (New York: Oxford University Press, 1988), 134–35; Charles J. Esdaile, *Spain in the Liberal Age: From Constitution to Civil War, 1808–1939* (Oxford: Blackwell, 2000), 153.

7. G. H. B. Ward, *The Truth about Spain* (London: Cassell and Co., 1911), 136.

8. Kaplan, *Anarchists of Andalusia*, 10–11.

9. Kaplan, *Anarchists of Andalusia*, 133; James Joll, *The Anarchists* (Cambridge, MA: Harvard University Press, 1980), 207; Pescatello, *Power and Pawn*, 23–24; George Woodcock, *Anarchism: A History of Libertarian Ideas and Movements* (New York: New American Library, 1962), 356–57.

10. Richard B. Saltman, *The Social and Political Thought of Michael Bakunin* (Westport, CT: Greenwood Press, 1983); Madariaga, *Spain*, 146; Joll, *The Anarchists*, 72–73; Fernando Savater, *Para la anarquía* (Barcelona: Tusquets Editor, 1977), 119–28.

11. Savater, *Para la anarquía.*

12. Bookchin, *The Spanish Anarchists*, 89–109; G. H. B. Ward, *The Truth about Spain*, 133.

13. Madariaga, *Spain*, 151; Brenan, *The Spanish Labyrinth*, 94; Marcelino García, interview with Paul Avrich, Palmerton, Pennsylvania, December 18, 1971, and Manuel Rey y García (Louis G. Raymond), interview with Paul Avrich, Stelton, NJ, December 14, 1989, in Avrich, *Anarchist Voices*, 390–95.

14. Joll, *The Anarchists*, 3, 117–274; Herr, *Spain*, 128–29; *Tampa Morning Tribune*, November 14, 1912; Rafael Núñez Florencio, *El terrorismo anarquista, 1888–1909* (Madrid: Siglo Veintiuno, 1983).

15. Duvon C. Corbett, "Immigration in Cuba," *Hispanic American Historical Review* 22 (May 1942): 302–8; Louis A. Pérez, *Cuba between Empires, 1878–1902* (Pittsburgh: University of Pittsburgh Press, 1983), 4–38.

16. Instituto de Historia del Movimiento Comunista y de la Revolución Socialista de Cuba, *El movimiento obrero cubano: Documentos y artículos, 1865–1925* (Havana: Instituto del Libro, 1963), 17–26; Ramiro Guerra y Sánchez et al., *Historia de la nación cubana: Antecedentes del movimiento obrero* (Havana: Editorial Historia de la Nación Cubana, 1952), 246–54.

17. Guerra y Sánchez, *Antecedentes*, 266; Gerald E. Poyo, *"With All, and for the Good of All": The Emergence of Popular Nationalism in the Cuban Communities of the United States, 1848–1898* (Durham, NC: Duke University Press, 1989), 87.

18. Ariel Hidalgo, *Orígenes del movimiento obrero y del pensamiento socialista en Cuba* (Havana: Instituto Cubano del Libro, 1976), 101–2.

19. José Rivero Muñiz, "El tabaquero en la historia de Cuba," *Islas* 5 (June 1963): 300–302; *El movimiento obrero durante la primera intervención* (Santa Clara, Cuba: Universidad Central de Las Villas, 1961), 211; Araceli Tinajero, *El lector: A History of the Cigar Factory Reader*, trans. Judith E. Grasberg (Austin: University of Texas Press, 2010), 41.

20. John Dumoulin, "El movimiento obrero en Cruces, 1902–1925: Corrientes ideológicas y formas de organización de la industria azucarera," *Islas* 62 (January–April 1979): 83–122; George E. Pozzetta, "An Immigrant Library: The Tampa Italian Club Collection," *Ex Libris* 1 (1978): 10–12.

21. Paul Estrade, "Las huelgas de 1890 en Cuba," *Revista de la Biblioteca de José Martí* (January–April 1979): 27–51.

22. Gaspar Jorge García Galló, "Influencia del tabaquero en la trayectoria revolucionaria de Cuba," *Revista Bimestre Cubana* 38 (1936): 108; Poyo, "With All," 35–52.

23. Dumoulin, "El movimiento obrero," 96; Gaspar Jorge García Galló, *Biografía del tabaco habano* (Santa Clara, Cuba: Universidad Central de Las Villas, 1959), 139.

24. L. Glenn Westfall, "Don Vicente Martínez Ybor, the Man and His Empire: Development of the Clear Havana Industry in Cuba and Florida in the Nineteenth Century" (PhD diss., University of Florida, 1977), 10–11, 16–21.

25. Westfall, "Don Vicente Martínez Ybor," 30–45; Gerald E. Poyo, "Key West and the Cuban Ten Years War," *Florida Historical Quarterly* 57 (January 1979): 289–308; L. Glenn Westfall, *Key West: Cigar City USA* (Key West: Historic Florida Keys, 1984).

26. For profiles of Spanish manufacturers, see *Tampa Morning Tribune*, April 10, 1895, 1; April 17, 1895, 1; November 17, 1896, 1; May 11, 1906, 1; November 12, 1915, 7; January 10, 1909, 1; March 17, 1926, 1.

27. Ybor City has become a cottage industry for historians. Note the inexplicable use of "Ybor" as the original name of the community. No one has ever explained why Martínez Ybor did not use the preferable family surname Martínez. For a treatment of the community's formative years, see Gary R. Mormino and George E. Pozzetta, *The Immigrant World of Ybor City: Italians and Their Latin Neighbors in Tampa, 1886–1985* (Urbana: University of Illinois Press, 1987), 63–70, 176–77; Durward Long, "The Historical Beginnings of Ybor City," *Florida Historical Quarterly* 59 (July 1971): 31–44; Emilio Del Río, *Yo fui uno de los fundadores de Ybor City* (Tampa: n.p. 1950), 9–11; Jesse L. Keene, "Gavino Gutierrez and His Contributions to Tampa," *Florida Historical Quarterly* 36 (1957): 33–41; Susan Greenberg, *More than Black: Afro-Cubans in Tampa* (Gainesville: University Press of Florida, 2002).

28. Gómez, "Spanish Immigration," 59–77; Carr, *Spain*, 10–11; *Gran Enciclopedia Asturiana*, s.v. "Emigración," 17 vols. (Gijón, Spain: Silverio Cañada, 1981), 7: 78.

29. Fermín Souto, interview, Federal Writers' Project volume, P. K. Yonge Library of Florida History, University of Florida (Tampa, 1936), 3–5.

30. María Ordieres, interview, Federal Writers' Project volume, P. K. Yonge Library of Florida History, University of Florida, 1.

31. US Bureau of the Census, *Compendium of the Eleventh Census: 1890*, table 20 (Washington, DC: Government Printing Office, 1892), 672–73; *Twelfth Census of the United States: 1900, Population*, vol. 2, table 27 (Washington, DC: Government

Printing Office, 1902), 214; *Thirteenth Census of the United States: 1910, Population,* vol. 2 table 2 (Washington, DC: Government Printing Office, 1912), 330.

32. *Tampa Guardian,* June 9 and 30, 1886; October 27, 1886; *Tampa Weekly Times,* April 16, 1886; *Tampa Journal,* January 12, 1888; January 2, 1890; Tampa City Council Minutes, March 26, 1888, Minutes Book 2; "Early Days in Ybor City, as Narrated by Fernando Lemos," Federal Writers' Project volume, University of Florida, 56.

33. Testimony of Ramón Williams, "Proceedings of the Cuba / Florida Immigration Investigation," US Senate Reports, Commission on Immigration, 1892 (Washington, DC: Government Printing Office, 1892), 4–6.

34. US Congress. Senate, *Reports of the Immigration Commission, Immigrants in Industries,* 61st Congress, 2d sess., 1910, pt. 14, "Cigar and Tobacco Manufacturing," tables 162, 163, and 191, p. 234; *Twelfth Census, 1900,* Manuscript Census Schedules; *Thirteenth Census, 1910,* Manuscript Census Schedules; Karen Weltz, "Boarders in Tampa, 1900 and 1910" (unpublished manuscript, University of South Florida, 1983).

35. Mormino and Pozzetta, *The Immigrant World,* 197–203; Dr. Frank Adamo, interview with Gary Mormino, April 20, 1980, Tampa; Catherine Bayless Slusser, "A Professional Opinion: A History of the Hillsborough County Medical Association, 1895–1970" (master's thesis, University of South Florida, 1982), 47–60.

36. *El Centro Asturiano en Tampa: Inauguración del Edificio Social 15 de Mayo de 1914* (commemorative program, n.p); Durward Long, "An Immigrant Cooperative Medicine Program in the South, 1887–1963," *Journal of Southern History* 31 (November 1965): 417–34.

37. Salatha Bagley, "The Latin Clubs of Tampa, Florida" (master's thesis, Duke University, 1948); *Tampa Tribune,* June 8, 1965, 3B.

38. Angelo Massari, *The Wonderful Life of Angelo Massari,* trans. Arthur D. Massolo (New York: Exposition Press, 1965), 144; Mormino and Pozzetta, *The Immigrant World,* 143–74.

39. This estimate is based upon a close reading of the surviving leftist press available for Tampa, citations from the English-language press, and oral interviews. Specific references will follow. Consuelo E. Stebbbins, *City of Intrigue, Nest of Revolution: A Documentary History of Key West in the Nineteenth Century* (Gainesville: University Press of Florida, 2007), 117–44, 194–213; Poyo, "With All," 87.

40. *El Internacional,* March 9, July 30, and August 27, 1915; December 8, 1911; August 4, 1905; Sirio Bruno Coniglio, interview with George Pozzetta, Clearwater, Florida, May 2, 1976, Oral History Collection, University of Florida, Gainesville.

41. Massari, *The Wonderful Life,* 107; *El Internacional,* March 1, 1918, 4.

42. Diego Abad de Santillán (pseud., Sinesio García Delgado), *Contribución a la historia del movimiento obrero español: Desde sus orígenes hasta 1905* (Puebla, Mexico: 1962), 188, 283, 392–93; García quoted in Avrich, *Anarchist Voices,* 391. See also pages

392–93; Jennifer Guglielmo, *Living the Revolution: Women's Resistance and Revolution in New York, 1880–1945* (Chapel Hill: University of North Carolina Press, 2010), 156–59. The best overview of Esteve's career in the United States is Joan Casanovas I Codina, "Pedro Esteve, A Catalan Anarchist in the United States," *Catalan Review* 5 (July 1991): 57–77.

43. Guglielmo, *Living the Revolution*, 292–93; José Alvarez Junco, *La ideología política del anarquismo español (1868–1910)* (Madrid: Siglo Veintiuno, 1976); Esenwein, *Anarchist Ideology*, 126–27, 187–89.

44. Massari, *The Wonderful Life*, 107.

45. *El Internacional*, November 17, 1905; *La Federación*, February 16, and March 9, 1900; *La Parola dei Socialisti*, Chicago, May 14 and 21, and July 2, 1910; Emma Goldman, *Living My Life*, 2 vols. (New York: Dover Publications, 1970), 1:150; Elizabeth Gurley Flynn, *The Rebel Girl: An Autobiography, My First Life (1906–1926)*, rev. ed. (New York: International Publications, 1976), 62, 184; Avrich, *Anarchist Portraits*, 143, 149, 158, 173, 180, 153; Avrich, *Anarchist Voices*, 391–97.

46. *La Cronaca Sovversiva* (Barre, VT), November 21, 1903; *Il Martello* (New York,) April 8, 1912; *La Questione Sociale* (Paterson, NJ), July 4, 1906. Another collection of Esteve's writings is contained in the pamphlet *Reformismo, dictadura, federalismo* (New York: n.p., 1922). This pamphlet, a copy of which may be found at the Biblioteca Pública Arús, Barcelona, contains articles published in *Cultura Obrera*. Professor Joan Ullman has kindly made a copy of Esteve's 1893 *Memoria* available to us. The Immigration History Center, University of Minnesota, Minneapolis, holds a copy of Esteve's *La Legge*.

47. *La Cronaca Sovversiva* (Barre, VT), September 19, 1903 and November 17, 1917; *El Despertar* (New York), September 10, 1901; *Il Diretto* (New York), February 15, 1919. See also Ramón Sempau, *Los victimarios: Notas relativas al proceso de Montjuich*, prologue by Emilio Junoy (Barcelona: García y Manent, 1900), 343. Professor James Amelang of the University of Madrid kindly made available this reference.

48. *L'Aurora*, Tampa, May 17 and 31, 1912; *La Voce della Colonia*, Tampa, June 10 and 17, 1911.

49. This assessment is based upon an examination of club holdings in Tampa, including the libraries of the principal Spanish ethnic organizations (Centro Español and Centro Asturiano). Italian groups in the city followed similar lines. See Pozzetta, "An Immigrant Library," 10–12.

50. Copies of these newspapers are available on microfilm at the P. K. Yonge Library of Florida History, University of Florida, Gainesville. The most extensive holdings are for *El Internacional*, 1904–1946.

51. Archdiocese of Saint Augustine, Florida, "Financial Statement, Ybor City Mission" (Tampa, 1911); Néstor Leonelo Carbonell, "El Catolicismo Romano," *Patria*,

February 5, 1898, 2; Julio Caro Baroja, *Introducción a una historia contemporánea del anticlericalismo español* (Madrid: Ediciones Istmo, 1980). For a spirited defense of the Catholic Church in Tampa, see Michael J. McNally, *Catholic Parish Life on Florida's West Coast, 1860–1968* (Philadelphia: Catholic Media Ministries, Inc. 1996), 162–84.

52. Louis A. Pérez, "Cubans in Tampa: From Exiles to Immigrants, 1892–1901," *Florida Historical Quarterly* 57 (October 1978): 129–40; Poyo, *"With All,"* 74–81.

53. Frank Fernández, "Los anarquistas cubanos (1865–1898)," *Guángara Libertaria* 5, no. 17 (1984): 4–5; José Martí, *Obras completas*, vol. 1 (Havana: Editorial Nacional de Cuba, 1963–1966); Pérez, *Cuba between Empires*, 16–17; José Ramón Sanfeliz, "Life History of José Ramón Sanfeliz," Federal Writers' Project, Special Collections, University of South Florida.

54. Poyo, *"With All,"* 104–5; Pérez, *Cuba between Empires*, 390.

55. *Patria*, November 7, 1902, cited in Fernández, "Los anarquistas cubanos," 7. Authorities had expelled Esteve from Spain after he denounced the government for turning Cuba into "a mere hacienda."

56. Fernández, "Los anarquistas cubanos," 7. More information on the career of Baliño is contained in *Carlos Baliño, Documentos y artículos* (Havana: Departamento de Orientación Revolucionaria del Comité Central del Partido Comunista Cubano, 1976); "Our Havana," *Tampa Tribune*, May 25, 1984, 1; *Patria*, May 6, 1896, 2; Joan Maria Steffy, "Cuban Immigrants of Tampa, Florida, 1886–1898" (master's thesis, University of South Florida, 1975), 63–67.

57. A. Rouse, "Tampa Camp Scenes Described," *New York Times Illustrated Magazine*, May 15, 1898, 10; Federal Writers' Project, "Ybor City Historical Data," 401; Tampa City Council Meeting, Tampa, Minutes, April 2, 1898; "Tampa's Dynamite Fiend," *Starry Flag Weekly*, June 18, 1898, Special Collections, University of South Florida Library. See also Ana Varela-Lago, "Conquerors, Immigrants, Exiles: The Spanish Diaspora in the United States (1848–1948)" (PhD diss. University of California, San Diego, 2008), 89.

58. John Higham, *Strangers in the Land: Patterns of American Nativism, 1860–1925* (New Brunswick, NJ: Rutgers University Press, 1955).

59. *Tampa Morning Tribune*, July 30, 1896.

60. *Tampa Morning Tribune*, July 30, 1899.

61. *Tampa Morning Tribune*, December 18, 1911; Roland Rerrick, *Memoirs of Florida*, 2 vols. (Atlanta: Southern Historical Association, 1902), 2: 22; US Congress (Senate), Immigration Commission Report, *Immigrants in Industries: "Cigar and Tobacco Manufacturing"* (Washington DC: Government Printing Office, 1911), 14: 88.

62. José Vega Díaz, interview with authors, May 3, 1980; Gary R. Mormino and George E. Pozzetta, "'The Reader Lights the Candle': Cuban and Florida Cigar Workers' Oral Tradition," *Labor's Heritage* (Spring 1993): 3–27; Tinajero, *El Lector*.

63. Louis A. Pérez, "Reminiscences of a *Lector*: Cuban Cigar Workers in Tampa," *Florida Historical Quarterly* 53 (April 1975): 443–49; Wilfredo Rodríguez, interview with Gary Mormino, April 1, 1982; Nancy Hewitt, *Southern Discomfort: Women's Activism in Tampa, Florida, 1880s–1920s* (Urbana: University of Illinois Press, 2001), 214–19; Tinajero, *El Lector*, 127–53. In the award-winning novel, *Anna in the Tropics* (2003), the playwright Nilo Cruz asserts literary license by having the cigar manufacturer's wife, not the workers, pay the reader.

64. Tinajero, *El Lector*, 144; Hewitt, *Southern Discomfort*, 214–19. The lyrics, "Women of Iberia," are from Ackelsberg, *Free Women*, 1. Luisa Capetillo, *Mi Opinión sobre las libertades, derechos, y deberes de la mujer* (San Juan, Puerto Rico: Times, 1911); Luisa Capetillo, *Influencias de las ideas modernas*, intro. and trans. Lara Walker (Houston, TX: Arte Público Press, 2009).

65. Pérez, "Reminiscences of a *Lector*," 443–49; Mormino and Pozzetta, "'The Reader Lights the Candle,'" 13–14; Tinajero, *El Lector*, 84–142; "Luisa Capetillo—a Biography," https://libcom.org/history/biography-luisa-capetillo.

66. Domínguez quoted in *Tampa Tribune*, September 12, 1977.

67. Emanuel LaRosa, interview with authors, Tampa, July 30, 1983; Coniglio quoted in José Yglesias, *The Truth about Them* (New York: World Publisher, 1971), 207; The Olay story, *"Mirando al mundo,"* is found in Varela-Lago, "Conquerors, Immigrants, Exiles," 212.

68. José Yglesias quoted in Studs Terkel, *Hard Times* (New York: Avon Books, 1970), 133; Robert P. Ingalls, "The Life and Work of José Yglesias," *Tampa Bay History* 18, no. 1 (1996): 5–28.

69. *Tampa Journal*, January 24 and 26, 1887, and March 12, 1887; Gerald Eugene Poyo, "Cuban Émigré Communities in the United States and the Independence of Their Homeland, 1852–1895" (PhD diss., University of Florida, 1983), 224–25. The Spanish consuls in Key West closely followed Rubiera's activities. See Stebbins, *City of Intrigue*, 136, 204–11.

70. Poyo, "Cuban Émigré Communities;" Tampa Board of Trade, Minutes, March 8, 1887; *Tampa Journal*, January, 24 and 26, 1887.

71. Rivero Muñiz, *Los cubanos en Tampa*, 42, 47; *Tampa Journal*, May 7, 1891.

72. *Tampa Morning Tribune*, July 7, 1891; Robert Ingalls, *Urban Vigilantes in the New South: Tampa, 1882–1936* (Knoxville: University of Tennessee Press, 1988).

73. *Cigar Makers' Official Journal* 14 (January–November 1889); Mormino and Pozzetta, *The Immigrant World*, 97–141.

74. *Tampa Tribune*, September 8, 1892. See also *Tampa Daily Tribune*, May 7, 1891.

75. *Tampa Tribune*, September 2, 6, 7, and 8, 1892; April 18, 1893; Stebbins, *City of Intrigue*, 129–43.

76. Gary R. Mormino, "Tampa and the New Urban South: The Weight Strike of 1899," *Florida Historical Quarterly* 60 (January 1982): 337–56.

77. *Tampa Morning Tribune*, July 11, 1899.

78. Durward Long, "La Resistencia: Tampa's Immigrant Labor Union," *Labor History* 6 (Fall 1965): 193–214.

79. *Tampa Morning Tribune*, November 1 and 10, 1900; Mormino and Pozzetta, *The Immigrant World*, 116–18; George E. Pozzetta, "¡Alerta Tabaqueros!: Tampa's Striking Cigar Workers," *Tampa Bay History* 3, no. 2 (1981): 19–29; Ingalls, *Urban Vigilantes*, 62–63, 69–82; *United States Tobacco Journal*, August 24, 1901.

80. Pozzetta, "¡Alerta Tabaqueros!"; Long, "La Resistencia"; Ingalls, *Urban Vigilantes*, 87–115; *Tampa Morning Tribune*, August 23, 1901.

81. *Tampa Morning Tribune*, August 12, 1910; George E. Pozzetta, "Italians and the Tampa General Strike of 1910," in *Pane e Lavoro*, ed. George E. Pozzetta (Toronto: Multi-Cultural History, 1980), 29–47.

82. Mormino and Pozzetta, *The Immigrant World*, 118–22; Sirio Esteve quoted in Avrich, *Anarchist Voices*, 393.

83. This information is derived from American and Spanish newspapers, 1910. Oral histories are also useful in understanding the strike of 1910. Emanuel LaRosa recalled helping hide José de la Campa from vigilantes.

84. James Weinstein, *The Decline of Socialism in America, 1912–1925* (New York: Vintage Books, 1967).

85. Investigative Case Files of the Bureau of Investigation, 1908–1922, National Archives (hereafter, ICFBI).

86. A. V. French to Bureau of Investigation, November 21, 1919, ICFBI, Old German Files, #362112.

87. M. E. Gillett and son to Bureau of Investigation, November 15, 1919, ICFBI, Old German Files, #631112.

88. Byrd Douglas to Bureau of Investigation, August 9, 1919, ICFBI, Old German Files, #362112.

89. Ibid., August 2 and 5, 1919; *United States Tobacco Journal*, November 15, 1919, 38; Hewitt, *Southern Discomfort*, 213–14.

90. Unnamed agent to Bureau of Investigation, January 27, 1920, ICFBI, Justice Department, #362112.

91. Justice Department Report on Anarchists, March 3, 1913, ICFBI, Justice Department, #5606; "Bomb Planned for Wilson," *New York Times*, February 24, 1919; Varela-Lago, "Conquerors, Immigrants, Exiles," 211–14.

92. "15,000 Cigar Makers Go On 2-Hour Strike," *Tampa Morning Tribune*, August 5, 1927; "5,000 Strikers at Meeting in Sacco Protest," *Tampa Morning Tribune*, August 11,

1927; Ana Varela-Lago, "'¡No Pasarán!' The Spanish Civil War's Impact on Tampa's Latin Community, 1936–1939," *Tampa Bay History* 19, no. 2 (1997): 5–34.

93. Ingalls, *Urban Vigilantes*, 120–22, 33–42; Mormino and Pozzetta, "'The Reader Lights the Candle,'" 20–22.

94. Gary R. Mormino, "Ybor City Goes to War: The Evolution and Transformation of a 'Latin' Community in Florida, 1886–1950," in *Latina/os and World War II: Mobility, Agency, and Ideology*, ed. Maggie Rivas-Rodriguez and B. V. Olguín (Austin: University of Texas Press, 2014), 13–42; "An Analysis of American Public Opinion Regarding the War," Presidential Personal Files (PPF) 4721, Franklin D. Roosevelt Library, Hyde Park, NY.

95. For example: Juan Avilés and Angel Herrerín, eds., *El nacimiento del terrorismo en occidente* (Madrid: Siglo XXI, 2008); Julián Casanova, ed., *Tierra y libertad: Cien años de anarquismo en España* (Barcelona: Crítica, 2010); Jesse Cohn, *Underground Passages: Anarchist Resistance Culture, 1848–2011* (Chico, CA: AK Press, 2015); M. Montserrat Feu-López, *Correspondencia personal y política de un anarcosindicalista exiliado: Jesús González Malo (1950–1965)* (Santander, Spain: Colección Cuatro Estaciones, Universidad de Cantabria, 2016); Christopher J. Castañeda and Montse Feu, eds., *Writing Revolution: Hispanic Anarchism in the United States* (Urbana: University of Illinois Press, 2019); Nicolás Kanellos, "Spanish-Language Anarchist Periodicals in Early Twentieth-Century United States," in *Protest on the Page: Essays on Print and the Culture of Dissent since 1865*, ed. James L. Baughman, Jennifer Ratner-Rosenhagen, and James P. Danky (Madison: University of Wisconsin Press, 2015), 59–84; Angel Smith, *Anarchism, Revolution and Reaction: Catalan Labor and the Crisis of the Spanish State, 1898–1923* (New York: Berghahn Books, 2007); Josep Termes, *Història del moviment anarquista a Espanya (1870–1980)* (Barcelona: L'Avenç, 2011); and Kenyon Zimmer, *Immigrants against the State. Yiddish and Italian Anarchism in America* (Urbana: University of Illinois Press, 2015).

4

"YOURS FOR THE REVOLUTION"

*Cigar Makers, Anarchists, and Brooklyn's
Spanish Colony, 1878–1925*

CHRISTOPHER J. CASTAÑEDA

Spanish-speaking immigrant cigar makers created an influential anarchist colony in Brooklyn during the late nineteenth century. Although studies of diasporic Spanish radicalism in this era typically identify Ybor City (Tampa) and Key West as the activist cigar makers' principal locations in the United States, New York's Spanish-speaking anarchist cigar makers established Brooklyn as a primary center for the support and promotion of anarchism, Cuba Libre, and of opposition to the Spanish monarchy and church. This chapter will examine the origins, development, and significant participants in Brooklyn's radical *colonia* within the transnational anarchist network of the late nineteenth and early twentieth centuries.[1]

Brooklyn's Spanish cigar makers represented a broad range of political, social and economic interests. A few became prosperous cigar shop or factory owners while many others struggled to make a living peddling cigars or working as rollers, strippers, or packers; some formed small partnerships to import, manufacture, or sell cigars. Most arrived in New York as single men seeking a new life; some came with a wife and family. Many of these

DOI: 10.5876/9781607327998.c004

immigrants settled in what became known as the "Spanish colony" adjacent to the East River near the Brooklyn Bridge as well as in "Little Spain" located in the area surrounding Fourteenth Street in Manhattan. Whether they arrived as anarchists or became radicalized in the United States, these cigar workers were an integral part of a rapidly changing tobacco industry in the process of being restructured by new manufacturing technologies. They were skilled craftsman in the disappearing hand-rolled cigar business that was at first slowly and then decisively decimated by automated machinery, the mass-produced cigar, and the increasingly popular cigarette.

By the late nineteenth century, Cuba had become the principal geographic and political link between Spain and the United States. Some Spanish immigrants in Cuba were landowners and tobacco growers; others joined the separatist movement. Many sympathizers were imprisoned or lost their lives in the ensuing civil strife; others left Cuba hoping for economic opportunity in the United States. For those in the cigar business, Florida and New York were the most common destinations (see table 4.1). The political situation in both Spain and Cuba infused many Spanish émigrés with a strong political awareness, if not radicalism, that they brought with them to the United States. Many Spanish cigar makers—along with dockworkers, seamen, and miners—had already joined the anarcho-syndicalist movement, supporting revolutionary labor activism, and voicing their opposition to Spanish government policies, tyranny in Cuba, and capitalism. These immigrants expressed themselves in strikes, anarchist periodicals, pamphlets, and labor clubs and organizations.[2]

INTRODUCING THE CIGAR

In the United States, the cigar manufacturing industry remained relatively small through the mid-nineteenth century.[3] Most cigar making took place within family units or very small shops consisting of one to four workers.[4] Many cigar smokers preferred imported cigars, either the less expensive brands from Belgium and Germany or the higher-grade Cuban cigars.[5] In Florida, due to its geographic and climatological proximity to Cuba, cigar manufacturing became a relatively significant part of the regional economy before it did in other parts of North America. As early as the 1830s, some Cuban cigar manufacturers had moved their operations from Cuba to Key

TABLE 4.1. Foreign-Born Population in the United States (1850–1920)

Year	Spain	Cuba	All Countries (millions)
1850	3,113	5,772*	2.2
1860	4,244	7,353*	4.1
1870	3,764	5,319	5.6
1880	5,121	6,917	6.7
1890	6,185	23,256*	9.2
1900	7,050	11,081	10.3
1910	22,108	15,133	13.5
1920	49,535	14,872	13.9

*Includes West Indies

Source: US Department of Commerce, *Historical Statistics of the United States: Colonial Times to 1970*, pt. 1 (Washington, DC: GPO, 1975), 117–18.

West to avoid import duties on cigars and tobacco leaf. Industry migration continued, as historian Louis A. Pérez noted, when the US panic of 1857 resulted in the imposition of higher tariffs on foreign goods, including Cuban cigars. This "had a catastrophic effect on the Havana cigar industry."[6] Many Cuban cigar manufacturers failed while others determined that one way around these tariffs, as well as new ones imposed during the Civil War years, was to move operations to the United States; the majority of tobacco leaf imported into the United States for cigar manufacturing continued to come from Cuba, where there were as many as 10,000 tobacco farms.[7] Not only was Cuban leaf in high demand, but consumers who valued prestige and authenticity demanded that Cuban manufacturers, even in the United States, use "Cuban tobacco, Cuban labor, and Cuban methods so that their product was typically Havana cigars."[8]

In the years after the Civil War, cigar manufacturing became an increasingly important part of the Brooklyn and New York City economies. "The real stimulus toward centering the manufacture of cigars in these cities," noted economic historian Willis N. Baer, "came as a result of the Civil War, at which time tobacco industries were moved northward in order to escape the impending hazards of war."[9] By 1869, there were approximately 4,631 cigar manufacturers in the United States, in cities such as Cincinnati, Baltimore, Chicago, and New York among other urban areas.[10] The New York City cigar industry continued to expand during the 1870s, and production began to shift, gradually, from tenements and small shops to larger factories. By 1877, about one-half of the city's cigar production came from seventy factories, that comprised only 5 percent of the total number of local cigar firms.[11]

Due in large part to the turmoil of the Cuban separatist movement, Florida attracted several large Cuban cigar manufacturers. One year after the beginning of the violent Ten Years' War (1868–1878) in Cuba, Vicente Martínez Ybor, a Spanish immigrant who had supported Cuban independence, moved his operations from Havana to Key West. Later, in 1885, he transplanted his manufacturing facilities to a coastal location near Tampa in central Florida. Known as Ybor City, this cigar-making town became the center of the US Havana cigar-making industry. During the following decades, cigar manufacturing increased in other Florida locales such as St. Augustine, Ocala, and Jacksonville. It was common for cigar makers to travel back and forth between those towns, Ybor City, Havana, and New York City. This movement facilitated the transference of business practices, labor, and ideology among these urban centers.[12]

By the mid-1870s, the cigar business in New York City was a significant economic activity. The *New York Sun* reported that about 25,000 persons in the city were "dependent upon cigar making for their daily bread."[13] Of this number about 15,000 were cigar makers including about 4,000 Bohemian women, 2,500 Bohemian men, 6,000 German (including Polish) men, 2,000 German women, 200 Americans, and a total of 500 Cubans and Spaniards.[14] If these numbers are accurate, then by the mid-1870s Cubans and Spaniards comprised only about 3 percent of New York City area cigar makers.

Conditions in tenement-based cigar making were harsh and posed particularly significant health problems in New York City. There is perhaps no better example of the nineteenth century urban sweatshop than the cigar makers' tenement. As legal historian Paul Kens observed, "Cigar making in New York City was an archetypical sweatshop industry. Workers were given the raw material to make cigars in their apartments, and they were paid on a piecework basis for the finished product."[15] Even worse, the unhealthy environment in which cigar workers spent much of their time, both in cramped factories and tenements, often led to early death. Cigar makers contracted respiratory illnesses including pneumonia and tuberculosis (about 50 percent of cigar maker fatalities in 1890 were related to tuberculosis). The common diagnosis for a cigar maker's respiratory disease at that time was "labor pneumonia." Cigar makers had an average life expectancy of only 37 years.[16]

The combination of poor working conditions and the influx of cigar makers from Germany and Britain, where cigar and tobacco unions already existed, prompted unionization in New York City.[17] There were early cigar maker unions in Cincinnati (1845) and Baltimore (1851), but the first successful national organization in the United States was the Cigar Makers' International Union (CMIU) formed in New York in 1864. In that year, a young English-born immigrant living in Brooklyn, Samuel Gompers, joined Local 144 of the CMIU; in 1886 he was elected its vice-president. In the same year, he became president of the newly formed American Federation of Labor (AFL) that he had helped to organize. He remained in these positions until his death in 1924.[18]

Spanish-speaking cigar makers tended to gravitate to their own labor organizations. Although CMIU Local 144 reportedly accepted Spanish-speaking members, Spanish and Cuban cigar makers made clear their desire for labor autonomy. It is important to note, however, that while non-Hispanics may have routinely classified Spanish and Cuban cigar workers into the same "Latin" ethnic category, Cubans and Spaniards (or *peninsulares*) often had very different cultural backgrounds and political beliefs.[19] Yet, generalized "racial" and cultural differences contributed to social divisions among various ethnic and cultural groups; while Spanish-speaking cigar makers were "white," they remained "different" and in any case generally preferred their own enclaves.[20] In 1883 a group of Spanish cigar makers formed the Gremio de Obreros de Nueva York, or New York Workers' Union, a "republican and reformist organization." Its membership quickly rose above 400, and it began publishing its own periodical, *La Cuestión Social*. In response, Cuban cigar makers in New York formed the Unión de Torcedores, or Cigar Makers' Union, closely linked to the Cuban separatist movement. Tensions between these unions grew, foreshadowing more strident disagreements later, as disputes over allegiance to Cuban independence became more intense.[21]

CUBANS AND SPANIARDS IN NEW YORK CITY

The nineteenth-century movement of Cubans to New York was not entirely distinct from Spanish migration. Since Cuba was a Spanish possession until it achieved independence after the Spanish-American War (1898), nineteenth-century "Cubans" were officially Spanish nationals. Cuban immigrants' naturalization papers identified their nationality as "King of Spain" or "Queen of Spain."[22] In addition, many Spanish immigrants to the United States traveled first through Cuba, further blurring the lines between Cubans and *peninsular* Spaniards. Immigrants typically self-identified to census takers, and while these records are highly useful, they are not precise. The 1870, 1880, and 1890 census reported 1,565, 2,073, and 3,470 Cubans respectively, living in New York City.[23]

Father Félix Varela y Morales, a Roman Catholic priest, was one of the first Cuban-born immigrants to move to New York City. He disembarked on December 23, 1823, from the *Draper C. Thorndike* that had sailed from Gibraltar to New York. Varela had met in Spain with King Ferdinand VII and advocated, to no avail, for Cuban autonomy.[24] In 1836, he established the St. James Church at 32 James Street in Lower Manhattan. St. James served New York City's Spanish-speaking residents through the century as a place of worship, baptisms, weddings, and funerals. Later in the nineteenth century, the area around Fourteenth Street in Manhattan became known as "Little Spain" due to the concentration of Spanish immigrants in the neighborhood.

While cigar making was an important industry in New York by 1850, there were few Cubans or Spaniards in the business at that time. An 1850 city directory listed twenty-four "Segar Importers" (partnerships and individuals) and another 119 "Segar Makers." Of the importers, three indicated that they imported Havana cigars. While country of origin is difficult to discern based solely upon surnames, it is evident that the vast majority of the cigar importers and makers in mid-nineteenth century New York were not of Spanish origin.

Miguel Francisco García Broint was one of the few Cubans who moved to New York City prior to 1850 to establish a cigar business. Born in Cuba on April 4, 1806, Broint was a "segar" importer who became well known to local authorities. In 1848, he was a co-defendant in an important legal case involving a $500 transaction, presumably concerning Havana cigars; the case rested upon a determination of who had standing to bring legal action.[25] In another instance, Broint accused Joseph Hignes, also identified as a "Cuban," of having falsely identified himself as Miguel Broint in order to pick up "a case of cigars valued at $800" from an express company. The real Miguel Broint appeared later to claim the same shipment, but he was told that the cigars had already been delivered. After he satisfactorily identified himself, the express company realizing "that there was a conspiracy on foot to defraud them," had Hignes arrested.[26] Authorities may well have been suspicious of Broint himself, as a year earlier he and an accomplice, described as "two Italians," had been arrested for stealing $197 worth of gold coins from one Francis Garibaldi.[27]

After settling in New York, Miguel Broint married Elizabeth, an Irish immigrant, and they had at least seven children. As was typical of Cuban and Spanish immigrant cigar makers and importers, the cigar trade was a family business passed on to the next generation. Their two sons, John and Joseph, became cigar makers. Both died fairly young, Joseph at age twenty-two and John at age thirty-five. John's death certificate listed his cause of death as "labor pneumonia," likely due to cramped and poorly ventilated working conditions.

All of Miguel Broint's daughters married peninsular cigar makers. Celina, the eldest, married Francisco Ynguanzo in 1874 at the St. James Church. Delores married Marcos Martínez and moved to Ybor City, where he worked as a cigar maker. Frances married Edward López, and lived for a time in Boston before returning to Brooklyn. Elizabeth married Antonio Sánchez. For unknown reasons that union did not last, and she later married Agustín Castañeda, a Spanish cigar maker who arrived in Brooklyn around 1890. These marriages suggest that the social divisions between the Cuban and Spanish communities in New York were not rigid and the cigar business contributed to creating a commonality, particularly among Spanish-speaking cigar workers.

The Cuban separatist movement intensified after the conclusion of the Ten Years' War in 1878, and New York became a center of resistance to Spanish colonialism. Cipriano Muñoz, a naturalized United States citizen who had migrated from Cuba to Brooklyn in 1872, encountered suspicion and distrust when he returned to the island with his sister-in-law to visit his elderly father in the fall of 1879. While spending time in the plaza at Cienfuegos, Cipriano and his sister-in-law were arrested. Their luggage was searched by Spanish authorities who claimed to have found dynamite. Both were charged with being spies. Spanish officials publically stated that New York City authorities had informed them in advance that Cipriano was a dangerous spy and should be carefully watched while in Cuba. Cipriano had three brothers, all of whom lived in Brooklyn, and they immediately sought their sibling's release. News reports noted that two of Cipriano's brothers had been actively involved with Cuban rebels, though Cipriano himself had not. He was eventually released following apparent diplomatic pressure.[28]

The arrival of José Martí (José Julián Martí y Pérez, 1853–1895) in New York in 1880 brought increased attention to the separatist movement.[29] Martí had supported the struggle of Cuban landowners to attain independence from Spain. During the Ten Years' War, he wrote articles defending their cause, and was subsequently arrested for treason and sentenced to six years in prison. In New York City, he worked as a foreign correspondent; consul for Uruguay, Paraguay, and Argentina; and poet and writer, and during the following years, he became known as one of the principal leaders of the Cuban separatist movement. He wrote essays, traveled, gave speeches, and continued to actively support an independent Cuba.[30] His influence soon galvanized many Spanish and Cuban cigar makers in New York and Florida into a solidly pro-separatist movement.

BROOKLYN'S SPANISH CIGAR MAKERS

By the 1880s, a sizeable community of Spanish immigrants resided in Brooklyn Heights, and part of this area therefore became known as the Spanish Heights or the Spanish colony. Many of these immigrants worked in the cigar business as shop owners, cigar rollers, packers, strippers or *teverianos* (cigar peddlers); others worked on the docks or in ships.[31] Brooklyn's Spanish colony offered a commercially viable location near the waterfront, in the shadow of the Brooklyn Bridge (figure 4.1).

The number of Spaniards living in New York City (including Brooklyn) by 1890 was relatively small, perhaps no more than 1,500. Although precise figures are difficult to obtain, they represented a community presence larger than their numbers suggest. The Spanish enclaves in Brooklyn and New York City were defined by a number of commercial, religious, and social landmarks, including the St. James Church in lower Manhattan. Another important social institution for the local Spanish community was La Nacional, a mutual aid society established in 1868 in Manhattan. Originally formed to assist with the health and welfare of new Spanish immigrants, its overall goal was to promote and maintain fraternity and solidarity among New York

FIGURE 4.1. Aerial view during construction of the Brooklyn Bridge, ca. 1876, Brooklyn slide collection, V1984.1.86; Brooklyn Historical Society.

City's Spanish-speaking residents.[32] La Nacional held annual festivals to celebrate Spanish culture and traditions. According to the *Brooklyn Daily Eagle*, Spanish residents also formed La Armonía, located in the late 1880s at 306 Fulton Street in Brooklyn. As a "sociedad de instrucción y recreo," its mission was primarily educational and social. It offered English- and Spanish-language lessons as well as dances and other entertainment. Other Spanish organizations included the Sociedad Española de Beneficencia (Spanish Benevolent Society) formed in 1884 and La Universal, a Masonic lodge for Spanish residents, established in Brooklyn in the early 1870s. In addition, several Spanish-language papers were published at different times, in both Brooklyn and Manhattan.[33]

The competitive cigar business became this community's economic center. In 1886, a reporter for the *Brooklyn Daily Eagle* conducted an investigation of the local cigar trade.[34] He noted that "in this city there are many cigar factories, all of which claim to manufacture the best brands of domestic goods" using Cuban tobacco. Reflecting uncertainty over the authenticity of the tobacco and the process, however, the reporter continued sardonically: "probably they do and probably they don't." Yet one Brooklyn-based Spanish cigar maker claimed that a person could not "tell the difference between these cigars"; the domestically made Havana cigar had a fine appearance and was "in every respect . . . as good as the imported" one.[35] While the imported Havana cost on a wholesale basis about five cents more per cigar, the price difference was due to the additional tax imposed on imported Havanas. Cigars made in the United States with Cuban leaf were typically called "clear Havanas" as there was a lower import duty on leaf compared to finished cigars.[36]

The cigar maker also described the differences between Cuban Havanas and Brooklyn Havanas. He argued that the best tobacco leaf grown in Cuba was exported to the United States and Europe. It actually stood to reason then that Cuban Havanas would be inferior to Brooklyn Havanas.[37] He explained, "the import duty on cigars is $2.50 per pound, while the import duty on raw leaf tobacco is 35 cents per pound . . . You can easily see what a difference this makes in the price of a hundred cigars."[38] Indeed, he said confidently, "I will state, and without fear of contradiction, that a cigar made in Brooklyn by a Spanish cigar maker is better than a cigar made in Havana of the same quality of tobacco by a Spaniard."[39]

Another Brooklyn cigar maker explained the difference between Spanish and northern European cigar makers. In particular, he criticized the use of molds, more typically used by German cigar makers. "The hand made cigar is the best," he said, "and as for the mold cigar I doubt very much if you could hire me to smoke one . . . almost any shoemaker can make a mold cigar and in factories where they employ German, Bohemian and English, the workmen are very careless." This cigar maker also stated that, during lunch breaks, Spanish and Cuban cigar makers left the work table to eat while workers of other nationalities ate their lunch "over the table and for all you know you may be smoking a piece of bologna or limburger in one of those mold cigars."[40] Clearly, cigar making was a craft that represented strongly felt ethnic and cultural practices and distinctions.

Spanish cigar makers confidently explained why their methods produced a superior product, but they were also realistic about the complexities of the cigar market. As new tobacco leaf from other sources, both domestic and international, became more prevalent, discerning consumers tended to retain an allegiance to the reputed superior quality of Cuban tobacco leaf—particularly that from the Vuelta Abajo region—as well as to Cuban and Spanish manufacturing.

A Brooklyn cigar maker implied that some non-Spanish cigar makers even used chemicals to enhance the flavor of the tobacco:

The different flavors of Spanish cigars are produced by combinations, not by chemicals. Many of the retailers I supply have customers who are as particular about their cigars as about their food. They have smoked the same shade, the same size and the same flavored cigar for years. I manufacture hundreds of brands, but each brand must never vary, or the retailer would soon lose his trade. The most delicate change in the shade of combination is sometimes fatal to a brand. American cigar smokers are intelligent. It is only the consumers of Havana cigars who know how to smoke, in my opinion.[41]

Ironically, this statement could also be interpreted as justifying the use of standardized production techniques to create a consistently high-quality cigar.

Enterprising cigar makers could still make a reasonably good living in these years. Spanish journeymen cigar makers typically earned between $18 and $35 per week, depending on skill and efficiency. The rate at which a cigar maker rolled cigars varied dramatically, from 150 to 400 per day. Typically, about twenty-five pounds of tobacco would be used for every 1,000 cigars produced.[42]

A unique feature of the cigar factory that performed both educational and entertainment functions was the reader (*lector*). Readers literally read to cigar workers as they made cigars. In her book *El Lector*, Araceli Tinajero traced the historical development and significance of the cigar factory reader. The lector became a fixture in cigar factories after reportedly being first introduced at the El Fígaro Cigar Factory in Cuba in December 1865.[43] Cuban immigrants to Spain, many of whom fled Cuba at the outbreak of the Ten Years' War in 1868, introduced this practice to Spanish cigar workers. Due in part to the illiteracy of some of them, as well as to the tedium of the cigar-making process, cigar factory workers found gratification and edification in having someone read to them while rolling cigars.[44]

The lector informed, educated, and often agitated, usually bringing a greater sense of community, if not cohesiveness, to cigar factory workers, whose attention was inevitably drawn to the subject of the reading. Typically, it was the cigar makers who determined what the lector would read to them, and the responsibility for reading rotated among workers. The reading material could include newspapers, novels, short stories, poetry, and political tracts. Indeed, cigar makers in factories that used readers participated in an educational forum by listening to the readers and then discussing the essays. Workers commonly provided the reading material to the reader, and these books or articles were often later donated to local ethnic organizations, churches, or schools.[45]

New York cigar factories commonly employed readers.[46] There are few firsthand accounts of readers in New York, but Samuel Gompers provided one of the earliest descriptions. "It was the custom of the cigarmakers to chip in to create a fund for purchasing papers, magazines, and books," he wrote. "One of our members would read to us perhaps for an hour at a time, sometimes longer . . . I had a habit of saving any interesting magazine or newspaper articles to read to my shopmates. Others did the same . . . In fact, these discussions in the shops were more like public debating societies or what we call these days 'labor forums.' This practice had a great deal to do with developing the interest of cigarmakers in leading economic questions."[47] Later in the nineteenth century, news about events in Cuba and Spain was certainly a common topic for Spanish and Cuban lectores.

While the trend toward consolidation of cigar factories continued unabated, many small partnerships struggled to survive. It is not clear whether the larger firms were more likely to outlive the smaller ones, but it is evident that smaller firms could easily become unstable due to personal disputes between the partners. Such was the case with one small manufacturing firm established on October 7, 1891, at 150 Adams Street in Brooklyn between Pedro Corrales and Francisco Ynguanzo, both peninsular cigar makers. Within three weeks of its establishment, disagreements between the partners led to formal legal action to dissolve the partnership. Celina Ynguanzo, Francisco's wife, apparently angered by the situation, "invaded the shop and carried away with her a lot of leaf tobacco." Corrales attempted legal action against her, but Ynguanzo's attorney replied that she had simply taken tobacco that already belonged to her. Since the "property involved amounts to a few hundred cigars . . . the case was adjourned."[48] Stories such as this one were most likely common among individual cigar makers seeking to establish and maintain small-scale shops and factories.

In addition to Brooklyn's small shop owners, cigar rollers, and cigar peddlers, a few Spanish residents became quite successful and wealthy. One of the best known was Serafín Sánchez, partner of cigar factory entrepreneur Ignacio Haya.[49] Haya had lived in New York City since 1867 but moved to Tampa in 1885 after Ybor City was founded. There, he opened a new cigar factory in partnership with Sánchez; Sánchez had lived continuously in Brooklyn since about 1870, and he oversaw the Sánchez and Haya factory in New York City. When Sánchez died in April 1894, the *Brooklyn Daily Eagle* declared that "the Spanish colony ha[d] lost one of its most prominent members and the City of Brooklyn a notable and valuable citizen." Sánchez had been the first president of the Spanish chamber of commerce in New York, and he was a former president of La Nacional, the Spanish benevolent society. He had also served as master of La Universal lodge of freemasons; his funeral was "in full masonic form." Indeed, on the day of his funeral, all Spanish cigar factories in New York and Brooklyn reportedly closed for the day, so that Spanish cigar workers could attend.[50]

Spaniards in Brooklyn also enjoyed an active social and cultural life. The celebrations hosted by La Nacional continued annually and brought a sense of cultural cohesiveness to the community. The *Brooklyn Daily Eagle* reported on one such event: "Spaniards Make Merry in Ulmer Park, Brooklyn." This was La Nacional's twenty-eighth annual festival, attended by more than 1,000 persons that included many dignitaries. These annual fiestas were celebrations of national identity, culture, and community. An observer described the scene: "There were black Spanish fans and *mantillas* to be seen in the hands or over the shoulders of the Spanish women, who did not fail to show by their dancing how well Spanish women have earned the reputation of having the finest step and the most graceful carriage of any of the peoples of Europe." These gatherings celebrated and stereotyped benevolent Spanish culture. As Brooklyn's sheriff was overheard saying: "a Spanish criminal was unknown in either the courts or prisons of Kings County."[51]

One particularly poignant depiction of a cigar maker's daily life in Brooklyn's Spanish Colony appears in Prudencio de Pereda's novel *Windmills in Brooklyn*. This is a fictional account of a young boy growing up in Brooklyn and the life of a close family friend, the cigar peddler Agapito López. López, de Pereda writes, was "the most popular man in the Spanish colony, but there were only two people who really liked him—grandmother and me."[52] Born in 1912 in Brooklyn, de Pereda was the son of a Spanish immigrant cigar maker and shop owner, so this novel can be considered a type of ethnographic account of Brooklyn's Spanish colony. For example, de Pereda writes that after Agapito arrived in New York, traveling by ship from Spain,

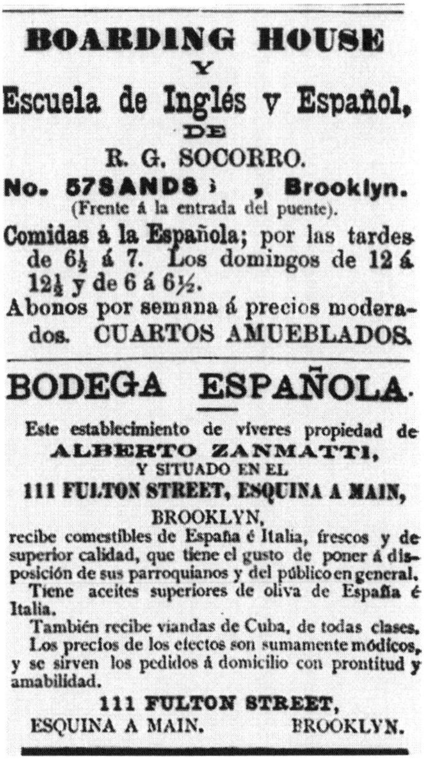
BOARDING HOUSE
Y
Escuela de Inglés v Español,
DE
R. G. SOCORRO.
No. 57SANDS ; , Brooklyn.
(Frente á la entrada del puente).
Comidas á la Española; por las tardes de 6½ á 7. Los domingos de 12 á 12½ y de 6 á 6½.
Abonos por semana á precios moderados. CUARTOS AMUEBLADOS.

BODEGA ESPAÑOLA.
Este establecimiento de víveres propiedad de
ALBERTO ZANMATTI,
Y SITUADO EN EL
111 FULTON STREET, ESQUINA A MAIN,
BROOKLYN,
recibe comestibles de España é Italia, frescos y de superior calidad, que tiene el gusto de poner á disposición de sus parroquianos y del público en general.
Tiene aceites superiores de oliva de España é Italia.
También recibe viandas de Cuba, de todas clases.
Los precios de los efectos son sumamente módicos, y se sirven los pedidos á domicilio con prontitud y amabilidad.
111 FULTON STREET,
ESQUINA A MAIN. BROOKLYN.

FIGURE 4.2. Advertisement for a Spanish boardinghouse and bodega located in Brooklyn's Spanish colony. *El Despertar*, June 1, 1891. (International Institute of Social History, Amsterdam.)

he moved from a boardinghouse near the docks in Manhattan to "one of the big, clean Spanish boardinghouses in Brooklyn Heights, in the heart of the Spanish colony" (figure 4.2).[53]

de Pereda's depiction of Agapito López provides a personalized view of a Spanish cigar peddler. Indeed, these peddlers led a difficult life, and honesty was not necessarily a virtue they upheld—in one episode, Agapito disguised himself as a Cuban priest in order to scam local Catholic priests in cigar transactions. The peddlers were quick to make shady deals and represent their cigars as Havanas, even though they were actually common cigars made from domestic tobacco. de Pereda's descriptions of Brooklyn's Spaniards telling stories, eating paella, and peddling cigars illustrate the shared traits of an ethnic community. He also describes the rampant anticlericalism among many Spaniards in Brooklyn: "I understood that Spanish men did not have to be Catholics—only women did . . . in fact, they talked against it."[54] Yet, it was Agapito who said, "Spain will always be Catholic—in spite of all the Anarchists. Don't ever doubt this! And you are always a Spaniard."[55]

SPANISH ANARCHISTS IN BROOKLYN

Within Brooklyn's Spanish immigrant enclave, an anarchist movement began to emerge in the late 1880s. It formed at the confluence of growing labor activism in the United States, José Martí's crusade for a free Cuba, and the increasingly outspoken opposition of many peninsulares to the Spanish monarchy and Catholic Church. Significantly, a potent labor movement had been brewing for years in Spain and was now sowing seedlings in the United States.[56] As historian Gerald Poyo observed, "the constant movement of workers between south Florida and Havana throughout the 1880s ensured the radicalization of Cuban and Spanish labor in Key West and Tampa."[57] This flow of radicalism traveled to Brooklyn and found a foothold there as well.

Although casual observers may have conflated the Spanish and Cuban supporters of separatism, anarchism, and labor activism into the same category, there were distinct differences among these groups. Separatists, led by Martí among others, focused on regime change and independence for Cuba. Many peninsular anarchists focused instead on the oppressive Spanish monarchy. Blaming the monarchy and the church for Spain's problems, they ardently sought structural change in Spain's ruling order as well as a broader social revolution. In principle, labor leaders, including Gompers and the CMIU, were on the same side as the Spanish and Cuban cigar makers in that they sought to empower workers, pursuing the traditional goals of higher wages and better working conditions. Even Gompers, who met with Martí during the late 1880s, noted that "it was important for us that not only Cuban cigarmakers in New York should be organized but that we should spread the gospel of unionism in Cuba."[58]

The Haymarket Square protest in Chicago on May 1, 1886, followed by the violence of May 4 and subsequent executions of four accused conspirators, became another immensely formative event for the Spanish-speaking labor activists in Brooklyn and worldwide. On May 4, during the end of a peaceful protest for a standard eight-hour workday, someone threw a bomb into the group of policemen who were attempting to disperse the crowd. Gunfire erupted, and by the time the melee ended, seven policemen and several civilians were dead, many more injured. Seven anarchists were put on trial and, despite the lack of good evidence, four of them were executed in 1887. Among the executed was Albert Parsons, who became an internationally recognized martyr for the anarchist cause. After the executions, protests and commemorations of the Haymarket affair took place in Havana, Barcelona, and many other cities in the United States and Europe.

Against this backdrop of the Haymarket Square episode, calls for Cuba Libre, increasing agitation in Spain against the church and state, encroaching mechanization of their industry, and growing labor activism generally, Spanish and Cuban cigar workers began to organize groups and newspapers to promote anarchism, labor rights, and Cuban separatism. José C. Campos, a Brooklyn-based Cuban-born cigar maker and printer, took up the cause. By 1887, he was already a leader of the local Unión de Torcedores, "an anarcho-collectivist group of Spanish-speaking people." At the same time, he began working as the New York correspondent for *El Productor*, a new anarcho-syndicalist paper published in Barcelona and described as "the most important anarchist periodical in Spain between 1887 and 1893."[59] Campos's work in Brooklyn was instrumental in facilitating the development of the city's anarchist community.

During 1890, the Spanish émigré Luis Barcia arrived in Brooklyn and joined Campos and others in a successful effort to establish a Spanish-language anarchist newspaper. A cigar maker and printer by trade, Barcia had traveled from Spain to Cuba and then Tampa before moving to Brooklyn, where he found employment in a cigar factory and felt "the spirit of organization and self-defense" among his fellow workers. Subsequently, a group of nine cigar makers formed the Grupo Parsons in memory of Albert Parsons. The Parsons Group then founded *El Despertar* (The Awakening; figure 4.3), a Spanish-language paper designed to "defend our common interest." Barcia later recalled that "this newspaper was not only the voice of the cigar workers, but also, the voice of all those who cherished freedom and economic redemption."[60] The founding members of the Grupo Parsons contributed $2.50 each to publish the first issue, and the newspaper quickly developed a large subscription base, locally and even internationally. *El Despertar* soon established itself as an integral and vital node in the international network of anarchist periodicals, becoming the longest-running Spanish language anarchist paper published in the United States during the nineteenth century.

EL DESPERTAR.

PERIODICO QUINCENAL ANARQUISTA.

| ANO II. | NEW YORK, ABRIL 1 DE 1892. | NUMERO 31 |

Dirección por Correo
para todo lo que se relaciona con este periódico:
Núm. 181 Adams Street,
BROOKLYN.

PRECIOS DE SUSCRIPCIÓN.
Interior y exterior, trimestre......25 centavos
Número suelto..... 05   "
COBRO ADELANTADO.

FIGURE 4.3. *El Despertar* masthead. This was the first issue that used the subtitle "Periódico Quincenal Anarquista." The subtitle for previous issues was "Periódico Quincenal dedicado á la Defensa de los Trabajadores." *El Despertar*, April 1, 1892. (International Institute of Social History, Amsterdam.)

Initially, Barcia and Campos served as *El Despertar*'s primary editors, though many others, including Manuel Martínez Abello, participated in editorial and administrative work. The newspaper promoted anarchist ideals that rejected an authoritarian state, the church, and capitalism. In practice, *El Despertar* promoted anarchism and reported regularly on labor conditions and strikes in New York, Tampa, Key West, and internationally. It also supported, and published accounts of collections to aid, striking cigar workers and workers around the country. In December 1891, for example, the paper printed a detailed accounting from the Comité de Huelga (Strike Committee) that consisted of Abelardo Petit, secretary; Joaquín Alvarez, treasurer; and Agustín Castañeda, accountant. José Díaz, Máximo Sánchez, and Luis Barcia reviewed the statement for accuracy, a common practice for large strike fund accountings. *El Despertar* actively promoted the eight-hour day movement, and published many anarchist and labor tracts along with other news related to local and international labor issues. Cigar workers in various cities throughout the United States and Cuba maintained a strong and resilient network that newspapers such as *El Despertar* played a significant role in supporting.

The crisis in Cuba also fueled the rising political tensions in New York City's Spanish and Cuban communities. In January 1892, José Martí had formed the Partido Revolucionario Cubano (PRC) to agitate for and promote an independent Cuba. The PRC drew essential financial support from Spanish and Cuban anarchists, and US tobacco workers became the PRC's primary source of income.[61] As Louis Pérez has shown, it was within the cigar maker communities, particularly in Florida but also in New York, where José Martí found "a wellspring of patriotic sentiment with a distinct affinity for his version of *Cuba Libre*." These workers "brought decades of labor militancy, political activism, and an enduring sense of cubanidad to the separatist cause."[62] Martí's vision of an independent Cuba appeared to take shape in February 1895, when the war for independence began. In May, he and a group of exiles traveled to Cuba to join the rebellion, but Martí was killed on May 19 at Dos Ríos, almost as soon as he had arrived in Cuba. Martí immediately became a martyr of the Cuban independence movement, but his life and death had other ramifications as well. He had forged an unprecedented and strong association among cigar makers, Cuban separatists, and anarchists, but his death also precipitated an unraveling of this alliance.

In Brooklyn, *El Despertar* and a variety of affiliated clubs provided intellectual and social cohesion for the anarchist community. Brooklyn's first Spanish-language anarchist club was the Círculo Anarquista, established under the auspices of the Grupo Parsons, and held its inaugural meeting on April 1, 1893, at 81 Fulton Street. The círculo's overarching theme was equality and fraternal harmony as expressed in the statement "Todos éramos anfitriones y huéspedes; todos nos sentíamos y considerábamos iguales" (We were all hosts and guests; we all felt and considered ourselves equal).[63] To propagate anarchist ideals, members of the Parsons Group formed another affiliated organization called *El Ideal*. Its purpose was to provide free-of-charge pamphlets and reprints of anarchist tracts printed in both English and Spanish. *El Productor*, the Barcelona-based anarchist periodical, noted and applauded the formation and plans of Brooklyn-based El Ideal.[64]

Pedro Esteve (figure 4.4) arrived in Brooklyn during summer 1892 and soon became one of the principal leaders of the city's anarchist community. Born in Barcelona in 1865, Esteve devoted himself to the anarcho-syndicalist cause as an editor and speaker. In his youth, he had trained to become a typesetter and printer. He joined a group of printers who, according to his biographer Joan Casanovas, were "very important in spreading anarchism in Spain, Cuba, Mexico, Argentina and the US, and most of them were Masons."[65] In Spain, Esteve worked as an apprentice at *La Academia* as well as at *El Productor*, and he became actively involved in the anarcho-syndicalist movement. Soon after

FIGURE 4.4. Pedro
Esteve, ca. 1920. *Cultura
Obrera*, September 19, 1925
(International Institute of
Social History, Amsterdam).

Spanish officials shut down *La Academia* (in May 1892), Esteve left Barcelona
for New York.[66] He arrived there on August 8, 1892, under the name Pierre
Esteve on the French steamship *La Bourgogne*, and he immediately joined
Brooklyn's anarchist community.

Adrián del Valle, one of Esteve's colleagues from Spain, had also traveled
to Brooklyn from Barcelona (via Cuba) and joined *El Despertar's* editorial
group. Del Valle, unlike Esteve, was firmly committed to Cuba Libre, and
these differences soon created deeper divisions in the anarchist community.
Del Valle was particularly engaged in writing plays and works of fiction. He
often signed his essays with the pseudonym Palmiro de Lidia.[67]

In Brooklyn, Esteve assumed a leadership role at *El Despertar* and in the
local anarchist community. During the summer of 1893, his calculated tactics were put on full display when he was blamed for causing the early end
of a festival sponsored by La Benéfica, the Brooklyn-based Spanish cultural
society. Initially, Esteve had encouraged community members to attend the
event, and he worked with the organizers to sell tickets. In fact, during the
festival, he was awarded a gold medal for selling the most tickets. But this

turned out to be a crafty ploy. When he was given the opportunity to speak to the gathering after receiving his award, he "started in to make an anarchist speech." While some of the attendees "hissed," the "friends to whom Esteve had sold tickets cheered." His speech was then "drowned out by the band," but this did not stop Esteve, who then began distributing an anarchist pamphlet, at which point the organizers apparently shut down the festival. Indeed, this episode also reflected tensions within Brooklyn's Spanish colony. The event, hosted to celebrate Spanish culture, attracted a wide range of attendees, but Esteve's attack against the political and economic power structure divided the festival attendees and led to its early ending.[68]

During 1895, *El Despertar's* office moved to Esteve's residence at 51 Poplar Place, near the Brooklyn Bridge, where he lived with his wife, the Italian anarchist Maria Roda, and where his first son, Pedro, was born.[69] Esteve's increasingly active role at *El Despertar* certainly contributed to its growing reputation as "the most important Spanish-language anarchist paper in the US during those years."[70] Esteve traveled frequently and became a prominent leader of the anarchist movement in the United States, observing that it was composed primarily of Jewish, Italian, and Russian immigrants residing in the larger cities. However, as Casanovas points out, "the anarchist groups in which Esteve became involved were those that emerged from the Cubano-Spanish tobacco workers' communities."[71]

Marcelino García, a self-described Spanish anarchist, later recalled Esteve's influence and the origins of Spanish anarchism in New York. He stated, "I was born in 1893 in San Martín (Oviedo) in the Asturias region of northern Spain, where all the rebels come from."[72] He continued, "Spaniards like [Pedro] Esteve began coming to the United States in large numbers during the 1890s. Many settled in port cities, like New York, Boston, and Baltimore, and worked as sailors and dockworkers. Spanish seamen were masters of the Port of New York. Over the years many moved inland to the mines and factories of West Virginia, Pennsylvania, and Ohio, and took up their former occupations. They were an important element in steel, mining, and metallurgy, as well as in cigarmaking . . . Spanish workers are by nature anarchists."[73]

Violent acts, or "propaganda by the deed," committed by self-identified anarchists brought increasing and largely unwanted attention to anarchist communities in the United States. After Italian anarchist Michele Angiolillo assassinated the Spanish prime minister Antonio Cánovas del Castillo on

August 8, 1897, Brooklyn's Spanish-speaking anarchist community attracted increased scrutiny from the press as well as from the authorities. A reporter visited a meeting of the Círculo de Estudios Sociales held in "a barber shop in Brooklyn, under the very shadow of the Brooklyn bridge." The reporter interviewed Gerardo Quintana, who defended Cánovas's assassination and said, "We all hope that Cuba will win her independence, because this means revolution in Spain and a step towards anarchy."[74]

While many Cuban and Spanish anarchists supported the Cuban separatist movement, there was a great divergence of opinion. Esteve was somewhat ambivalent about Cuban independence, believing that simply replacing one regime with another would not solve Cuba's problems. Such views contributed to an increasingly contentious rift in Brooklyn's anarchist community and at *El Despertar*. Tensions grew further after the United States declared war against Spain on April 25, 1898. The anarchist community became increasingly factionalized, and *El Despertar* lost subscribers. Esteve then wrote a brief message to *El Despertar*'s readers, noting a lack of community support and interest in the newspaper's fate. It needed more contributors and subscribers to continue operating (only three issues were published between late February and mid-September 1898). In June 1898, Esteve announced that he was moving the editorial offices of *El Despertar* to 350 Clay Street, his personal residence, in Paterson, New Jersey. According to its masthead, *El Despertar* maintained a separate administrative office at 1255 Fifth Avenue in Brooklyn, the tenement of Agustín Castañeda.[75] Paterson had an active Italian immigrant community, many of whose members worked in local silk factories, and Esteve found a supportive environment there. His Italian wife most likely preferred living in Paterson's Italian enclave.[76]

Another indication of the ongoing tension within Brooklyn's cigar-making community became evident in a dispute between Agustín Castañeda (figure 4.5), at that time *El Despertar*'s administrator and treasurer of the newly formed Sociedad de Torcedores de Habano, and some of its 250 members. After electing Castañeda to the treasurer's post, the society's membership decided to create a new position of president in order to avoid the appearance of being an anarchist organization. Castañeda unsuccessfully opposed this reorganization and then resigned, stating that he was opposed to presidencies and would not serve under one, reflecting the anarchist principle of rejecting positions of political hierarchy and authority. This conflict erupted

FIGURE 4.5. Agustín Castañeda with his wife, Elizabeth Broint Castañeda, ca. 1905. Courtesy of the Carol Carey Godwin family archives.

into further community division and incrimination. Defending himself against rumors of having destroyed pages from an account book, he brought those books to the meeting and then accused the society's "despicable slanderers" of damaging the Spanish cigar-making community's cohesiveness: "this accursed race of *rodents*," he wrote, "is responsible, to a great extent, for the anemic period our institutions are going through."[77]

The now clear rift between the peninsular anarchists and the Cuban separatists resulted in the establishment of a new Spanish-language anarchist newspaper in Brooklyn. Several of *El Despertar*'s original founders and editors—including Luis Barcia, José C. Campos, Adrián del Valle, and Gerardo Quintana—formed *El Rebelde* (The Rebel), which focused on the Cuba situation. *El Rebelde* appeared in September 1898 just as *El Despertar* resumed publication. But the editors' attempts to reinvigorate the local Cuba Libre cause were not successful. After only five issues, *El Rebelde* ceased publication. Luis Barcia and Adrián del Valle soon left Brooklyn for Tampa and Havana, respectively. In Havana, del Valle established *El Nuevo Ideal*, a much more successful paper that remained in print for several years. J. C. Campos, perhaps the person most responsible for establishing *El Despertar*, remained in Brooklyn until his death in 1901.

As the rifts among Spanish-speaking anarchists, Cuban separatists, and those with other causes and affiliations continued to fracture the Spanish-speaking community, several of *El Despertar*'s contributors formed the Círculo de Trabajadores (Workers' Circle), located in the heart of the Spanish colony. Founded in January 1899, the círculo was based on the organization of the same name established in Havana in 1885.[78] It was located first at 154 Fulton Street and then at 72 Liberty Street before moving to 102 Pineapple Street—all of these addresses were within close proximity of the Brooklyn Bridge. Initially a meeting place for Spanish-speaking cigar workers and anarchists, the círculo welcomed and included other laborers and political activists. It received perhaps its most high-profile anarchist visitor in 1900, when the famed Italian anarchist Errico Malatesta presented a lecture to the assembled group on March 30.[79] The círculo served as a social and entertainment venue as well. At one event, a group of singers entranced the audience with songs, including "El Pirata" (The Pirate); and one Señora Boada delighted the crowd with her exquisite voice.[80] At another meeting, "Cuban songs were sung to the beat of the guitar . . . [and] there was dancing until two-thirty, when we left very satisfied and willing to return soon to savor the sweet meetings in the *Círculo de Trabajadores*."[81]

Spanish-speaking cigar makers confronted tensions within their community, but they also dealt with opposition, distrust, and, at times, manipulation from those outside the community, including the powerful Cigar Makers' International Union led by Samuel Gompers. On December 10, 1900, *El Despertar* printed in English on the front page a letter titled "To the Cigarmakers of the International Union." It was both a defense of an independent Spanish-speaking cigar makers union and their members' high-quality work, and an appeal for mutual acceptance. It began:

> COMRADES: Being convinced that the struggle which you sustain against the Havana Cigarmakers' Unions, has become very bitter, owing principally to a prejudice inculcated and nutrified in your minds by those, who, instead of looking after your interests and for the interests of labor in general, solely look after their own, we address our friendly voice . . . we have obtained respect and considerations superior, very superior, to that obtained by you. We enjoy many advantages which you do not, such as: to enter and leave the factory whenever it is convenient to us or whenever we desire, to have a reader paid by us to read while we work, the periodicals of our choice without the slightest interference from the proprietor.[82]

In the meantime, Esteve had become an active participant in the Italian anarchist community in Paterson, and he remained deeply committed to the anarcho-syndicalist cause. Another Italian anarchist newspaper, *La Questione Sociale* (1895–1908), cofounded by Italian anarchist Gaetano Bresci, was already active in Paterson, and Esteve worked as one of its editors as well.[83] During these years, anarchism and violence became increasingly seen by the American public as one and the same, and some events seemed to confirm this perception. In 1900, Bresci decided to put his anarchist ideology into action: he traveled to Italy and assassinated the Italian monarch King Umberto I. Esteve publically defended Bresci's regicide. After avowed anarchist Leon Czolgosz shot President McKinley in 1901, authorities again questioned Esteve to determine whether he had any involvement; he was cleared. The US Secret Service increased its own surveillance of anarchists, and it employed agent Maurits Hymans to befriend and report on the activities and discussions of anarchists in Paterson and New York City. Hymans became an habitual visitor to Esteve's printing shop as well as various anarchist meeting places and saloons. He sent regular, sometimes daily, reports of what he had heard and seen to John E. Wilkie, chief of the US Secret Service in Washington, DC.

The political and financial strain on the anarchists translated into significantly less community support. Both *El Despertar* and *La Questione Sociale* fell on hard times in 1902. The Paterson's silk makers' strike of that year had created a significant rift between laborers and anarchists, and Esteve reported that "the majority of silkworkers . . . do not want to mix with the anarchists."[84] Suffering from lack of resources, fractures within the Spanish immigrant community, and the lessening popularity of anarchism due in part to the proliferation of anti-anarchist laws passed after the assassination of President McKinley, *El Despertar* published its last issue in December 1902. *La Questione Sociale* continued irregular publication until 1908.[85]

During these years, Esteve became directly involved in the wider US labor movement. He reportedly participated in some early planning for the creation of the Industrial Workers of the World (IWW, aka "Wobblies"), and this work continued to bring more aggressive attention from the authorities. He also sought to reinvigorate Brooklyn's anarchists after *El Despertar* ceased publication. In early 1905, Esteve met with friends and colleagues in Brooklyn to discuss forming a new anarchist group. Out of this meeting, they developed plans for a new periodical that Esteve would edit. The first issue of *Doctrina anarquista-socialista* appeared on February 1, 1905. More a serial pamphlet than a periodical in the style of *El Despertar*, it had a short life and ceased publication by the summer of 1905.

Disappointed by the fragmentation and overall decline of the anarchist movement there, coupled with police harassment, Esteve decided to leave Paterson. He, María Roda, and their children moved to Ybor City (Tampa) where they lived for several years. In Tampa, Esteve worked at various times as a printer, cigar maker, and lector in cigar factories.[86] While there, his son, Pedro Jr., died in a tragic accident that Esteve believed to have been an attempt on his own life. From New York, Secret Service agent Hymans wrote to Esteve: "Let me begin to say how sorry I feel on account of the death of your little boy . . . you are still the same old active comrade, and all your troubles do not seem to lessen your ambition for our movement." Hymans encouraged Esteve to keep up his anarchist work, as he continued to report on those activities, along with his correspondence with Esteve, to the Secret Service headquarters in Washington.[87]

ANARCHISM AND EDUCATION: THE SPANISH CONNECTION

Spain's resolute military defeat in the Spanish-American War exacerbated issues of divided loyalties and ethnic pride for many Spaniards. Indeed, Spanish anarchists could acknowledge a victory against the Spanish monarchy in that defeat, but in Brooklyn, as elsewhere in the United States, authorities often viewed Spaniards even more so with suspicion, concerned that they might be spies or anarchists, or both.[88] Perhaps more important, in terms of national and cultural identity, that war symbolized a final epitaph of the once great Spanish empire, and Spaniards had to resituate their own sense of personal and national identity within the final chapter of their once imperial nation. In Spain, however, the government sought to contain discontent and exercise whatever colonial muscle it retained, leading to disastrous results several years later during the Spanish military's escapades in Morocco.[89]

Popular opposition to the Moroccan conflict combined with serious labor unrest in Barcelona led to a series of events that culminated in the execution of Francisco Ferrer Guardia in Barcelona in 1909, reigniting widespread out-rage against Spain's monarchy. Born in Catalonia in 1859, Ferrer had become the founder of the Escuela Moderna (The Modern School) in Barcelona in 1901 and the related Modern School movement. He drew inspiration from other progressive education reformers as well as from the dire state of educa-tion in Spain, where less than one-third of the population was literate; indeed, only about one-third of Spain's 45,000 towns even had public schools.[90]

Many observers believed that Ferrer's only "crime" had been his aggressive attempt to bring modern rational thinking to Spain through a new secular educational system. Reportedly not impressive in stature or oratorical skills, he had nevertheless attracted many followers due to his personal warmth and sincerity, if not his insistent promotion of rational thinking in both France and Spain. As a young man, he had become involved in "an abortive republican rising" and subsequently fled to France with his wife and children in 1885; he lived in Paris for the next sixteen years.[91] Supporting himself and his family by teaching Spanish and selling wine, he immersed himself in anar-chist literature. All the while his anticlerical views became more extreme. After divorcing his Spanish wife in 1899, he became involved with a wealthy middle-aged French teacher who died soon after and left him nearly 1 million francs. Ferrer was then able to return to Barcelona, where he planned to implement his dream of opening a Modern School to free the Spanish people from the stultifying control of the state and the church.[92]

Ferrer opened his first Escuela Moderna in Barcelona on September 8, 1901. The school's attendance grew from thirty students in 1901 to 126 in 1905, but Spanish authorities closed the school in 1906. The pretext for closing it was

Mateo Morral's unsuccessful assassination attempt against King Alfonso XIII; Morral was a twenty-five-year-old anarchist who worked at the Escuela Moderna's publishing house.[93] Spanish authorities tried to implicate Ferrer in the assassination plot, but there was no direct evidence. Still, he was jailed for over a year. Upon his release he traveled again to France but later returned to Barcelona, where he resumed his publishing operation; he was not able to reopen his school.

Ferrer returned to Spain at a tumultuous time. He continued to be associated with the protests and attacks on the government, and opposition to Spanish militarism in Morocco combined with social unrest and labor strikes culminated in what became known as the Semana Trágica (Tragic Week) in August 1909. Violent clashes between protestors and the military resulted in hundreds of deaths. During these events, the *New York Times* published an article on the turmoil in Spain. Interestingly, the author, Stephen Bonsal, drew a comparison between Francisco Ferrer and the Barcelona exile, Pedro Esteve. In a poignant description of the two men, Bonsal wrote: "Both Ferrer and Esteve are men of high character, and of tried unselfishness; their private lives are pure and admirable; they are indeed dangerous enemies of the civilization which they combat and yet credit should not be withheld from the society which has produced two such remarkable and, in many ways, admirable men under the most untoward circumstances, for they are both children of the slums."[94] Spanish authorities arrested Ferrer on trumped-up charges falsely claiming that he was the primary instigator of the Semana Trágica. He was quickly convicted and subsequently executed by firing squad on October 13, 1909.[95]

One of Ferrer's associates in Barcelona, according to historian Bieito Alonso Fernández, was Jaime Vidal. Vidal's early life is not well known, but by 1896 he had become associated with Barcelona's *El Productor* and was working with Ferrer in the Escuela Moderna movement. He had also served as the secretary of the Federación de Sociedades Obreras de Barcelona. Some accounts indicate that Vidal had been exiled to London in the mid-1890s and he did travel to New York in 1904. He also spent some time in Los Angeles, working with Ricardo Flores Magón, the Mexican anarchist and publisher of *Regeneración*. By 1906, Vidal was living again in Brooklyn, where he joined other Spanish immigrant anarchists and pro-labor activists.[96] Ferrer's execution became a new focal point for Vidal and other anarchists to rail against

the Spanish Crown, and the well-known anarchist Emma Goldman organized a planning meeting four days after Ferrer's death.

In Brooklyn, fifteen members of the Spanish *colonia* formed the Spanish
Pro-Revolution Committee of New York in response to Ferrer's execution;
Jaime Vidal served as secretary of the group.[97] Established during a meeting at Arlington Hall on the evening of October 22, the committee included
"representatives of the radical Spanish colony" and was "a branch of the
'Revolutionary Party,' with headquarters in Paris, composed of Spanish revolutionists, but enjoying the co-operation of intelligent and generous foreign
fighters, who conduct an international agitation in all the principal cities of
Europe."[98]

The execution of Francisco Ferrer set off a series of protests in the United
States and Europe that both condemned the Spanish government and celebrated Ferrer's life and work. In New York, the day after the formation of the
Spanish Pro-Revolution Committee a "Ferrer Protest Meeting" of more than
1,500 persons took place at Carnegie Hall on the evening of October 23, 1909.
Undercover agent Maurits Hymans reported that Vidal, Alexander Berkman,
and Emma Goldman spoke at the rally. At its conclusion, the participants
adopted a resolution that, according to Hymans, read in part: "A great educator and lover of the children, comrade Francisco Ferrer died a victim of cler-
icalism, capitalism and autocracy." Hymans regularly reported on anarchist
activities in Paterson and New York City, and he apparently had no trouble
obtaining information from local anarchists at various saloons, liquor stores,
and meeting halls.[99]

The newly formed Spanish Pro-Revolution Committee also sought to use
Ferrer's execution as a vehicle to call for the overthrow of the Spanish monarchy. The group drafted a manifesto that was published in *Mother Earth*, the
journal coedited by Emma Goldman and Alexander Berkman. The manifesto decried the execution of Ferrer but also reflected the divisions within
the Spanish colony by stating that "we wish to fight all together, without
regard to individual principles or separatist ideas." The committee called
for the "overthrow [of] the present regime, and to open the road for more
advanced institutions."[100] The manifesto requested contributions be sent
to its treasurer, Agustín Castañeda, at 72 Liberty Street (the address of the
Círculo de Trabajadores) in the heart of Brooklyn's Spanish colony; Jaime
Vidal reportedly was living at this address as well.[101]

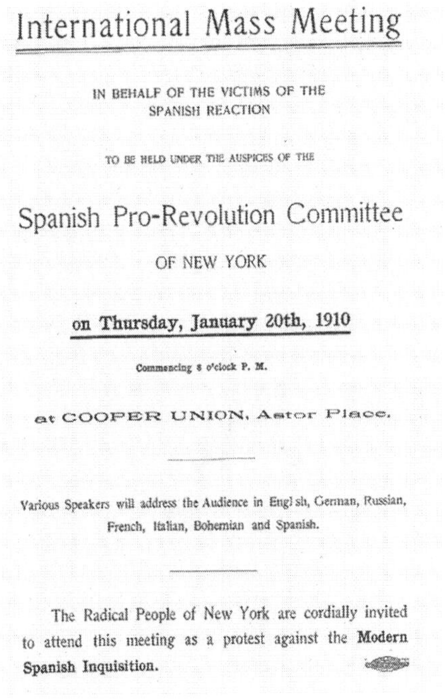

International Mass Meeting

IN BEHALF OF THE VICTIMS OF THE
SPANISH REACTION

TO BE HELD UNDER THE AUSPICES OF THE

Spanish Pro-Revolution Committee

OF NEW YORK

on Thursday, January 20th, 1910

Commencing 8 o'clock P. M.

at COOPER UNION, Astor Place.

Various Speakers will address the Audience in English, German, Russian, French, Italian, Bohemian and Spanish.

The Radical People of New York are cordially invited to attend this meeting as a protest against the **Modern Spanish Inquisition.**

FIGURE 4.6. Spanish Pro-Revolution Committee flyer (back page). The text of the manifesto refers to the group as the "Pro-Spanish Revolution Committee." (Reports of Agents, Maurits Hymans, National Archives and Records Administration, Record Group 87.)

The Spanish Pro-Revolution Committee also sponsored its own Ferrer rally (figure 4.6). Held on January 20 at Cooper Union in New York City, about 400 persons attended, mostly anarchists and socialists of different nationalities. Speakers included Leonard Abbott and Bolton Hall. At the rally, Jaime Vidal "explained the necessity for revolution in Spain" and "made an appeal for money . . . for the Spanish revolutionist movement." The committee's manifesto for this event, titled "An Appeal for Solidarity," was then distributed as the collection of funds commenced. Each of the committee members signed the manifesto after the closing phrase, "Yours for the revolution."[102]

It is not clear whether Pedro Esteve, who was still living in Tampa, was involved with the formation of this group, but he had made it known that he wanted to return to Spain and take revenge on King Alfonso XIII for the execution of Ferrer. Instead, another anarchist, Manuel Pardiñas, whom Esteve knew in Tampa, pursued this objective on his own. Pardiñas returned to Spain and assassinated Prime Minister José Canalejas in Madrid on November 12, 1912. Importantly, Pardiñas was not unknown to authorities. Agent Hymans had noted in a report written during January 1912 that "an anarchist named Pardiñas . . . is said to be endeavoring to raise funds to send some one to Spain to assassinate the King." It is unclear whether Pardiñas remained under surveillance, but rather than provide someone else to carry out "propaganda by the deed," he carried it out himself.[103]

ANARCHISM TO ANARCHO-SYNDICALISM

The movement from anarchism generally to anarcho-syndicalism became more pronounced in the first decade of the twentieth century. In the Spanish immigrant community, this transition manifested during January 1910, when Jaime Vidal established a new periodical, *Cultura Proletaria*, that served as the propaganda arm of the newly formed group Solidaridad Obrera. It was published at 310 Fulton Street, the new headquarters of the Círculo de Trabajadores. Pedro Esteve served as the Tampa correspondent for the paper. However, *Cultura Proletaria* had a short publishing life; it ceased operation the following October due to pressure from postal officials. In the meantime, Vidal was becoming increasingly active as a labor organizer. He became the Spanish organizer for the Marine Firemen, Oilers and Water-Tenders' Union of the Atlantic and Gulf (MFOW), the offices of which were located adjacent to the docks at 229 West Street in Manhattan. Vidal worked with the Atlantic Coast Marine Firemen, initially affiliated with the International Seamen's Union (ISU). About 85 percent of its membership was Spanish.[104] He remained deeply committed to the seamen's union as well as the anarcho-syndicalist movement.[105]

In 1912, Pedro Esteve returned to Paterson, New Jersey. He had left Tampa in part because of persecution from authorities and a sense that the anarchist movement there was on the decline, but he also desired to resume his writing and editorial work in New York. The ongoing turmoil in Spain and reinvigoration of the peninsular anarchist movement in Brooklyn and New York, particularly after the execution of Ferrer, likely attracted Esteve back to the New York area's intellectual milieu.[106]

The closure of *Cultura Proletaria* a few months earlier provided Esteve with the opportunity to establish a new periodical. Working with Vidal, he produced *Cultura Obrera* (Labor Culture), a weekly paper similar in format and coverage to both *Cultura Proletaria* and *El Despertar*. *Cultura Obrera* was first printed in Brooklyn during 1911 at the círculo, and it served as the voice of the MFOW.[107] Esteve and *Cultura Obrera* took up the cause of seamen, cigar makers, and other workers in frequent articles on labor, anarchism, the Mexican Revolution, and feminism among a variety of other topics. The newspaper published several regular sections, including one for cigar makers typically titled "Entre Tabaqueros" or "De Tabaqueros" (Tobacco Workers), while the section for maritime workers was called "Los Trabajadores del Mar" (Seamen). The weekly cost five cents per issue, usually of four pages, or two dollars for an annual subscription. Each issue listed new subscribers and donations from cigar factories and shops, as well as Spanish cigar workers and seamen, and from others around the nation. Many contributors used pseudonyms to protect their identity.

During summer 1912, the Marine Union organized a large strike against New York shipping companies for higher wages. *Cultura Obrera* both promoted and covered the strike with frequent articles and appeals. A journalist with the *New York Herald* investigated the leadership of the strike and identified the strike leaders as Jaime Vidal, Pedro Esteve, Violetta Esteve (Esteve's daughter), and Milo H. Woolman. The article began: "Perhaps the most varied assortment of personalities that ever conducted a labor strike involving thousands of men in New York city is the odd quartet which is now captain, pilot, lookout and stoker of the striking seamen." Vidal, the "chief moving spirit of the strikers," the writer continued, "has fought his way up from the hold and ought to know what he is battling for. He is about thirty-five years old, dark, tall and with that raw boned strength that can well explain how he is able to work with his men for fifteen and sixteen hours a day." The reporter described Pedro Esteve as the "quiet, unassuming power that counts," and Woolman as the Harvard graduate. But Violetta Esteve, her father's stenographer and editor, received most of the reporter's attention. Underlying the stereotypical image of the female Spaniard in New York, the reporter asked Violetta if she, "a slip of a little Spanish beauty," had been born in Barcelona. She replied "in the most perfectly spoken English [and] said: If you please, I was born in Brooklyn and never saw Spain . . . I am thoroughly in sympathy with the movement . . . [but] I am just like other American girls who are trying to improve every moment they can."[108]

During the seamen's strike, a violent incident became a new flash point for the anarchist cause: the case of Alejandro (Alexander) Aldamas. Aldamas was a fireman and delegate to the Brooklyn branch of the MFOW. During the strike on the evening of July 8, 1912, he was at the union's Brooklyn office at 17 Hamilton Avenue. A representative of the steamship line entered the office and requested that firemen be sent immediately to the Morgan Line. Aldamas replied that, due to the strike, he could not send any men to the ship. A fight then broke out between Aldamas and the representative. A policeman was just outside the offices, apparently hiding and waiting for an altercation, and he attempted to arrest Aldamas during the fight. Instead, Aldamas shot the policeman as well as two others who were also nearby and attempting to arrest Aldamas. In the end, Aldamas was severely beaten, arrested, and charged with attempted murder.[109]

The Aldamas case attracted a great deal of attention from Emma Goldman's *Mother Earth* and Esteve's *Cultura Obrera*, which took up the cause and began a fund-raising campaign for Aldamas's defense. Jaime Vidal, the Brooklyn cigar maker Aquilino Chao, and William Sanger (husband of birth control advocate Margaret Sanger), among many others, contributed funds and fund-raising efforts to support Aldamas. The case became a cause célèbre, and on the evening of October 29, 1912, several hundred members of the MFOW gathered to protest his incarceration. Speakers included Emma Goldman and Alexander Berkman as well as Andrés Rodríguez of the Cigar Makers' Union and a representative of the Brooklyn Workingmen's Circle. Jaime Vidal told the crowd how Aldamas had been attacked and had merely attempted to defend himself. Emma Goldman asked the attendees to contribute to a defense fund, but only $40.15 was raised at the event. Subsequently, a committee of thirty men and women of various nationalities and occupations formed to support Aldamas and collect more funds for his defense. They raised thousands of dollars. On February 1, 1913, after diligent work by his defense team, paid for in large part by these fund-raisers, Aldamas was convicted of only the lesser charge of "injury to an agent" and sentenced to eighteen months in Sing Sing penitentiary. Upon his release, he was deported to Spain.[110]

Cultura Obrera maintained its offices in Brooklyn through August 1913, though it moved several times. On February 1, 1913, it relocated from Brooklyn's Fulton Street to 102 Pineapple Street, the new location of the Brooklyn Círculo de Trabajadores. To inaugurate the periodical's new location, Esteve announced an evening of dramatic musicals. He expected that the event would be morally uplifting to the Spanish colony in "the great metropolis."[111] Sharing an address with the círculo, the weekly advertised and promoted the círculo itself. Apparently with Jaime Vidal's involvement, Local 105 of the IWW also held regular meetings there.[112] During the spring 1913, *Cultura Obrera* also supported the cause of Brooklyn's striking barbers, estimated at 8,000 strong.[113]

Jaime Vidal had taken an active role in *Cultura Obrera*, contributing essays and likely helping with editing, but he desired his own paper. In February 1913, he announced in *Cultura Obrera* that he was starting a new anarchist periodical. It followed his earlier short-lived paper, *Brazo y Cerebro* (Arm and Brain) published briefly in 1912. The new one, *Fuerza Consciente* (Conscious Force), would "emulate and surpass, if possible" the example set by *Brazo y Cerebro*; the new paper would be "dedicated to propagating the ideals of anarchism and revolution." Its offices were initially located at 266 West 154th Street.[114] Rather abruptly, however, Vidal and *Fuerza Consciente* moved to Los Angeles in October 1913 and again, soon thereafter, to 958 Pacific Street in San Francisco.[115] Vidal traveled to California with José Vilariño, whom he knew in New York, and Vilariño served for a time as business manager for *Fuerza Consciente*. In San Francisco, Vidal's new periodical advocated anarcho-syndicalism as well as anarchism of social conventions: "free love" and the dissolution of "matrimonial slavery."[116] Vidal reported that the anarchist movement in San Francisco was in good shape, but he lamented that many people simply believed that "anarchy is to get drunk and beat [your] wife."[117]

Pedro Esteve continued to publish pamphlets, articles, and essays about labor politics in New York. He also published in *Cultura Obrera* an array of articles on other progressive topics. Luisa Capetillo, the activist Puerto Rican lectora, contributed important essays on feminism. In "Por la libertad femenina," she asked "Women of the Universe! What are you doing?" In a powerful challenge to traditional sexual and gender norms, she critiqued the criminality of adultery and oppression of women. "One of the biggest human mistakes," she wrote, "is to want to legislate human sexual desire, the manifestations of sexual growth, between different sexes, should be free, like everything else." She concluded with the statement: "Freedom from religious fanaticism [and] social formulas. It's time."[118]

Finances and the lack of adequate printing equipment continued to present a challenge to Esteve. In March 1913, Andrés Rodríguez called a meeting at the

FIGURE 4.7. Advertisement for a social event at the Brooklyn Círculo de Trabajadores to raise funds for *Cultura Obrera*: *Cultura Obrera*, March 1, 1913 (Author's Collection).

círculo to discuss the need for a new linotype press.[119] Apparently, sufficient funds were not forthcoming, and *Cultura Obrera* (figure 4.7) moved its offices, in September 1913, from 102 Pineapple Street in Brooklyn to 114 Roosevelt in New York City, where it shared space with the Círculo de Estudios Sociales.[120] Although *Cultura Obrera* remained at this new address for less than one year, the association between the círculo and *Cultura Obrera* continued and was a clear indication of the strong ties between Brooklyn's Spanish laborers and the ongoing anarcho-syndicalist movement.

The círculo remained an active meeting place for Brooklyn's cigar workers and other laborers through at least that decade. According to Bernardo Vega, a Puerto Rican cigar maker living in New York who visited the círculo in 1918, it "was largely made up of *tabaqueros*. They were all progressive in their thinking—anarchists, socialists, or at the very least left-wing republicans . . . most of them were getting on in years, but their minds were young and alert, their hearts were filled with optimism." Bernardo Vega recalled: "I went to the *Círculo* often. On any given night, in wintertime, they would get together at tables to play dominoes, checkers, or chess, or just to talk." At the círculo, and more than twenty years after the death of José Martí, Vega heard laments of those who remembered Martí with affection if not reverence. "I went from one group to another," Vega remembered, "The venerable old man Castañeda would be sitting in a corner. I can still hear him saying, 'It was a shame that Martí took that rumor-mongering by Trujillo and Collazo so much to heart, and that his own pride brought him to his end in Dos Ríos. If he had only stayed on to direct and guide the revolution, Cuba today would be the freest and most democratic republic in the world . . .'"[121]

END OF AN ERA

The laments of Brooklyn cigar makers at the Círculo de Trabajadores about Martí's death twenty years earlier tell us more about the cigar makers' changing world than Martí's hubris or tactical miscalculations. Indeed, the lives of the skilled Spanish cigar makers were changing dramatically. Consolidation of cigar and cigarette factories and the rising mass production of the increasingly popular cigarette led to the demise of the artisanal cigar makers. Cigar rollers lost their jobs, displaced by machinery. Even the celebrated and popular lectora Luisa Capetillo lost her job, as there was no reason for lectores to read to machines.[122] Small cigar shops continued in operation, but they often had to sell other items in order to remain profitable, typically becoming small drug stores or "five & dimes."

Willis Baer succinctly described the end of the cigar makers' era: "Since 1910 the independent wholesale cigar distributor has been waging a losing battle."[123] National statistics showed a significant increase in the number of cigar manufacturing firms in the United States from 1859 to 1904 after which, and particularly by the end of the second decade of the twentieth century, the number of independent firms declined precipitously as larger firms consolidated their market control over the cigar and cigarette manufacturing business (see table 4.2).

The rise of large tobacco corporations resulted in the inevitable consolidation and concentration of the cigar manufacturing business. By 1907, the American Tobacco Company, which also owned the American Cigar Company, controlled "eighty-nine percent of the little cigar trade; fourteen percent of the large cigar trade and purchased seventy percent to eighty percent of all the tobacco leaf used by the tobacco industry for domestic consumption."[124] While the United States government successfully prosecuted an antitrust case against American Tobacco that led to its dissolution in 1911, the tendency toward consolidation and the use of new and efficient manufacturing technology continued to squeeze small and independent manufacturers out of the cigar-making business. In 1926, the *New York Times* echoed this theme in an article titled "Age of Hand-Made Cigars Gives Way to Machine Era: One-Man Factory Passes as Mechanical Devices Greatly Increase Production." The article reported that "less than 5 per cent of the country's total cigar production is now made entirely by hand"[125] The dramatic decline in the number of independent artisanal cigar manufacturers during these

TABLE 4.2. Trend in the Number of Cigar-Manufacturing Establishments in the United States (1859–1931)

Year	Manufacturers	Year	Manufacturers
1859	1,478	1919	9,926
1869	4,631	1921	4,146
1879	7,145	1923	3,466
1889	10,956	1925	2,445
1899	14,522	1927	1,960
1904	16,394	1929	1,587
1909	15,362	1931	1,044
1914	13,515		

Source: Willis N. Baer, *The Economic Development of the Cigar Industry in the United States* (Mansfield Centre, CT: Martino Publishing, 2008), 260.

years presaged not only the end of the hand-rolled cigar but the Hispanic cigar makers' work culture, as the mass production and consumption of the much smaller cigarette skyrocketed (see table 4.3).

Several years later, during the New Deal, the Works Progress Administration (WPA) sponsored a series of studies titled "Effects of Industrial Change on Labor Markets." The first study, published in December 1937, focused on the cigar industry. The report noted that since about 1909, cigarette production had risen dramatically while cigar production continued to decline. This trend only increased the economic pressure on cigar businesses to become more efficient and translated into consolidation and mechanization. For the majority of cigar makers, this was truly the end of their livelihood and profession as independent craftsmen. Noting that the cigar maker was a "skilled artisan" whose "skill is not transferrable to other industries," the report's authors stated that these skilled craftsmen did not have much of a future making cigars in the era of the machine-made five-cent cigar.[126] "The principal finding," the report concluded ominously, "is that many thousands of workers, formerly or now attached to the cigar industry as skilled artisans, will be primarily dependent for their wellbeing on public relief for many years."[127]

The fiercely independent Spanish cigar makers did not easily give in to the dramatic social, political, and economic changes buffeting their world. Many held on to their craft as it was so much an integral part of their worldview and identity. Pedro Esteve remained as a leading figure of this community,

TABLE 4.3. Production of Cigars and Cigarettes
in the United States (millions) (1870–1930)

Year	Cigars	Cigarettes
1870	1,183	16
1875	1,828	59
1880	2,510	533
1885	3,294	1,080
1890	4,229	2,505
1895	4,099	4,238
1900	5,566	3,870
1905	6,748	4,477
1910	6,810	9,782
1915	6,599	18,945
1920	8,097	48,091
1925	6,463	82,712
1930	5,894	124,193

Source: US Department of Commerce, *Historical
Statistics of the United States: Colonial Times to 1970*,
pt. 2 (Washington, DC: GPO, 1975), 689–91.

and he continued publishing *Cultura Obrera* until his death in 1925 (he died suddenly in Paterson after attending a picnic). In 1927, *Cultura Obrera* was replaced by a new version of *Cultura Proletaria*, which remained in print until 1953. In Brooklyn, the Spanish colony and the círculo vanished as well. Suffering from urban decay, the former Spanish colony was reshaped and redeveloped, and in the mid-1930s much of it was forever lost to the project that created Cadman Plaza Park (figure 4.8).

It was not only mechanization and consolidation that led to the cigar makers' demise; the passions evoked by the political turmoil in both Cuba and Spain years earlier were becoming memories. Cuba was now independent, and the death of Martí and the execution of Ferrer were fading into history. Even undercover agent Maurits Hymans signaled the end of this era—along with his eleven-year career spying on the anarchists—when he wrote his last report in 1915 to William Flynn of the US Secret Service and explained his recent inability to work and write reports: "It was impossible for me to attend to my duties on account of terrible headaches and nervousness."[128]

A new era, nationally and internationally, was dawning. European tensions erupted into World War I followed by the Russian Revolution. In the

FIGURE 4.8. The area once described as the Spanish Colony of Brooklyn under redevelopment in 1936 for the Cadman Plaza Park. The Círculo de Trabajadores was located just inside the lower-left junction of the elevated road. Liberty Street, the street in between the elevated roadways, no longer exists as it was fully covered by the new park. (US Works Progress Administration, 1936.)

United States the Red Scare and the Palmer Raids, the Sacco and Vanzetti case, and the xenophobia associated with the National Origins Act of 1924 marked even more dangerous times for many immigrants and radicals. Authorities continued to aggressively target anarchists, socialists, and other radical movements during these years, but the "jazz age," rising consumerism, and hope for prosperity and middle-class social status changed the cultural tone of the 1920s for many Americans. By the mid-1930s, the Spanish Civil War became the new flash point for Spaniards in New York and internationally.[129]

Brooklyn's Spanish immigrants, particularly those cigar makers who espoused anarchist ideals, had forged a small yet cohesive and internationally influential community; they committed to the principles of anarchy as well as labor rights, educational reform, and egalitarianism. Due to its very nature, this movement was at its core radical and threatening to the state and capitalism. In Brooklyn, as in other locales, a significant number of those current and former anarchists continued their crafts; some opened shops, raised families, and often appeared to assimilate into the very socioeconomic construct that they had once tried to change. Yet some of these aging immigrants among newer arrivals still remained committed to the struggle for the rights of labor in the burgeoning capitalist system, social equality, and the pursuit of liberty. The means to achieve those ends had become more complex, but the idea remained the same.

NOTES

I express appreciation to CSU, Sacramento, for the Provost's Research Incentive Fund as well as travel grants from the College of Arts & Letters and Department of History to support research and travel costs for this essay. I also thank this book's coeditors, Phylis Cancilla Martinelli and Ana Varela-Lago, and the many persons who graciously answered my research questions and provided helpful information, including (but not limited to): Joan Casanovas, Montse Feu, Lily Litvak, Susana Sueiro Seoane, Jennifer Guglielmo, Bieito Alonso Fernández, James D. Fernández and Manuel Amador.

1. For background on Spanish anarchism see, George R. Esenwein, *Anarchist Ideology and the Working Class-Movement in Spain, 1868–1898* (Berkeley: University of California Press, 1989); Murray Bookchin, *The Spanish Anarchists: The Heroic Years, 1868–1936* (New York: Free Life Editions, 1977); and Temma Kaplan, *Anarchists of Andalusia: 1868–1903* (Princeton, NJ: Princeton University Press, 1977). On nationalist movements in Spain at the turn of the century see, Enric Ucelay Da Cal, "The Restoration Monarchy and the Competition of Nationalisms," in *Spanish History Since 1808*, ed. José Alvarez Junco and Adrian Shubert (London: Arnold, 2000), 121–136; and Sebastian Balfour, *The End of the Spanish Empire, 1898–1923* (Oxford: Oxford University Press, 1997).

2. Anarcho-Syndicalism refers to revolutionary industrial unionism through which workers gain control of production and have a broad influence on society. Louis A. Pérez Jr., *Cuba between Empires, 1878–1902* (Pittsburgh: University of Pittsburgh Press, 1982); Joan Casanovas, *Bread, or Bullets!: Urban Labor and Spanish Colonialism in Cuba, 1850–1898* (Pittsburgh: University of Pittsburgh Press, 1998); John Lawrence Tone, *War and Genocide in Cuba, 1895–1898* (Chapel Hill: University of North Carolina Press, 2006).

3. Willis N. Baer, *The Economic Development of the Cigar Industry in the United States* (Mansfield Centre, CT: Martino Publishing, 2008), 63; first published in Lancaster, PA: Art Printing Co., 1933.

4. Patricia A. Cooper, *Once a Cigar Maker: Men Women, and Work Culture in American Cigar Factories, 1900–1919* (Chicago: University of Illinois Press, 1992), 10.

5. Cooper, *Once a Cigar Maker*, 10.

6. Pérez, *Cuba between Empires*, 96.

7. Baer, *Economic Development of the Cigar Industry*, 63, 49. See also pages 108–110, 114.

8. Baer, *Economic Development of the Cigar Industry*, 107.

9. Baer, *Economic Development of the Cigar Industry*, 41.

10. Baer, *Economic Development of the Cigar Industry*, 260.

11. "Samuel Gompers and Early Cigarmakers' Unions in New York City," in *The Samuel Gompers Papers: The Making of a Union Leader, 1850–86*, vol. 1, ed. Stuart B. Kaufman (Urbana: University of Illinois Press, 1986), 45.

12. For the development of Ybor City, see Gary R. Mormino and George E. Pozzetta, *The Immigrant World of Ybor City: Italians and Their Latin Neighbors in Tampa, 1885–1985* (Gainesville: University Press of Florida, 1998); and Robert P. Ingalls and Louis A. Pérez Jr., *Tampa Cigar Workers: A Pictorial History* (Gainesville: University Press of Florida, 2003).

13. Quoted in Stuart B. Kaufman, ed., *The Samuel Gompers Papers*, 50.

14. Quoted in Stuart B. Kaufman, ed., *The Samuel Gompers Papers*, 50–51.

15. Paul Kens, *Lochner v. New York: Economic Regulation on Trial* (Lawrence: University Press of Kansas, 1998), 68.

16. Robert Mendel, *"A Broad and Ennobling Spirit": Workers and Their Unions in Late Gilded Age New York and Brooklyn, 1886–1898* (Westport, CT: Praeger, 2003), 88.

17. Mendel, *"A Broad and Ennobling Spirit"*, 87–89; Baer, *Economic Development of the Cigar Industry*, 89–90.

18. Gompers served as second vice-president of the CMIU from 1886–96 and first vice-president from 1896 until his death in 1924. See Baer, *Economic Development of the Cigar Industry*, 94–96.

19. Mendel, *"A Broad and Ennobling Spirit,"* 25.

20. See Thomas A. Guglielmo, *White on Arrival: Italians, Race, Color, and Power in Chicago, 1890–1945* (New York: Oxford University Press, 2003). While this work addresses concepts of race and ethnic identity among Italian immigrants, Spanish immigrants found themselves in a comparable situation.

21. Casanovas, *Bread, or Bullets!*, 168.

22. When Alfonso XII died in 1885, Queen Maria Cristina served as regent during Alfonso XIII's minority.

23. Evan Matthew Daniel, "Rolling for the Revolution: A Transnational History of Cuban Cigar Markers in Havana, Florida, and New York City, 1853–1895" (PhD diss., New School for Social Research, New York, 2010), 338.

24. Lisandro Pérez and Guillermo J. Grenier, *The Legacy of Exile: Cubans in the United States* (Boston: Pearson Education, 2003), 15.

25. E. D. Smith, *Court of Common Pleas Reports for the City and County of New York* (New York: Jacob R. Halsted, 1855), 1:273–79.

26. "Charge of Obtaining Goods under False Pretenses," *New York Herald,* December 17, 1855.

27. "Charge of Grand Larceny," *New York Tribune,* July 30, 1854.

28. "High Handed: Dastardly Outrage upon Two Brooklynites in Cuba," *Brooklyn Daily Eagle,* November 20, 1879.

29. John M. Kirk, *José Martí: Mentor of the Cuban Nation* (Gainesville: University Presses of Florida, 1983), 48.

30. Daniel, "Rolling for the Revolution," 29.

31. Rita Bird, "Spanish Heights Recalled for Good Talk, Poor Cigars," *Heights Press,* July 7, 1960.

32. http://lanacional.org/centro-espanol-nyc-spanish-benevolent-society-history/ (accessed March 22, 2017).

33. "Spanish Residents Enjoy an Annual Dinner at the Clarendon Hotel," *Brooklyn Daily Eagle,* January 24, 1887; "Spaniards Enjoying Themselves: Tobacco Importers and Cigar Manufacturers at a Hop," *Brooklyn Daily Eagle,* June 16, 1885. See also *El Despertar,* September 15, 1891.

34. "Brooklyn Cigar Making: Difference between Foreign and Domestic Brands," *Brooklyn Daily Eagle,* October 24, 1886.

35. "Brooklyn Cigar Making." There are many descriptions of the cigar-making process. See, for example, Cigar Institute of America, Inc., *The Story of Cigars* (New York: Cigar Institute of America, Inc., 1942), 36; Cooper, *Once a Cigar Maker,* 10–19; Daniel, "Rolling for the Revolution," 38–39; Baer, *Economic Development of the Cigar Industry,* 77–80; Mendel, "A Broad and Ennobling Spirit," 84.

36. "Brooklyn Cigar Making," *Brooklyn Daily Eagle,* October 24, 1886.

37. "Brooklyn Cigar Making."

38. "Brooklyn Cigar Making."

39. "Brooklyn Cigar Making."

40. "Mysteries of Cigars: A Conversation with a Brooklyn Dealer," *Brooklyn Daily Eagle,* July 1, 1888.

41. "Brooklyn Cigar Making."

42. "Brooklyn Cigar Making."

43. Araceli Tinajero, *El Lector: A History of the Cigar Factory Reader*, trans. Judith E. Grasberg (Austin: University of Texas Press, 2010), 16–17.

44. Tinajero, *El Lector*, 48–49.

45. Tinajero, *El Lector*, 150–51.

46. Tinajero, *El Lector*, 150.

47. Samuel Gompers, *Seventy Years of Life and Labor: An Autobiography* (New York: E. P. Dutton, 1948), 80–81.

48. "Corrales and Ynguanzo Could Not Agree," *Brooklyn Daily Eagle*, October 31, 1891.

49. Glenn Westfall, "Ignacio Haya, Pioneer Cigar Entrepreneur," *Sunland Tribune* 4, no. 1 (November 1980): 12–15.

50. "Funeral Service of Serafine Sanchez: A Well-Known Member of the Spanish Colony Buried in Greenwood," *Brooklyn Daily Eagle*, April 25, 1894.

51. "Annual Fete of 'La Nacional,'" *Brooklyn Daily Eagle*, July 4, 1896.

52. Prudencio de Pereda, *Windmills in Brooklyn* (New York: Atheneum, 1960), 22.

53. de Pereda, *Windmills in Brooklyn*, 26.

54. de Pereda, *Windmills in Brooklyn*, 41.

55. de Pereda, *Windmills in Brooklyn*, 43.

56. See George R. Esenwein, *Anarchist Ideology and the Working-Class Movement in Spain, 1868–1898* (Berkeley: UC Press, 1989); and Temma Kaplan, *Anarchists of Andalusia, 1868–1903* (Princeton, NJ: Princeton University Press, 1977).

57. Gerald E. Poyo, "The Anarchist Challenge to the Cuban Independence Movement, 1885–1890," *Cuban Studies* 15, no. 1 (Winter 1985): 31.

58. Gompers, *Seventy Years of Life and Labor*, 64.

59. Casanovas, *Bread, or Bullets!*, 169.

60. Luis Barcia, "Autobiography of Luis Barcia Quilabert" (unpublished manuscript at Special Collections, University of South Florida Tampa, 1957), 26–27.

61. Joan Casanovas I Codina, "Pedro Esteve (Barcelona 1865—Weehauken, N. J. 1925): A Catalan Anarchist in the United States," *Catalan Review* 5, no. 1 (1991): 69. See also Poyo, "The Anarchist Challenge," 40.

62. Pérez, *Cuba between Empires*, 17. See also Bernardo Vega, *Memoirs of Bernardo Vega: A Contribution to the History of the Puerto Rican Community in New York*, ed. César Andreu Iglesias, trans., Juan Flores (New York: Monthly Review Press, 1984), 73–75.

63. *El Despertar*, March 15, 1893.

64. See *El Productor* (Barcelona), July 20, 1892; and *El Despertar*, January 1, 1893.

65. Casanovas I Codina, "Pedro Esteve," 61.

66. Casanovas I Codina, "Pedro Esteve," 66–67.

67. On Adrián del Valle see Shane L. Thomson, "Recovering Adrián del Valle's 'Por el camino' and Building Transnational Multitudinous Communities" (PhD diss., Ball State University, Muncie, Indiana, 2013).

68. "A Spanish Anarchist," *Brooklyn Daily Eagle*, August 1, 1893.

69. For Maria Roda and the Italian anarchist community, see Jennifer Guglielmo, *Living the Revolution: Italian Women's Resistance and Radicalism in New York City, 1880–1945* (Chapel Hill: University of North Carolina Press, 2010).

70. Casanovas I Codina, "Pedro Esteve," 67. See also Daniels, "Rolling for the Revolution," 289.

71. Casanovas I Codina, "Pedro Esteve," 67. See also Kenyon Zimmer, "'The Whole World is Our Country': Immigration and Anarchism in the United States, 1885–1940" (PhD diss., University of Pittsburgh, 2010).

72. Marcelino García interview in Paul Avrich, *Anarchist Voices: An Oral History of Anarchism in America* (Princeton, NJ: Princeton University Press, 1995), 391.

73. Avrich, *Anarchist Voices*, 392.

74. "Anarchists from Spain: Thriving Clubs in New York Whose Members Uphold Assassination," *Los Angeles Herald*, September 19, 1897.

75. Pedro Esteve, [untitled], *El Despertar*, June 20, 1898. See also, Casanovas I Codina, "Pedro Esteve," 70–71.

76. For more on Italian radicalism, see Guglielmo, *Living the Revolution*; and Philip Cannistraro and Gerald Meyer, eds., *The Lost World of Italian-American Radicalism* (Westport, CT: Praeger, 2003).

77. A. Castañeda, "Comunicado," *El Despertar*, April 15, 1899. Translation by Héctor Urrutibeheity.

78. *El Despertar*, January 30, 1899. See also Frank Fernández, *Cuban Anarchism: The History of a Movement* (Tucson, AZ: Sharp Press, 2001), 22.

79. *El Despertar*, May 1, 1900.

80. "Desde el Círculo de Trabajadores," *Cultura Obrera*, May 3, 1913.

81. "La Fiesta del Círculo," *Cultura Obrera*, March 1, 1913.

82. "To the Cigarmakers of the International Union," *El Despertar*, December 10, 1900.

83. See George Carey, "'La Questione Sociale,' an Anarchist Newspaper in Paterson, N.J. (1895–1908)," in *Italian Americans: New Perspectives in Italian Immigration and Ethnicity*, ed. Lydio F. Tomasi (Staten Island: Center for Migration Studies of New York, 1985), 289–97.

84. Maurits Hymans, Special Operations, to John L. Wilkie, chief of the Secret Service Division, April 2, 1904; Daily Reports of US Secret Service Agents, 1875–1936: Hymans, M.; Records of the US Secret Service, Record Group 87, National Archives at College Park.

85. See "Rise and Fall of Anarchy in World-Famed Paterson," *Washington Post*, December 9, 1906, 8. See also Casanovas I Codina, "Pedro Esteve," 72–73.

86. Casanovas I Codina, "Pedro Esteve," 73.

87. Maurits Hymans to John E. Wilkie, December 5, 1906, Daily Reports Agent: Hymans, M., Records of the US Secret Service, Record Group 87.

88. Ana María Varela-Lago, "Conquerors, Immigrants, Exiles: The Spanish Diaspora in the United States (1848–1948)" (PhD diss., University of California San Diego, 2008), 92.

89. See Sebastian Balfour, *Deadly Embrace: Morocco and the Road to the Spanish Civil War* (Oxford: Oxford University Press, 2002).

90. Paul Avrich, *The Modern School Movement: Anarchism and Education in the United States* (Princeton, NJ: Princeton University Press, 1980), 6.

91. Avrich, *The Modern School Movement*, 4.

92. Avrich, *The Modern School Movement*, 6–7.

93. Avrich, *The Modern School Movement*, 27–28.

94. Stephen Bonsal, "The Situation in Spain and its Meaning," *New York Times*, August 8, 1909.

95. Avrich, *The Modern School Movement*, 31–32. See also, John A. Crow, *Spain: The Root and the Flower: An Interpretation of Spain and the Spanish People*, 3rd ed. (Berkeley: University of California Press, 1985), 284–87.

96. Bieito Alonso Fernández, "Migración y sindicalismo: Marineros y anarquistas españoles en Nueva York (1902–1930)," *Historia Social* 54 (2006): 119. Immigration records indicate that Jaime Vidal was born in 1878. It is possible that Vidal came to New York earlier, but immigration records are not clear on this point.

97. "In New York Tonight," *New York Call*, October 26, 1909. See also Susana Sueiro Seoane, "El asesinato de Canalejas y los anarquistas españoles," in *El nacimiento del terrorismo en Occidente: Anarquía, nihilismo y violencia revolucionaria*, ed. Juan Avilés and Angel Herrerín (Madrid: Siglo XXI, 2008), 176–77. See also Alonso, "Migración y sindicalismo," 116.

98. Jaime Vidal et. al., "For the Revolution in Spain: An Appeal for Solidarity," *Mother Earth* 4, no. 11 (January 1910): 359.

99. Maurits Hymans to John L. Wilkie, October 23, 1909; Daily Reports of US Secret Service Agents; Records of the US Secret Service, Record Group 87, National Archives at College Park.

100. Vidal et al., "For the Revolution in Spain," 359.

101. *The New York Call*, October 26, 1909. Note that Liberty Street was located in Brooklyn Heights, where Cadman Plaza Park is now located.

102. Hymans to Wilkie, January 22, 1910; Records of the US Secret Service, Record Group 87, National Archives.

103. Hymans to Wilkie, January 16, 1912; Records of the US Secret Service, Record Group 87, National Archives. See also, Sueiro Seoane, "El asesinato de Canalejas," 177. Pardiñas was arrested soon thereafter and then committed suicide.

104. This union reportedly left the ISU in 1913 and then joined the IWW. See Stephen Schwartz, *Brotherhood of the Sea: A History of the Sailors' Union of the Pacific, 1885–1985* (San Francisco: Sailors' Union of the Pacific, AFL-CIO, 1986), 38. See also Nancy A. Hewitt, *Southern Discomfort: Women's Activism in Tampa, Florida, 1880s–1920s* (Urbana: University of Illinois Press, 2004), 214. Hewitt also identifies Jaime Vidal as a member of the Maritime Workers' Union.

105. Casanovas I Codina, "Pedro Esteve," 74–75.

106. Hymans to Wilkie, January 27, 1912; Records of the US Secret Service, Record Group 87, National Archives.

107. *Cultura Obrera* was published from 1911 to 1917 and from 1922 to 1927.

108. "Beautiful Young Spanish Woman Is a Manager of Seamen's Strike," *New York Herald*, July 15, 1912.

109. "Recuerdos de una huelga sangrienta," *Cultura Obrera*, January 25, 1913.

110. "To Start Agitation for Marine Fireman: Comrades Decide to Work for Release of Alexander Aldamas," *New York Evening Call*, October 30, 1912. See also "The Case of Aldamas," *Mother Earth*, 7, no. 8 (October 1912): 254–55.

111. "El Círculo de Trabajadores," *Cultura Obrera*, February 8, 1913.

112. "El Círculo de Mudada," *Cultura Obrera*, February 1, 1913.

113. "Movimiento Obrero," *Cultura Obrera*, May 16, 1913.

114. J. Vidal, "'Fuerza Consciente,'" *Cultura Obrera*, February 15, 1913.

115. Zimmer, "The Whole World Is Our Country," 243–44. Also Pedro Castillo, "Urbanización, migración y los chicanos en Los Angeles: 1900–1920," in *El México olvidado: La historia del pueblo chicano*, ed. David R. Maciel (El Paso: University of Texas and Ciudad Juárez: Universidad Autónoma de Ciudad Juárez, 1996), 367.

116. William Wilson McEuen, "A Survey of the Mexicans in Los Angeles" (master's thesis, University of Southern California, Los Angeles, 1914), 93. World War I draft registration records indicate that Jaime Vidal was married to Josefine Cipresso in 1918 while living in Los Angeles. The 1920 census indicates that Cipresso was then married to José Vilariño. Vilariño was deported ca. 1931 for being a communist. Records indicate that Vidal lived much of his life after 1930 as an itinerant cook in several locations in California until his death in 1961.

117. Hymans to William Flynn, March 11, 1915 and February 13, 1915; Records of the US Secret Service, Record Group 87, National Archives.

118. Luisa Capetillo, "Por la libertad femenina," *Cultura Obrera*, February 22, 1913.

119. A. Rodríguez, "A los socios de Solidaridad Obrera," *Cultura Obrera*, March 8, 1913.

120. "A todos cuantos interese la vida de 'Cultura Obrera,'" *Cultura Obrera*, September 7, 1913. By December 27, 1913, the journal had moved again, this time to 100 James Street.

121. Vega, *Memoirs of Bernardo Vega*, 102.

122. Tinajero, *El Lector*, 152.

123. Baer, *Economic Development of the Cigar Industry*, 264.

124. Baer, *Economic Development of the Cigar Industry*, 102. Note that "A small cigar is one whose weight per thousand is not over three pounds; a large cigar is one whose weight per thousand is over three pounds" (103).

125. "Age of Hand-Made Cigars Gives Way to Machine Era: One-Man Factory Passes as Mechanical Devices Greatly Increase Production," *New York Times*, August 22, 1926.

126. Daniel Creamer and Gladys V. Swackhamer, *Cigar Makers—After the Lay-Off* (Philadelphia: WPA, December, 1937), xvi.

127. Creamer and Swackhamer, introductory letter from Corrington Gil to Harry Hopkins, December 16, 1937, in Creamer and Swackhamer, *Cigar Makers—After the Lay-Off*.

128. Maurits Hymans to Flynn, July 23, 1915; Records of the US Secret Service, Record Group 87, National Archives.

129. See Peter N. Carroll and James D. Fernández, eds., *Facing Fascism: New York and the Spanish Civil War* (New York: New York University Press, 2007).

5

PAGEANTS, POPULARITY CONTESTS, AND SPANISH IDENTITIES IN 1920S NEW YORK

BRIAN D. BUNK

In April 1925 over 1,000 people from all over New York City came to Hunts Point Palace in the Bronx to attend a grand festival hosted by the Galicia Sporting Club. Revelers enjoyed the music of three different bands, competed in dance contests, and perused the 120-page program. One of the evening's most anticipated events was the crowning of the "Queen of Beauty," a title that was sure to be "tenaciously contested" by girls and young women of Spanish descent from the United States, Spain, and other countries. The Queen would receive a number of prizes including a crown, pearls, and a perfume case. At 10:30 p.m. the procession of candidates began, and afterwards the winner was proclaimed: an eleven-year-old girl named Mercedes Anca.[1]

The young Queen had been born in New York City to Spanish immigrant parents who lived in Greenwich Village, one of several peninsular enclaves in the metropolitan area. During the 1920s numerous Spanish societies such as Galicia Sporting Club thrived in the city, and many families from Spain, including the Ancas, were closely involved with these associations. The organizations, many linked to particular regions of Spain, provided a variety of

DOI: 10.5876/9781607327998.c005

services for families and played a significant role in organizing the social and cultural lives of the community. The groups offered mutual aid benefits, built clubhouses, and hosted exhibits of art and literature. The social lives of people of all ages and genders revolved around these centers and the events they sponsored, especially dances, picnics, and soccer games. The societies created spaces for Spanish New Yorkers to move between the social and cultural traditions and practices of both the Old and New Worlds.

The recreational opportunities provided by the clubs were especially important to young female members of the community, since many parents adhered to traditional gender proscriptions and thus limited their daughters' participation in activities outside of the home. As researchers Loretta Baldassar and Donna Gabaccia have argued, events sponsored by voluntary associations should not be seen exclusively as public activities but instead occurred in areas where the domestic and the public combined to create "intermediate spaces."[2] The activities taking place within this intermediate space often involved or resembled domestic rituals, the "purposive and expressive ceremonialized performances" marking important life events such as births, deaths, and marriages.[3] Rituals such as these allowed participants to express continued membership in a traditional community while at the same time acknowledging the changing nature of that community. As a result, the intermediate spaces "become arenas of contestation about wider issues: power, status and boundaries of 'community,' history and identity."[4] The cultural rituals performed at dances and other events reflected the ways that Spanish immigrants used these public/private gatherings not only to reinforce old customs but also to establish new ones. The belief that a woman's proper role centered almost exclusively on the household sat at the heart of widening circles of affiliation ranging from the domestic to the international. For many, a subnational regional heritage based on place of origin within Spain remained a primary characteristic. Others celebrated a Spanish national identity, while many young people came to embrace new American traditions. Finally, during the 1920s, as the population of nonpeninsular Spanish speakers increased, the concept of a transnational cultural identity known as *hispano* received widespread attention. It was the notion of a hispano identity that ultimately proved the most elusive to Spanish New Yorkers. Defined not so much as a biological concept, the word instead invoked the shared heritage, language, and culture between people from

Spain and Latin America. Fear over the loss of their unique cultural background as a result of population changes, however, ultimately led Spaniards to cling more tightly to regional and national identities even as they espoused a more broadly inclusive one.[5]

In many ways the history of the Anca family was typical of Spanish immigrants to the United States in the first decades of the twentieth century. Juan Anca was born in La Coruña (Galicia, Spain) around 1880.[6] While still in Spain he married María Antonio Díaz Vasquez (born c. 1879) around 1897, and their first daughter, Carmen, was born on January 4, 1899.[7] At some point Juan traveled to Cuba—the length of his stay is unknown—before continuing on to the United States. His experience reflects a series of common decisions made by Galicians during the period. The region had long been one of Spain's top producers of immigrants, and Cuba emerged as a leading destination during the early twentieth century as almost 750,000 Spaniards arrived between 1902 and 1925.[8] Instead of settling in Cuba, like many of his countrymen, Anca sailed from Havana aboard the *S.S. Saratoga* and arrived in New York City on January 2, 1909. The ship's passenger list cites his occupation as clerk and indicates that he was literate.[9] His wife and daughter joined him in the city four years later. They had sailed from Spain to Liverpool, England, before arriving in the United States on February 20, 1913, aboard the *S.S. Celtic*. A second daughter, Mercedes, was born in New York City on December 10, 1913, and by 1915 the family was living at 353 West Eleventh Street in Greenwich Village (figure 5.1). Juan Anca worked in a variety of jobs over the next several years including as a clerk, building superintendent, and ice puller. The census records consistently list Maria's occupation as "none" indicating that she did not work outside the home.

The neighborhood, along with areas of Brooklyn and Manhattan's Lower East Side, was one of several Spanish areas in the city, and originally its busy waterfront attracted a mostly transient, male population many from Galicia. The figures compiled by historian Caroline Ware for her 1935 study of the area show that 100 men and only 18 women of Spanish descent lived in the Village before 1910. By 1920 the total population of Spanish-born persons had reached 416 (113 of them women). The movement of families such as the Ancas to the neighborhood resulted in demographic and cultural shifts, as more American-born children helped to create mixed Spanish-American households.[10] Despite the compact size of the colony, only about eight square blocks, the Village

FIGURE 5.1. Hudson river piers a few blocks south of the Anca residence at 353 West Eleventh Street in Greenwich Village. Library of Congress, Prints & Photographs Division, Detroit Publishing Company Collection.

contained a variety of businesses and institutions catering to the Spanish population. At 82 Bank Street, for example, less than a quarter mile from the Ancas' home, was the Hotel Santa Lucía. Valentín Aguirre, one of New York's most prominent Spanish residents, owned the hotel and its associated restaurant called Jai-Alai. Aguirre, who grew up in the Basque country, left Spain to work the shipping routes between Europe, Latin America, and the United States when he was just ten years old.[11] By 1895 he had settled in New York and established a rooming house that was enormously popular with Basque immigrants, many of whom passed through the city on to destinations in the American West. Later Aguirre opened the restaurant and an agency that sold tickets for everything from transatlantic voyages to boxing matches.[12]

Just a few more blocks east, a grand terracotta-clad building at 154 West Fourteenth Street housed the Spanish Consul's office, a bookstore, and the Banco de Lago.[13] Spanish immigrant James (Jaime) V. Lago founded the state-certified private bank in 1917 (figure 5.2). He also operated a ticketing agency, boardinghouse, and import business and even sold his own patent medicine. On July 3, 1928, just a day before many Spanish residents of New York

FIGURE 5.2. Showing 154 West Fourteenth Street. Designed by
Herman Lee Meader and built in 1912, during the 1910s and 1920s
the building was home to the Spanish Consul's office, a Spanish-
language bookstore, and the various business interests of Jaime V.
Lago, including the bank that closed in 1928. Image by Beyond my
Ken, 2011. Wikipedia Commons.

attended holiday picnics, the state closed the bank citing "irregularities" in its
records. As early as 1921 the accounts were in trouble, and eventually Lago
admitted to changing a $211 deposit from a Spanish bank into a $200,000 one
in order to mask the institution's growing indebtedness. He also pled guilty
to accepting deposits while knowingly being insolvent and was sentenced to
two years in prison. The bank catered to thousands of customers, including

many who had invested much of their meager life savings with Lago. A petition filed by a handful of depositors a few days after the bank's closing listed some of the amounts at risk, ranging from a high of $2,098 to a low of just $85. Once the case was settled, former customers of the Lago Bank received only about 65 percent of their original funds.[14]

In 1930, when the Spanish presence had declined somewhat, the Village was still home to seven pool rooms, six boardinghouses, three restaurants, three tailors, four barbers, three grocers, two pharmacies, and one speak-easy catering primarily to the Spanish-speaking community.[15] A Spanish Catholic church named Nuestra Señora de Guadalupe (Our Lady of Guadalupe) served the district, and several voluntary associations had been organized with many of them headquartered in the neighborhood. The oldest of these groups, the Spanish Benevolent Society La Nacional, founded in 1868, still exists today just north of Greenwich Village at 239 West Fourteenth Street. Eventually Spaniards in the United States, like those in other countries, established a number of different voluntary associations, mostly centered on the region of origin in Spain.[16] These societies offered members various services including mutual aid, health care, and insurance. The organizations also sponsored recreational activities in the form of sports, dances, and picnics.

The decade of the 1920s saw a dramatic growth in the number of new organizations, and, within a few years, groups representing several different regions of Spain had appeared. Between 1923 and 1926, for example, supporters from Cataluña, Asturias, Galicia, and Cantabria founded new soccer clubs.[17] The growth of these associations was likely associated with the large numbers of immigrants who had arrived in the previous decade. Between 1911 and 1920, nearly 70,000 Spaniards came to the United States, many of them settling in New York.[18] The Anca family became closely involved with two regional groups: Galicia Sporting Club and the Casa de Galicia. The impetus for the creation of a new organization centered on Galician origin began as early as 1922. According to press reports many immigrants from Galicia felt the universal Spanish associations did little to protect or promote their interests.[19] A year later the athletic club had been organized, and Juan Anca served on the commission that helped form the Casa de Galicia in 1925. Originally both groups were located in Greenwich Village at 108 West Fourteenth Street, but in 1927 they purchased and renovated a building at 109–111 East Fifteenth Street for $125,000 (about $1.57 million today).[20]

Although the voluntary organizations served a number of different functions, one of the most important was to organize what historian Lizabeth Cohen has called "ethnically based leisure."[21] Likely, Spanish New Yorkers experienced the same fears as the immigrant groups Cohen studied in Chicago, namely, that the near closure of the United States to new arrivals, combined with the pernicious effects of American popular culture, spelled the end of their native traditions. Spanish New Yorkers also faced an additional challenge as large numbers of nonpeninsular migrants arrived in the city during the 1920s. Estimates indicate that the Spanish-speaking population of New York City more than doubled between 1920 and 1930 despite the limitations placed on arrivals from Spain. As a result, the nature of Spanish culture in the city was changing from one dominated by Spaniards to one more closely associated with Puerto Ricans.[22] Immigrants from Spain, like those from other nations, responded by attempting to strengthen the voluntary associations they believed were crucial to preserving traditional identities. In that same decade many organizations began to increase efforts designed to involve women and young people in the groups.[23] The opening of a social center such as the Casa de Galicia seemed a perfect way to organize and direct efforts aimed at preserving and encouraging a sense of both regional and national identity.

The physical space of the Casa de Galicia's headquarters served as both a tangible expression of community identities and as a site for individuals and groups to perform those identities. The Spanish daily *La Prensa* ran a long front-page story describing the opening of the new center in July 1928. The building, fixtures, and decoration symbolically aimed to support both a Galician regional identity and a Spanish national one. Two lights of "pure Spanish style" with the name Casa de Galicia etched in the glass lit the façade. On the night of the opening, club officials planned to have special electric lights paint the building in the colors of the Spanish flag. Another Spanish-style lamp hung suspended from the ceiling above the long marble staircase to the interior. After passing by tapestries embroidered with Spain's coat of arms, visitors moved into the vestibule where lamps designed in a manner typical of Seville illuminated the space. The basement housed a restaurant and bar as well as a gymnasium complete with changing rooms and showers. The first floor contained a number of areas including office space and meeting rooms. A library displaying the soccer team's trophies and a ladies lounge were on the second level while the top floor held office space for the club, medical facilities, and a photography studio. At the heart of the building were two great open salons, each festooned with regional and national symbols. Medallions depicting the crests of the four Galician provinces adorned the main floor room, and velvet curtains featuring the crest of the region itself covered its windows. In the second-level hall gold-framed paintings depicting the family emblems of Christopher Columbus and other notable Spanish families lined the fifty-foot-long space. The first floor room was named for Concepción Arenal, a nineteenth-century writer and social reformer from Galicia, and the large space on the second floor honored another Galician woman, the poet Rosalía de Castro.[24] The naming of the main gathering areas of the building confirms the notion of them as intermediate spaces between public and private. It was in these rooms, named for distinguished daughters of Galicia, where rituals such as banquets, receptions, and dances took place.

A dance card from an event held at the Casa de Galicia around 1929, much like the decorated space of the building, demonstrates the multiplicity of identities on display. Printed on the small booklet was a poem celebrating the Galicians' love for their homeland. The card also reveals the importance of other identities: of the fifteen dances played, six were classified as Spanish, six as American, and three as both Spanish and American.[25] The circumstances of the dance, such as the location, the poem on the card, and much of the music aimed at perpetuating a sense of Galician and Spanish identity. The inclusion of American songs, however, introduced an element of broader mass culture into the seemingly controlled world of the Casa de Galicia and at least offered the possibility of nontraditional identifications, especially for young people. Evidence suggested a growing distance between generations as many institutions, the neighborhood church, for example, no longer resonated with youths because these institutions had become too closely associated with their parents' culture. Although the Catholic Church did not generally play as central a role in the community as it did in Spain, Nuestra Señora de Guadalupe did function as a place for women to participate in activities outside the home. The adults also tended to cling to heritage traditions, especially regarding language and food, while resisting assimilation into broader American culture. In part this distance was also a result of the children's involvement with influences outside of the Spanish colony. Education, for example, reinforced the growing cultural divide between adults and young people because, as Caroline Ware explained, "the school experience of these children had no continuity with their cultural past or with that of their families."[26] Ware's researcher conducted a series of interviews with Spanish residents of the Village that generated detailed information about the attitudes and practices of immigrant families. Researchers only administered a handful of surveys to young people, and all of them were given to women between the ages of fifteen and eighteen—the same age as Mercedes Anca in 1929.[27]

The questions reveal important details about what practices researchers considered to be important markers of the ways people identified with a particular national heritage. The surveys given to Spanish residents of the Village asked whether the respondent ate and enjoyed Spanish and/or American food. In this context, the answers given could be seen to reflect the respondents' degree of cultural assimilation. The results showed that unlike the vast majority of the adults, the young women, all born in the United States, enjoyed both Spanish and American food. In some ways, the findings illustrate the ongoing process of Americanization that took place as the respondents became exposed to traditions and practices outside the Spanish colony. Nevertheless, the process of total cultural change had not been completed, and many also retained a sense of Spanish heritage. While the majority answered yes or "I am" to the question "do you wish to become Americanized?" some also expressed a desire to return to Spain, even though they had grown up outside of it. One fifteen-year-old, whose answers were called "typical" of Spanish girls born in the United States, declared herself to be totally Americanized but to enjoy and eat both types of food. She also answered yes to the question "Are you planning to return to your country?"[28] Although only a small sample, the results of the survey point to the development of an array of traditions and identities existing simultaneously: Galician-Spanish-American.[29]

Exposure to American schools, music, and food was not the only way that young people became integrated into the broader mass culture outside the Spanish colony. Images of Spain had achieved widespread popularity and permeated many aspects of American popular culture during the 1920s, including art, music, and fashion. For the children of immigrants the images appearing in magazines, newspapers, and advertisements displayed a limited vision of their parents' homeland. The vogue for Spain began in the

184 BRIAN D. BUNK

late nineteenth century as European and American writers and artists constructed an "Orientalized Spain" that was primitive, sensual, and erotic. Many
of the works depicted the characters and cultural practices of Andalusia and
involved gypsies, bullfighters, and flamenco dancers. Such imagery was distributed in a variety of forms such as advertising and film. Between 1921 and
1926, for example, Hollywood produced at least eight major Spanish-themed
pictures, many of them based on the work of writer Vicente Blasco Ibáñez.
The movies featured some of the era's biggest stars, including Rudolph
Valentino (1922, *Blood and Sand*; figure 5.3), Pola Negri (1921, *Gypsy Blood*; 1923,
The Spanish Dancer), Mary Pickford (1923, *Rosita*) and Dorothy Gish (1923, *The
Bright Shawl*).[30]

How this external vision of Spain merged with representations from inside
the Spanish colony can be shown in the response to the 1925 visit of Spanish
painter Ignacio Zuloaga. Although he had exhibited in the United States
before, his January show at the Reinhardt Galleries in New York was a sensa-
tion. The artist quickly became a high-society favorite, and the show proved
equally popular, attracting some 75,000 visitors in less than three weeks.[31]
Within the Spanish colony Zuloaga's visit also generated a great deal of attention, especially from *La Prensa*. The newspaper ran a number of front-page
stories chronicling the painter's many appearances and activities. The coverage culminated with the publication of large reproductions of six paintings
from the exhibit along with an article describing many of the others.[32] The
popularity of Zuloaga both outside and inside the Spanish colony was partly
a result of the style and subjects of his work. Art historian Leigh Roethke
describes his paintings as "romanticized simplifications deliberately vague
in time frame but realistic in execution." The canvases omit references to
contemporary society and instead offer the viewer "nostalgic figures placed
amid identifiable landscapes."[33]

The paintings satisfied the needs of many upper- and middle-class
Americans who longed for a vision of an exotic and slightly dangerous place
removed from their ordinary lives. It also reflected the carefully constructed,
mostly idealized vision of a country many Spanish New Yorkers had either left
behind or never seen at all. The decoration of the Casa de Galicia, for example,
was focused on the region itself but also contained elements similar to those
appearing in mainstream popular culture. The decision to name one of the
central halls for Rosalía de Castro reflected the poet's tremendous popularity

FIGURE 5.3. Poster for the 1922 movie *Blood and Sand*. The film was one of several made during the 1920s, when Spanish-themed art and literature were popular within the United States. Wikipedia Commons.

among Galician immigrants. Many of her poems, like Zuloaga's canvases, invoked nostalgic feelings for people or places now absent.[34] Nevertheless, the Andalusian lamps in the building's entryway, an upstairs lounge decorated in the style of Philip II and the paintings in the salon honoring aristocratic families all coincided with broadly popular themes including the culture of southern Spain and the nation's Golden Age of discovery and empire.[35]

Another event showed how Spanish immigrants combined these stereotyped representations of Spain with depictions of their own regional customs. For second-generation Spanish Americans such imagery may have characterized much of their exposure to a broader Spanish culture outside the regional one of their parents. In March 1927 the Ancas attended a costume ball at the Manhattan Casino. By that time the family had grown, as the eldest daughter, Carmen, had married Juan Díaz in 1917. Díaz had come to the United States from Spain in 1907 when he was just seventeen years old. After the marriage the two continued to live in Greenwich Village, just a few doors down from Carmen's parents and sister. The couple had three children, all daughters: Electra was born on April 13, 1917, Maria came about five years later, and Iberia arrived in 1925. Although the Galician society hosted the dance, attendees came dressed in clothing representing a variety of regional and national traditions. Organizers gave prizes for the best costume in both adult and youth categories. While some of the clothing reflected the traditions of particular regions, others appeared almost like collages of elements taken from popular images of Spain. Several people wore traditional Galician outfits, including one young woman who donned traditional wooden clogs, or *zuecas*. Mercedes Anca, daughter of Galician parents, appeared as a *maja*, customarily an image of lower-class women from Madrid. Another party-goer wore a *mantón de Manila*, the silk shawl often associated with southern Spain, as well as a *boina*, or beret typical of northern Spain.[36] While each outfit and item were not exclusive to those geographic regions, they all served as potent symbols of a generalized Spain, much like the people in Zuloaga's paintings.[37] Other outfits reflected an emphasis on Spanish national culture, including the prizewinning suit worn by young Electra Díaz. Her clothes were made in the colors of the Spanish flag and had a label pinned to the front reading *¡Viva España!* The identities expressed through the costumes, like the music played at previous dances, also included a nod toward a growing sense of Americanization. One couple arrived dressed as Spain and America, while another appeared as Charlie Chaplin and his wife Lita Gray.[38]

The events sponsored by associations also demonstrate the ways participants used the intermediate spaces to enforce traditional gender roles and to control female sexuality, things they believed necessary for the preservation of other regional and national identities. Such notions fit the conclusions made by researchers who studied the Spanish population during this period. Caroline Ware described the community as strongly patriarchal and noted that marriages typically involved "the complete subordination of the woman." Parents often arranged unions for their children and tried to control the ethnicity of the partner. Some aimed to make certain that their daughters wed only other Spaniards.[39] A later investigation done for a proposed Work Projects Administration Writers' Project, "Spanish Book," claimed that after marriage women rarely appeared in public and that in some homes the wife was not allowed to sit with her husband at the same dinner table.[40]

Other stories in *La Prensa* promoted the idea that uncontrolled women posed a threat to both the community and themselves. In early 1925, the daily published an article titled "The Madness of Jazz." In it, the author argued that modern music caused young women to crave excitement and led them into lives outside traditional boundaries. Jazz encouraged behaviors inappropriate to women such as sexual promiscuity and violence. The solution, according to the author, was a reliance on Europe's "many centuries of tradition" to help guide women away from poor choices.[41] Another story published on the front page of *La Prensa* in spring 1926 concerned the disappearance of a young Puerto Rican woman named Regina Quiñones. Her father had contacted the paper to help locate her after she failed to return home after work. Eventually, she read about her family's pleas in the newspaper and came back to the residence. Along with her parents' worries about her personal safety, the incident revealed concerns over the increasing independence of young women. Quiñones already had a job outside the home, and the story reported that the reason she had left was so she could live on her own and enjoy more freedom. The newspaper indicated that the danger was not limited to economic autonomy but also involved questions over the control of her sexuality. Evidence of this struggle can be found in *La Prensa*'s declaration that in the neighborhood Quiñones was known for being "too beautiful." The paper also took care to assure readers that while away from her parents she had been staying with a respectable American family, and the case did not involve a love affair or kidnapping as had been rumored.[42] In many ways the events became a very public way of restoring parental authority and limiting the freedoms of a young working woman. By asserting her continued virtue, the author of the story also made known that by returning home she had also returned to her proper role and her proper culture.

The dances and pageants performed in Spanish New York during the 1920s show how the colony emphasized and argued particular roles for women. The staging of beauty and popularity contests in particular highlight the values of gender and morality important to a community, and the winner often represents the ideal form of these beliefs.[43] The tradition of selecting a queen had long been a feature of May festivals in Europe and the choice of winner could be made on a number of criteria including beauty, likeability, or status.

Such activities reinforced community solidarity through shared participation in ritual celebration.[44] In the United States photographic newspaper contests had become popular by the late nineteenth century, and eventually live pageants were commonplace at beach resorts along the East Coast.[45] The growing belief that being beautiful was a woman's main goal led to the rapid commercialization of the beauty industry and an increased acceptance of such competitions. The first Miss America pageant, for example, took place in Atlantic City in 1921 and had only eight contestants, but just six years later there were seventy-five.[46] The developments also related to broader changes in attitudes toward young people, especially women. Fears associated with the growing liberty of youth grew especially intense during these years. For many, this advancing freedom had the potential to lead women into sexual promiscuity and to undermine the existing social order.[47] As a result, beauty pageants developed into rituals designed to harness and control the "immaterial powers" of young women. The awarding of a title linked the holder to the sponsoring institution and imposed a requirement that she properly represent the community and its values.[48]

Two examples from the 1920s illustrate how competitions centered on beauty and/or popularity functioned to control both the emergent sexuality of girls and the extant but as yet latent potential of young women. The Queen of Beauty competition described at the start of this chapter demonstrated the way the community employed the public ritual of the beauty pageant in order to establish appropriate roles even before a girl had reached marriageable age. The second contest, a newspaper pageant framed as a popularity contest, aimed to reorient the behavior of young women before they deviated too sharply from appropriate female norms.

As an American-born Spanish girl of Galician parents, Mercedes Anca embodied all of the gender, regional, and national traditions central to the community's sense of itself. The society organized the Queen of Beauty event so as to highlight each of these traditions in different ways, although with a particular emphasis on gender. Since the celebration was held in an intermediate space between the private and the public, it took on the characteristics of a domestic ritual. The ceremony crowning Anca closely resembled a wedding, and the ritual became representative of the bonds connecting the young woman to her broader community. Although too young to be truly married, Anca nonetheless was approaching an age where such a notion was not unrealistic. Given the uneven distribution of men and women in the Village's Spanish colony, competition for female partners was intense. Young women rarely made it to the end of their teens before marrying.[49] Carmen Díaz, Mercedes's sister, gave birth to her first child just a few months after her eighteenth birthday; she had become pregnant while still only seventeen years old.

The event began with a procession and ended with Anca on display at the center of the ritual surrounded by a "court of honor." Once named, a crown was placed on her head and she received a bouquet of flowers. Many of the gifts awarded to the queen seemed of the sort typically given to a woman by a suitor or spouse: jewelry, perfume, and other objects designed to enhance her physical appearance. As part of her winnings, Anca even earned a honeymoon-like two-week vacation at a Catskills resort called the Glenbrook Hotel.[50] The Queen of Beauty event also featured dancing with music played by three different orchestras. The selection of bands reflected the multiple identities on display. A Galician ensemble called Os Novos Trinta allowed for the performance of traditional regional dances while La Regional Española played more widely popular Spanish music. Finally, guests jived to that most American of genres—jazz—thanks to the sounds of the Virginia Six.[51]

The symbolic joining of the girl to the community channeled her sexual potential into the service of the patriarchal family. Families needed to produce future generations so that the colony could survive. The belief by Spanish men that motherhood served as the foundation of all cultural tradition can be seen in a letter published by *La Prensa* in 1928. The note also confirmed the inherent power of women and explained why asserting control over procreation was deemed of such vital importance. The author, quoting from an article in the journal *Guide of Galicia,* illustrates how multiple layers of identity all traced back to women. A person's fundamental sense of community, he wrote, came from the mother, who, as the "sacred receptacle of our most pure endearments, is the heart of the *patria* from which radiate our affections for those others, the family, the neighborhood, the province, the region, the nationality . . . with diminishing intensity of feeling in relation to the distance [from the mother]".[52]

Pageants contain an implicit transaction in which the community places responsibilities and constraints on female behavior in exchange for public recognition and sometimes a platform to speak. Such events generate symbolic inversions where the powerless are given a temporary authority usually denied them.[53] The granting of the royal title and other honors elevated Mercedes Anca into a figure of supposed authority. The process of symbolic inversion also played itself out in the physical space of the event hall. Socially important families of the community purchased box seats at the center of the ballroom. Such locations were reserved for those with enough wealth or prominence to afford them. La Prensa confirmed the group's status by publishing the list of families seated in this prominent area, and the Ancas were not among them. Nevertheless, her election as Queen of Beauty allowed Mercedes Anca entry into this socially powerful territory. Following her coronation she was seated next to the president of the association in the box located at the very heart of the physical and social space. Being placed in the middle of the room also put Anca at the center of the community's attention. Her role carried with it some privilege but also put her in a position where the community could scrutinize and evaluate her actions. At another event in 1926, Anca had been tasked to distribute medals to the association's soccer team. Apparently, she had failed to properly do so the year before and as a result was publically chastised in the pages of La Prensa.[54] The incident reveals how even such ostensibly honorific titles carried with them an actual/physical responsibility to the larger community to uphold its values and expectations.

The Galicia Sporting Club was not the only organization to sponsor competitions reflecting the performance of various traditions and revealing how the community sought to impose control over women. One of the most visible events of the decade took place in the spring of 1926 and was co-sponsored by the Pro-Cuba Committee and La Prensa. The "Popularity Contest" featured working girls from different Spanish-speaking nations competing to be elected queen of the Festival of Flowers. The goal in this case was not to harness the emerging sexual potential of girls but rather to restrain young adult women who seemed in danger of pursuing lives that did not reflect traditional roles centered on domesticity. In this newspaper pageant all of the contestants worked outside the home, and many lacked a protecting male presence since they lived in homes with absent fathers and none admitted to having a boyfriend or spouse.[55]

To enter La Prensa's Popularity Contest, the young woman herself or a sponsor submitted information about the candidate's family, job, and personality traits. The initial call also asked for a photograph and indicated that the Pro-Cuba committee would contact the women to arrange a personal interview. The all-male committee members decided what candidates would be included in the competition, and it was announced that some applicants had been rejected for unspecified reasons. Each day during the month of April the newspaper published a ballot that readers could fill out with the name of a contestant before returning it to the paper. In a telling gesture, the paper felt it necessary to confirm that women could also cast ballots. The top vote getter of each nationality continued to the final round, where the woman with the highest total was crowned queen.[56] During the next few weeks *La Prensa* ran front-page profiles and photographs of most of the contestants as well as brief stories containing updates and information about the competition. According to the newspaper, the contest quickly became one of the most popular and talked-about events in the history of the Spanish-speaking colony. Such a claim may not be an exaggeration, since by the end of the competition readers of *La Prensa* had submitted just over 160,000 votes, a figure close to the total of the entire Spanish-speaking population of the city.[57] Ultimately, twenty-seven women participated in the general competition, and eight became finalists. Spain had the most candidates, with seven; followed by Puerto Rico, with four; and Mexico, with three. Other women came from Cuba, Colombia, Argentina, Venezuela, and the Dominican Republic. The winner, Lilly Martínez, was Cuban and the runner-up, Pilar Fuentes, was Spanish.[58]

The profiles and stories published in the newspaper contain important details about the candidates and their lives but also reflect the concerns and interests of the committee who selected them. In many ways the candidates seem to have been chosen to signify ideal types who would have broad appeal. As in other forms of pageants, the contestants represented qualities the community prized and deemed most worthy of celebrating and preserving. Such values related directly to the contestant's physical appearance but also included personality traits and attitudes. In addition to representing their homeland in the contest, many of the young Spanish women embodied regional identities. The descriptions often praised them for their perceived faithfulness to certain regional characteristics. The paper called Leonor Menéndez y Díaz a "typical Asturian woman" and labeled Manuela Escariz authentically Galician. From Valencia, a region described as being famous for flowers, fruit, and gorgeous women came María Satorres, whom the paper characterized as "very young and much more beautiful than young."[59]

In general, the profiles of the Spanish contestants were longer than those of other countries, and the only other contestant said to fully embody her nationality was Esther Gómez de la Vega from Argentina. This could represent a bias toward European contestants as Argentina, with its large immigrant Spanish and Italian population, was often considered the most European of the Latin American countries.[60] The contest seemed to reflect the way that Spanish societies negotiated institutions and activities that aimed to link all nationalities into a single Spanish-speaking community. Despite the growing imbalance in the population of peninsular immigrants and those from the Americas, Spanish groups sought to lead and control the unified organizations. The predominance of Spanish contestants and the attention given to them could also illustrate the latent tensions that existed between the peninsular community and those from Latin America. Despite references to an often racialized hispano identity, some members of the Spanish community increasingly came to view Puerto Ricans as nonwhite. Such attitudes often resolved themselves in the discriminatory behavior of some societies and helped prevent the formation of a single common social organization.[61]

Many of the descriptions invoked characteristics often linked to proper femininity, such as kindness, modesty, and likeability. At other times *La Prensa* praised a Cuban and Dominican contestant for being especially beautiful. Through participation in such a public competition the young unmarried women were transformed, not only into symbols of community values, but also into commodities themselves. In a sense the contest advertised the sexual availability of the women as the newspaper itself acknowledged by informing readers that if they desired to communicate with a candidate, they should send a request to the committee. At the same time the profiles stressed that though they were unattached, the women remained essentially chaste. A few declared that they did not wish to have a boyfriend or had stayed single because they had not yet met the ideal partner. One even reportedly gave a look of terror when asked if she had a boyfriend. Sometimes the stories emphasized that the women preferred the company of Spanish speakers or liked Americans only as friends.[62] Such statements indicated that once married they would fulfill their obligation to preserve and perpetuate Spanish-speaking cultures and traditions.[63] In the case of Pilar Fuentes, from

Salamanca, the descriptions linked a regional and ethnic authenticity to sexual wholesomeness. The paper described Fuentes as "an authentic Spanish girl" whose perfect husband would be of Spanish descent, and because of this attitude she "remained pure from her head to her feet."[64]

Some articles worked to connect the women to domesticity. The profiles of most candidates described their families including any siblings who were married or still at home. Candidates won praise for their helpfulness and diligence. Other stories subverted the impression of the women as leading lives in the public sphere. On May 4, 1926, for example, *La Prensa* contained an article describing an "intimate gathering" hosted by a widow. Young men and women gathered in honor of Lillian Soneira, who had been chosen to represent Mexico in the final round of voting. The event brought the women together with men but in a culturally safe place. The home functioned as another intermediate space between the public and private. Since her mother and sister were also in attendance, the party reconnected Soneira with domesticity by locating the performance of national and gendered identities into a familial space.[65]

The majority of candidates announced that dancing was one of their favorite pastimes. For many immigrant parents in the first half of the twentieth century, dancing represented a pernicious and dangerous force corrupting modern youth. Historian Sarah Chinn argues that the combination of economic independence, delayed marriage, and the rapidly expanding commercial amusement industry created the modern adolescent. For these young adults dance halls became "the space of adolescent independence, of fun and heterosociality, of flirting, of asserting a specific kind of urban American identity."[66] Since the women in the newspaper contest shared all of the characteristics of the young people Chinn studied, it is possible that many Spanish adults felt such activities threatened not only their sexual honor but also their ethnic heritage. One way to combat the danger was to provide the young women with an opportunity to indulge their passion for dancing while insuring that the venue and the partners could be carefully controlled. A group called Club La Prensa held just such a dance at a Spanish society hall in Brooklyn. Young employees of the paper had formed the organization and likely represented appropriate escorts for the competitors. The event featured poetry as well as exhibitions of traditional dances including flamenco and tango.[67] In this way the activities directed young women toward both socially and culturally appropriate behaviors and company.

As with the ritual that resulted in the selection of Mercedes Anca as Queen of Beauty, the coronation of Lilly Martínez also had characteristics associated with wedding ceremonies.[68] The event took place in the Grand Ballroom of the Waldorf Astoria Hotel in Manhattan, and the decorations included the flags of all Spanish-speaking nations as well as large numbers of flowers. Although the Pro-Cuba committee was all male, a special women's section had been formed to organize different aspects of the ceremony. Once again the selective inclusion of women and the nature of the ritual transformed the public space of the ballroom into an intermediate space. The event began with a procession of important people representing different aspects of the community. First came military personnel from the New York garrison along with trumpeters. Next, the Flowers Committee appeared, each member holding a different bloom symbolizing each of the eight finalists. The six ladies of the Escort Committee came next, wearing pale blue dresses. The flag bearers of the Pro-Cuba committee directly preceded the arrival of Martínez, who was followed by maids of honor carrying bouquets of flowers. As if to further link the coronation to matrimony, the queen wore a specially designed white dress. The male leaders of the Pro-Cuba committee walked next along with consular officials from each of the nations represented in the contest. Members of the various women's committees who organized the ceremony followed, and finally came people selected by each of the finalists.[69]

As in the earlier occasion celebrating Mercedes Anca, the event showcased Lilly Martínez as a symbol of the community, not only of Cuba but also the whole family of Spanish-speaking nations. The music and entertainment too reflected the multiple cultures on display. Performers from Mexico, Spain, and Chile sang songs, and the Hawaiian band that played music from "the land of volcanoes and palm trees" was reportedly a big hit. The long article recapping the event that appeared in La Prensa clearly stated how the ceremony had brought all members of the colony together "from the luxuriously dressed lady of the aristocracy to the simple working girl, and from the highest representative officials to the most humble laborers." Such diverse people came to be united not only in a celebration of their shared cultural heritage but also in a new American context. According to La Prensa, the event signified a true "demonstration of democratic fellowship." Speeches given by men at the ceremony also reinforced the idea of the event as a site for the performance, not only of national and supranational identities, but also gendered ones. Felipe Taboada, the consul general of Cuba, praised the representatives of "the peoples of noble Spain" and other nations by high-lighting the stereotypically feminine traits of "charm, likability and virtue."[70]

During the 1920s Spanish societies such as the Casa de Galicia used the intermediate spaces of the clubhouse and other venues to reflect a multiplic-ity of emerging identities. Some were traditional ones, rooted in the regional and national origins of first-generation immigrants, while others showed the complex process of assimilation into American culture and a desire to reach out to other Spanish speakers.[71] All of these identities, however, posited the maintenance of proper gender roles for women as central to the perpetua-tion of traditions. As a result, the associations sponsored a variety of events where all of these identities could be performed. Some of these activities, such as the Queen of Beauty pageant or the Popularity Contest, developed into elaborate rituals but the dances, banquets, and events that took place on a daily or weekly basis were likely far more important. It was here that the community attempted to define and enforce what they believed to be proper feminine actions, attitudes, and traits.

Although the society halls often accommodated events designed to reaf-firm existing hierarchies of gendered power, they could also be spaces where authority was contested. Despite the strong patriarchal nature of the com-munity, women could and did assert real agency beyond the symbolic inver-sion of the pageants and contests. In February 1928 *La Prensa* published a short note describing a visit from the Casa de Galicia's newly organized "Spanish Ladies Pro-Casa de Galicia Committee." The group's governing board included Mercedes Anca and Electra Díaz, who both served as mem-bers at large. The women came to the newspaper to talk about their upcom-ing projects including plans to offer a variety of classes for girls and to raise money in order to purchase a gift for the Galician society. Since the gift was to be presented to the Casa from the entire Spanish community, the women solicited donations from other societies and from business owners such as Valentín Aguirre, who gave twenty dollars, more than any other person listed. It appears that the colony responded generously—Juan Anca chipped in five dollars—and within a few months the committee had purchased a piano.[72]

By early summer, however, tensions developed between the leadership of the women's section and the all-male governing board of the Casa de Galicia. The row culminated with the publication in *La Prensa* of a long open letter written by the society's president, Juan Gallego. In the text, the association's board sought to reassert control of the women by publically chastising them. According to the letter, Gallego initiated the formation of the committee by inviting a group of women to meet with the goal of creating a Casa de Galicia Ladies' Section. After he left the building, the women proceeded to organize the group on their own, even choosing a different name. The relationship between the ladies' committee and the leadership of the society quickly deteriorated. Gallego wrote that the board at no time had authorized them to collect money for any purpose. He also claimed that the women had visited *La Prensa* without the knowledge or approval of anyone at the Casa de Galicia. The ladies' section had no power to initiate programs; instead, all activities needed to be submitted to the organization's board for approval. Gallego believed that by prematurely advertising the committee's actions, the women had "sinned by indiscretion." To make matters worse, the ladies had violated other regulations too, including opening a bank account without prior authorization. Gallego seemed especially concerned that only the president and treasurer of the ladies' committee could withdraw money from the account. To the male leadership of the association such disregard for the rules was "a question of social and moral order and discipline."[73]

The usurpation of traditional male authority over the activities and finances of the committee angered the society's administrators, and they moved quickly to reprimand the women. The board of the Casa de Galicia met with the leadership of the group to present an ultimatum: the committee could submit to the authority of the board, or they could disband. When confronted with this demand, the president, treasurer, and several other women protested "violently" and abruptly left. The remaining members of the committee then voted to depose the current president and treasurer and authorized a statement saying that those women had acted without the support of the majority. They also agreed to send a letter petitioning the board not to dissolve the committee and asking for permission to replace the ousted leaders. Gallego included the names of the eight women who had agreed to these demands but at no point did he specifically identify the dissidents, though they would already have been widely known.[74] Indeed, the names of the president, Enriqueta de Borines, and treasurer, Concepción de Callejo, had been published in the earlier article describing the visit to the offices of *La Prensa*.[75] Gallego's decisions about whom to name and whom to leave out rewarded those who had submitted to the authority of the society and marginalized the women who remained outside its control.

These actions, however, did not end the controversy, because the committee's ex-officials refused to turn over the collected funds to either the reconstituted ladies' organization or to the casa itself. In the remainder of the published letter, Gallego described how attempts were made to convince the women to relinquish the funds. He claimed that although the society could have used legal means to compel them, they wished to avoid such unpleasant action. Despite this "courtesy," the women who "had declared rebellion" went ahead and purchased a piano. They had even had the nerve to contact the society's president, asking when the gift could be delivered. As a result, the executive claimed it had no choice but to refuse the piano, since it "would enter into this Casa bringing notes of insubordination and discord."[76]

For Spanish immigrants in the 1920s the creation of associations centered on regional origin was an important part of efforts aimed at retaining identities, and they believed that without such support their traditional heritage would be lost. The anti-immigrant legislation passed by Congress early in the decade, along with the onset of the Great Depression and the effects of the Spanish Civil War, ended the golden age of the associations.[77] The twin blows of economic hardship and military conflict damaged the stability of many Spanish associations as membership levels declined and several, including the Centro Catalán and the Centro Valenciano, were forced to close.[78] A similar fate seems to have befallen the Casa de Galicia, as it sold its clubhouse building in 1932 for just $77,000.[79] Eventually a new Centro Galicia would be formed but only after the Spanish Civil War, and its new headquarters was located outside of Greenwich Village. It is unclear what, if any, role the Anca family played in the new organization. In a history of the Centro hosted on the society's website, Juan Zapata relates that the list of founding members has been lost and does not appear in the organization's archives.[80]

The lives of the Anca and Díaz families again reflected some of these broader trends within the Spanish colony. By the end of the decade, they had left Manhattan and purchased a home together in South Brooklyn valued at $12,000 (about $159,000 today). Over the course of the decade, Greenwich Village had undergone a dramatic transformation. Dozens of large concrete and steel buildings had been constructed largely to house the neighborhood's growing graphic arts industry.[81] Such changes directly affected the area's Spanish colony. Road construction along Seventh Avenue and the opening of the Holland Tunnel greatly increased the amount of traffic into the Village. The needs of the expanding transportation network forcibly broke up the Spanish community by destroying the tenements where many had lived.[82] Such disruptions might have influenced the Anca family's decision to abandon the city. The building of an elevated railroad on West Street, about a block from where they lived, was completed only in 1927. Other projects, including the construction of a freight terminal and warehouse as well as a gas station and garage, happened right on the street where both families lived.[83]

The family's decision to relocate could also be seen as part of what has been described as "a tremendous working-class exodus" out of Manhattan during these years. Many of the former residents of the Village cited "a search for better living conditions" as the main impetus for the move. Indeed, a study conducted in 1942–43 called the western portion of the Ancas' new Brooklyn neighborhood "one of New York's choicest residential areas."[84] Although a Spanish community had long existed in Brooklyn, the Anca-Díaz residence was located in South Brooklyn and not within this traditional area. Despite remaining connected to the Spanish colony and attending society events, the family's neighbors were now mostly Italians, Scandinavians, and native-born Americans. The 1930 United States Census showed that only one other Spanish family lived within several blocks of the Ancas.[85] As a result, the Anca family, whose experiences closely mirrored that of other Spanish immigrants, slowly began to withdraw from that traditional world. They had moved out of the Village, and by 1940 Juan Anca had died. Mercedes Anca, who had once symbolized the ideal of Spanish-American girlhood, married a man of Italian, not Spanish, descent. She along with her niece Electra Díaz, who also married outside the Spanish community, had grown up to join a new ethnic American community.

NOTES

1. "El festival del Galicia Sporting C.," *La Prensa*, April 11, 1925; "Sociedades Hispanas," *La Prensa*, April 14, 1925.
2. Loretta Baldassar and Donna R. Gabaccia, "Home, Family, and the Italian Nation in a Mobile World," in *Intimacy and Italian Migration: Gender and Domestic*

Lives in a Mobile World, ed. Loretta Baldassar and Donna R. Gabaccia (New York: Fordham University Press, 2010), 3, 17.

3. Katy Gardner and Ralph Grillo, "Transnational Households and Ritual: An Overview," *Global Networks* 2, no. 3 (2002): 185–186, 187.

4. Gardner and Grillo, "Transnational Households and Ritual," 183.

5. Brian D. Bunk, "Boxer in New York: Spaniards, Puerto Ricans and Attempts to Construct a Hispano Race," *Journal of American Ethnic History* 35, no. 4 (Summer 2016): 34, 36.

6. It is unclear whether he came from the city or the province of La Coruña. Unless otherwise noted biographical information on the Anca family in this article comes from the following: Ancestry.com, *1920 United States Federal Census* [database online] (Provo, UT: Ancestry.com Operations Inc., 2010); Ancestry.com, *1930 United States Federal Census* [database online] (Provo, UT: Ancestry.com Operations Inc., 2010); Ancestry.com, *1940 United States Federal Census* [database online] (Provo, UT: Ancestry.com Operations Inc., 2012); Ancestry.com, *New York State Census, 1915* [database online] (Provo, UT: Ancestry.com Operations Inc., 2012); Ancestry.com, *New York, Passenger Lists, 1820–1957* [database online] (Provo, UT: Ancestry.com Operations Inc., 2010); Ancestry.com, *U.S. City Directories, 1821–1989* [database online] (Provo, UT: Ancestry.com Operations Inc., 2011); "United States Social Security Death Index," *FamilySearch*, https://familysearch.org/ (accessed May 24, 2013).

7. The name Maria Antonio Diaz Vasquez is recorded on the passenger list, but it is likely an Anglicized version of María Antonia Díaz Vázquez.

8. The exact figure was 743,597. Moisés Llordén Miñambres, "Las asociaciones españolas de emigrantes," in *Arte, cultura y sociedad en la emigración española a America*, ed. María Cruz Morales Saro and Moisés Llordén Miñambres (Oviedo, Spain: Universidad de Oviedo, 1992), 14.

9. Anca once again fit the profile of a Galician immigrant to the United States. About one in three Spanish immigrants to New York were from Galicia, and many of them came from towns and regions in the province of Coruña. The vast majority, 89 percent, were literate. Nancy Pérez Rey, "Unha achega á emigración galega a Nova York," *Estudos Migratorios* 1, 2 (2008): 34, 38, 40.

10. Caroline F. Ware, *Greenwich Village 1920–1930: A Comment on American Civilization in the Post-War Years* (Boston: Houghton Mifflin Company, 1935), 40, 227, 228.

11. Jerónima Echeverria, *Home Away from Home: A History of Basque Boardinghouses* (Reno: University of Nevada Press, 1999), 45–47.

12. Gloria Totoricagüena, *The Basques of New York* (Reno: University of Nevada Center for Basque Studies, 2004), 73–74, 76.

13. Landmarks Preservation Commission, "Designation List 444 LP-2419" (2011), 7, www.nyc.gov/html/lpc/downloads/pdf/reports/2419.pdf (accessed May 30, 2013).

14. "Lago's Private Bank is closed by State," *New York Times*, July 4, 1928; "Mancuso on Bench . . . ," "Business Records," *New York Times*, July 8, 1928.

15. Interview notes, P. Meléndez, folder: Spanish Section, Caroline F. Ware Papers, Box 54: Ethnic Studies, Greenwich Village Study, Franklin D. Roosevelt Library, Hyde Park, New York (hereafter, Caroline F. Ware Papers).

16. Studies have been made on Spanish immigrant communities in Argentina, Cuba, Mexico, and the United States: José C. Moya, *Cousins and Strangers: Spanish Immigrants in Buenos Aires* (Berkeley: University of California Press, 1998); Michael Kenny, "Twentieth–Century Spanish Expatriates in Cuba: A Sub-Culture?" *Anthropological Quarterly* 34, no. 2 (April 1961): 85–93; Michael Kenny, "Twentieth-Century Expatriates in Mexico: An Urban Sub-Culture" *Anthropological Quarterly* 35, no. 4 (October 1962): 169–80; Ana María Varela-Lago, "Conquerors, Immigrants, Exiles: The Spanish Diaspora in the United States (1848–1948)" (PhD diss., University of California, San Diego, 2008).

17. In 1925 many of the clubs organized the Liga Hispano Americana de Balompié (Spanish American Soccer League). See Brian D. Bunk, *"Sardinero* and Not a Can of Sardines: Soccer and Spanish Ethnic Identities in New York City during the 1920s," *Journal of Urban History* 41, no. 3 (May 2015): 444–59.

18. Varela-Lago, "Conquerors, Immigrants, Exiles," table 3, p. 136. By 1930, more Spaniards lived in New York than in any other American state. Varela-Lago, "Conquerors, Immigrants, Exiles," table 5, p. 138.

19. "Tribuna Libre," *La Prensa*, January 2, 1923.

20. "Galicia Buys Clubhouse," *New York Times*, October 20, 1927. Contemporary value computation from www.measuringworth.com (accessed June 26, 2013).

21. Lizabeth Cohen, *Making a New Deal: Industrial Workers in Chicago, 1919–1939* (Cambridge: Cambridge University Press, 1990), 55.

22. Gabriel Haslip-Viera, "The Evolution of the Latino Community in New York City: Early Nineteenth Century to the Present," in *Latinos in New York: Communities in Transition*, ed. Gabriel Haslip-Viera and Sherrie L. Baver (Notre Dame, IN: University of Notre Dame Press, 1996), 8.

23. Cohen, *Making a New Deal*, 54, 71–72.

24. "Hoy inaugura la Casa de Galicia su nuevo y espléndido edificio social," *La Prensa*, July 7, 1928.

25. Caroline F. Ware Papers.

26. Ware, *Greenwich Village*, 140, 141, 318, 439.

27. A Panamanian graduate student named Próspero Meléndez completed most of the interviews using a form with a set group of questions. From his written notes, the majority seem to have been conducted in Spanish. Ware refers to fifty interviews in her book but the research files contain sixty-three records, though

some are only partially complete and a few others were with non-Spaniards. Ware, *Greenwich Village*, appendix A, p. 434; Caroline F. Ware Papers.

28. Caroline F. Ware Papers.

29. The term was inspired by Jaine Beswick, who identified something similar in contemporary Britain. Jaine Beswick, "Galician-Spanish-British? Migrant Identification Practices, Transnationalism and Invisibility in Guildford, England," in *Contemporary Galician Cultural Studies: Between the Local and the Global*, ed. Kirsty Hooper and Manuel Puga Moruxa (New York: Modern Language Association of America, 2011), 127.

30. Leigh S. Roethke, "The Spanish Hour: Imagining and Selling Spain in 1920s America" (PhD diss., University of Minnesota, 2009), 3–4, 7, 32–42, 130. See also James D. Fernández, "The Discovery of Spain in New York, circa 1930," in *Nueva York, 1613–1945*, ed. Edward J. Sullivan (London: Scala, 2010), 217–33.

31. Roethke, "The Spanish Hour," 119, 124–25.

32. "El arte glorioso de Ignacio Zuloaga triunfa por su regio vigor, su colorido y sobriedad," *La Prensa*, January 22, 1925. Other stories appeared on January 20, 21, and 23.

33. Roethke, "The Spanish Hour," 145.

34. The Galician word *saudade* captures this feeling. John P. Dever and Aileen Dever, *The Poetry and Prose of Rosalía de Castro* (Lewiston, ME: Edwin Mellen Press, 2010), iii.

35. "Hoy inaugura la Casa de Galicia su nuevo y espléndido edificio social," *La Prensa*, July 7, 1928. On the popularity of such imagery to Spanish immigrants in the United States see Varela-Lago, "Conquerors, Immigrants, Exiles," especially ch. 2.

36. "Sociedades Hispanas," *La Prensa*, March 1, 1927.

37. Roethke writes extensively on the popularity of the mantón de Manila, "The Spanish Hour," 54–62 and 190–212.

38. "Sociedades Hispanas," *La Prensa*, March 1, 1927. Díaz's suit was probably a hand-me-down from her aunt Mercedes, who had worn a similar outfit to an event in 1925. On that night, however, another girl took the prize for a costume featuring the Spanish coat of arms. "Sociedades Hispanas," *La Prensa*, April 14, 1925.

39. Ware, *Greenwich Village*, 404, 409.

40. Gerald Fitzgerald, "Spanish Customs Preserved in New York," August 14, 1939, WPA Federal Writers' Project, NYC Unit, Spanish Book, Municipal Archives, New York City, New York. Fitzgerald may have been influenced by popular stereotypes as he wrote that such attitudes came from Spain's "Moors."

41. Amarilis, "La locura del jazz," *La Prensa*, January 20, 1925.

42. "Regina Quiñones, desaparecida ocho días, oye la llamada de 'La Prensa,'" *La Prensa*, March 16, 1926.

43. Coleen Ballerino Cohen and Richard Wilk with Beverly Stoeltje, "Introduction: Beauty Queens on the Global Stage," in *Beauty Queens on the Global Stage*, ed. Coleen Ballerino Cohen and Richard Wilk with Beverly Stoeltje (New York: Routledge, 1996), 2.

44. Lois W. Banner, *American Beauty* (Chicago: Chicago University Press, 1983), 250, 254.

45. Cohen and Wilk, "Introduction," 4.

46. Banner, *American Beauty*, 249.

47. Paula Fass, *The Damned and the Beautiful: American Youth in the 1920s* (New York: Oxford University Press, 1977), 23, 24.

48. Beverly Stoeltje, "The Snake Charmer Queen: Ritual Competition and Signification in American Festival," in *Beauty Queens on the Global Stage*, ed. Coleen Ballerino Cohen and Richard Wilk with Beverly Stoeltje (New York: Routledge, 1996), 14, 26.

49. Ware, *Greenwich Village*, 41–42.

50. The Glenbrook, located in Shandakan, New York, was one of many Spanish-owned or -operated resorts in the area. The hotel had been built in 1888 and had room for 150 guests. "Summer Hotel Brings $17,000 at Auction," *Catskill Mountain News*, February 11, 1944. Thanks to Laura Miller for the reference.

51. "El festival del Galicia Sporting C.," *La Prensa*, April 11, 1925; "Sociedades Hispanas," *La Prensa*, April 14, 1925.

52. Letter of José M. Gil, "De nuestros lectores," *La Prensa*, December 25, 1928. Ellipsis in the original.

53. Stoeltje, "The Snake Charmer Queen," 14, 15, 27, 28.

54. "Sociedades Hispanas," *La Prensa*, September 21, 1926.

55. For example, "La segunda candidata al Certamen de Simpatía de Obreritas, española," *La Prensa*, March 9, 1926; "Vizcaya presenta una candidata al Certamen de Simpatía de Obreritas," *La Prensa*, March 18, 1926; "Dos candidatas colombianas en el Certamen de Simpatía de Obreritas," *La Prensa*, March 31, 1926; Lorrin Thomas, *Puerto Rican Citizen: History and Political Identity in Twentieth-Century New York City* (Chicago: University of Chicago Press, 2010), 34.

56. "La coronación de la triunfadora en el Concurso de Simpatía sera el 15 de Mayo," *La Prensa*, March 4, 1926; "Un gran entusiasmo popular acoge al Concurso de Simpatía iniciado," *La Prensa*, March 2, 1926; "La segunda candidata al Certamen de Simpatía de Obreritas, española," *La Prensa*, March 9, 1928.

57. In comparison, a poll from the year before to determine the most popular soccer player born in a Spanish-speaking country drew only 31,172 votes. "El jugador F. González quedó clasificado en 1er. lugar entre los once jugadores más populares," *La Prensa*, July 20, 1925. Exact population figures are open to debate.

Lawrence R. Chenault, *The Puerto Rican Migrant in New York City* (1938; repr., New York: Russell and Russell, 1970) gives a figure of 136,615 by 1930, while Virginia E. Sánchez Korrol, *From Colonia to Community: The History of Puerto Ricans in New York City* (Berkeley: University of California Press, 1994) cites (page 59) contemporary surveys indicating that 100,000 Puerto Ricans alone resided in the city by 1926. See also Haslip-Viera, "The Evolution of the Latino Community in New York City," 4, 5.

   58. I was unable to locate profiles of all the candidates, including one for Lilly Martínez. In part this was due to missing issues in the newspaper archives, but it also had to do with inconsistencies in *La Prensa*'s reporting. Some names on early lists of candidates are not included on the final vote tally and vice versa. "Aumenta por días el entusiasmo por el Certamen de Simpatía para obreritas," *La Prensa*, March 6, 1926; "Ocho candidatas al Certamen de Simpatía elegidas en el escrutario," *La Prensa*, April 17, 1926; "La cubanita Lilly Martínez está al frente en el Certamen de Simpatía," *La Prensa*, April 27, 1926.

   59. "Asturias da su candidata para al Certamen de Simpatía de Obreritas," *La Prensa*, March 16, 1926; "Galicia da su candidata para el Certamen de Simpatía de Obreritas," *La Prensa*, March 20, 1926; "Valencia da su candidata para el Certamen de Simpatía de Obreritas," *La Prensa*, April 1, 1926.

   60. It could also be a consequence of the lack of sources; see note 58. "La Argentina da su candidata al Certamen de Simpatía de Obreritas," *La Prensa*, March 23, 1926; "Aumenta por días el entusiasmo por el Certamen de Simpatía para obreritas," *La Prensa*, March 6, 1926 and "La capital mejicana da candidata al certamen de simpatía de obreritas," *La Prensa*, March 13, 1926; "Dos candidatas colombianas en el Certamen de Simpatía de Obreritas," *La Prensa*, March 31, 1926; "Valencia da su candidata para el Certamen de Simpatía de Obreritas," *La Prensa*, April 1, 1926.

   61. Bunk, "Boxer in New York," 36, 49–50.

   62. "Vizcaya presenta una candidata al Certamen de Simpatía de Obreritas," *La Prensa*, March 18, 1926; "La capital mejicana da candidata al certamen de simpatía de obreritas," *La Prensa*, March 13, 1926; "Méjico da una candidata para el Certamen de Simpatía," *La Prensa*, March 11, 1926.

   63. Thomas, *Puerto Rican Citizen*, 34.

   64. "La segunda candidata al Certamen de Simpatía de Obreritas, española," *La Prensa*, March 9, 1928.

   65. "La coronación de la reina del Certamen de Simpatía tendrá brillante sin rival," *La Prensa*, May 4, 1926.

   66. Sarah Chinn, *Inventing Modern Adolescence: The Children of Immigrants in Turn-of-the-Century America* (New Brunswick, NJ: Rutgers University Press, 2009), 5, 103–4.

67. "Las candidatas al Certamen de Simpatía asistirán al baile del Club 'La Prensa,'" *La Prensa*, March 20, 1926.

68. The festivities actually included a number of different events. The announcement of the winner took place at the Sixty-Second Street Armory, but the coronation ceremony itself was held at the Waldorf Astoria Hotel. The committee also scheduled a garden party and river excursion for future dates. "Mañana se cierra la admisión de votos del Certamen de Simpatía," *La Prensa*, April 13, 1926.

69. "La coronación de la reina del Certamen de Simpatía tendrá brillante sin rival," *La Prensa*, May 4, 1926; "La reina y las damas del Certamen de Simpatía presidirán el festival," *La Prensa*, May 6, 1926.

70. "Una nutridísima concurrencia aplaudió delirante y disfrutó sin res . . . [newspaper damaged], *La Prensa*, May 11, 1926. The article begins on the front page although in the copy on microfilm I consulted, most of the first section had been torn away. The article continues and is intact on a subsequent page. All of the quotations and most of the information cited here came from the interior story.

71. On the relationships between Spaniards and other Spanish speakers, especially Puerto Ricans, see Bunk, "Boxer in New York."

72. "Sociedades Hispanas," *La Prensa*, February 13, 1928; "Sociedades Hispanas," *La Prensa*, March 28, 1928.

73. "El piano regalado a la 'Casa de Galicia' crea un conflicto," *La Prensa*, July 5, 1928.

74. "El piano regalado a la 'Casa de Galicia'."

75. The names of Mercedes Anca and Electra Díaz appear in the February article but not in the letter published in July. As girls of just fourteen and ten years old, they probably had little do to with the events. "Sociedades Hispanas," *La Prensa*, February 13, 1928.

76. "El piano regalado a la 'Casa de Galicia.'" Apparently, the piano remained with one of the rebellious women until just over a year later, when the affair flared up once again. In July 1929 a group of twenty-eight men signed an open letter protesting the pending donation of the piano to another Spanish society. The letter ran in the newspaper *Gráfico* because *La Prensa* had refused to publish it. The passage of time and a change in leadership at the Casa de Galicia seem to have encouraged a more conciliatory tone. They argued that the society's governing board and general membership had never officially rejected the gift. Instead they claimed that the now ex-president had exceeded his authority by refusing the piano. The letter continued by acknowledging that both sides had been at fault for creating the atmosphere of tension. The former president had been wrong to snub the women, but they did not own the piano and should have consulted those who donated money about its final disposition. Eventually they concluded that if an agreement could not be

reached, the piano should be donated to charity. It is not clear what happened to the piano. "Se protesta contra la donación del piano de Casa de Galicia al Centro Hispano," *Gráfico*, July 27, 1929.

77. Legislation passed in 1921 set Spanish annual quotas at 912. In 1924 it was revised downward to 131 before being altered again to 252 in 1929. Varela-Lago, "Conquerors, Immigrants, Exiles," note 12, p. 135.

78. Gerald Fitzgerald and Barney Conal, "Spanish Clubs and Societies in New York," WPA Federal Writers' Project, NYC Unit, Spanish Book, Municipal Archives, New York City, New York.

79. "Manhattan Plans Filed," *New York Times*, October 29, 1932.

80. Manuel Zapata, "La Historia de Casa Galicia" unpublished article, n.d., n.p., available at https://www.casagaliciany.com/historia.htm (accessed June 20, 2013). Despite Zapata's account, Fitzgerald and Conal, "Spanish Clubs and Societies in New York," wrote in 1939 that a Centro Gallego had been formed in 1933 and was headquartered at 153 Sixty-Fourth Street. According to Zapata, however, the society only acquired that building in the 1950s.

81. Stuart Waldman, *Maritime Mile: The Story of the Greenwich Village Waterfront* (New York: Mikaya Press / Greenwich Village Community Task Force, 2002), 50.

82. Ware, *Greenwich Village*, 15, 230.

83. Waldman, *Maritime Mile*, 51; Regina M. Kellerman, ed., *The Architecture of the Greenwich Village Waterfront* (New York: New York University Press, 1989), 65, 66.

84. Ware interviewed mostly Italians who had left the area, but it is likely the motives were equally true for Spanish families. Ware, *Greenwich Village*, 23, 29; *New York City Market Analysis* (New York: The New York Times Co., Daily Mirror Inc., Hearst Consolidated Publications Inc., 1943), www.1940snewyork.com (accessed May 5, 2013).

85. *1930 United States Federal Census* [database online] (Provo, UT: Ancestry.com Operations Inc., 2010).

6

MINERS FROM SPAIN TO ARIZONA COPPER CAMPS, 1880–1930

PHYLIS CANCILLA MARTINELLI

Serafín Arduengo was a teenager in 1919, when he left his village in Santander, Spain's northern mining region, now Cantabria. A *paisano's* (friend) letters lured him to Arizona in hopes of good wages in mining. The first leg of his journey was by a steamship headed for New York City. From New York Serafín traveled west by train and took a bus to Gila County, his final destination.[1] This route was different from that of many Spaniards heading to Arizona at that time who entered the United States via southern ports in Louisiana and Texas, or from Cuba or Mexico. However, in many ways Serafín certainly fits the profile of Spanish migrants to the United States in this period. According to Spanish historian Germán Rueda, around 70 percent of them were single men (or married men without their spouses). Eighty percent of them were aged between fifteen and fifty years old.[2]

Serafín had few skills when he arrived in Arizona, so he began working for the Miami Copper Company as a lowly mucker, shoveling ore in the Number Four shaft and earning some $4.20 per day. As a bachelor he likely lived with paisanos in a boardinghouse, such as the one managed by Angelina Bairo,

DOI: 10.5876/9781607327998.c006

which catered to immigrants from Italy and Spain.³ In 1930, he married Aurora Gómez, a Spanish widow also from Santander. Her first husband, Baldomero Cisterna, a Spanish merchant, had died in 1926.⁴

Serafín and Aurora were part of an unrecognized stream of Spanish immigrants who came to Arizona during the 1920s. By 1931 Serafín's lot had improved; he worked at the Miami Cleaning Company, exactly what he did is not mentioned, and he supported Aurora so she could be a housewife. Their son, Serafín, Jr., was born then; it is not known if the children from her first marriage lived with them.⁵

When speaking of Spaniards mining in the Southwest, images of *conquistadores* take precedence over those of wage workers: men such as Alvar Núñez Cabeza de Vaca searching for Cities of Gold as early as 1535; explorer Antonio de Espejo staking claims on rich copper ore veins in Arizona's Black Mountains in 1583; or Juan de Oñate finding rich silver ore in the Prescott Valley in 1598, even though the remote site was not mined until centuries later, in the 1880s.⁶ Spaniards are also credited with introducing metallurgy techniques, which were still used by early prospectors until modern technology and knowledge allowed large-scale corporate mining. Otis Young, for example, noted their contributions derived from a history of mining begun when Phoenicians and Romans extracted minerals from the Iberian Peninsula. The best-known Spanish techniques were the inexpensive and effective dry-washing method that used the *batea*, a conical pan rather than the flat typed used by others for panning gold; the *arrastra* to pulverize ore; and the *patio* process, an early chemical system able to refine minerals.⁷ This technology was superseded in the Progressive era by more sophisticated mining systems, which permitted large-scale mining of inferior ores. By the time Spanish immigrant workers arrived in Arizona to work in the mines, the historic contributions of Spaniards to early mining were practically forgotten. Their later contributions to mining and to ethnic history deserve to be acknowledged.

Introducing Spaniards into Arizona's early labor history serves to both "re-envision" Western history and to further diversify immigration history. A call for a new, more inclusive paradigm for Western history went out in 1991.⁸ As William Robbins notes in discussing David Emmon's book, *The Butte Irish*, "Emmon's study emphasizes that immigration and ethnicity, class consciousness, and industrialism are vital components to understanding the

West."[9] The inclusion of Spanish migrants also contributes to this new paradigm. The lack of attention to Spaniards extends beyond Western history. For example, immigration expert Vincent Parrillo's popular textbook offers an expanded catalog of "Other Hispanics," but he only briefly mentions the 275,000 immigrants from Spain who arrived in the United States since 1820.[10] Spanish historian Germán Rueda was unaware of the presence of Spanish miners in Arizona. He noted that while Arizona had interesting traces of the Spanish language and customs, this was not enough to attract Spanish emigration in the twentieth century.[11]

The migration of thousands of Spaniards to Arizona is often hidden. Their existence is frequently conflated in the documents with the much larger group of Mexican miners under general labels, such as "Spanish-surnamed" or "Spanish-speaking." In addition, some Mexican groups identified themselves as "Spanish Americans," which further muddies the waters. For example, in New Mexico by the 1920s Mexican origin people often used the term, regardless of their class, trying to create a more positive public label for themselves.[12] No single self-designation worked for all Mexicans; a fairly comprehensive list includes Mexican, Mexicano, Latin American, Spanish American, Latino, Hispanic, Hispano, Chicano, Mexican American, and American of Mexican descent.[13] Further complicating the recognition of Spanish miners in the West was the presence of Spanish Basques, a distinct ethnic subgroup in Spain with their own language. While they did migrate to parts of the West, their occupational niche was primarily sheepherding, not mining.[14]

In this chapter the terms for the different ethnic groups follow these definitions: "Anglos" describe both English-speaking native born and English-speaking white Protestant immigrants.[15] "EuroLatin" designates, when appropriate, Spaniards and Italians, following the work of Spanish economist Gabriel Tortella.[16] "Latin," as was used in this time period, includes Mexicans, Spaniards, and Italians. "Latino" is not used, to avoid confusion with today's use of the term.

THE GROWTH OF THE MODERN EXTRACTIVE INDUSTRY

Spaniards arrived in mining as a late but important addition to Arizona's labor force, as mining corporations in the early 1900s shifted to industrialized copper mining. The quest for gold and silver, begun by Spaniards in the sixteenth century, continued as Anglo treasure seekers combed Arizona's rugged mountains that sliced at an angle through the land. Once the Apache threat was curtailed, after the Civil War, explorers also found rich copper deposits previously overlooked in favor of more precious metals. The Arizona Territory experienced a boom in copper mining, when the mundane metal soared in price due to modern uses such as the telephone and in pipes. Copper can be spun into fine wire, will not rust, and is an excellent conductor of heat and electricity. While copper was first mined some 9,000 years ago, modern applications later turned it into a highly prized commodity.[17]

Technological advances allowed the use of low-paid workers as surface mining spread, which made low-grade ore profitable. Prominent among investors/inventors was Daniel C. Jackling. He discovered how to mine low-grade ore on a major scale with open-pit mining and milling the low-grade ores into profitable copper. His work began in Utah mines in Bingham Canyon and then expanded to Arizona. Production and profit soared. The extractive field needed and got, within a relatively short span of time, new technologies to refine and smelt copper ore, new transportation routes, and a new workforce of semiskilled, low-paid miners.

The initial need to ship copper from Arizona to England for refining that stifled early efforts to make Ajo, Arizona's, ore profitable, ended with the growth of train lines. A series of railroad lines were built to connect the territory's mineral wealth to major markets.[18] Small-time investors gave way to global companies with deep pockets. The United States–based Phelps Dodge mercantile company parlayed its early investments in Arizona mines into an international copper empire, while investors from Scotland, for example, supplied the capital to fund the growth of mines in Clifton, Arizona.[19]

The final piece needed to rocket Arizona's fabulous mineral wealth into national prominence was waves of Mexicans, Chinese, and Southern and Eastern Europeans arriving to the United States looking for work. By the 1900s the new extractive techniques allowed companies to reduce their need for highly skilled workers, such as Cornish miners. A multiethnic labor force filled the need for labor. These immigrants were often poor, uneducated, and willing to work for wages that undercut more skilled miners. Among these new arrivals was a significant group of Spanish laborers. Their numbers were small enough in 1900 that the group might be easily overlooked; but as the century progressed, Spanish migration increased. In 1910 Arizona had almost

TABLE 6.1. Southern European Immigrants in Arizona (1890–1920)

	1890		1900		1910		1920	
	Number	Percent	Number	Percent	Number	Percent	Number	Percent
Spanish	21	8	51	7	855	34	1,013	38
Greek	7	3	10	1	77	3	329	12
Italian	207	81	699	90	1,531	61	1,261	48
Portuguese	19	7	18	2	29	1	30	1
Total	254	100	778	100	2,492	100	2,633	100

Source: US Bureau of the Census, *Sixteenth Census of the United States* (1940); *Arizona. Characteristics of the Population*, Foreign-born White, 1910 to 1940, and including Total Foreign Born, 1850–1900, Origin of Birth, for the State, table 15. (Washington, DC: Government Printing Office, 1941). The designation of Southern Europeans as those from Greece, Italy, Spain, and Portugal is based on the 1940 Census, as are the percentages. Table compiled by author.

doubled in population (from 122,931 in 1900 to 204,354 in 1910). In the same period, the number of Spanish residents grew from 51 to 855. These numbers put them at 34 percent of the Southern Europeans, a group whose languages and cultures made them very distinctive from the dominant Anglo group[20] (see table 6.1).

ECONOMIC, POLITICAL, AND SOCIAL FACTORS IN SPANISH MIGRATION

Spaniards were pushed to emigrate by many factors. Economic stagnation was a major factor because Spain and other Mediterranean nations were behind industrializing Northern Europe, remaining basically agricultural. Modern agricultural techniques were still unused by poorer peasants who labored in poverty, as their ancestors had, making a living but not really advancing their families. Monies to support social services, such as education and health care, were diverted to Spain's bloated military budget. The nation's unsettled political system was another reason to leave. Napoleon invaded Spain in 1808; however, once the French were ousted, peace did not return. A Republic reigned briefly, followed by a restored constitutional monarchy and continued unrest. The main stream of migrants to first leave Spain went to rapidly emerging former Spanish colonies such as Argentina or those still under Spanish control: Cuba and Puerto Rico; Uruguay and Mexico received fewer numbers. The period between 1903 and 1914 saw one-twelfth of the population leave the Spanish heartland, due to increased agricultural problems such as the importation of cheap wheat and a plague of phylloxera attacking the vineyards.[21]

In the United States, Tampa, Florida, became a magnet for Spaniards who found work in cigar manufacturing. There they connected with Italians and Cubans of all races to form a unique Southern version of a tripartite class system, consisting of nonwhites, Latins, and Anglos.[22] Other Spaniards were attracted by recruiting agents looking for workers in American mines and agriculture. After the American Civil War some labor bosses wanted docile workers to replace freed blacks. Spaniards were recruited to work in Hawaiian sugar cane plantations. They were seen as tractable "white" labor, replacing Asian immigrants who did not take to plantation work.[23] West Virginia, too, came to rely on Spanish immigrants in its booming coal-mining and zinc industries.[24] Immigrants who found riches in the Americas returned home or wrote letters describing their success, thus establishing powerful immigrant networks.

I compiled data from fifty-three Spaniards, using information found in their petitions for naturalization. The data came from several mining counties in Arizona, and the petitions covered the period between 1901 and 1920. I found that most Spanish immigrants in the state emigrated from northern Spain. The regions of Galicia, Asturias, and Cantabria were known for mining iron and coal. As industrialization increased in Europe, Spain's coal deposits received the attention of foreign investors in the period from 1860 to 1880. Unfortunately, this brief spurt of success ended when cheaper, better-quality coal from Wales undercut Spain's output and abruptly displaced workers from Galicia and Asturias.[25]

A number of these coal miners from the north migrated to Andalusia in southern Spain when coal producing closed down in their regions. There they worked in Huelva's resurgent copper mines, once mined by Romans. Spain's copper riches in Huelva were certainly known to Americans interested in copper mining. An early tie between Huelva and New Mexico began when Lieutenant Colonel José Manuel Carrasco was sent by the Spanish governor of New Mexico to rid the western district of Apaches. Carrasco was born in Huelva's Río Tinto mining area. When he saw an Apache's copper sample of exceptional quality, he realized its worth and quickly claimed the land. The Santa Rita del Cobre Mine that he started in 1799, and was developed by others, produced 41 million pounds of copper by 1845. Santa Rita del Cobre, now named the Chino Mine, developed into the largest open-pit copper mine in the world and is currently owned and operated by the Kennecott Copper Corporation.[26] However, for the story of copper mining in Arizona, it is important to know that Santa Rita was only eleven miles from Silver City, New Mexico. There resided investors in Arizona's Clifton copper area, as well as early, skilled Mexican workers.[27]

The widespread mineral wealth of the Río Tinto and the entire Huelva area suffered a lack of development by the Spanish government. The area remained basically poor and agricultural. An extensive effort, from 1798 to 1854, by a Spanish administrator, Vicente de Leonta, to improve Río Tinto ended in financial disaster due to the political unrest that wracked the peninsula.[28] That changed in 1855, when investors from Britain, France, and Scotland, who were looking for profitable projects during the Industrial Era, rediscovered the area and made Spain's legendary mines profitable again.

Mining had begun with the Phoenicians and Romans; both left tantalizing traces indicating the potential for profitable use of newer mining techniques. The Romans had mined silver at Río Tinto, called Corta Lago. They also found gold, iron, lead and copper, but only scratched the surface of one of the planet's largest pyrite lodes in the mountainous region near the port of Cadiz.[29] Huelva's Tharsis and Río Tinto mines catapulted modern Spain into prominence as a global copper producer due to British investors. Miners in this area, some from Northern Spain, others farmers looking for added income, turned to Huelva for work. Here they perhaps learned of United States copper-mining opportunities from ties between British and American copper interests. In 1900 the Río Tinto Company, today still a global mining force, hired American William Carlyle as general manager. Carlyle had honed his tough management skills in the United States mining industry. After a falling out with management, he returned to the United States, replaced by Walter Browning, another North American with mining experience in Mexico.[30] These Americans opened a pathway from Spain to the United States.

Miners also heard of Arizona opportunities from another source in Huelva: the Tharsis mines. The Spanish government was in no position to tackle modern mining techniques. A French company showed interest in developing the mines, but was undercapitalized. A group of British investors took over from French interests and began profitable mining in the 1870s.[31] This group, based in Glasgow, Scotland, wanted to produce sulfur, a copper byproduct extracted from pyrites. Like copper, sulfur was in increasing demand in the Industrial Era as a component in making items such as glassware and textiles.[32]

Segregation between Anglo managers and Spanish laborers was found at the company towns of Río Tinto and nearby La Zarza and Tharsis. Some miners were local men anxious to make a steady income, but many were miners from Asturias, Galicia, the Basque Country, and Portugal looking for new places to use their mining skills. In Spain labor unrest in the late nineteenth century affected the British mining areas. Tharsis workers began to strike in 1900; the company quickly squelched the rebellion, which left some workers thinking that their best option was to emigrate. In 1901 the Tharsis Company looked into further global expansion. Representatives explored properties in Pinal County, Arizona, as did other British companies, which beat them out.[33] However, another pathway to Arizona had been opened for Spanish workers.

THE SPANIARDS' SOCIAL LOCATION, AN INBETWEEN "RACE" IN ARIZONA

In the American mindset of the era so-called Latins formed a "race," similar to what would be termed an ethnic minority group today. They were identified by cultural markers such as Romance languages and adherence to Catholicism; some alleged personality traits, such as impulsiveness; and perceived distinctive phenotypes, such as swarthy skin, and dark eyes and hair. The Dillingham Commission, formed in 1907, in part to address fears caused by the increasing migration of Southern and Eastern Europeans to the United States, classified groups according to their supposed race. The commission characterized Spaniards as a generally homogenous group physically resembling South Italians.[34]

As historian Oscar Handlin noted, racist doctrines beginning in the 1890s claimed that "the peoples of the Mediterranean region were biologically different from those of Northern and Western Europe in that the differences sprang from an inferiority of blood and could be observed in certain social characteristics."[35] From this belief came a designation of race used at that time, which merged cultural and physical traits. These designations used by Anglo-American political leaders formed images in the public mind about alleged Latins. Theodore Roosevelt even used this pseudo-scientific idea in trying to rally Americans to fight Spain, siding with Cubans in their fight for independence. Drawing on Charles Darwin and Edmond Demoulins, a social Darwinist popular at the time, Roosevelt, then governor of New York, claimed that the Spanish were "shiftless and of weak moral fiber."[36] These traits made Spaniards unfit to rule Cuba. In contrast, Anglo-Saxons were a people known for their love of independence and education. In other words, Anglo-Saxons were naturally meant to rule.[37]

The "Latin Race" was a category used at times by whites to designate darker-skinned people who spoke a Romance language. Cubans, Puerto Ricans, and Mexicans—along with Portuguese, Spaniards, Italians, and Romanians—were included in this designation. Other Mediterranean peoples, such as Greeks, were also considered nonwhite, as were some Eastern Europeans, including Slavic peoples. Here I differ from the binary concept of racialization, as it is widely recognized in sociology, due, in part, to the work of Michael Omi and Howard Winant.[38] They posit that racialization in a multiracial society is part of the process of competition over scarce resources when groups struggle over which group will be defined as the racial norm, leaving remaining groups to become "Others." Being an Other places a group in a subordinate status, which carries perceived negative and supposedly permanent racial characteristics. These social categories are "autonomous fields of social conflict, political organization, and cultural-ideological meaning" in racially based societies. They suggest that this process occurred fairly quickly in the United States, when Anglo-American nativists ended their resistance to the inclusion of "Southern Europeans, the Irish, Jews and other 'non-white' categories" in the 1870s, after the Civil War, to counter the potential power of freed African Americans.[39] This model asserts a racial binary, which comprises all Whites versus all nonwhites. However, the historical record shows a much longer period, some sixty years, of divisiveness before Southern and Eastern Europeans were gradually shifted from Other and accepted into the dominant White group.

Some historians—such as James Barrett, David Roediger, and Robert Orsi—have suggested the use of the term "inbetween" to describe this Other, shifting category.[40] I agree with their term and will show how it was prevalent in Arizona. Ironically, labor solidarity shown by new immigrants began to promote acceptance among their economic working-class peers.[41] Covington Hall, a member of the militant International Workers of the World (IWW), also called Wobblies, lauded Southern Europeans as part of the "Latin race," which he saw as more militant than Southern whites.[42]

Preliminary research in Arizona suggests that Spanish immigrants were seen as part of a different race by some Anglo clerks. Data collected on naturalization papers for fifty-three Spanish men showed that most (40, or 75 percent) were listed as being of dark complexion, rather than having a light or medium complexion. Drawing on this group to further explore their status through data linkage with other Arizona records (birth and death certificates), I found a surprising detail. Clerks often wrote in "Spanish Race" or "Latin" rather than check off "White," which was a category on forms. The tendency for clerks to improvise on forms was also found by historian Coleen Stitt in her examination of census records for the white man's town of Globe, Arizona. Globe was a self-designated "white camp," which meant that those of Northern European ancestry openly got the best jobs, while Mexicans were routinely placed in lower-skilled jobs regardless of their level of skill. Stitt found that in the 1910 Census, those collecting information let their personal prejudices seep into their recording: "Apparently some of the local numerators could not bring themselves to count people commonly seen as darker among the white population. Thus some persons of Mexican and Italian descent were simply listed as 'Other'; they were not perceived as 'white' but neither were they 'Negro,' Asian or American Indian."[43] This is another indication of their inbetween status.

Since this information was collected across eight counties, it was apparent that no one person in one county decided to enter Other.[44] Likewise, Italians were sometimes classified as "Italian race," not "White." The other main Latin group, Mexicans, was categorized as "Mexican race." This meant that in Arizona, Spanish and Italian immigrants were often closest in status to Mexicans, since all three groups were considered Latin.[45] The import of this designation could be negative or at best ambivalent. William Davenport, a Massachusetts politician whose views were published in *Charities* in 1904, claimed that Italian immigrants should admit that their Latin race was "dishonest, hot-blooded, ignorant and dirty." But he held out hope for the third generation, indicating the conflation of ideas of race and ethnicity prevalent at that time.[46]

Mexicans faced an even more problematic status, since, despite their ability to become citizens, their so-called Latin blood was further stigmatized by the societal pollution of Native American lineage.[47] The other side of the label was that these groups used at times a form of positive self-identification, calling themselves Latin, providing some basis for unity. Self-identification can be most easily found in the designation of social organizations, for example La Liga Protectora Latina, formed by Mexican Americans to fight discrimination, or the Italian bilingual Il Branch Latino IWW.[48]

A tripartite economic and social division existed among people in Arizona focused on whites versus inbetween whites and nonwhites. Imagine a kaleidoscope with each color representing a different racial-ethnic group. The patterns changed according to the social and cultural climate of the time. In some cases, European groups of the late migration (1880–1930) are shifted so that their color becomes white, almost like northern Europeans. But in other instances, the shifting of colors and perceived swarthiness makes Southern Europeans become dark, almost comparable to Asians and Mexicans. This shifting of patterns brings greater subtlety to our history and allows us to look at our contemporary race relations and ethnic identities as part of a shifting kaleidoscope rather than a fixed mosaic.

Historian Linda Gordon explicates this complexity when she examines the copper camps of central-eastern Arizona: Clifton and Morenci. A simple binary division of races into whites and nonwhites misses the actual multilayered gradations of race. In mining towns racial microclimates formed, according to Gordon, which varied from one town to another and also changed within one place over time. Thus, Mexicans in the Clifton area were originally enfranchised and generally accepted members of local society, since their invaluable aid during the pioneer days was appreciated. Mexicans were involved in building the town, transporting essential goods from Silver City, New Mexico, over treacherous terrain, and, when needed, fighting the Apaches, who resisted incursions into their territories. In time, however, a middle stratum in the local hierarchy formed populated by lighter Mexicans and EuroLatins as more Anglos moved into positions of power.[49]

The reception given to Spanish immigrants can be looked at two levels: one would be that of Anglo mine owners and miners, the other that of Mexican miners. Spaniards became an inbetween group in Arizona because, while they were European, they were also from a Catholic Romance-language-speaking culture quite different than the dominant English Protestant culture. Spaniards' European origins brought them some white privilege. For example, they could opt to become citizens, intermarry with Anglos, and vote. In contrast, Asians were excluded from these significant advantages. Furthermore, immigrants could take pride in Arizona's Spanish cultural heritage. The Spanish empire colonized, through religion and military forces, a wide swath of the Southwest. Tucson was the commanding urban presence in the new territory, with a distinct Spanish and Native American culture. This cultural amalgam continued to influence southern Arizona after the land was ceded to the United States by Mexico in 1848 in the treaty of Guadalupe Hidalgo and the Gadsden Purchase of 1853.[50]

The early Spanish influence remains evident today in Spanish place-names and in the Spanish red and yellow rays in Arizona's flag. Efforts to eradicate the Spanish colonial influence grew as more Anglos moved in. Some influential Anglos held prejudiced views of Spanish culture. Influential Americans proposed annexing northern Mexico, as part of the Manifest Destiny ideology of the time. Mining entrepreneur Sylvester Mowry wanted Arizona to be a thoroughly American state dominated by white English-speaking Protestants. Similarly, Senator Albert Beveridge wanted Arizona admitted into statehood, which would allow Anglo migrants to dominate the territory's political scene. Beveridge saw both Mexicans and Indians as deficient in the supposedly Yankee traits of self-sufficiency and love of democracy. For example, a major city like Tucson should be under Anglo rule.[51]

In Arizona's mines Spaniards' legal standing as whites did not prevent discrimination at the hands of employers. In terms of wages Mexican workers were often paid less than Anglo workers, even with the same skill set. Spaniards could be subsumed into the general Mexican category by employers since surnames, such as García, were common to both groups. However, some mine managers, for example, in Jerome, recorded a worker's nationality in which case a Spaniard would be recorded as such and paid accordingly.[52]

In many mining districts the records show how being inbetween hurt EuroLatins. The Dillingham Report (1911) included scant information on Spaniards in western states, with the exception of Arizona since in Arizona there were enough data to merit their inclusion. The report singled out the Clifton and Bisbee Copper Districts for unfair wage differences. It documented that native whites and Northern Europeans were mostly in the top two wage categories, earning between $3.50 and 4.00 per day. In contrast, most Spaniards earned between $2.50 and $3.00, Italians a notch below that at $2.00–2.50, and Mexicans even lower at $1.75–$2.00. These wages, and the gap between the Anglos and other categories of workers, led the commissioners to conclude that while generally Southern and Eastern Europeans did not face wage bias, in Arizona "discrimination has been shown against the . . . Italians, Spaniards, as well as against the Mexicans."[53] The Dillingham report's comment on discrimination is noteworthy, considering the anti-immigrant bias of the commission.

Their place in the wage scale helps explain how Mexican workers received their Spanish cousins. As the settlement patterns of Spaniards will show, these Europeans preferred to live apart from Mexicans when possible. Given the racially stratified housing patterns in mining towns, however, immigrants from Spain and Mexico were likely to live in proximity and certainly neither was integrated with Anglos. Some interviews show Mexicans according, perhaps grudgingly, the Spaniards a social rank somewhat above theirs.[54] However, the discriminatory wages paid both groups meant that when unity counted Latins stuck together, as will be seen.

SPANIARDS IN ARIZONA'S MINING TOWNS

To follow Linda Gordon's research on Arizona copper towns means looking at those towns with recognized Spanish populations as possessing racial microclimates that changed from one town to another and within a given town during changing times, such as mining booms and busts. Here, I will examine each distinct climate to see if patterns emerge to describe Spaniards: do we see them accepted as whites or do they have an inbetween status?

Jerome

Jerome is in the western part of the state and early on was explored by Spaniards looking for precious metals. (See map 6.1.) The next major reference linking Spaniards to Jerome came in the 1900s, when they were a specialized fire fighting force in the United Verde mine. The birth of a real copper town was financed by eastern investors who consolidated small claims on Cleopatra Hill into a company in 1883. Struggling in its infancy,

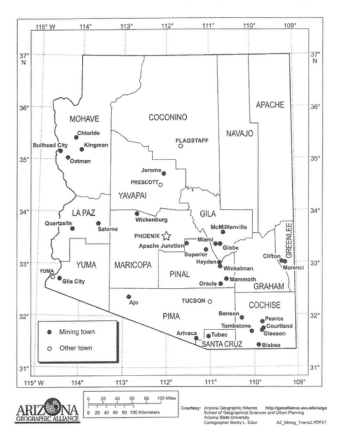

MAP 6.1. Arizona's mining towns. Map by Becky L. Eden.
Courtesy of the Arizona Geographic Alliance.

multimillionaire William A. Clark developed the site, pumping in capital and knowhow, learned in mining in Butte, Montana, to turn Jerome into a success. It did not hurt that the Verde District sat atop an enormous ore body opened up in 1914 by a second mining company, the United Verde Extension.[55]

However, the future of copper mining in Jerome in the 1890s and early 1900s was plagued by serious underground dangers, which made miners' work even more hazardous than usual. It was Spanish miners who eased one of these serious problems: long-burning underground fires. While the smelting, railroad, and support shops turned the mines into veritable "sophisticated industrial plants," Jerome's reputation as a difficult workplace prompted the local union, which the company had instituted, to use safety issues as a point of contention between workers and management.[56] In Jerome mines heavy sulfide ore often caused fires, especially when trolley motors were still used, because the trolley wires could spark a conflagration, with stubborn fires scorching extensive underground areas.[57] A fire in 1902 reached the fifth level of the mine, which caused a shutdown of the mine and smelter. Not only did this result in lost profits, but unsafe working conditions gave union organizers an issue they could take on, thus encouraging membership growth. The inventor of an innovative system for fighting stope fires, J. J. Shaw, was hired to solve the problem; he had solved similar problems in Pennsylvania and California. When Shaw arrived in Jerome, he brought his crew of specially trained Spaniards; the exact number in the crew is not known, but twenty per team was mentioned.

Using Shaw's Plenum method, a chamber containing cooler air at a positive pressure, the twenty Spaniards reduced the scorching temperature while reducing the sulfur fumes so ore could be removed. The fire still burned, but decreased temperature and less fumes made it possible for work to continue (in thirty minutes shifts), albeit under difficult conditions of heat and smoke.[58] Shaw's Plenum System not only reduced the sulfur fumes; it also improved safety, as well as copper production, which hit a new record in 1904, with less time lost to fires. In 1905 Shaw and his team continued to remove ores from the fire district of the United Verde mine. This success allowed the company to bring a larger workforce underground, some 540 men, which included Spaniards who stayed on in Jerome.

According to historian Nancy Prichard, the 1900 census showed only one Spaniard in Jerome; by 1910 they totaled 118, or 5 percent of the population.[59] Most were men (90 percent), with twelve women in the minority. Their average age was slightly younger than that of the Mexican population, and they tended to have arrived in Arizona later than the Mexican immigrants.[60] Since underground fires continued to plague this area, the need for the original core of Spaniards persisted. Showing their intent to settle in Arizona some, like Juan (John) Gago, brought their families to Jerome. Gago came from Navarre, entering the United States in 1907 through New Orleans. His wife, Ermelinda García, was also Spanish.[61] Other Spaniards married into the Mexican community. The Holy Family Catholic Church in Jerome served a large immigrant community, composed mainly of Spanish speakers and Eastern Europeans.[62]

Priests and Brothers from across Spain, such as Father Autimo Nebruda, served Jerome's Catholics during this period, some of them opting to become naturalized.[63] By the 1920s the church was staffed by five priests who held three Sunday masses and had Sunday schools in English and Spanish.[64]

Spaniards, like Mexicans, at times faced de facto segregation. Historian Antonio Rios-Bustamante notes that Mexicans lived in segregated *barrios* in a number of major copper camps in Arizona. He suggests several factors that influenced where groups lived, including the physical setting, placement of mines and smelters, transportation routes, and copper companies' policies that included support for racial and class divisions. His findings are shared by historian Andrea Huginnie, both noting that Spaniards and Italians sometimes lived in mixed ethnic neighborhoods with Mexicans.[65]

Temporary lodging for newly arrived bachelors was near the mines, a place called "Tent Town." Mexicans lived in Jerome's "Mexican Town." This area reflected de facto segregation and, like Bisbee's Mexican barrio, Chihuahua Hill, had substandard living conditions. As Huginnie learned, only after a fire demolished this part of Jerome did the city extend full water services to this area.[66] It was in this barrio that local Spaniards lived in their own enclaves, such as El Verde. As Prichard noted, "the Spaniards kept to their own section of Mexican Town and had their own lodging houses. Although the two groups generally interacted in a positive manner in both social and occupational settings, tempers between the Spanish and Mexican born populations ran hot on occasions."[67] However, some housing mixing did occur. Aureliano Sandoval of Mexico, for example, listed his residence in the 1910 census with "Spaniards."[68] The time card for Gabino Zalba (figure 6.1) of Spain listed him as living in Mexican Town. We cannot know if he was in El Verde, however.

Jerome also hosted organizations, termed Hispanic by some locals; most likely some included Spaniards as members.[69] EuroLatins have been found as members in Mexican organizations in other Arizona towns. Since there is no evidence of the existence of separate organizations for Spaniards, we can infer that they probably joined the Alianza Hispano-Americana, La Liga Protectora Latina, and perhaps the Sociedad Mutualista Funeraria y de Ahorros, which aided families of deceased miners.[70] Furthermore, in 1916 La Liga member C. R. Dominguez established a Spanish-language newspaper in Jerome, which would keep Spaniards not yet fluent in English apprised of developments in Arizona and beyond.[71]

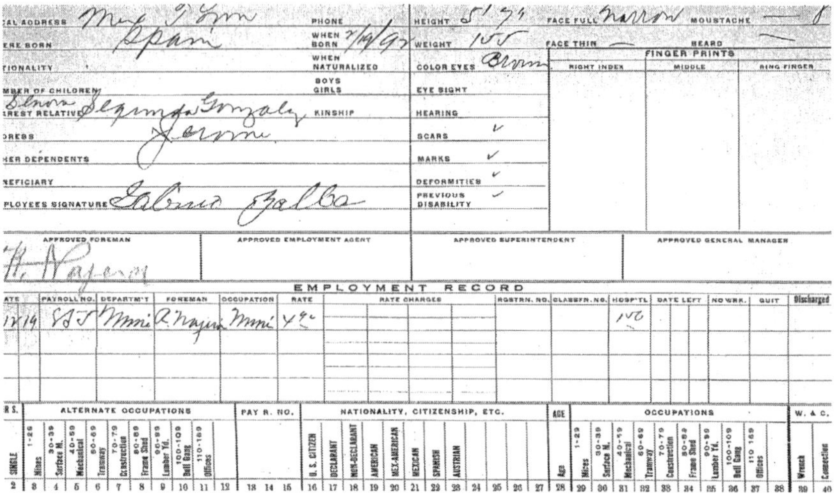
:AL ADDRESS Mex Town
ERE BORN Spain
TIONALITY
MBER OF CHILDREN
EREST RELATIVE Señora Segunda Gonzalez
DRESS Jerome
HER DEPENDENTS
NEFICIARY
PLOYEES SIGNATURE Gabino Zalba
PHONE
WHEN BORN 7/14/92
WHEN NATURALIZED
BOYS
GIRLS
KINSHIP
HEIGHT 5' 7½
WEIGHT 155
COLOR EYES Brown
EYE SIGHT
HEARING
SCARS
MARKS
DEFORMITIES
PREVIOUS DISABILITY
FACE FULL Narrow
FACE THIN
MOUSTACHE
BEARD
FINGER PRINTS
RIGHT INDEX
MIDDLE
RING FINGER
APPROVED FOREMAN
APPROVED EMPLOYMENT AGENT
APPROVED SUPERINTENDENT
APPROVED GENERAL MANAGER
EMPLOYMENT RECORD
ATE | PAYROLL NO. | DEPARTM'T | FOREMAN | OCCUPATION | RATE | RATE CHANGES | RGSTRN. NO. | CLASSFN. NO. | HOSP'TL | DATE LEFT | NO WRK. | QUIT | Discharged
ALTERNATE OCCUPATIONS
PAY R. NO.
NATIONALITY, CITIZENSHIP, ETC.
AGE
OCCUPATIONS
W. & C.
SINGLE
Mines
Surface M.
Mechanical
Tramway
Construction
Frame Shed
Lumber Yd.
Bell Gang
Offices
U. S. CITIZEN
DECLARANT
NON-DECLARANT
AMERICAN
MEX-AMERICAN
MEXICAN
SPANISH
AUSTRIAN
Wrench
Connection

FIGURE 6.1. A work card for Gabino Zalba, one of the Spanish workers employed in the mines at Jerome. The local address is registered as "Mex[ican] Town." Courtesy of the Jerome Historical Society.

As mentioned before, working conditions were among the outstanding issues that gripped miners in Jerome. The main corporate presence was William A. Clark. His strategy was to address some union demands by granting an eight-hour day to miners in 1907 and paying acceptable wages.[72] On the other hand, when requests were deemed unworthy the mine might be shut down. Workers might also find themselves laid off due to a slowing demand for copper. This was the case in 1906, when smelter workers wanted their twelve-hour day cut to eight hours while continuing to be paid $2.75 per day. Rather than acquiesce to this change, the smelter simply closed for a bit only to reopen later.[73]

The Clark United Verde Organization (UV) kept an eye on the local union. When necessary, the UV nudged workers to favor company candidates. Since the UV had started the Jerome Miners' Union, company managers felt it permissible to keep out any so-called radicals. In a 1909 letter to Charles Moyer, president of the Western Federation of Miners, labor organizer Joseph D. Camon explained how the company manipulated union meetings and decisions. The UV aided the election of company candidate John Opman as secretary-treasurer by sending men loyal to the company to the election meeting. Charges of packing the meeting were ignored at the next meeting. Those in charge wanted to stifle radical tendencies and keep in place the system of men paying foremen to get a job. Camon also noted that the company feared attempts by outside organizers, like Ben Goggins, "to try to get the Spaniards and Italians into the Union." "The Company does not like it," Camon explained, "and it is a mistake to go against the wishes of the company in matters of this kind."[74]

The pointed reference to Spaniards in Camon's letter reflects the reputation Spaniards had for being willing to stand up for their rights. In Jerome, however, strike activity was minimal, due to a combination of factors. The company favored stable loyal workers and their relatives, paid decent wages, and tried to control the local union as much as possible. In 1912 the state legislature put the issue of an eight-hour workday to rest, by declaring that all workers in dangerous jobs, whether above- or belowground, should work only eight-hour shifts. Buoyed by better wages, ranging from $2.75 for laborers to $5.25 for shift bosses, union membership for stable workers grew.[75] Ever cautious the company kept watch on any workers that might cause trouble. It was not until 1917, when labor conflict broke out throughout the state, that Jerome became embroiled in a strike.

In 1917, the International Union of Mine, Mill, and Smelter Workers decided it was time to organize a branch in Jerome. Henry McCluskey, an able organizer, sparked miners' interest in joining. At the same time, UV management used spies to identify miners who should be fired for union preferences. A key issue was a better salary scale, which managers refused, as well as the union proposal to have Jerome become a closed union shop. The role of Spanish miners in the strike is unrecorded; they may have sided with the Mexican workers of La Liga Protectora Latina, who decided to ignore the strikers and went to work. Or, like their countrymen in Ray and Morenci, they may have joined the strikers. All that is known is that a compromise was reached in a little over a week with better wages but no closed town.[76]

Prichard's contention is that, unlike in other copper towns, most Mexican, Italian, and Irish immigrants were integrated into Jerome over time, with a fair number enjoying stable employment as miners. We know that some Spaniards did have longtime employment in the mines. However, we do not know if the Spanish found pathways to upper mobility through starting small businesses, as did the Irish, Mexicans, and Italians. Given that the other Latins prospered, it is reasonable to assume that Spaniards did well, since when Latins faced discrimination so did Spaniards. Thus, some upward mobility would be expected, particularly if Spaniards became fluent in English. Not speaking English was the major factor Prichard saw limiting upward mobility. This topic remains to be explored.[77]

Ray

In 1901 the British corporation controlling the Spanish Tharsis Mines looked into acquiring the Ray, Arizona mines in rugged Pinal County. Ray was built in 1873 when the Mineral Creek Mining district was formed; the future looked promising. Within a decade, the copper mineral wealth led to the organization of the Ray Copper Company. The Tharsis Company was hungry for new reserves of cupreous ore; four prospecting engineers were sent out on a global quest for new mines. The United States drew a lot of interest, but Ray proved to be incompatible with their needs. Instead, the Tharsis Company acquired property in the Bunker Hill mining district, also in the Pinal area.[78] The Globe Exploration Company of London got the option on Ray and other mines in Pinal County, forming the Ray Copper Mines Ltd. The Ray mine area did not really take off, however, until an American group, led by D. C. Jackling, an inventor and mining developer, and his associates took over. As the area began to grow, so did the need for less-skilled workers.[79]

Spanish workers may have originally come from the Tharsis region, in Andalusia, which, as noted, had captured British mining Tharsis Sulfur & Copper Company interests.[80] The average miner probably spoke little or no English, but news of the company's explorations in Arizona could have traveled via bilingual Spaniards, such as "Miss America." An outspoken Spanish woman working as a servant for an American employed at Río Tinto earned the derisive nickname from British employees of "Miss America." Perhaps she regaled fellow Spaniards of mining opportunities in the United States.

Or, the company's four prospecting engineers might have brought a few talented Spanish miners with them when they investigated sites. However the word spread in Spain, once a few men learned of good opportunities, they sent for family and friends. The Spanish presence was important to American mine managers. As D. C. Jackling noted in a 1914 article, "The Spaniards who work here generally come direct [*sic*] from their native land. They are a fine looking lot of men and are said to be good workers. When they have accumulated a couple of thousand dollars they return to Spain to live in ease the balance of their lives."[81] Sojourners might return, but some remained, like "Tata Tacho," who brought his skills from Spain to work in Ray as mason and carpenter and stayed to build his rancho in Barcelona.[82]

The most vivid physical representation of the racialized housing patterns in Arizona mentioned above was found in Ray, a company town that grew with housing supplied by the Mining Company. Ray's construction was taken on by a development company that owned the townsite. In 1910 the owner, Mr. Dunham, claimed he had been building houses at a fast clip, twenty homes per month. The little town of Ray, called "El Rey" by Spanish speakers, one Mexican youngster recalled as "the prettiest mining town with all white houses built in straight rows."[83] The Spanish-speaking communities, he noted, was where residents were responsible for building their own places.[84] Here, the Spanish community was literally between whites and Mexicans.

According to Leonor López, "the Spaniards who were attracted to the new mining area selected an area nearby but adjacent to the town of Sonora, the Mexican enclave. They developed their own village of Barcelona. By 1911, emigrating Spaniards enlarged Barcelona to about 1,000 families. The immigrants seemed interested in maintaining their own social and cultural identity by residing in their own Spanish village."[85] Kathy Quiroz, of Sonora, remembers that Spaniards were distrusted by Anglos in Ray and Mexicans in Sonora, so they kept to themselves. However, their children went to school in nearby Sonora, at Washington Elementary. Kathy Quiroz's mother recalled that once open pit progressed and dynamite literally blew them out of their homes in Barcelona, her Spanish classmates of the 1930s and 1940s scattered like the wind, which is why making contact was difficult.[86]

According to one source, Barcelona was named for the Spanish city by the displaced Spaniards who built up their little enclave above Sonora. Another possible source for the name could be the local priest, Father Angel Esteve (figure 6.2), who ministered to both Spanish-speaking communities. He was born near Barcelona and was ordained a priest in that city. The local Catholic Church was St. Helen Church, which Esteve ministered to for many years.[87] Over the years, the church struggled to survive. Once it was rebuilt from a fire; it was later moved to nearby Kearney as open-pit mine encroachment took the land.[88]

FIGURE 6.2. Father
Angel Esteve.
Courtesy of the
Diocese of Tucson.

The Spaniards' settlement was remembered by one young woman as a
beautiful area overlooking Teapot Mountain. Barcelona boasted many trees
and plants brought from Spain, such as lime, peach, apricot, pomegranate,
and fig trees. The community of Españoles had homes surrounded by large
yards, where chickens, goats, turkeys, and pigs were raised. "This was their
way of keeping their ranches, 'Spanish style,'" Joe Bittick recalled, "There
was a large slaughter house in Barcelona. Dad herded cattle from his ranch in
Winkelman, Arizona to sell there."[89]

The Mexican settlement of Sonora, Arizona, was described by newspaper
reporter, Ralph Mahoney, as "Tucked away on a hillside overlooking . . . the
Ray mine." "Sonora," Mahoney wrote, "resembles a town that could, indeed,

be a part of Old Mexico itself."[90] The largest Latin group was Mexicans, who, like other immigrant groups, including Spaniards, were sometimes used as strike breakers. However, in Arizona their labor activism grew, fueled by Mexico's own anarchists and labor leaders as well as expatriates fleeing their Civil War. At Ray the residential divisions were not enough to prevent Spanish-speaking workers from unifying. Various theories exist about what sparked the 1915 Strike in Ray. Not surprisingly, outside agitators were blamed. One factor was that workers tired of their lower wages compared to other mining camps, and the many direct or indirect insults that Spanish speakers had to put up with.[91] It did not help the workers' morale when local papers trumpeted the company's economic success right before the strike. Ray Consolidated was one of Pinal's biggest mines, having made a net gain of $741,539 for the first quarter of 1915 compared to $174,954 for the prior quarter. The dip in 1914 copper prices had allowed companies to slash salaries. The red ore, due to the start of World War I, had rebounded by 1915.[92] Workers wanted to share in this profitable moment, as they had gained in nearby Miami, Arizona. In June of 1915 Ray's Spaniards and Mexicans fought together to end a racially divided pay scale, which favored whites. Spanish and Mexicans were conflated into a group paid $2.25 a day as muckers and $3 for machine workers. In contrast, Anglos in nearby Miami were unionized, and muckers made $3.75 per day, with machine workers at a high of $4.15.[93] At this point in time, unions were still struggling with the thorny issue of whether or not to include Latins as members.

Lacking a union to back them as the Western Federation of Miners (WFM) had done for Miami's Anglo workers, Ray's Latin workers formed their own organization, a Committee for Workers that functioned as a surrogate union. As Philip Mellinger noted, the strikers contacted the governor and said they were not asking to bring in a union but simply wanted equal pay for equal work.[94] Ray strikers probably knew that they would not get the major increases they demanded, Mellinger suspected, but tactically they could move closer to this goal; indeed, they won a sixty-cent flat rate daily wage increase and several other concessions. This labor activism did not mean that the Latin workers rejected American society, as claimed by some who distrusted the loyalty of immigrants, especially as the world war grew in size and the Mexican revolution raged just across the border. Miners wanted their fair share of the tremendous profits being produced by their labor. During World War I a local newspaper praised the little Spanish colony of Barcelona as well as Sonora's Mexicans for their sacrifices in the war effort.

When most Arizona camps burst into unrest during World Word I, Ray was quiet. Arizona's governor Thomas Campbell credited this to Ray's general manager Lewis Cates. Cates was known as the "Czar of the Pinals." He was a career mining engineer who saw Ray as another rung up the corporate ladder. Ray, Cates knew, could only be reached by a single county road or a little-used and difficult-to-traverse road connected to the mining town of Superior. The only other route in was by a company-controlled railroad. Any organizer hoping to recruit the Spanish and Mexican miners would be spotted by the company's deputy sheriffs under Cates's command. Anyone suspected of being a labor agitator was caught and brought before the local justice of the peace. Quickly sentenced as a vagrant or trespasser, the outsider would be swiftly "floated" out of the District.[95]

Ray is now a ghost town, which is more than the Spanish and Mexican residents can claim. As open-pit mining took over, both settlements vanished. One of the last residents of Barcelona had no memory of the Spaniards' ranchos; he only remembered a few houses awaiting destruction by bulldozers. Sonora is kept alive in the memories of those who grew up after the Great Depression; today a few books and memories on their Facebook website are of a very unique and fondly remembered Sonora.[96]

Clifton-Morenci-Metcalf District

Here early workers were also skilled miners. The so-called Mexican Camp—composed of Clifton, Morenci, and Metcalf—was a mining area in several, but interrelated, locales. The mines were owned by different companies. Clifton was a town located in a valley nearby Chase Creek. Morenci was perched in the mountains high above Clifton; Metcalf's rich copper deposits were in canyon walls close to Clifton and Morenci. Various companies ran the numerous mines. The label Mexican camp came from the important role Mexican laborers and mining specialists played; they came from nearby Silver City, New Mexico, located to the east. The Lesinsky family, of New Mexico, who funded early Robert Metcalf's mining in Clifton had good relations with and respect for Mexican workers, so much of early Clifton's development is credited to their efforts.[97]

Linda Gordon noted that before the district assimilated into the Anglo-Mexican binary racial system, it had its own tripartite system. At the bottom were the poor Mexicans; in the middle were prosperous and usually lighter-skinned Mexicans, Spaniards, and other dark or "Latin" European immigrants; while above them were Anglo Americans. Local wages reflected this triple pattern, with Mexicans at the lower end of the scale. Spaniards' and Italians' wages were usually higher than Mexicans' but definitely lower than what Anglos earned. Furthermore, Gordon explains, "patterns of sociability also pointed to a 'Latin' identity that included Mexicans. Intermarriage among Mexicans, Spaniards, and Italians was common."[98]

Fermín Palicio, born in Asturias, was hired to work in the mines while in Spain. Fermín had graduated from a technical school and trained as a blacksmith. His knowhow made him well regarded by the Americans he met when working in Huelva.[99] The Arizona Copper Company in the Mexican camp of Clifton-Morenci hired him in 1906. Arriving at El Paso, Texas, he crossed into Arizona from Juárez, Mexico, according to his naturalization papers. He was described as white, with a dark completion.[100] Fermín worked for eleven years in Arizona Copper's foundry before leaving to become a merchant.[101] The presence of a sizeable number of Spaniards in the Clifton-Morenci-Metcalf District stems from such pioneers. Fermín was accompanied by his wife, Carmen Cota, and daughter, from Spain.[102] The birth certificate for their son, born in 1909, shows both parents listed as "Latin Race."[103] Fermín remained in Greenlee County until his death in 1949.[104]

There was indeed a Spanish mercantile group in Clifton, unlike Jerome. Amelia Oñate, a local Chicana, recalled the overall diversity of the area, commenting that in Clifton there were many Mexicans, Italians, Chinese, and Spaniards. She saw Spaniards as an upwardly mobile group: "Spaniards would work for themselves and they eventually accumulated a fortune. When they would retire, they were very rich."[105] She mentioned, as did others, the Zorrilla family, who came from Santander, Spain, to Clifton in 1910. Gerardo Zorrilla, the family patriarch, went into ranching and established a meat market that his sons, Jesús and Manuel, eventually took over. In 1914 Gerardo's sister and her husband, Fabian Fernández, arrived and opened a grocery store. The Cueto family, from Spain, also had a store.[106]

In Clifton Spaniards lived among Italians near Chase Creek. These Spanish families intermarried to some extent. For example, Cipriano Cueto married

Matilde Zorrilla. Others married Italians or Mexicans. Charles Spezia, an Italian, married Teresa Palicio, while Al Fernández, a Mexican, married Pilar Palicio. Over time the Zorrilla family became established in both the Spanish and Mexican communities. Joaquín Oviedo suggested that in Spain the Zorrilla family would have been called *una familia rancia*, an old established family. When Jesús took over the family store on Chase Creek during Prohibition, their warehouse became a meeting place where Joaquín's father and other friends would go to enjoy an illicit beer.[107] Many of these mercantile Spanish families—who also included the Márquez, Aja, Esteves, Rivas, and Lavins—would have socialized among each other; they were generally not part of the Anglo social circle.

According to the recollections of Mexican American Pedro Gómez, it seems that Spaniards maintained subtle cultural differences as social boundaries; for example, their importation of special foods and drinks from their homeland. The Spanish drank *clarete* (claret) when they ate and "did not get drunk." Another difference Gómez noted related more to their social status: Spaniards in Morenci could afford to have coffins transported by train for burial in Clifton's Bunker Cemetery, albeit in a separate section from Anglos, while poorer Mexicans were carried by family members to nearby La Bendición Cemetery.[108] Some divisions between Spaniards and Mexicans can be gleaned from these two interviews. In this settlement Spaniards were, perhaps, ethnocentric. They would have considered their version of Spanish superior to the Spanish of Mexicans. Also, they would have preferred their own cooking. Finally, though some Mexicans were merchants, the Spanish upward mobility through businesses would have been noted by those who remained working class.

Many Spanish bachelors lived near Metcalf on Shannon Hill, also known as Cerro Prieto, or Dark Hill. According to local memory about 300 Spaniards lived there. Mrs. Gustablados, who ran a boardinghouse, would get food from Spain at Al Fernández's store. The camp was on top of a deep incline above Chase Creek, north and east of Metcalf. Spanish food preferences included drinking clarete and eating garbanzo beans. Burros owned by the Loya family supplied the boardinghouse. The Shannon Copper Co. seemed to prefer Spaniards, not only because they were good workers, but because they were daring. They did not balk at working in dangerous places where cave-ins and landslides were known to occur.[109]

Metcalf was a mining camp with a large Mexican population and enough Spaniards to warrant their own store. According to David Myrick, Fabián Fernández owned the store in Metcalf that "catered to the small colony from Spain."[110] Here Gabriela Valverde could shop for family meals she prepared for Félix, her husband, and children, Celestino and Rosa. Bachelors living together, like Fernando Santiago and his four friends, who ranged in age from eighteen to twenty-two, probably took turns with shopping and cooking. One section of Metcalf had six all male households; some with older men who had left their wives in Spain and decided to room with bachelors.[111]

Morenci was the largest settlement in the area, but it had a poor reputation. As historian Roberta T. Watt noted, an article in the local newspaper, the *Morenci Leader*, described Morenci as "a crude Spanish-speaking community with two Mexican settlements—with few whites, one big company Store."[112] Her later reference to "white Spaniards" indicates a shift of the kaleidoscope here, since Watt makes a point of calling Spaniards whites, unlike the reporter in the *Morenci Leader*, who said there were few whites in the Spanish-speaking settlement. Watt mentions that the town was built on the steep grade and that "white Spaniards" who bought "a keg of wine would roll it down to their shacks."[113]

Morenci was established on seven hills and generally, with the exception of Burro Alley where some Spaniards lived, there were no street names. Morenci's hills were, unimaginatively, named alphabetically or numerically. The hill you lived on was more relevant to your social standing than the size of your home, since some hills were mostly "American." Some 1910 Census pages were mainly filled with Mexican names, like B Hill, a pattern that continued for decades as Víctor Velásquez recalled.[114]

Concentrations of Spaniards were found, in the 1910 census, on Devil's Back Hill, as locals called it, intermixed with Mexicans and Italians, with almost no Anglos. A young Spanish wife of nineteen, young by today's standards, found herself with five boarders plus her husband to care for. On Hill Six Beatriz Gonzales managed a household with her husband, brother-in-law, and two daughters. Nearby was Mrs. Diego, with five lodgers. These women would have found housework unending. In New Town, a separate part of Morenci, other family groups were found, such as the father and son Gutiérrez or the Gómez brothers.

It was from these hills that the unity to defy the copper companies was forged. Latins found themselves living together and working at roughly the same wages. They were also exposed to the radical ideas of anarchists who were giving voice to workers' dissatisfaction in Europe and the Americas. According to Linda Gordon, "Mexican anarchism overlapped with Mexican liberalism and anticlericalism—in short, it was by no means an isolated sectarian ideology."[115] Spaniards too were infused with ideas of class conflict. As other chapters in this volume show, anticlericalism and anarchism were powerful ideologies among Spanish workers. Socialism and anarchism had found a warm reception among landless peasants in Andalusia and urban workers in industrial and mining areas in northern Spain.[116] Miners from Asturias and Andalusia had a long history of activism and militancy, which they brought to the United States, where Spanish anarchist leaders such as Pedro Esteve preached a philosophy of liberty and justice to a variety of immigrant workers.[117] Miners coming to Arizona from the Río Tinto Mining District in Huelva had their class consciousness awakened in part by the British mine owners who established a system of control workers saw as unfair. While miners' wages (fifteen *reales*) were higher than that of peasants, who earned about eight *reales* a day, the working conditions in the mines were hard. Organizing the workers in the period from 1883 to 1887 was Cuban-born Maximiliano Tornet. He had been exiled from Cuba due to his anarchist ideas and in Spain was unknown in Huelva for his radicalism, which enabled him to find work.[118]

Here is an example of not only ideas but also activists crossing the Atlantic from the New World to Europe. Grievances came to a head in February 1888, when workers struck to protest not only labor conditions but also the environmental devastation caused to local farms by fumes from the reduction system used by the British, which was, ironically, outlawed in England but practiced in Spain. The protest culminated in a mass gathering in the town square, where soldiers brought in to control the crowd opened fire, killing at least fifty people; some estimates range as high as two hundred. The event went down in Spanish mining history as "The Year of the Shots."[119]

Thankfully, Arizona did not have an equivalent atrocity; however, the Territorial years saw a number of anti-immigrant bills. When Arizona finally became the forty-eighth state, in 1912, legislators worked on restricting Mexican and, later, all foreign workers. The First Bill (House Bill No. 54) was aimed at restricting Mexicans and other non-English speakers from mine work. The bill stated that those who could not understand English would be prohibited from hazardous jobs particularly underground mining. Mining corporations and immigrant groups quickly mustered opposition, and the bill failed. However, an even broader bill was quickly prepared to limit all non-citizens. In 1914, the ink was barely dry on Arizona's statehood papers when voters overwhelmingly passed a major anti-immigrant law: 80 Percent Law, as it was popularly known. Senator Kinney's bill required that any employer with more than five employees had to hire a minimum of 80 percent native-born or naturalized American citizens. A multinational coalition formed to have the bill brought down; included in this effort were Mexican organizations such as La Liga Protectora Latina (LPL), started in 1914 in Phoenix.[120] Chinese businessmen joined the Spanish, British, and Italian governments in protests of the bill.[121] The Arizona law was found to be in conflict with the Fourteenth Amendment to the Constitution, and therefore was ultimately declared void in 1915.[122] Undeterred, lawmakers drafted another bill restricting those who were not fluent in English from hazardous jobs. The Claypool-Kinney Bill of 1915 drew strong resistance and was ultimately defeated as being un-American by excluding Spanish-speaking American citizens who might not be fluent in English.[123]

Still trying to reduce the numbers of Spanish-speaking workers another bill was proposed in 1915 that would prohibit the employment in hazardous occupations of anyone deaf and dumb or who could not speak or read the English language. Six hundred Mexican miners signed a petition to be given to the State Legislature in session in Phoenix. They argued that this bill discriminated in favor of English men and against people of Mexican descent. Although mine safety was an overt concern, the state, through Attorney General Wiley Jones, defended this act as necessary to "police powers over dangerous gatherings. Labor troubles in the mining camps gave birth to the act."[124] The sentiments against Mexicans certainly would have carried over to Spaniards, as indicated in a letter from the Spanish vice-consul in San Francisco to the governor of Arizona protesting a similar bill (No. 57) in 1919. This bill, too, was defeated.[125]

By 1911 the Morenci mines had 700 workers. Mexicans provided 74 percent of the men, followed by Spaniards at 12 percent and Italians at 10 percent, totaling 96 percent of the workforce.[126] Companies recognized the potential for unity among Latin workers, so shrewd managers played up ethnocentric hostilities. Mexicans had been first on the scene, but remained lowest in social status below Spaniards and Italians. However, in the Clifton District this divisive tactic failed. As Canuto Vargas, a union organizer, remembered, "the workers, forgetting . . . the antagonism of races which the company had inculcated into them, determined to join the union and risk everything."[127]

In 1915, three months after Spaniards and Mexicans struck in Ray, a major strike hit the Clifton District, where the workforce was 96 percent Latin, in this case EuroLatins and Mexicans. The confrontation began in September under the aegis of the Western Federation of Miners. The workers wanted to eliminate the ethnically and racially stratified wage system. Hardships for the estimated 5,000 workers, as winter hit, led the WFM to appeal for aid to keep the strike going. Some workers left, looking for work elsewhere, and some were forcibly ejected for not being loyal to the union side. The strikers finally won in 1916. A formal agreement, signed by the three main corporate representatives and a group of workers, laid out the new higher wage scale as well as other concessions, such as an employee grievances board, the end of foremen extracting gratuities from workers, and the right to refuse to shop at the company store in Morenci.[128]

At the 1917 International Union of Mine, Mill, and Smelter Workers' convention a Mexican delegate shouted, referring to the 1916 strike, "They were sure that the Mexican element and the Spaniards and Italians would not hold together [but] the times in which the master class were imposing on us are past and gone . . . the times of slavery are gone forever . . . and the United States is going to be more free than it has ever been."[129] A major concession from the workers was agreeing to have the WFM banished from the district, while retaining the right to organize. Management had reserved the right to fire workers considered attached to the radical IWW and shortly after the settlement began bringing in newer Mexican workers to replace those union men deemed "dangerous."[130]

Ironically, the workers' advancement led to increased tensions between the rapidly unionizing workers and management. Wage gains were significant for the state's most poorly paid area, but there was only a 39 percent increase for miners and a 60 percent improvement for laborers. At the same time the cost of copper ore skyrocketed 56 percent in the six months between August 1915 and February 1916.[131] A series of minor strikes, called *strikitos*, began. This continued friction neatly fits the concept of "rising expectations." Sociologist

James Davies found that when a long suppressed group, such as the miners, obtained positive changes their repressed expectations flared up.[132] This happened in the Clifton area. The improved salary was only part of what workers wanted; they wanted to be treated with respect. So when, in 1916, Metcalf workers shut down the ore concentrator it was because the foreman's order to speed up had ignored their union representative. Latin workers became upset by management slights that were accepted in years past. A decent salary was not the only issue occupying miners classified as nonwhite; men had long wanted respect from their Anglo supervisors.

In 1917 dissatisfaction broke out again. This time the WFM had many Spanish-surnamed workers in charge, such as Pascual M. Vargas. The Vargas brothers, Pascual and Canuto, became important supporters of the local International Union of Mine, Mill and Smelter Workers (IUMMSW) and Pascual Vargas was a leading spokesman in the large 1917 strike in Clifton-Morenci.[133] Companies continued to work at the "division of races" by promoting some EuroLatins over Mexicans. Norman Carmichael, who represented the copper companies, declared that Clifton-Morenci District workers were slackers, lagging far behind Miami's laborers. He blamed this on the attitudes of local workers, who were mostly Latins (Mexican, Spanish, and Italian). Carmichael thought that workers seemed to think that being unionized (the WFM developed again in 1917) they could call the shots and defy the commands of shift bosses.[134] In 1917 the Latins struck again and held on winning their demands.[135]

Canuto Vargas, the labor organizer, later coeditor, of the American Federation of Labor's English/Spanish newspaper, reported that between 1915 and 1918 overall wages rose by 20 percent.[136] Miners who had earned $2.55 now made $5.10 and surface workers saw an increase from $1.60 to $3.83 per shift.[137] However, throughout Arizona most copper camp workers faced demoralizing losses. While miners in Jerome and Bisbee experienced the humiliation of deportation, Globe's workers saw their demands ignored because the Old Dominion copper mine shut down rather than give into workers' demands. The mine later reopened without the changes being asked for. By the end of 1917 Edward J. Moreno, who later became active in the League of United Latin American Citizens (LULAC), appealed for aid for Arizona's Mexican and Spanish workers. Noting that 66 percent of Arizona's copper miners were Spanish speakers, he suggested that unless workers got some help, not welfare, they might leave Arizona and cripple the state's output, which was roughly 35 percent of the national copper production.[138]

Historian Philip Mellinger stated that the cooperation of nonunionized Latin workers in 1913 and 1914 was worth noting because of the unique coalitions formed. Mellinger also included Southern Slavs in addition to Latins.[139] The rough times in Arizona's mining districts did not seem to discourage Spaniards; the 1920 Census showed 1013 or 26 percent more Spaniards than in 1910. However, after the turbulent decade of the 1920s, the passage of restrictive immigrant laws, the harassment of the resurgent Ku Klux Klan with its anti-immigrant and anti-Catholic views, and the Great Depression, the number of first-generation Spaniards dropped to 558 in 1930.[140]

In conclusion, as a social meteorologist, I suggest a pattern for the microclimates that Spaniards found in Arizona. All areas showed a cool climate toward residential proximity of Anglos and Spaniards. Even in Jerome, where Spanish fire fighters did not displace Anglo workers but actually helped save or produce more jobs, Spaniards lived in a segregated *barrio*. These places, one could argue, might reflect self-segregation. New immigrants might prefer to live among other Spanish speakers. However, these segregated areas were generally substandard in terms of basic amenities, like a supply of clean water. In turn, the lack of water contributed to both fires and the spread of diseases; workers faced dangers both at work and in their homes. Segregated areas had more of a health hazard than other areas in a given town. Another factor was education for the children of residents. Children in segregated areas were more easily shunted off to inferior schools than those that served Anglos. In Morenci, Spaniards lived in more diverse residential settings. Scattered on the town's seven hills, they dwelled among other Latins in an area which was not an actual slum. Here the climate heated up, as these somewhat diverse groups worked together on strikes. But, wages were a colder part of the climate. Generally, Latins earned less than Anglos and were not in higher supervisory positions.

An unintended consequence of such residential separation and a wage scale divided by "race" was that in some places, such as in Ray and the Clifton-Morenci area, it led to Latin unity. For employers the only significant racial difference was the gap they perpetuated between Anglos and the group, or "race," they considered Latins. It was to close this gap that Latins united, albeit briefly in strikes.[141] They cooperated when a strike for better wages was taking place. According to a letter to Governor Hunt at the end of the Clifton Morenci strike, what we would today call the psychological effects of the strike "are shown in the elimination of race prejudices, and the development of the solidarity of brotherhood among the workmen, which bears fruit in unity of purpose and willingness to suffer & sacrifice for their common good."[142]

Future research can show if and when Spaniards worked for the same wages as whites. Their status in some of the public work projects they were involved in early in the last century brought them lower wages than white workers, but, sometimes, higher wages than workers from other ethnic groups. For example, historian Julie Greene documents how in the building of the Panama Canal, Spaniards were not placed in the gold roll status of wages, reserved for whites. Instead they were on the lesser-paid "silver roll," along with Afro-Caribbean workers.[143] On the island of Pigeon Key, Florida, the railroad camp held up to 400 workers at peak times. The 1910 census taker found 211 people on the island; the majority of them were nonnatives. Seventy-seven Spaniards constituted the largest immigrant group, some 51 percent of the total immigrant population. In Florida, where Spanish laborers were part of an impressive project to link the island of Key West to the mainland, they were considered a notch above African Americans, whose labor was relegated to clearing land.[144] The examples of Panama and Florida illustrate two important aspects of the migratory experience of Spaniards in the United States, also shown in the Arizona mining camps: they were an "inbetween" racial group, and most were unskilled workers who served, as stated in Varela-Lago's chapter, as the "hands of America," doing work native white Americans would not do or would be paid more for doing.

NOTES

1. Guy Anderson and Donna Anderson, eds., *Honor the Past, Mold the Future* (Globe, AZ: Gila Centennials, 1976), 72. In the book his name is spelled Zerafin, but other documents indicate that his name was Serafín.

2. Germán Rueda, *La emigración contemporánea de españoles a Estados Unidos, 1820–1950: De "dons" a "misters"* (Madrid: Editorial Mapfre, 1993), 56.

3. Anderson, *Honor the Past*, 104. Given the mobility of low-paid immigrant workers city directories, when available, can tell us more about where people lived. In this case, I am making an "educated guess" that Serafín possibly lived there.

4. Arizona's genealogy site, http://genealogy.az.gov (accessed 2007).

5. Arizona's genealogy site, http://genealogy.az.gov (accessed 2011).

6. Marshall Trimble, *Arizona: A Cavalcade of History* (Tucson, AZ: Treasure Chest, 1990), 60.

7. Otis Young, "Spanish Tradition in Gold and Silver Mining," *Arizona and the West* 7 (Winter 1965): 299–314.

8. Patricia Nelson Limerick, Clyde Milner II, and Charles E. Rank, eds., *Trails: Toward a New Western History* (Lawrence: University Press of Kansas, 1991).

9. William G. Robbins, "The Emergence of a New Paradigm," in *Trails: Toward a New Western History*, ed. Patricia Nelson Limerick, Clyde Milner II, and Charles E. Rank (Lawrence: University Press of Kansas, 1991), ch. 12, p. 206. See David Emmons, *The Butte Irish: Class and Ethnicity in an American Mining Town, 1875–1925* (Urbana: University of Illinois Press, 1990).

10. Vincent Parrillo, *Strangers to These Shores: Race and Ethnic Relations in the United States*, 3rd ed. (New York: Macmillan, 1990), 427.

11. Rueda, *La emigración contemporánea*, 138.

12. Charles Montgomery, "Becoming Spanish American: Race and Rhetoric in New Mexico Politics, 1880–1928," *Journal of American Ethnic History* 20, no. 4 (Summer 2001): 59–84.

13. Phylis Cancilla Martinelli, "Mexican American Identity: An Interdisciplinary Approach," in *Mexican American Identity*, ed. Martha Bernal and Phylis Cancilla Martinelli (Encino, CA: Floricanto Press, 1993), 25.

14. R. A. Gómez, "Spanish Immigration to the United States," *Americas* 19 (July 1962): 76.

15. The Irish would be classified by their national origin if their religion was Catholic, since nativists did not welcome people of that faith. The Protestant Irish case is more complex. Noel Ignatiev carefully delineates the process of how the Irish [Protestants] became white. Noel Ignatiev, *How the Irish Became White* (New York: Routledge, 1996), 187.

16. Gabriel Tortella, *The Development of Modern Spain* (Cambridge, MA: Harvard University Press, 2000), 4–7. Historian Linda Gordon also uses this term, with a hyphen, specifically in discussing Arizona. Linda Gordon, *The Great Arizona Orphan Abduction* (Cambridge, MA: Harvard University Press, 1999), 101.

17. Gail Lichenhan, *Copper the Mighty Metal* (Phoenix: Arizona Mining Association, 2001).

18. Gordon Chappell, *Rails to Carry Copper: A History of the Magma Arizona Railroad* (Boulder, CO: Pruett, 1973).

19. Thomas Sheridan, "Silver Shackles and Copper Collars: Race, Class and Labor in the Arizona Mining Industry from the Eighteenth Century until World

War II," in *Social Approaches to an Industrial Past*, ed. A. Bernard Knapp, Vincent Pigott, and Eugenia Herbert (London: Routledge, 1998): 174–87.

20. US Bureau of the Census, *Thirteenth Census*, Arizona Population, Foreign Born (Washington, DC: Government Printing Office, 1911).

21. Joseph Harrison, "Spanish Economic History: Restoration to the Franco Regime," *Economic History Review* (May 1, 1980): 260.

22. Gary R. Mormino and George E. Pozzetta, *The Immigrant World of Ybor City: Italians and Their Latin Neighbors in Tampa, 1885–1985* (Urbana: University of Illinois Press, 1987).

23. See Beverly Lozano, "The Andalucia-Hawaii-California Migration: A Study in Macrostructure and Microhistory," *Comparative Studies in Society and History* 26, no. 2 (April 1984): 305–24 (chapter 2 in this volume).

24. See Thomas G. Hidalgo, "From the Mountains and Plains of Spain to the Hills and Hollers of West Virginia: Spanish Immigration into Southern West Virginia in the Early Twentieth Century" (chapter 7 in this volume).

25. Adrian Shubert, *The Road to Revolution in Spain: The Coal Miners of Asturias, 1860–1934* (Urbana: University of Illinois Press, 1987), 33.

26. John L. Sinclair, "Santa Rita: The Town that Vanished into Thin Air," *New Mexico Magazine* (March 1985).

27. William Conger, "History of the Clifton-Morenci District," in *The History of Mining in Arizona*, ed. J. Michael Canty and Michael Greeley (Tucson: Mining Club of the Southwest Foundation, 1987), 99–128.

28. David Avery, *Not on Queen Victoria's Birthday: The Story of the Rio Tinto Mines* (London: Collins, 1974), 91.

29. S. J. Keay, *Roman Spain* (Berkeley: University of California Press, 1988), 65.

30. Avery, *Not on Queen Victoria's Birthday*, 270.

31. Richard West, *River of Tears: The Rise of the Rio Tinto-Zinc Mining Corporation* (London: Earth Island Limited, 1972), 21.

32. The Tharsis Sulphur & Copper Co. Ltd. took over the copper mines in the Sierra de Tharsis. The company became a global distributor of sulfur and on the side made some profit on copper as well. https://uoginternationalstory.wordpress.com/tag/rio-tinto-mines/ (accessed 2011).

33. S. G. Checkland, *The Mines of Tharsis: Roman, French and British Enterprise in Spain* (Glasgow: Allen and Unwin, 1967).

34. Dillingham Commission Report, *Dictionary of Races or Peoples* (Washington, DC: Government Printing Office, 1911), 5:136. Northern Italians were believed to be of Alpine racial stock. The Bureau of Immigration classified the Spanish as Iberic or a Romance group of Aryan origins (136).

35. Oscar Handlin, *Race and Nationality in American Life* (Boston: Little, Brown, 1957), 77.

36. Douglas Brinkley, *The Wilderness Warrior, Theodore Roosevelt and the Crusade for America* (New York: Harper Collins, 2009), 317.

37. Brinkley, *The Wilderness Warrior*, 318.

38. Michael Omi and Howard Winant, *Racial Formation in the United States: From the 1960s to the 1980s* (New York: Routledge,1987), 52.

39. Omi and Winant, *Racial Formation in the United States*, 64.

40. James Barrett and David Roediger, "Inbetween Peoples: Race, Nationality and the 'New Immigrant' Working Class," *Journal of American Ethnic History* 16, no. 3 (Spring 1997): 3–44; Robert Orsi, "The Religious Boundaries of an Inbetween People: Street *Feste* and the Problem of the Dark-Skinned Other in Italian Harlem, 1920–1990," *American Quarterly* 44, no. 3 (September 1992): 313–47.

41. David Roediger, *Working toward Whiteness: How America's Immigrants Became White; The Strange Journey from Ellis Island to the Suburbs* (New York: Basic Books, 2005), 149.

42. Roediger, *Working toward Whiteness*, 85.

43. Coleen Stitt, "Fickle Friends: Copper and Community in Globe, Arizona" (PhD diss., Arizona State University, 1999), 110.

44. This is preliminary research. Naturalization papers are useful since the person has made a commitment to become a US citizen, which omits *golondrinas*, or birds of passage. The data linkage was used to see if these men stayed in Arizona and if they began families. However, the classification as Spanish race was unexpected.

45. Both Mexicans and Italians were considered by white Americans as part of the "Latin Race," since at this time race was often loosely equated with nationality or geographical region (for example, the Alpine race). As David Roediger demonstrates, some labor leaders considered Mexicans and Italians as members of the Latin race. Roediger, *Working Toward Whiteness*, 85. Linda Gordon makes a similar point, *Great Arizona Orphan Abduction*, 102.

46. William Davenport, "The Exodus of a Latin People," *Charities*, vol. 12 (1904): 465–67, reproduced in Francesco Cordasco and Eugene Bucchioni, eds., *The Italians, Social Backgrounds of an American Group* (Clifton, NJ: Augustus Kelley, 1974).

47. Clare Sheridan, "Contested Citizenship: National Identity and the Mexican Immigration Debates of the 1920s," *Journal of American Ethnic History* 21, no. 3 (2002): 3–35.

48. Poster with "Latin" in author's personal collection.

49. Gordon, *Great Arizona Orphan Abduction*, 98.

50. Henry F. Dobyns, *Spanish Colonial Tucson. A Demographic History* (Tucson: University of Arizona Press, 1974).

51. Jed Woodwroth, "Public Schooling in Territorial Arizona; Republicanism, Protestantism, and Assimilation," *Journal of Arizona History* 46 (Summer 2005): 95–134.

52. Nancy Prichard, "Paradise Found?: Opportunity for Mexican, Irish, Italian and Chinese Born Individuals in Jerome Copper Mining District, 1890–1910" (PhD diss., University of Colorado, 1992), 163.

53. Dillingham Commission Report, *Japanese and other Races* (Washington, DC: Government Printing Office, 1911), 136, 150.

54. Pedro Gómez, interviewed for "In the Shadow of the Smokestack" by Elena Diaz Bjorkquist; Mrs. Amelia Oñate, interview by author, Phoenix, Arizona, June 15, 2000.

55. Eric Clements, *After the Boom in Tombstone and Jerome, Arizona: Decline in Western Resource Towns* (Reno: University of Nevada Press, 2003).

56. Thomas Dorich, "This Is a Tough Place to Work: Industrial Relations in the Jerome Mines, 1900–1922," *Journal of Arizona History* 38 (Autumn 1997): 233–56.

57. T. W. Quayle, *Mining Methods and Practices at the United Verde Copper Mine, Jerome, Arizona* (Washington, DC: US Bureau of Mines, 1931): 27–28.

58. Prichard, "Paradise Found?" 96. No more was found on J. J. Shaw or how he found the original team of Spaniards. This is an area needing more research.

59. Prichard, "Paradise Found?" 96; Quayle, *Mining Methods*, 27–28.

60. Prichard, "Paradise Found?" 97.

61. Superior Court Yavapai County, Arizona, Declaration of Intention, John Gago.

62. Eastern Europeans were also subjected to discrimination, but are not the focus of this chapter.

63. Superior Court Yavapai County, Arizona, Declaration of Intention, Father Autimo Nebruda.

64. Clements, *After the Boom*, 63.

65. Antonio Rios-Bustamante, "As Guilty as Hell: Copper Towns, Mexican Miners and Community, 1920–1950" (unpublished document, Chicano Collection, Arizona State University Library, CHMS-336, 1993); Andrea Huginnie, "Strikitos: Race, Class, and Work in the Arizona Copper Industry, 1870–1920" (PhD diss., Yale University, 1991).

66. Huginnie, "Strikitos," 209.

67. Prichard, "Paradise Found?" 97

68. Prichard, "Paradise Found?" 96. This is one of several names that may have been recorded incorrectly, due to incorrect spelling or the difficulty of reading some written archival materials. It could have been Sandoval. Unfortunately at this point a more correct Spanish spelling was not found.

69. In Phoenix some Italians were active members in some Mexican organizations, for example, the Alianza Hispano Americana and the Phoenix Mexican Athletic Club. Phylis Cancilla Martinelli, "Transformation of an Ethnic Community: Phoenix's Italians, 1880 to 1980," in *Phoenix in the 20th Century, Essays in Community History*, ed. G. Wesley Johnson (Norman: University of Oklahoma Press, 1993), 71.

70. Lily S. Hernández, *Los Pioneros Mexicanos* / "The Mexican Pioneers," Manuscript 90-458 (Jerome Historical Society, 1990).

71. "Local News," *Jerome News*, September 1, 1916, 7. Unfortunately, no further information was available regarding this paper. In many cases local foreign-language newspapers vanished. According to email correspondence with Professor Chris Marin (longtime archivist of Arizona State University Chicano Collection), these newspapers focus on the events going on in those times in Arizona, Mexico, New Mexico, and Texas, as these are places that affected Mexican immigrants in the copper industry. Chris Marin, email message to author, December 13, 2013.

72. Clements, *After the Boom*, 50.

73. Herbert V. Young, *They Came to Jerome* (Jerome, AZ: Jerome Historical Society, 1952).

74. Joseph D. Camon to Charles Moyer, Western Federation of Miners, July 7, 1909, Henry McCluskey Collection, Arizona State University Library, Special Collections.

75. Young, *They Came to Jerome*, 53.

76. Dorich, "This Is a Tough Place to Work," 233–56. The more famous Bisbee Deportation that year was not brought about by the local union, but by the IWW; the failure of that movement insured Wobblies had no place in Jerome.

77. Prichard, "Paradise Found?" 271.

78. Checkland, *Mines of Tharsis*, 187.

79. Frank Tuck, *History of Mining in Arizona*, 2nd ed. (Phoenix: Arizona Department of Mines, 1962), 22.

80. More research is needed in Spain. Company records may clarify how workers found out about jobs in Arizona's copper mines, or a family history may emerge, or diaries of the mining experts.

81. Jackling papers, Bancroft Library, University of California, Berkeley, Ray mine file, Carton I, Scrap Book: Arizona & New Mexico, February 21, 1914.

82. El Club Sonorense, *Recuerdos de Sonora*, 2nd ed. (self-published) (Arizona: El Club Sonorense, 1999), 71.

83. El Club Sonorense, *Recuerdos de Sonora*, 46.

84. "Ray Is Booming," *Arizona Republican*, October 13, 1910, 1.

85. Leonor López, *Forever Sonora, Ray, Barcelona: A Labor of Love* (self-published, n.d.), courtesy of Kathy Quiroz, email message to author, August 17, 2012.

86. Kathy Quiroz, email message to author, August 20, 2012.

87. El Club Sonorense, *Recuerdos de Sonora*, 17–18.

88. www.copperarea.com/pages (accessed September 2012).

89. Joe Bittick, email correspondence with author, August 2012.

90. Ralph Mahoney, "Retains Atmosphere of Old Mexico," *Arizona Days and Ways Magazine*, December 7, 1986, 7–10.

91. Philip Mellinger, *Race and Labor in Western Copper: The Fight for Equality, 1896–1918* (Tucson: University of Arizona Press, 1992), 145.

92. "Ray Consolidated Makes Big Gain," *Casa Grande Dispatch*, June 22, 1915, 5.

93. Eric Meeks, *Border Citizens: The Making of Indians, Mexicans and Anglos in Arizona* (Austin: University of Texas Press, 2007), 103.

94. Mellinger, *Race and Labor*, 146.

95. True Copy of the Notes of Honorable Thomas E. Campbell (former Arizona governor) written between 1934 and 1939, Arizona State Capitol: History and Library Division (ASCH&LD).

96. https://www.facebook.com/groups/61350512177/about/, Ray Sonora and Kearney, organized and monitored by Chris Marin.

97. Ted Cogut and Bill Conger, *History of Arizona's Clifton Morenci Mining District* (Thatcher, AZ: Mining History, 1999), 1: 39.

98. Gordon, *Great Arizona Orphan Abduction*, 101–2.

99. Charles Spezia, *Walking Tour of Historic Chase Creek, Clifton, AZ 1900–1929* (Clifton, AZ, 1990). The surname appears also as Pallacio on the genealogy website http://genealogy.az.gov.

100. Superior Court, Greenlee County, Arizona, Declaration of Intention, Fermín Palicio.

101. Spezia, *Walking Tour*, 7.

102. Information available on Ancestry.com.

103. Arizona Territorial Board of Health, Bureau of Vital Statistics, Clifton, Arizona, November 20, 1909.

104. Arizona's genealogy site, http://genealogy.az.gov.

105. Mrs. Amelia Oñate, interview by author, Phoenix, June 15, 2000.

106. Mrs. Amelia Oñate, interview by author, Phoenix, June 15, 2000.

107. Joaquin Oviedo, *Morenci Memories: True Tales of a Copper Town* (New York: Universe, 2004), 96.

108. Pedro Gómez, interviewed for "In the Shadow of the Smokestack," website by Elena Diaz Bjorkquist, http://www.geocities.ws/shadowofthesmokestack (accessed 2008).

109. Cogut and Conger, *History of Arizona's Clifton-Morenci*, 175.

110. David Myrick, *Railroads of Arizona*, vol. 3: *Clifton, Morenci and Metcalf* (Glendale, CA: Interurban Trans-Anglo Press, 1984), 247.

111. US Bureau of the Census, *Thirteenth Census, 1910*. Arizona, Graham County, Manuscript Census, Metcalf Precinct (Washington, DC: Government Printing Office, 1911).

112. Roberta Troxell Watt, "History of Morenci, Arizona" (master's thesis, University of Arizona, 1956), 61; *Morenci Leader*, July 8, 1905, 25.

113. Watt, "History of Morenci," 52.

114. Víctor Velásquez, interview with author, 2008.

115. Gordon, *Great Arizona Orphan Abduction*, 229.

116. Murray Bookchin, *The Spanish Anarchists: The Heroic Years, 1868–1936* (New York: Free Life, 1977).

117. Mormino and Pozzetta, *The Immigrant World of Ybor City*, 80. See also chapters by Christopher Castañeda, and Gary Mormino and George Pozzetta in this volume.

118. Avery, *Not on Queen Victoria's Birthday*, 194.

119. R. A. Davis, A. Welty, J. Borrego, J. Morales, J. Pendon, and J. Ryan, "Rio Tinto Estuary (Spain): 5000 Years of Pollution," *Environmental Geology* 39 (September 2000): 1107–15; Juan Manuel Pérez López, "Los conflictos sociales de febrero de 1888: Causas y consecuencias," *Catálogo monográfico N. 1* (Huelva, Spain: Fundación Río Tinto, no date): 20–24. Translation courtesy of Parkin Kent and Irene Cedillo Kent. Smelting consisted of placing tons of minerals in large outdoor mounds, called *teleras*, that were burned, releasing sulfur fumes. When the remaining material was washed with the waste water from the mines, pure copper was the result. This method was environmentally a disaster, however, and Spaniards objected to its use since it contaminated crops; furthermore, this method was not allowed in England.

120. James McBride, "The Liga Protectora Latina: a Mexican-American Benevolent Society in Arizona," *Journal of the West* 14, no. 4 (October 1975): 82–89.

121. Lawrence Michael Fong, "Sojourners and Settlers: The Chinese Experience in Arizona," *Journal of Arizona History* 21 (1980): 13.

122. "80% Law Void," *Arizona Republic*, January 8, 1915.

123. J. Morris Richards, *History of the Arizona State Legislature, 1912–1967*, vol. 3 (1913): 1; vol. 4 (1914–1915) (Arizona State University Library, microfiche).

124. J. Morris Richards. *History of the Arizona State Legislature 1912–1967*, vol. 4 (Arizona State University Library, microfiche).

125. My thanks to Ana Varela-Lago for a copy of the letter from Spanish vice-consul in San Francisco, Arturo Brand, to the Arizona governor. The original is located at the Archivo General de la Administración (Alcalá de Henares, Spain), Ministerio de Asuntos Exteriores, box 8172.

126. F. Remington Barr, *A History Of the Detroit Copper Company, Ltd, 1872–1924* (Morenci, AZ: n.p., 1940), 67.

127. Canuto Vargas, "A Short History of the Organized Labor Movement in Clifton-Morenci-Metcalf District, Arizona," *Pan-American Labor Press*, October 16, 1918, 3, Bancroft Library Collection, University of California, Berkeley.

128. Hywel Davies and Joseph Myers, *Report from Federal Commissioners of Conciliation*, correspondence file, Governor George Wilson Hunt Files, February 1916, Arizona State Archives, University Special Collections.

129. Canuto Vargas, "A Short History of the Organized Labor Movement in Clifton-Morenci-Metcalf District, Arizona, Continued," *Pan American Labor Press*, December 4, 1918, 7, Bancroft Library Collection, University of California, Berkeley.

130. Governor George Wilson Hunt, letters, February 1916, Arizona State Archives, University Special Collections.

131. Michael E. Parrish, *Mexican Workers, Progressives and Copper: The Failure of Industrial Democracy in Arizona during the Wilson Years* (La Jolla: Chicano Research Publications, University of California, San Diego, 1979), 13.

132. James C. Davies, "Toward a Theory of Revolution," *American Sociological Review* 17 (1962): 5–19.

133. Parrish, *Mexican Workers*, 17.

134. Mellinger, *Race and Labor*, 196.

135. Watt, "History of Morenci," 73–77.

136. Mellinger, *Race and Labor*, 197.

137. Vargas, "Short History," 2.

138. "Need Spanish-Speakers," *Arizona Silver Belt*, December 1, 1917, 1.

139. Mellinger, *Race and Labor*, 19

140. US Bureau of the Census, *1930 Census*, Arizona (Washington, DC: Government Printing Offices, 1931), table 15, 363.

141. Mellinger, *Race and Labor*, 47.

142. Davies and Myers, *Report from Federal Commissioners of Conciliation*, correspondence file, Governor George Wilson Hunt Files, February 1916, Arizona State Archives, University Special Collections.

143. Julie Greene, "Spaniards on the Silver Roll: Labor Troubles and Liminality in the Panama Canal Zone," *International Labor and Working Class History* (Fall 2004): 78–98.

144. Dan Gallagher, *Florida's Great Ocean Railway: Building the Key West Extension* (Sarasota: Pineapple Press, 2003).

7

FROM THE MOUNTAINS AND PLAINS OF SPAIN TO THE HILLS AND HOLLERS OF WEST VIRGINIA

*Spanish Immigration into Southern
West Virginia in the Early Twentieth Century*

THOMAS HIDALGO

On New Year's Eve, 1919, my grandfather, Cayetano Hidalgo Sánchez, boarded the ship *P. de Satrústegui* in Cádiz, Spain, and set sail for the United States. He landed in New York City three weeks later, on January 20, 1920. A farm laborer in Spain, Cayetano planned to stay in the United States for four years and then go back home to Peñarroya, a small town in the province of Córdoba, in Andalusia. From New York, he headed to Stotesbury, West Virginia, a small coal-mining community in Raleigh County, to join his friend Lorenzo Tocado, who had left Peñarroya for the United States in 1912. On December 2, 1920, my grandfather on my mother's side, Valeriano Santos Núñez, also from Peñarroya, left Spain aboard the *Mongolia* from Vigo. He sailed into Ellis Island on December 10. His first stop was Freeport, Pennsylvania, where he met up with Vidal Victoria Catena, a friend who had left Peñarroya for the United States several years earlier. Valeriano quickly moved on to West Virginia, where he planned to stay indefinitely.

I never knew either of my grandfathers. Cayetano did not return to Spain after four years as he had planned. On April 16, 1928, he was killed in a mining

DOI: 10.5876/9781607327998.c007

accident. My grandmother Esperanza, who had followed my grandfather to the United States in 1920 with their firstborn son, my uncle Cayetano, was thus forced to return to Spain, but now with four children: little Cayetano, along with my father, Manuel, my aunt Astrea, and my uncle Benito, all born in West Virginia. My father eventually returned to the United States in 1941. Astrea and my grandmother followed a few years later. Benito died as a child in Spain, and Cayetano lived the rest of his life in France. When Valeriano said he was staying in the United States, apparently he meant it. In 1929 he sent for my grandmother Agrícola and my mother, Flor, who had been born a month after he left Spain, in 1920. In 1943, he took out citizenship papers. He died in 1946.

All I know about my grandfathers is what I have heard through family stories and read about in a few documents I have found. Like several thousand Spaniards who were drawn by the prospect of work in the coal mines, my grandfathers immigrated to West Virginia early in the twentieth century, but their story is virtually unknown. There is almost nothing in the history books to document that they lived and worked there.

I left West Virginia for New England in 1986, and I am often asked where I am from. People are no doubt intrigued by my Appalachian drawl. "My family is from Spain, but I grew up in West Virginia," is my standard answer. The response is usually something like "Spaniards in West Virginia? That's interesting. I've never heard of that. Why did they go to West Virginia?" In this chapter I will provide some answers to that question using the words of immigrants and their families as well as information gathered from a variety of documents.

The inspiration to write about the Spanish immigrants in West Virginia came to me when I was visiting there in 1993 with my Puerto Rican wife, Dr. Maria Idalí Torres, an anthropologist who is now the director of the Mauricio Gastón Institute for Latino Public Policy and Community Development at the University of Massachusetts Boston. She was fascinated with the story of Spanish immigrants in West Virginia. Through her encouragement I interviewed Avelino Cartelle, a dear family friend who came from Spain in 1920 when he was seventeen years old and lived many years in Oak Hill. The next morning, Idalí and I visited the Raleigh County Library in Beckley to see if we could learn more about Spaniards who had lived in West Virginia. I perused a few standard West Virginia history books that told me nothing. With the help of the librarian, we found some information on Spanish immigrant coal miners in labor department records. Idalí and I rifled through the documents, and I was so excited I could barely keep from yelling *¡olé!*

The next year I began work on a doctoral degree in multicultural education at the University of Massachusetts at Amherst. As a dissertation topic I decided to write a history of Spaniards who had immigrated to West Virginia. I wrote my dissertation, "Reconstructing a History of Spanish Immigrants in West Virginia: Implications for Multicultural Education," and graduated with my EdD in 1999. Since then I have gathered additional information. Fourteen oral history interviews form the foundation of this chapter. Spanish immigrants and their families tell their stories as they remember them. A variety of records and documents buttress the interviews and help bring the stories alive.

This chapter addresses several basic questions: Where in Spain did the immigrants come from, what was life like for them, and why did they leave? Of all the places to settle in the Americas, why did they choose West Virginia? Once in West Virginia, what was life like for them? What type of work did they do? How did Spaniards maintain their identity? Did they suffer discrimination?

LIFE IN SPAIN: WHERE THEY CAME FROM

I examined 163 documents (a sampling of citizenship papers and immigration records), 123 from Raleigh County and 40 from adjoining Fayette County. These were popular destinations for Spanish immigrants because of the booming coal industry that needed immigrant labor.[1] The documents also contain some information on forty spouses. Spaniards came to West Virginia from throughout Spain, but most emigrants to Raleigh and Fayette Counties came from the southern region of Andalusia and the northern regions of Galicia and Asturias. In this sampling of Spaniards, 88 came from Andalusia, 30 from Galicia, and 21 from Asturias. Smaller numbers came from other regions: the Balearic Islands of Mallorca and Menorca, the Basque Country, Cantabria, Castilla y León, Cataluña, Extremadura, Madrid, and Valencia. This pattern differs somewhat from what Phylis C. Martinelli found in her study of Spanish immigrant coal miners in Arizona, most of whom were from Galicia and Asturias in the North of Spain.[2] She found little evidence of immigrants from Andalusia.

Many Spaniards faced economic difficulties at the turn of the twentieth century, conditions that probably influenced their decision to leave. At that time 70 to 80 percent of the population of Andalusia worked for low wages in agriculture, mostly on large estates owned by a few landlords who had held the land for centuries. Adding to these poor labor conditions, workers were forced to attend churches located on the big *latifundios* and pay into Catholic worker associations organized by the landowners.[3] In Asturias, emigration was a response to the scarcity of jobs in agriculture due to growth in the population. Coal mining was an important industry there, but not enough jobs were available for the inhabitants.[4] In Galicia, the land was divided into *minifundios*, plots too small for subsistence, forcing many to leave.[5] Life became so difficult that sometimes an entire Spanish village, including the priest, would leave Spain for the Americas, driven out by dire poverty.[6]

Farming, or jobs related to farming, provided the livelihood for many Spanish families I spoke with. The family of Dolores García's father owned a farm in Bélmez, Córdoba. "They had olive orchards and grape arbors, but mostly olives," Dolores remembers."For miles it was like acres of olive trees." She was able to see the orchards when she visited once.[7] Not all migrants worked in agriculture. Asunción Marquis Richmond's parents came also from Bélmez, where her father was a carpenter and her mother worked in a pub.[8] Women were no strangers to work. Toney Pallares's mother, Patrocinio Castillo, from Almería, was the town baker.[9] In Galicia, Josephine Meijide Midkiff's mother went to work outside the home as a seamstress when she came of age.[10] My aunt, Rose Santos Parkins, recalled only that her father, Valeriano Santos, worked in a factory of some sort and in a grocery store: "He seemed to like to work in a grocery store. That is what I remember him talking about."[11] Rose's maternal grandmother, my great-grandmother Rosa Porras Robas, became a baker in Peñarroya, after her husband was killed.

LEAVING SPAIN

All the folks I spoke with agreed that economics was a key factor in leaving Spain. However, it was not the only reason. Toney Pallares said his parents, Ramón Pallares Navarro and Patrocinio Castillo, left Spain to escape an oppressive Catholic Church. "They were Catholics in Spain, and that was the real reason they came to this country, to get away from the religion,"

Toney recalled. "They didn't like the Catholic Church. My mother told me the priests ran Spain. I mean, whatever they said was law."[12] Aversion to the power of the Catholic Church also influenced José Torrico's decision to leave Spain. His son, Pedro Torrico, explained: "Neither one of them liked the Catholic Church. They ruled the country. I've heard them say that they'd never go back on account of that, especially my mother, and they never did go to church while they were here."[13]

Avoiding military service was another motivating factor among many of the men who left Spain, because of the length of service (twelve years, counting reserves) and the risk of being drafted to fight in the very unpopular colonial war in Morocco.[14] That was the case with one of Josephine Midkiff's uncles, José Fernández. "He came to this country when he was only nineteen years old. I think some of the young men came to dodge the military service that they were expected to do, so he came just a young man," she said.[15] Similarly, Manuel Cartelle's uncle, Avelino Cartelle, left Galicia at age seventeen to avoid being drafted into the Spanish Army and risk being sent to fight in North Africa.[16]

Union politics forced Alejos ("Alex") López's maternal grandfather, Antonio Castañón, to leave Spain. He explained: "My grandpa was a coal miner in Spain. The reason he immigrated here is because he was a very strong-minded person, and he was a very strong union person, and he had to leave Spain because he was kind of a political activist. And they said if he hadn't left Spain, they would probably have killed him or imprisoned him."[17]

A sense of adventure motivated some migrants. Josephine Meijide Midkiff said that her father was an adventurous person who had traveled a great deal before ending up in West Virginia.[18] Adventure, not necessity, seemed to motivate Libby Martínez Keadle's maternal grandfather, Nicasio Sánchez, to leave Spain with her grandmother Adela when her mother, María Antonia Sánchez, was only four years old. She remembered: "My grandmother Adela always said that they were better off in Spain. My grandfather just wanted, I guess he was adventurous. He was bent on coming to the United States."[19]

Emigrants often left their hometowns in groups, some going to the same destination in the United States, but often splitting up once they arrived. Chain migration was typical. Once a settlement of Spaniards established itself, relatives and friends from the old country naturally followed.[20] When my grandfather, Cayetano Hidalgo Sánchez, left Spain from Peñarroya he was accompanied by eleven young men from his town. He and four others headed for West Virginia, while the rest went to Dover, New Jersey; New York City; and Waterbury, Connecticut.

Spanish emigrants were typically young, male, and single, like those from other European countries. Men accounted for 70 percent of all emigrants between 1882 and 1914.[21] Of the Spaniards in my sample, nearly 80 percent were under the age of thirty. Of those who filled out the documents, 103 were single at the time of their arrival in the United States, and 60 were married.

THE PATH TO WEST VIRGINIA

West Virginia was a popular destination for Spanish immigrants. In 1920, the state had the seventh-highest number of residents originally from Spain, behind New York, California, Florida, Pennsylvania, New Jersey, and Hawai'i.[22] However, many Spaniards did not come directly to West Virginia from Spain. A common experience was to stop along the way, including in other countries. The documents I have consulted show that of the Spaniards who settled in Raleigh and Fayette Counties, at least one-fourth had lived in another state (Indiana, Kentucky, Massachusetts, Michigan, New Jersey, New York, Ohio, Pennsylvania, and Wyoming). These documents also indicate that before settling in West Virginia, some of these Spaniards had lived in other countries (Argentina, Bermuda, Chile, Cuba, France, Mexico, and Panama). Francisco Ubeda Guirado, for example, went to Panama first. His son Frank explained: "Daddy came over in 1908. They stopped, he and a friend of his from Spain, stopped off at the Panama Canal when they were building the Panama Canal and they just worked there a very short while, wasn't too long, wasn't very long because they were so afraid of the malaria mosquitoes, him and a Mr. Rubin, a Spanish fellow. They thought they had better leave that and come to the coal camps where they had originally intended to anyway.[23]

Alex López's father, Dositeo, went to Cuba, where he worked cutting sugar cane, and then to Cleveland before coming to West Virginia. Libby Martínez Keadle's father, José, first went to Cuba and worked on the railroad for about three years before entering the United States through Key West, Florida. Josephine Meijide Midkiff's father made several stops before coming to West Virginia, including Argentina, Cuba, and Bermuda.[24]

In 1920, seventeen-year-old Avelino Cartelle was in New York City, down to his last fifty cents, with no job and no job prospects. A few months earlier he had left Arnoya, in Galicia, and was thinking about trying his luck in Uruguay where a brother had emigrated. That is, until Manuel Básquez paid him a visit. Básquez had sailed with Cartelle from Spain to the United States earlier that year and had gone to Logan County, West Virginia, to join an uncle. Básquez asked Cartelle to return with him to Logan County and get a job in the coal mines. West Virginia? Coal mines? That was not what Cartelle had in mind when he set sail for the Americas, but it would have to do. "I wanted to stay in New York. I wanted to go to school. I didn't want to go to the mines," he told me in a 1993 interview, when he was ninety. He decided to go, taking with him a $2 guitar he had brought from Spain. "I wore it over my shoulder all the way to Logan County," Cartelle recalled. Arriving in Logan County, he received one day's training and went to work for the Guyandotte Coal Company at $10 a day, big money in those days.[25]

Although Cartelle never intended to go to West Virginia, he lived there for the rest of his life, leaving only for a one-year visit to Spain in the late 1920s and to work in a defense plant in Detroit during World War II. After the war, he opened a car dealership in Oak Hill, about sixty miles from the city of Logan. After that venture, Cartelle and Joe Benito, another Spaniard from Galicia, together opened "punch mines," small operations that sold coal to large companies. Later, Cartelle opened the Skyline Drive-in, a popular restaurant-bar near Oak Hill, which he operated until he retired. Cartelle died in 1996 at the age of ninety-three.

Frank Troitiño was a stonemason in Pousada, Galicia. Stonemasonry was a family as well as a community tradition. "My grandfather was a stonemason. My father was a stonemason. That's where I learned the trade," he recalled. Troitiño was working in Madrid in 1936 when General Francisco Franco led an uprising against Spain's democratically elected government, plunging the country into a brutal and bloody civil war. Troitiño joined the Spanish Republican Army in 1937 to fight against Franco, but the fascists won the war, primarily because of extensive assistance from Hitler and Mussolini. At war's end, Troitiño found himself in one of Franco's concentration camps, sentenced to thirty years! Through the intervention of his brother, Joe, who had left Spain years earlier and was living in Asheville, North Carolina, Frank was released and allowed to emigrate. "My brother got me out and then he brought me over here," he said. Troitiño later joined the United States Army and returned to Europe to fight the Germans as part of General Patton's force. After the war, he returned to Asheville and eventually to Mt. Hope to open a strip-mining operation. He lived there the rest of his life.[26]

Asunción Marquis Richmond's father, Manuel Márquez Cabrera (figure 7.1), first went to Chicago alone and worked in a meat-packing plant. Somehow the last name was changed to Marquis. He returned to Spain for Asunción's mother and then came back to the United States. The family lived for a while in Indiana before eventually settling in Stanford, West Virginia, not far from Beckley. Asunción said that her father was drawn to the coalfields, having learned that jobs were available and knowing English was not needed to work in the mines.[27]

Immigrants were required to prove that they were in good health to enter the United States. At Ellis Island, one can look at registers and see that people were examined and forced to return home because of an illness. Frank Ubeda had a copy of a document signed September 14, 1910, from the Tabernas Health Department (Almería, Spain) certifying that his mother, Josefa López Plaza, was married to his father, Francisco Ubeda Guirado, who was her sponsor, and that their two children, Mercedes and Juan, had been declared to be "of good health and free of contagious diseases," by the city health inspector.[28]

In some cases, a US resident had to guarantee to support the new immigrants. I found the original affidavit that my grandfather filed in April 1929 in support of an application for a visa for my grandmother and mother. It reads in part:

> Valeriano Santos Nuñez, aged 36 years . . . is a resident of Concho, West
> Virginia . . . he was born in Peñarroya, Province of Cordoba, Spain . . . he
> was admitted to the United States in December 1920, and he came at once to
> Concho . . . he has fourteen hundred seventy five dollars ($1,475.00) on deposit
> in the Comercial Italiana of New York City and . . . he is employed at Rock
> Smokeless Coal Company of [Fayette] County, where he earns one hundred
> fifty dollars ($150.00) per month . . . His wife Agricola Moraño Porras . . .
> and his daughter Flor Adela Santos Moraño . . . desire to come to Concho
> to live with him and . . . he desires to have his wife and child come to the
> United States to make their home with him. That if his wife and daughter are

FIGURE 7.1. Manuel Márquez Cabrera, one of thousands of Spaniards who worked in the mines of West Virginia. (Author's personal collection.)

admitted to the United States he will guarantee the United States that his wife and child shall not become a public charge, that he will make a home for them and that they will be under his care.

LIFE IN WEST VIRGINIA: COAL MINE CONDITIONS

Spaniards started arriving in West Virginia in the early 1900s, when the coal industry was expanding rapidly and there were not enough native-born Americans to do the work. The greatest numbers went to Raleigh and Fayette Counties because strikes had caused many Americans to leave for organized fields in the Midwest or elsewhere, and coal production was increasing proportionately at the greatest rate there. There was also the growing tendency for Americans to enter other industries and leave mining.[29]

Spaniards entered the mines in West Virginia in 1908, when seven were working at New River Coal Company mines in Raleigh County. The first Spaniard to die in a mining accident was killed in 1909 in a roof fall. In an investigation of immigrants in coal mining between 1909 and 1910, employers were asked about the relative efficiency of immigrants and natives on the job.[30] At that time, Spaniards were evident in only one mine. The commission reported:

> At another mine where Spaniards, Poles, and natives were employed, the Spanish miners were said to be slightly more industrious than the Poles and the Poles more industrious than the natives. Spaniards and Poles were more tractable than the natives and required less supervision. The Spaniards and Poles usually drank large quantities of beer and whiskey, but seldom became intoxicated, and lost less time from work from this cause than the natives. The natives were progressing more rapidly, it was claimed, but the inability of the immigrants to use English had little influence upon their work or usefulness as miners.[31]

Most Spaniards immigrated between 1912 and 1922, a violent period in United States labor history, which included a "mine war" between miners and coal operators.[32] Coal companies recruited immigrant labor from Eastern cities or other mining localities. They also sent labor agents to immigration ports and to Europe to procure workers, a practice discussed in other chapters of this book as well. John H. Nugent, commissioner of the Immigrant Bureau for West Virginia, was little more than an agent of the coal companies. From 1907 to 1913 the New River Company and the Consolidation Coal Company paid his salary and expenses.[33] As a result of these recruiting efforts, the number of Spaniards working in the mines in West Virginia grew steadily from 1911, when 18 were employed in six counties, to 1921 when their number peaked at 2,212 and they were working in 19 of the state's 55 counties. Southern West Virginia counties accounted for 1,744 miners.[34]

In 1921, nine Spaniards were killed as the result of mine accidents. Coal mining was physically demanding and hazardous, and the mines of southern West Virginia were the most perilous in the country. Working in the mines was more dangerous for southern West Virginia miners than going to war in World War I, according to historian David Corbin.[35] Mine safety laws were deficient, and mine inspectors were unqualified political appointees.

Meanwhile, operators refused to take responsibility for accidents, blaming injuries or deaths on the miners themselves.[36] W. P. Tams Jr., a southern West Virginia coal operator who started the town that bore his name, insinuated in his 1963 memoir that accidents were more the result of errors in judgment or procedures on the part of the miner, rather than the lack of safe conditions.[37]

Death and serious injury from mining accidents visited many Spanish homes. The coal mines took Toney Pallares's father when Toney was only two years old. "I really don't know how long he worked or how long we lived in Ethel [Logan County], but my father was killed in Ethel in the mines in 1929. A slate fall," Toney recalled.[38] Frank Ubeda remembered his father coming home after a long day in the mine and the obvious pain he was suffering, but like many of his generation, Frank quit high school to go into the mines to help the family:

> Coal mine [roofs] are not very high. You had to crawl on your belly in some
> of them. There was a whole lot of water in all the mines, naturally; it's
> underground. It would drop down all the time. So many [miners] had to
> work on their knees. My brother Joe and I were working one time at number
> 2 Lillybrook in what they called the peewee section because it was so low
> [there was barely enough room] between the top of the car and the top of
> the mine. Where me and my brother Joe were working, we had to work on
> our knees and water just pouring down everywhere. It's the nature of the
> brute, but that's what you had to do. You had to work on your knees, or sit
> on your butt or whatever, but you had to load that coal. Dad ruined his health
> by working in the mines. My brother John, he lost a leg due to working in the
> mines. I would from time to time stop and think [pointing], "That guy's a coal
> miner. He can barely walk. He's all stooped over." You could see men walking
> around, couldn't hardly breathe, dying from suffocation because they had
> the black lung. The mines have ruined the health of many, many, many men.
> [Eventually, Frank gave up mining and became a firefighter.][39]

John Ubeda, Frank's brother, was five years old when he came with his family from Spain to Prudence (Fayette County) in 1910. He learned the dangers of working in a coal mine early in life:

> I went to school to the fifth grade and then went to working in the mines
> when I was about twelve years old. Dad wanted me to go in with him to help

him. That's when I went in the mines. When I was twelve years old. Back in them days, even on a tipple [where coal is taken after leaving the mine] they had little boys like that picking dirty coal out, the slate and rock and stuff like that. [Coal] went over a table and they'd pick it out. I run a motor in there and I got hurt. Motor run over my foot when I went to get on it. It slipped off and just hit the wheel, that's all. It smashed [my foot], got blood poisoning, and they had to cut it off. After the accident, I went back to work at the same place. After I got my foot cut off with this motor, when I went back in I got used to wearing my [artificial] leg and went to run the motor and that was it. I hadn't worked at that mine but about a couple weeks when I got hurt.[40]

Most coal companies permitted boys to work in those days because there were no minimum age laws.[41] However, even after West Virginia established a minimum working age of fourteen, coal operators took advantage of loopholes or ignored them altogether to put children to work in the mines. Operators even had the gall to blame parents for this exploitation, claiming that they willingly sent their children to work in the mines.[42] John received $12 a week for 160 weeks as compensation for losing his leg. He worked nearly twenty years in the coal mines before starting his own trucking business, John Ubeda's Motor Truck Delivery (figure 7.2).[43]

Alex López was a college graduate, but worked in the mines for several years because the job paid well, and it was a challenge. Danger was always present and rock falls were common, he recalled:

You look up, man, you see that rock falling. You talk about something that will scare you. When you see that mountain coming in on you, man, you're scared, you're going to run. Everybody runs. I've experienced it. It's scary man. I mean, in the mines, at times I could sit and feel just as secure as you and I are sitting here talking. You know, not a concern in the world. And all of a sudden things can change so quick, and you're in mortal danger. That's the way it is. There's so many ways you can get killed in the mines. Rocks fall on you, explosion, get run over, get caught in the belt, get electrocuted. I almost got electrocuted twice. I thought I was a dead man a couple of times. [The company] sent in an order, said don't leave oil cans littered all over the section because it's against mining laws and we'd get written up when the inspector comes. I had two empty cans. I put these cans on the buggy, a rubber-tired vehicle run by electricity. The cable wasn't grounded properly, but I didn't

FIGURE 7.2. John Ubeda, pictured with the truck of the company he started with his brother Frank in the late 1930s—Ubeda Motor Truck Delivery. (Author's personal collection.)

know that. I set them two cans down on that buggy and when I did, that hit me, 440 volts. I was screaming. I think I was, I don't know. I, finally, it either knocked me loose, or I kicked myself [loose]. But the thought came to me: I'm going to die here, I'm going to die here. Because when it hit me I was just [paralyzed], you know. It hit me twice. I don't know if you've ever been—440 volts now. But if I'd had leather shoes on, I'd have died right there, been electrocuted. I was screaming and everything, and I couldn't work no more [that day]. My chest was hurting. And it scares you to death.[44]

That near-death experience did not force Alex López from the mines, but he did reach a point when he decided he had had enough. The deciding incident happened at Itmann (Wyoming County) when a group of miners with whom he worked were killed in an explosion. He recalled the incident: "Last time I worked was on a Saturday. We were coming out, they were coming out. And the man car, a spark off a cable, set off methane gas, killed five or six men. This was on a Saturday. And right at Christmas, too. I guess all those factors is what—Christmas, thinking of family, going home. And they're gone, just like that. So I said, that's it; I'm getting out of here, now."[45]

My grandfather, Cayetano Hidalgo, died as the result of a mining accident in 1928. Avelino Cartelle and my grandfather were close friends, and Cartelle was present when my grandfather died. "'Déjame descansar [let me rest]'" were his last words, Cartelle recalled.[46]

My grandfather's brother, Gabriel Hidalgo, suffered a broken back in a slate fall in 1935, when he was thirty-six years old, that left him disabled for the rest of his life. His daughter, Joyce Hidalgo Cook, explained that the accident left him unable to stand up straight. Gabriel's situation worsened when he developed Parkinson's disease, which was related to the mining accident. "My memory of him is that he was constantly shaking," Joyce recalled. For his injury, Gabriel received a compensation check for $60 a month, for him, his wife and two children. "That was what we lived on," Joyce said. It was not easy to get the compensation, despite his injuries. Joyce said that her mother, my Aunt Dora, had to wage a "tremendous fight" to get compensation. "I was very close to my dad. I adored him. I took care of him. I shaved him. I fed him. I have one precious thing that belonged to my father, a little bowl he drank tea in. I think I developed my compassion for the underdog from my dad."[47]

Laura Torrico was one year old when her maternal grandfather, Lauriano Ruiz, was killed in a mine explosion at McAlpin (Raleigh County) in 1928. Her father developed black lung from his many years underground. "I don't know which of them didn't have [black lung] because that dust was just, just terrible."[48] Lauriano is one of at least twenty-six Spaniards buried in what is called the Old Catholic Cemetery in Beckley. His tombstone reads:

Lauriano Ruiz

July 4, 1881 / Oct. 22, 1928

Su desconsolada/esposa e hijos/le dedican este/recuerdo D. E. P.

(His disconsolate/wife and children/dedicate this/memorial to him R. I. P.)

Knowing that your father or other loved one might be the next one killed was something that everyone in the coalfields lived with. Dolores García's father worked forty-nine years in the mines and had two close calls. She remembered one accident:

We thought that daddy got killed, but daddy just got a broken leg. We heard the ambulance coming and the whistle blowing and it scared us to death. We all ran to the tipple, all the kids. We ran as hard as we could run, and it wasn't daddy but daddy got hurt. It was terrible. It was terrible especially, when we found out that the mine caved in. That was the first news that we had. They went around in a car with a loudspeaker telling us that there had been a slate fall . . . and that there were men under it. So you know, it just scared every-body in Minden to death. It was just horrible. Nobody knew who it was . . . all of them that got killed was super friends of ours. It was a terrible time. It was just awful. I think I was about ten or eleven when all of this happened. It was a sad time in Minden.[49]

Rose Santos Parkins remembers hearing the sirens, signaling that some-thing bad had happened: "I remember in the mining camps, the most dread-ful thing was to hear the ambulance. The minute you heard the siren, oh it was scary. You wondered if it was your dad who got hurt or killed. Oh, it was awful. The way I remember it was that it happened often. It really scared you."[50]

The mine death of one Spanish immigrant was reported in the May 19, 1927, *Raleigh Register* under the headline "Slab Fork Spaniard Killed in Accident":

Vincent Lopez, of Slab Fork, was killed instantly on Tuesday in the mines at that place while engaged in getting out coal. The accident that caused his death occurred when a mine car struck a mine machine, catching Lopez between the two.

Lopez was 25 years of age and was a native of Spain. His parents live in Spain and he has an uncle in this county, Manuel Lopez. He came to America about eight years ago and had but recently returned from a visit to his rela-tives in the old country. He was unmarried.

Asunción Marquis Richmond recalled that work in the mines became spo-radic. One day her dad would have a job, and the next he would be cut off. When she was a child, she used to wait for her dad to come home:

I'd go sit on that path and wait on my dad to come every evening. I was real faithful to do it. I just had to wait on my dad. I remember that just as plain as day . . . Let me tell you what my mother did. My mother had a (scarf), it was as long as from here to that wall [gesturing] over there . . . and it had all kinds of colors, blue and green and yellow, and it come from Spain. Well, dad got hurt in the mines a time or two and hurt his back and so mama wrapped him, every time he went to the mines . . . It's cold in the mines anyhow, no heat or nothing down there, and she wrapped that thing around him every day. When he went to work, he always wore that thing to support his back. Mama wrapped him every day before he went to work.[51]

UNITED MINE WORKERS OF AMERICA

Spaniards accepted the hard work they faced each day in the mines and reluctantly tolerated the unhealthy and often deadly working conditions. What they refused to accept, however, was the abuse and exploitation from the coal companies. The treatment of miners was described as reminiscent of the way Blacks were treated in the South.[52] The concept of one man, one vote was unknown in West Virginia. A man's rights were stripped from him when he went to work in the southern West Virginia coalfields. Evictions from company housing were a commonplace way to punish miners.

Frank Ubeda recalled an example of the abuse. Miners had to "clean up" all coal that had been cut that day, along with the rock and debris from their section by the end of their shift. Even if a large amount was left when it was time to go home, a miner could not continue the task the following day:

If you didn't get all of it and load it up and have it pulled out before you went home, whether it was midnight and you were supposed to have went home at five o'clock, you still had to do it. If you didn't do it, let's say you're in the mines today—tonight they'd put your wife and kids and furniture out on the road whether there was mud, snowing, raining—your kids and your wife and furniture out in the road. I didn't like that, but that's what happened. They talk about Russia—buddy it was hell here for the coal miners because that's what happened during them times *and that's history* [Ubeda's emphasis]. It's a wonder there weren't more killings than what did occur, the way that the companies treated the coal miners, like slaves. There's a lot of this that people don't know about.[53]

As was the case in the camps studied by Phylis Cancilla Martinelli in Arizona, labor strife contributed to the unionization of the workers. In West Virginia, Spanish miners were actively involved in this process. These conditions contributed to the formation of the United Mine Workers of America (UMWA). The union was founded in Columbus, Ohio, in 1890, but did not take hold in Raleigh and Fayette Counties until the 1930s, pushed by the federal government as part of the New Deal. Libby Martínez Keadle's father, José Martínez, worked in the mines for forty years and was one of the organizers who helped bring the union in. Besides opposition from the coal companies, many miners did not want the union coming in. Some would accuse her father of starting trouble when he was organizing. Later, after the union was in and conditions had improved, people changed their tune. She recalled:

> I was born in '32. And I remember being six, seven and eight, and the neighbors would holler at me because my daddy was so involved in the union . . . And my daddy was treasurer of the union. So if they had a strike or if anything would go wrong, the first thing you would do is blame the workers [laughing] . . . It would cause problems between mom and dad because people would jump on her—"your husband's causing trouble." And the very people that said that to her, ten years later were so thankful for the benefits they were getting. I mean to tell you that pension was wonderful, with hospitalization. But when they were organizing, it was nothing. But he really did a lot to establish the union down in the Gulf area. He was one of the main men that brought it in. *Antiunion forces were not beyond playing hardball* [Martínez Keadle's emphasis]. I remember once, evidently someone must have reported him because he was involved so strongly in the union. Then they came—I guess it was immigration—came and checked his papers and everything to make sure he was in this country legally. But everything was correct, or as it should have been. But I guess they thought they could get rid of him that way. [Laughing] He was an instigator, you know [sarcastically]. But he really worked at it.[54]

Alex López supported the union although he was a foreman and, therefore, ineligible for membership. He explained: "A lot of people are antiunion in this country. I'm not. I saw what it did for the workers in West Virginia. For my dad and many like him. It's a lot safer than when my dad, most people, worked because we had the Federal Bureau of Mines, State Bureau of Mines, had a lot of mining laws that were enacted because of the labor movement. If it hadn't been for that, we wouldn't have the laws that we have today that make mining safer."[55] My grandfather Cayetano was killed in 1928, long before the United Mineworkers organized the Southern West Virginia coalfields, but my grandfather Valeriano was a UMWA member, and I still have his union card.

DAILY LIFE

While most of the 151 Spanish men in my sample became coal miners, some had other occupations: seven were stonecutters or stonemasons, four were merchants, and four appear listed as "laborer." There was a pool-room proprietor, a machine runner, a transit engineer, a clerk, a newspaper worker, a fireman, a bricklayer, a plasterer, a bookkeeper, a teacher, a mechanic, a student, and a restaurant worker. Twelve women filled out forms: eight were housewives; one was unemployed. The other three were a beautician, a student, and a restaurant worker.

Most miners in West Virginia lived in "coal camps," towns that coal companies built around the mines they developed. The landscape was dotted with them. Typically, the company that owned the mine also owned the houses where the miners and their families lived and the only store in the town (the company store), where the miners and their families shopped. When Tennessee Ernie Ford sang his classic song "Sixteen Tons," he was referring to the kind of places in West Virginia where these Spanish immigrants came. More miners in West Virginia (94 percent) lived in these coal camps than did miners in any other state. In southern West Virginia, the proportion was probably as high as 98 percent. Illinois was second with only 53 percent.[56] The proliferation of small independent mines led to a concentration of coal camps, one after another, for miles along many narrow valleys and hollows. These mining towns were the rural equivalents of the ethnic ghettos that served as transitional communities for foreign immigrants in the cities.[57]

Foreign-born miners and Blacks often lived in restricted sections of these communities, usually with the least desirable housing.[58] Strong community ties typically developed. Frank Ubeda recalled: "[In] the coal camps, the people were very clannish. They stayed together. If something happened to a certain family, here come all the rest of the families; you didn't have to ask for any help. They came to see if you needed help. In the coal camps the people were together like that. Like say, one of the miners gets hurt in the mines, buddy, it wasn't long that the people were right there."[59]

Some "enlightened" operators believed that creating a congenial environment was good for business. They contributed to schools and churches, built theaters and clubhouses, for example. Some larger companies established model company towns, such as Tams in Raleigh County.[60] Laura Torrico grew up in Tams and described the community:

> Everybody was kinda close-knit, one of those things where you don't have to close the doors, and everybody was there to help you if you needed it. It was very dirty as far as that dust goes. You could clean every day and you'd still have a dusty house. But I don't guess anybody minded it because it was a way of life there. We didn't know anything else, so that was a way of life with us. We didn't know to want for a lot. When you live in a community like Tams was, that's all you had. You didn't know if you were poor, or if you were rich, or if you were better off. You had what you needed, and that made you happy.[61]

These model company towns attracted public attention, but they comprised less than 2 percent of all coal company towns. According to historian Ronald Lewis, abuses of coal company power led many critics to characterize West Virginia as "Russia" and coal towns as "relics of feudalism."[62]

When the Depression hit, most people in the coalfields faced hard times. Pedro Torrico explained what was like growing up one of nine children during hard times:

> It's a rat race [laughing]. It's a lot of hand-me-downs. I used to be handed down girls shoes and stuff like that, and there was very little to eat. That was the worst. When you were a certain age, you got like one egg for breakfast and then at a certain age you got two. You never did get three [laughing] [and] a little piece of *chorizo*. You got a bigger piece when you were older and so forth. They'd kill a chicken on Sunday and that thing—it's hard to split one chicken between nine kids and two parents, but mother made all kinds of stuff out of that chicken. We'd eat everything but the damn bill on that thing. We never starved or anything, but stayed hungry.[63]

Children were expected to work to make a few dollars to help the family when they were old enough. From the time Pedro was twelve to about fifteen, he caddied at a country club and turned over his pay to his parents. He kept the tips, he recalled with a big grin, because his parents were unaware of the custom of tipping. Getting a job there was difficult and reflected the hard times of the Depression. Young boys eager to earn a little spending money were competing with unemployed men desperate for any type of work. When he was fifteen or sixteen Pedro landed a job working Saturdays at the Valencia Café, owned by Spaniards Joe Moran, Eladio García, and Felisa Garrido. He worked from 6 a.m. to 12 midnight and was happy to have it: "They paid me a dollar and all I could eat."[64]

Gardening and raising livestock were common activities, critical to the well-being of families, especially during the Depression. With some families so big, a garden was needed to feed everyone because the miners' pay often would not do it.[65] Growing vegetables and raising animals also reduced expenditures at the company store. Manuel Marquis had a huge vegetable garden. Besides being a good farmer, he knew how to use his bounty creatively; he paid doctor bills with it, his daughter Asunción recalled:

> He couldn't afford to pay [the doctor] from one baby to the next, so by the
> time that I was born dad got tired of calling the doctor and not being able
> to pay. So dad told the doctor if he had any money he'd pay him, but he just
> didn't have any [money] to pay him. So he took the best things out of his
> garden and took it to the doctor. Because the doctor wasn't raising no garden,
> he's probably tickled to death to get those nice vegetables. Dad had a big cab-
> bage, he saved it for the doctor. He had a big tomato; he saved it for the doctor.
> He saved the best for him. Dad would tell us not to pick this and not to pick
> that. "Saving it for the doctor." He tried to do the best that he could.[66]

Joyce Hidalgo Cook's family had only her father's $60 a month disability check coming in; so they planted a huge garden at their home. "We lived on the food we raised in that garden," she recalled. Her disabled father would help work in the garden the best he could: "I remember him hoeing, and then he would be very sick." Joyce also earned a few dollars for the family by selling vegetables from a wagon in the neighborhood.[67]

Dositeo López's family in East Gulf was practically self-sufficient. His son Alex recalled:

> We had chickens, we had a cow, we raised a calf every year. We raised our
> own chickens. Hatched our own eggs. We didn't buy much. My dad had big

gardens. We raised everything. Potatoes, onions, celery, peppers, carrots, peas, beans, lettuce, onions. You name it, we grew it. My mother would can. We had our own milk. We'd make butter. She'd take the fat and even make soap. He'd buy the feed sacks and my mother'd make pillowcases and sheets. That's what they were, old feed sacks. We didn't go to the store and buy these fine linens and things, you know. We made our own sheets and pillowcases out of feedsacks. My job in the evenings, I'd come home, I'd gather eggs, I'd feed the chickens, feed the dogs, feed the cows. A lot of people had cows in the coal camps, and you just let your cows run loose. Put a bell on here. We had a black and white one and we called her Morita. It means Blacky in Spanish. In the evenings I'd have to go get the cow if she wouldn't come home. And I knew her bell over all the others. I'd start calling her, "Morita!" and she'd move and I'd hear that bell and I then I could go find her.[68]

Juan Meijide contracted cancer in 1932. He died in 1934, at age fifty-two, when his daughter Josephine was eight years old. She recalled the family's struggle to survive:

[My mother] had to do all sorts of creative things to make ends meet. She began to have foreign boarders in our house, and she would cook for them and gave them a place to sleep. She washed clothes for people and ironed. And then we were janitors. My sisters and I were at that time able to help. Then we did babysitting, all of us girls after we got old enough. I can remember starting babysitting when I was only nine years old, and some of the children I babysat were as old as I was. I [did] domestic work for people and even during the summer when they would go on vacation I used to take care of their dogs, their turtles, any kind of pets, they had birds. I used to do that, take care of them while they were on vacation. So we did all sorts of creative things to make ends meet.[69]

After Toney Pallares's father was killed in the mines in Logan County, his mother, Patrocinio Castillo, moved with her six children to Minden, then to Sullivan where she ran a boardinghouse, and finally to Beckley, around 1931, when he was four years old. "My mother received back then I think it was 55 dollars a month compensation for my father had gotten killed in the mines. And she worked. Cleaned houses and she took in laundry, stuff of this nature. We had a rough time growing up. I suppose I got my first new pair of socks when I was ten, twelve years old. Because when holes came in the end of them, they were cut off and sewed and passed down to the next one. Shirts, pants, everything was like that."[70]

As a youngster, Toney worked at Tamayo and Co., operated by Spaniards José Tamayo and Nick Secador. Tamayo and Co. catered primarily to Spanish people, who represented a huge community in Raleigh and surrounding counties in those days. "At one time I'd say there were four or five, six thousand Spaniards," Toney recalled.[71] Other immigrants, such as Hungarians and Poles, were also regular customers because Tamayo and Co. carried items they enjoyed. Typically, the storekeepers went out to coal camps on Monday and Tuesday to take orders and then deliver on Thursday and Friday.

Mining families moved regularly, especially those living in southern West Virginia. Historian David Corbin believes that this pattern surpassed that of other American workers, and was typical of European miners who may have moved frequently to escape a particular coal company's prejudice against foreigners.[72] Whether it was to escape prejudice or to find better jobs, families commonly lived in half dozen places or more in a relatively short period. The Ubeda family might have set a record by moving nineteen times. John Ubeda recalled: "Moving so much, that beat everything I ever seen [laughing]. Dad would get mad and hell he'd quit and go somewhere else 'cause you could get a job back in them days in the mines anywhere, anytime. They wasn't mechanized like they are now."[73]

LIFE IN A BOARDINGHOUSE

Many Spanish families took in boarders, a common practice among immigrants.[74] Occasionally coal companies set up boardinghouses that would cater to one ethnic group. The Ubeda family ran a company-owned boardinghouse known as the "Spanish clubhouse" for fourteen to sixteen Spanish miners in Fireco (Raleigh County). "These men had their wives in Spain, or were single. Instead of them going out and staying in separate homes with different people, they stayed together in the coal camp house we called the Spanish clubhouse," Frank Ubeda explained.[75]

The Meijide family had an ethnic mix of boarders, often representing several nationalities, which made for interesting experiences. Josephine Meijide Midkiff recalled:

We had a couple or three who were Greeks, we had Hungarians, we had Italians. We really learned a lot from all these people and they liked staying in our place and eating my mother's food. There was also a boardinghouse for Americans in another part of the mining town, but they preferred staying with us. We would gather around in the evenings around this fireplace and they would tell the stories about how life was back in their countries. It was very interesting. And I can remember this one fellow that stayed at our place. He was Italian, he and his son. He was kind of jolly, a sunny person. He and his son played the guitar, and they taught us some songs, and we would get around in the evening and sing.[76]

Laura Torrico's family ran a boardinghouse in Tams. Most boarders were married men who came to the United States to make money and then go back. The whole Torrico family pitched in to run the house:

The house wasn't that big. We had four bedrooms upstairs and two bedrooms downstairs and a dining room and a kitchen. That was it. At times we had as many as twelve boarders that lived with us. Some of them stayed here many, many years. We would do their [lunch] buckets, we would fix their meals and they paid rent. The dining room was theirs. There was a big porch, and the porch belonged to them too. We had the kitchen. My mother and dad raised us in the kitchen and we had two bedrooms downstairs. Mom and dad had one bedroom and the other one, the rest of us slept in that one room. Mom and dad always had boarders there that I could remember since I was just a little girl.[77]

Rose Santos's family kept boarders in its small home, which had only a kitchen, living room, and two bedrooms. "The boarders slept in one bedroom, and the whole family, like so many of them did when they had boarders, slept in one room," Rose recalled. "So in our house, when great-grandma came [from Spain], there was my mother and father, grandmother, me and your mother, all in one bedroom. Can you imagine? And I remember I slept in the baby bed until I was eight years old [laughs]."[78]

THE STING OF PREJUDICE

Some native-born Americans, especially those who traced their ancestry to northern European or English-speaking countries, considered Southern and

Eastern European immigrants a problem because too many retained their language and customs and associated with people from their own ethnic or national group. Organizations that deemed themselves patriotic, like the Daughters of the American Revolution (DAR) or the Young Men's Christian Association (YMCA), believed that immigrants needed to be "Americanized," educated in behavior and principles characteristic of middle-class native-born Americans. These groups, and those who shared their philosophy, assumed that immigrants had no concept of responsible self-government and would be a destabilizing force unless fully assimilated into American society.[79] They claimed that foreigners violated the law more than native-born Americans, or those of northern European descent, that they were ignorant, that they spawned radical organizations such as the Industrial Workers of the World (IWW), and that they had to be taught to conform to American ideals and institutions. Clearly, these beliefs were based on assumptions of Anglo-Saxon superiority, a sentiment that eventually culminated in the restrictive immigration legislation passed by the United States Congress in 1921 and 1924. Many in the coal industry blamed immigrants for much of the labor unrest in the coalfields. Educators joined the front lines in the Americanization movement to save the United States from immigrants. Americans also blamed their economic frustrations on immigrants, especially after World War I and the postwar boom.[80]

This prejudice was added to the daily struggles of most immigrants. "There was bad feelings against all foreigners in the 1920s and 1930s. There was discrimination, not only against Spaniards, but all foreigners," recalled John Ubeda. "[The White, native-born Americans] would just ignore them and not have nothing to do with them mostly."[81] John's brother, Frank, took up music as a young man and along with several other Spaniards formed a band that played dances regularly. In some circles, having this talent for music—or anything else, such as sports—rubbed the native-born white Americans the wrong way, if you were of the "wrong" background.

As in the mining camps studied by Martinelli in Arizona, segregation was also prevalent in West Virginia. However, I did not find evidence of pay disparity according to ethnicity.[82] Typical of coal camps, especially the "model" towns, Tams was segregated along racial and ethnic lines from its beginning in 1909. Before then, Blacks and immigrants had not been segregated from the rest of the community. In Stanaford, Blacks and immigrants lived together until the early 1920s, when strict segregation was introduced to the town.[83] Laura Torrico grew up in Tams and described how the community was segregated:

> We had three sections there, and this is probably so strange, there was a colored community, a white community and a foreign community. The foreign community was at the bottom of the town and then there was a church and a school, two churches and a school, and then it was the white community. And then there was the mines and then it was the colored community. There was, segregation is what you call it, even the foreigners were segregated from the American people. We had a Catholic church, they had an American church and the colored people had their church. We didn't know to feel anything. It didn't matter to us at that time of our lives because we were in the foreign town, but they called us hunks, whether you were Spanish, Polish, whatever you were, that was hunk town, that's how they referred to us, the foreigners, they called them hunks regardless of their nationality.[84]

The Marquis family felt the sting of prejudice. Asunción Marquis Richmond recalled:

> A lot of people didn't like us because we were Spanish. A lot of people called us hunky all the time, but you know what our dad told us? Dad said, "Don't pay any attention to it. If they call you that, don't pay any attention to it." He said, "You're just as good as anybody and hold your head high." That's what dad always told us. "Hold your head high and just go on." They didn't want to associate with the others. But in school you didn't have much trouble. It's just at home your neighbors wanted to fight. Not all of them, some of them.[85]

Josephine Meijide Midkiff also recalled the prejudice her family experienced:

> I can remember my mother being out in the yard hanging her clothes and the kids would throw rocks at her, just because she was a "hunky." And that was a hurtful thing. And I can remember picking up, maybe I had left a textbook lying and then go pick it up and there would be some derogatory things written in the textbook. Like being a hunky, and poor. Of course we were poor. We knew we were poor; we didn't have to have anyone tell us that. As if being a hunky or being a foreigner would cause you to be poor, which was not the case.[86]

Pedro Torrico remembered how Spaniards were mistreated at Blue Jay where he grew up: "We were outcasts. I mean we were called hunks, laughed at. The older kids beat our ass and all that stuff. You had to scrap a little bit. They didn't like hunks. I thought 'damn hunk' was one word [laughs loudly]. Now the teachers seemed to treat us good."[87]

Coal companies typically built schools in the camps, recruited good teachers, and even built housing for the teachers.[88] This practice was followed for a number of reasons. The company directors believed that a better-educated workforce would decrease accidents and increase coal production. They believed that education could help preserve the social structure; in other words: those on top stayed on top. They also wanted to Americanize the immigrants.

MAINTAINING SPANISH CULTURAL IDENTITY

While adapting to life in the United States, Spanish immigrants and their children in West Virginia maintained their cultural identify and cohesion in many ways, a pattern consistent with that of Spaniards who immigrated to other parts of the country.[89] The tendency of Spaniards to cling to their Spanish roots was demonstrated by the high percentage who did not become American citizens.[90] It is also evident in some of the aspects I will mention in the last section of this chapter, such as the maintenance of the Spanish language and Spanish traditions (food, wine making, *matanza* [hog slaughter]) and the connections with the homeland, through visits and cultural associations, such as El Ateneo Español.

Most of the people I interviewed grew up speaking Spanish at home. Typically, adult immigrants never learned to speak English fluently, although some could "get by." Frank Ubeda grew up bilingual, but his parents did not learn English. He remembered: "At home we spoke Spanish. Mom and Dad never could speak English. So we had to talk Spanish. As soon as you got outside the door it was English."[91] Josephine Meijide Midkiff experienced a similar situation: "I can remember that even after we started school that we were always expected to speak Spanish in our household. Once you stepped over the threshold into the house it was Spanish, and it became just automatic, like you turned on a switch. We wouldn't think of talking English in the house."[92] Laura Torrico's family spoke only Spanish at home. Laura spoke no English until she started school. She recalled: "I didn't even know what American language was until I went to school. My grandmother always spoke Spanish to us and mom and dad, so we just knew Spanish until we went to school. To the day my dad died, I never spoke to him in American. It was always Spanish."[93]

The Marquis family had a strict "Spanish only" rule at home, Asunción Marquis Richmond said, "You wasn't allowed to come in the house and speak English. When we come in the house and we said something in English, my mother said, 'In this house we speak Spanish.'"[94] But the Spaniards did the best they could with their limited linguistic skills and would improvise when necessary to be understood. Asunción recalled a story about her father going to the grocery store: "He wanted to buy ham. He said 'hama.' They brought him a hammer. 'No, I don't want a hammer. I want a *jamón*.' He couldn't get across to [the clerk] what he wanted. So you know what he did? He got on his hands and knees and said 'oink, oink' and patted right there [patting her behind] and he said they ran and got it then."[95]

Spaniards brought their foodways with them to West Virginia. Spanish food was about all they ate at home. *Arroz con pollo* (chicken and rice), *bacalao* (dried cod fish), *chorizo* (smoked, highly spiced pork sausage), *garbanzos* (chickpeas), *gazpacho blanco* (a cold soup made of eggs, garlic, vinegar, olive oil, and bread), and *tortilla* (egg, potato, and onion omelet) were some of the foods that people ate regularly. Spaniards also used *azafrán* (saffron), cumin, garlic, and olive oil, products that were pretty much unknown to the Appalachian culture. There were enough Spanish people in the area to support two Spanish-owned grocery stores: Tamayo and Co. in Mabscott, and José Rodríguez's market in Beckley. They catered primarily, although not exclusively, to Spanish immigrants. Along with the day-to-day Spanish fare, two other customs flourished for a time in West Virginia—wine making and matanzas.

Making wine was an autumn event. It was customary for groups of Spaniards to order large amounts of grapes and have them shipped in. Frank Ubeda (figure 7.3) remembered: "Buddy they'd have a hell of a time I'll tell you. You see, that kind of life, or that type of activity was what kept them going because that's what they liked (figure 7.4). That was common for them. Very rich and very good, and buddy you couldn't beat that. People just loved that."[96]

FIGURE 7.3. Frank Ubeda loved music and learned to play guitar at an early age. He and many other Spaniards played regularly in the coalfields at dances and parties and informal gatherings (figure 7.4). (Author's personal collection.)

Laura Torrico still has her father's grape grinder and press at her home. "Wine making was very interesting to me. It was something that fascinated me," she recalled. "We would make white wine and the dark wine. I could just hardly wait for the season to come, so that we could do the wine, and it was hard work."[97] Libby Martínez Keadle's grandfather and father both made wine and she helped both of them, even when they did it the old-fashioned way: "I remember back when my grandfather used to mash them [the grapes] with his feet. Sometimes he'd tell me to get in [the barrel] . . . And then he bought the press. In fact my daughter has it over her house out in the yard on display."[98]

"He was a great one for making wine," Rose Santos Parkins said of her father. "[They] would get their white boots and romp around in those grapes

FIGURE 7.4. Gathering of Spaniards in West Virginia (Author's personal collection.)

to mash them because we didn't have anything to crush the grapes." The white boots stand out vividly in her memory: "They were always shiny, white and clean . . . Later dad got a press."[99] In East Gulf, the López family also made wine. "I helped my dad make wine many times," Alex López recalled. "Oh, it'd smell so good. I used to love to walk in our basement and smell that wine when it was working."[100] Dolores García's father made wine in their basement, and the family was always worried that he would get in trouble because wine making was illegal. "When you came up the stairs to our house, you could smell it when he was making it," she remembered. "I would say, 'You are going to get put in jail,' and he said, 'I don't care. We are going to make it.'"[101]

Matanza literally means killing. For the Spaniards, it meant butchering hogs to make sausages such as *chorizo* and *morcilla*, but also to have feasts and celebrate. It was a special time, Frank Ubeda recalled: "It looked like a fever hit 'em. Time to kill hogs. Whenever that came about, you didn't have to go out and hire any help—man they all came. They'd get together and come and help each other. Back then chorizo was the thing. All the Spanish people did that. It was a custom that I soon missed because it was good eating. It was a ritual you had to do."[102]

The Marquis family also raised a hog, sometimes two, to butcher every year to make chorizo. Asunción Marquis Richmond pointed out that it was an important custom: "They did that because that's the way they lived in Spain."[103] Alex López fondly remembered the annual ritual, which resembled a huge feast:

Every Thanksgiving we'd kill pigs and that's when they'd make the chorizo. It was big, like a holiday fair. All of the guys that worked in the mines, because miners didn't work Thanksgiving. So for two or three days, it was just like a fiesta, or like a picnic there. They'd eat and drink wine and at night we'd play music and sing songs. They'd sing Spanish songs. Grandpa'd play the *gaitas* [bagpipes]. They'd dance. Oh, it was just great times. Best times in my life. Family all together, all Spanish people. And the American people would come watch. [104]

Toney Pallares described the process of making chorizo:

They would grind the pork, [add] salt, pepper, garlic, paprika, oregano, mix it up, put it in a tub and let it marinate. Then they would start packing it into the intestines of the pig, squeezing it down and tie it off in pieces six or eight inches long. Then it was ready to be smoked. The job I hated the most was the smokehouse. We'd have to build a fire and you couldn't let the fire flame up, just the smoke to smoke the chorizo. And it would drip on you and everything. It was terrible. We'd hang the chorizo on nails, get the fire going, put it out, and just let it smoke. Anytime you saw any flame you had to put it out and just let the smoke go into there. You had to stay right there. You'd go outside to get some fresh air and then you'd go back in. At night you'd let it die down, and then you'd go back up again in the morning and start her up again.[105]

Josephine Meijide Midkiff remembered a family story about chorizo:

When my mother came to this country, another family wanted her to bring some chorizo to somebody here in this country. Well, you weren't allowed to bring foodstuff and that kind of thing. So mother said that she'd try. My father said you shouldn't do that; you're doing the wrong thing. They knew that she could get on the boat OK; her problem was going to be when she got here to the states. So you know what she did? She put those chorizos hanging on her arms, put her coat over that and walked right through customs. So she was able to take those people the chorizos.[106]

My family was no exception to the chorizo-making ritual, which we did every fall. We would hang the chorizos in a little shed behind our house which we called the "watchihou"—Spanglish for wash house—and smoke them. It was quite a production, but I will never forget the heavenly aroma and wonderful taste of those links of Spanish sausage.

Spaniards who left their homeland for the Americas during the early part of the twentieth century were embarking on quite an adventure. The mythology of the immigrant experience is that Europeans came to the United States, severed all ties to the homeland, and never returned. That is not the whole story. Many Spaniards migrated to the United States and countries such as Argentina and Cuba only to earn enough money to go back to Spain after a few years and live better.[107] It was common for Spaniards to "commute" between Spain and somewhere in the Americas over a period of many years. Citizenship documents show that many returned for at least one visit, and some returned multiple times over a number of years. Many Spaniards went back for good.[108] From 1908 to 1940, about 72,000 Spaniards returned to Spain from the United States for good, about 41 percent of those who immigrated during that period.[109]

Andrés García Gómez was one of those immigrants who returned to Spain several times. His nephew, Pedro Torrico, remembered: "He'd work in the mines four or five years and then he'd go back and stay four or five years and spend the money and then come back. Three times I know of."[110] Juan

Meijide made several trips across the Atlantic before he was married, according to his daughter, Josephine. She said: "He went back periodically to visit the family. He really never intended to live here until he died. He always had it in mind to go back to Spain and take his family back there sometime. His Spanish heritage meant a lot to him."[111]

Juan's brother, Manuel, was the only other family member who came to West Virginia. After a few years in the United States he returned to Spain to live. Josephine met him years later on a visit there: "I never will forget the day when we walked into the room, and he kind of saluted us and said 'Beck-a-lee Vest-a-virhinia.' He was still proud of the fact that he could still say the name of the place where he had lived. But he was quite a character, and he still remembered and liked to talk about his experiences here."[112]

A number of Spaniards returned to Spain during the 1920s, repatriated by the Spanish government, which even paid for their return ticket home. Avelino Cartelle said he almost went back to Spain, but decided to stay in the United Sates. His good friend Manuel Básquez, the *compañero* who came with him on their first trip from Spain and later found him a job in Logan, took Spain up on the deal and went back home to Galicia. In 1929, Cartelle went to Spain to visit Básquez and many other repatriated "West Virginia" Spaniards.[113]

In 1938, more than thirty years after the first Spaniards arrived in the area, a group of them decided to form their own organization and construct their own building. The Ateneo Español was born. Its first meeting was called to order on October 30, 1938. *Ateneo* is the Spanish word for athenaeum. Colloquially, it was known as the Spanish Club. The Ateneo was similar to mutual aid societies and social clubs that Spanish immigrants formed in other parts of the United States.[114] According to the bylaws (written in English and Spanish), its goal was to promote the "best interest and general welfare of all Spaniards in and around Raleigh, Wyoming, Fayette, Mercer, Summers and Boone counties." Dues were $1 a month. A women's membership of fifty cents per month was established "with the goal of having women participate in social life and give them the opportunity to participate in all discussions of the Ateneo."[115]

When the Spaniards got together to form the Ateneo, nine Spaniards put up the $8,800 to buy the property and construct the club's building, which became known as the "Spanish house" (figure 7.5).

The club provided many activities and benefits. It held regular dances; made loans to members; donated to charities, such as the Red Cross, and

FIGURE 7.5. In 1938, a group of Spaniards in Beckley, West Virginia, started the
Ateneo Español. Pictured is the building façade and the interior of the main hall as it
looked for the formal dedication in January 21, 1939. (Author's personal collection.)

the United Service Organizations; had picnics; provided support to widows;
held dinners for members and their families; and served as a gathering place.
The Ateneo also collected money, clothing, and other supplies to send to

Spain during the Spanish Civil War. Acting troupes also came and performed plays at the Ateneo to raise money for the loyalist side. The Ateneo was also a place where entire families could go together to have fun, as Laura Torrico explained:

> We were young, we started going [when] we were just little fellas, and we enjoyed the dances. It was good fun. You would dance with everybody, and everybody knew everybody and the whole family would go. It just wasn't the young group; it was everybody. The whole family went. The little ones, and the big ones and the old folks—whether they could dance or not they could sit and watch. There were lots of people, just hundreds. All the people from the little coal camps would come on Saturday. They did have some Spanish plays there. They had several weddings there at the ateneo, too. They made money and sent it to [Spain] during the civil war. I guess we felt in our own way we were contributing too.[116]

When the Ateneo Español opened its doors, it was an exciting moment for Libby Martínez Keadle's family. She recalled: "Every time they had a dance, we all came. We didn't have a car. We had to get somebody to bring us, but the whole family—mom, dad, grandfather, grandmother, aunts, uncles—everybody came. It was a big deal to us. We made friends up here with other Spanish people. Sometimes you couldn't move [it was so crowded]."[117]

The Ateneo Español was a happening place not just for Spaniards (figure 7.6). People of all ethnic groups would often go with their Spanish friends, as Toney Pallares remembered: "You talk about a place rock man—that place rolled. They had tremendous parties down there. The ateneo was really quite the thing with Spanish people. There were a large number of other people besides Spaniards who attended the dances and get-togethers. Polish, Italian, Hungarians, Americans, you name it. They would flock to the Spanish hall. It was the spot for everybody in the coal camps."[118]

I have often wondered how the Spanish community in the area might have developed had it not been for World War II, when many left the area. The war was not the only event that pulled Spaniards away, but it was a major cause of the community's decline. The Ateneo, with its clear objectives, would have been a place where Spanish identity and culture flourished, even as the newer generations became more acculturated to the new homeland. That is what

FIGURE 7.6. The Ateneo Español, also known as the Spanish Hall, was a popular gathering place for many Spaniards and people of Spanish descent. This photograph (March 1940) shows a gathering in the hall's lower level. Upstairs were a stage and large dance floor. (Author's personal collection.)

the founders intended. Who knows? If not for the war, there still might be a huge Spanish community in southern West Virginia.

Spaniards began arriving in West Virginia, primarily to work in the coal mines, in the early part of the twentieth century and in such large numbers that by 1920 the state was ranked seventh in the number of residents originally from Spain. Yet, few people realize this fact. Many are probably shocked to hear that any Spaniards ever were there, living and working in the state. This lack of knowledge is not surprising given that in this country we promote an "official history" that emphasizes an Anglo-Saxon heritage and the exploits of the wealthy and powerful, while ignoring stories of other ethnic groups, immigrants, workers, and minorities. Fortunately, some of us are rediscovering the history of Spanish immigrants and documenting the experiences of some of the Spaniards who came to West Virginia almost a century ago. Gavin González's memoir, *Pinnick Kinnick Hill*, and the online Asturian-American Migration Forum, created by descendants of immigrants from Asturias, many of whom settled in West Virginia, are good examples of this.[119] There remain many other stories about Spaniards who immigrated to

West Virginia, as well other parts of the United States. They are still waiting for someone to tell them.

NOTES

1. David Corbin, *Life, Work, and Rebellion in the Coal Fields: The Southern West Virginia Miners, 1880–1922* (Urbana: University of Illinois Press, 1981), 7–8; United States Senate, *Reports of the Immigration Commission* (Washington, DC: US Government Printing Office, 1911), 69: 219–28.

2. See Phylis Cancilla Martinelli, "Miners from Spain to Arizona Copper Camps, 1880–1930" (chapter 6 in this volume).

3. Charlotte Erickson, *Emigration from Europe, 1815–1914* (London: Adam and Charles Black, 1976); Beverly Lozano, "The Andalucía-Hawaii-California Migration: A Study in Macrostructure and Microhistory," *Comparative Studies in Society and History* 26, no. 2 (April 1984): 305–24 (chapter 2 in this volume).

4. Rafael Anes Álvarez, *La emigración de asturianos a América* (Colombres, Spain: Archivo de Indianos, 1993), 85.

5. R. A. Gómez, "Spanish Immigration to the United States," *Americas* 19 (July 1962): 59–78.

6. Erickson, *Emigration from Europe*, 235.

7. Dolores García, interview by author, Beckley, WV, March 1998.

8. Asunción Marquis Richmond, interview by author, Stanaford, WV, March 1997.

9. Toney Pallares, interview by author, Beckley, WV, March 1997.

10. Josephine Meijide Midkiff, interview by author, Beckley, WV, March 1997.

11. Rose Santos Parkins, interview by author, Raleigh, NC, March 1998.

12. Toney Pallares, 1997.

13. Pedro Torrico, interview by author, Beckley, WV, March 1997.

14. Anes Álvarez, *Emigración de asturianos*, 108.

15. Josephine Meijide Midkiff, 1997.

16. Manuel Cartelle, interview by author, Beckley, WV, March 1998.

17. Alejos "Alex" López, interview by author, Sophia, WV, March 1997.

18. Josephine Meijide Midkiff, 1997.

19. Libby Martínez Keadle, interview by author, Beckley, WV, March 1997.

20. Gómez, "Spanish Immigration."

21. Blanca Sánchez-Alonso, "Those Who Left and Those Who Stayed Behind: Explaining Emigration from the Regions of Spain, 1880–1914," *Journal of Economic History* 60 (2000): 730–55.

22. Gómez, "Spanish Immigration."

23. Frank Ubeda, interview by author, Beckley, WV, March 1997.

24. Josephine Meijide Midkiff, 1997.

25. Avelino Cartelle, interview by author, Oak Hill, WV, June 1993.

26. Frank Troitiño, interview by author, Mt. Hope, WV, March 1997.

27. Asunción Marquis Richmond, 1997.

28. Frank Ubeda, 1997.

29. United States Senate, *Reports of the Immigration Commission*, 219–28.

30. United States Senate, *Reports of the Immigration Commission*, 219–28.

31. United States Senate, *Reports of the Immigration Commission*, 227.

32. Corbin, *Life, Work, and Rebellion*.

33. Otis K. Rice and Stephen Wayne Brown, *West Virginia: A History*, 2nd ed. (Lexington: University Press of Kentucky, 1993), 189. On recruitment of Spanish immigrants, see essays by Ana Varela-Lago, Beverly Lozano, and Phylis Cancilla Martinelli (chapters 1, 2, 6, and 8 in this volume).

34. West Virginia Department of Mines, *Annual Report* (Charleston, 1922), 322.

35. Corbin, *Life, Work, and Rebellion*, 10.

36. Corbin, *Life, Work, and Rebellion*, 128.

37. W. P. Tams Jr., *The Smokeless Coal Fields of West Virginia: A Brief History* (Morgantown: West Virginia University Foundation, 1963), 38.

38. Toney Pallares, 1997.

39. Frank Ubeda, 1997.

40. John Ubeda, interview by author, Beckley, WV, March 1997.

41. Tams, *Smokeless Coal Fields*, 34.

42. Corbin, *Life, Work, and Rebellion*, 15–16.

43. John Ubeda, 1997.

44. Alejos "Alex" López, 1997.

45. Alejos "Alex" López, 1997.

46. Avelino Cartelle, 1993.

47. Joyce Hidalgo Cook, interview by author, Shady Spring, WV, December 2008.

48. Laura Torrico, interview by author, Beckley, WV, March 1997.

49. Dolores García, 1998.

50. Rose Santos Parkins, 1998.

51. Asunción Marquis Richmond, 1997.

52. Corbin, *Life, Work, and Rebellion*, 61–62.

53. Frank Ubeda, 1997.

54. Libby Martínez Keadle, 1997.

55. Alejos "Alex" López, 1997.

56. Corbin, *Life, Work, and Rebellion*, 8.

57. Ronald L. Lewis, "Appalachian Restructuring in Historical Perspective: Coal, Culture and Social Change in West Virginia," *Urban Studies* 30 (1993): 299–308.

58. Rice and Brown, *West Virginia*, 189.

59. Frank Ubeda, 1997.

60. Rice and Brown, *West Virginia*, 189.

61. Laura Torrico, 1997.

62. Lewis, "Appalachian Restructuring."

63. Pedro Torrico, 1997.

64. Pedro Torrico, 1997.

65. Corbin, *Life, Work, and Rebellion*, 33–34.

66. Asunción Marquis Richmond, 1997.

67. Joyce Hidalgo Cook, 2008.

68. Alejos "Alex" López, 1997.

69. Josephine Meijide Midkiff, 1997.

70. Toney Pallares, 1997.

71. Toney Pallares, 1997.

72. Corbin, *Life, Work, and Rebellion*, 40–43.

73. John Ubeda, 1997.

74. Rice and Brown, *West Virginia*, 189.

75. Frank Ubeda, 1997.

76. Josephine Meijide Midkiff, 1997.

77. Laura Torrico, 1997.

78. Rose Santos Parkins, 1998.

79. John Hennen, *The Americanization of West Virginia: Creating a Modern Industrial State, 1916–1925* (Lexington: University Press of Kentucky, 1996), 74–76.

80. Hennen, *Americanization*, 74–76

81. John Ubeda, 1997.

82. In Arizona and other locales, Martinelli explains, Spaniards had an in-between racial status, and they were paid less than Anglos, but more than Blacks or Mexicans. See chapter 6 in this volume.

83. Joe W. Trotter, *Coal, Class and Color: Blacks in Southern West Virginia 1915–1932* (Urbana: University of Illinois Press, 1990).

84. Laura Torrico, 1997.

85. Asunción Marquis Richmond, 1997.

86. Josephine Meijide Midkiff, 1997.

87. Pedro Torrico, 1997.

88. Corbin, *Life, Work, and Rebellion*, 127.

89. See, for example, Carlos M. Fernández-Shaw, *Presencia española en los Estados Unidos*, 2nd ed. (Madrid: Instituto de Cooperación Iberoamericana, 1987); Gary R.

Mormino and George E. Pozzetta, *The Immigrant World of Ybor City: Italians and Their Latin Neighbors in Tampa, 1885–1985* (Urbana: University of Illinois Press, 1987); Anne Santucci Aguilar, *Memories of Spain* (Sacramento: Griffin Printing, 1994); Loy G. Westfall, "Immigrants in Society," *Americas* 34 (1982): 41–45.

90. Gómez, "Spanish Immigration."

91. Frank Ubeda, 1997.

92. Josephine Meijide Midkiff, 1997.

93. Laura Torrico, 1997.

94. Asunción Marquis Richmond, 1997.

95. Asunción Marquis Richmond, 1997.

96. Frank Ubeda, 1997.

97. Laura Torrico, 1997.

98. Libby Martínez Keadle, 1997.

99. Rose Santos Parkins, 1998.

100. Alejos "Alex" López, 1997.

101. Dolores García, 1998.

102. Frank Ubeda, 1997.

103. Asunción Marquis Richmond, 1997.

104. Alejos "Alex" López, 1997.

105. Toney Pallares, 1997.

106. Josephine Meijide Midkiff, 1997.

107. Gómez, "Spanish Immigration."

108. Gómez, "Spanish Immigration"; Mark Wyman, *Round-Trip to America: The Immigrants Return to Europe, 1880–1930* (Ithaca: Cornell University Press, 1993), 11.

109. Gómez, "Spanish Immigration."

110. Pedro Torrico, 1997.

111. Josephine Meijide Midkiff, 1997.

112. Josephine Meijide Midkiff, 1997.

113. Avelino Cartelle, 1993.

114. Germán Rueda, *La emigración contemporánea de españoles a Estados Unidos, 1820–1950* (Madrid: Mapfre, 1993); Mormino and Pozzetta, *Immigrant World*.

115. Ateneo Español, *Reglamento del Ateneo Español de Beckley, W. Va.* ([Beckley, WV?], 1938), 6.

116. Laura Torrico, 1997.

117. Libby Martínez Keadle, 1997.

118. Toney Pallares, 1997.

119. Gavín W. González, *Pinnick Kinnick Hill: An American Story* (Morgantown: West Virginia University Press, 2003); the Asturian-American Migration Forum, https://www.asturianus.org.

8

"SPANISH HANDS FOR THE AMERICAN HEAD?"

Spanish Migration to the United States and the Spanish State

ANA VARELA-LAGO

In May 1902, as Cubans welcomed the new century celebrating the procla-mation of the Cuban Republic, Spaniards joined in the festivities marking the beginning of the reign of Alfonso XIII.[1] Surprisingly, perhaps, the royal cere-monies served to highlight the harmonious relations between Spain and the country that had so enthusiastically contributed to the independence of the island and to Spain's colonial losses in 1898. President Theodore Roosevelt's choice of special ambassador to the occasion, J. L. M. Curry, received much praise, as the diplomat had headed the American Legation in Spain at the time of Alfonso's birth sixteen years earlier. In his message to the king at a royal audience, Curry stated: "I voice the universal sentiment of my country when I say Spain and the United States should be interlinked in chains of mutual interest, good will, and happiness."[2] To the American secretary of state Curry wrote of the kindness shown by the Spanish government to his representation and, therefore, to the government and people of the United States.[3]

Diplomatic relations between the two countries following the Spanish-Cuban-American War reflected the cordial interactions that marked the

DOI: 10.5876/9781607327998.c008

king's inauguration. A few weeks into Alfonso's reign, a new treaty of friend-ship between the two nations was signed.[4] Spaniards who had left the United States in anticipation of a formal declaration of war returned to American shores. In Tampa, where the American troops had embarked to fight Spain in Cuba in 1898, Spanish immigrants resumed their work in the Clear Havana cigar factories that would make the city the "Cigar capital of the world." In fact, 1902 saw the establishment in Ybor City (Tampa's Latin quarter) of a delegation of the Centro Asturiano de la Habana, one of several mutual aid societies founded by Spanish immigrants in Cuba.[5] In the next three decades, thousands of Spaniards would join millions of immigrants from Europe and elsewhere who journeyed to the United States in search of a better life. While this migration was comparatively small, its steady increase throughout this period presented a number of challenges to the migrants themselves, as well as to the Spanish state, still dealing with the aftermath of the "disaster," as the war of 1898 came to be known in Spain.[6]

This chapter uses the lens of migration to analyze some of the opinions and policies that helped define Spanish-American relations in the first quar-ter of the twentieth century. It begins with the recruitment of Spaniards to work in Hawai'i and the Panama Canal. Although small in size, this migra-tion became a crucial factor in the debate that led to the passage of the 1907 Emigration Act, the most comprehensive emigration law in Spain up to that point. The fact that these territories had become the outposts of the emerg-ing American empire added a new dimension to the discussions. Spanish emigrants were often portrayed as the victims of American exploitation, and the failure of the Spanish state to protect them underscored its short-comings vis-à-vis the American powerhouse. As more Spaniards migrated to the United States in the 1910s and 1920s, a new set of challenges faced the Spanish state. Among them were the demands that a growing and widely dis-persed population of immigrants placed on the perennially deficient Spanish consular system. These are discussed in the second part of the chapter. The reported ill treatment and discrimination experienced by Spanish immigrants at the hands of American officials were also a matter of concern, causing, in 1914, the Spanish ambassador in Washington to recommend to his govern-ment a temporary halt of Spanish migration to the United States. In fact, migration from Spain increased in the following years, in part due to the out-break of World War I. But the conflict also posed new challenges, as scores of Spanish subjects were illegally drafted into the American Army, in contra-vention of the treaty of friendship between the two countries. The postwar economic recession, and the anti-immigrant legislation that ensued, limiting the entry of Southern and Eastern Europeans to the United States, practi-cally stopped the new migration of Spaniards to North America. By the time the Immigration Act of 1924 came into effect, General Primo de Rivera had established a military dictatorship, and the reign of Alfonso XIII had started down a perilous path that would end in 1931 with the fall of the monarchy and the proclamation of the Spanish Republic.

THE EMIGRATION ACT AND THE RECRUITMENT OF
SPANIARDS TO HAWAIʻI AND THE PANAMA CANAL

"Why should Spain allow her people to do America's labor?" The question, posed by Spanish prime minister Segismundo Moret to LeRoy Park, an agent from the Isthmian Canal Commission seeking to recruit Spanish workers for the Panama Canal, encapsulated Spanish official sentiment about this enterprise. W. Leon Pepperman, the chief of administration of the Second Isthmian Commission, and author of the book where this 1906 conversation is reproduced, described Moret's reply as "disconcerting."[7] Yet, it was pre-dictable, given Moret's background and the course of Spanish-American rela-tions at the turn of the twentieth century.

Moret had been the minister of Overseas Colonies (Ultramar) at the time of the Spanish-American War, and the architect of a failed attempt to prevent Cuba's independence by offering Cubans autonomy instead. In the aftermath of the Spanish-American War, the circumstances that led to the independence of Panama from Colombia in 1903, and the subsequent appro-priation of the Isthmus by the United States were followed with concern by the Spanish government, which saw in it a repetition of the American tactics and European acquiescence that had occurred in 1898.[8] It probably did not help LeRoy Park's case that in his efforts to soften the minister's position regarding the recruitment of Spaniards, he reminded Moret that the United States was building the canal "for the benefit of the commerce of the entire world" and that "it was a high privilege Spain was offered in the opportunity to pay her part of the universal debt of gratitude by allowing her people to assist in its excavation."[9] This comment, Pepperman tells us, is what sparked

Moret's remark: "If America needs common labor, let her seek it among her own people. The American is too proud to work with his hands! He must work with his head, and Spain must be his hands! Spain refuses to be hands for the American head."[10]

The construction of the Panama Canal can be seen as one of the scenarios where the Social Darwinist discourse that imbued the imperialist narrative of the late nineteenth century was played out. Spain, as Lord Salisbury had hinted in his famous speech on "living" and "dying" nations, seemed to belong to the latter. The victory in 1898 placed the United States squarely among the "living" nations. American initiative in the building of the Panama Canal, an enterprise at which France had previously failed, appeared to lend support to this theory of racial superiority of the Anglo-Saxons over the Latin races.[11]

The Spanish elites, however, did not share this view. In 1907, as LeRoy Park continued his recruiting efforts in the peninsula, Juan Mateos was busy writing a book on his impressions of the Canal Zone. Besides warning potential Spanish immigrants about poor working conditions, he used his conversations with an American engineer as a foil to highlight, among other things, the differences between (materialistic) Americans and (cultured) Europeans.[12] Mateos also reminded his readers that, as early as the sixteenth century, under Charles V, Spaniards had contemplated building a canal connecting the two oceans.[13] In 1915, as Americans celebrated the opening of the canal, Modesto Pérez Hernández published *Los precursores españoles del Canal Interoceánico* (The Spanish Precursors of the Interoceanic Canal), a book whose opening pages stated: "to Spain, whose blood has been spilled in the construction of the marvelous Canal, should go the glory of having been the first one to conceive the idea of interoceanic communication." The United States, the author claimed, "have done nothing more than to execute initiatives and plans thought out, conceived, and tried by illustrious Spanish captains upon the discovery of the New World." In this reading of history, Spaniards could then celebrate the achievement of the opening of the canal as an "homage to the [Spanish] race."[14] In an interesting reversal of Moret's metaphor, in this narrative Americans had become the "hands" for the Spanish "head."

Another aspect of Segismundo Moret's background made him the least likely candidate to agree to LeRoy Park's requests: his views on emigration. As a member of the Instituto de Reformas Sociales (Institute for Social Reform), an institution created to study and address Spain's "social question," Moret had eloquently expressed his opinion against an emigration bill proposed to the Spanish Parliament in 1905. He argued that the government ought to prevent the emigration of its citizens and instead promote the colonization of Spain's unpopulated regions. Moret categorized emigration as a "social ill"—such as prostitution, theft, or fraud—and contended that the government should not encourage it, nor give it a sense of normalcy. While sensitive to the needs of the poor and the working class, Moret had little sympathy for the plight of the emigrants, whom he considered unpatriotic. Those who "abandon" their motherland, he declared, have no right to ask for her protection.[15]

Despite Moret's statements on the need for the government to curb emigration by stimulating the internal colonization and development of Spain, little was done to improve the conditions that would keep Spaniards at home, especially at a time when other world regions were in dire need of labor and aggressively recruiting in the country. A headline in the *New York Times* summed up this blunt economic reality: "Spaniards for Canal Work. Attempt to Attract Immigrants from Famine-Stricken Region."[16] The region referred to was Galicia, in the northwest corner of Spain, an area that sent so many emigrants to Latin America that the term Galician (*gallego*) became synonymous with anyone from Spain.

Much to Moret's chagrin, Spanish migrants did become the hands of America. Thousands participated yearly in a cycle of "swallow migration" to Latin America. In Cuba, where Spaniards had returned soon after the end of the 1898 war, they worked in agriculture, harvesting sugar cane, but also in a number of public works, such as railroads, promoted during the American administration of the island. It was there that American officials became aware of the quality of Spanish labor. A 1902 report from the US Department of Labor stated: "Some American employers consider them [Spaniards] the best unskilled laborers of Europe. They are physically robust and not addicted to many of the vices of laborers of the same class in the United States."[17] It was from Cuba that the first Spanish workers to work in the Panama Canal arrived in 1905, when the resourceful LeRoy Park spirited away 300 of them against the will of the Cuban authorities.[18] The success of this initial force led the Isthmian Canal Commission to send Park to Spain to recruit workers there.

From 1906 to 1908, over 8,000 workers were hired in Spain to work in the Panama Canal. While most of these laborers came from Galicia, Park's networks of agents extended throughout northern Spain and areas of Old

Castile and Aragon.[19] At the same time, in the Southern region of Andalusia, agents hired by the Hawaiian Sugar Planters' Association sought Spanish peasants to work on the islands' sugar plantations. If the recruitment of workers for the Panama Canal targeted single men, the one directed to Hawai'i wanted entire families, who, it was hoped, might eventually settle there. On March 10, 1907, the first steamship, the *Heliópolis,* sailed from the port of Málaga to Honolulu with 2,269 men, women, and children. From 1907 to 1913, six other ships made the journey, transporting approximately 8,000 Spaniards to the sugar plantations in Hawai'i.[20]

While broader global economic forces were at work in this transfer of labor from Europe to America, this migration underlined the dislocations of the Spanish national economy and the inability of the state to provide for its subjects. American praise of Spanish workers as reliable, sturdy, and sober only underscored the enormous potential of this labor force if conditions in Spain had been more favorable to economic enterprise. The migration of Spaniards to Latin America had often been couched in terms of the "spirit of adventure" manifested by modern-day emigrants, a legacy of the intrepid "conquerors" of yore who had explored and populated the American continent.[21] But it was difficult to maintain this uplifting narrative in the outposts of the new American empire. Relegated to the hardest tasks in manual labor, often in insalubrious environments, Spaniards were forced to compete with other ethnic and racial groups (West Indians in Panama, Asians in Hawai'i). Their difficulty learning English limited their opportunities to advance, increased the chances of misunderstandings and accidents, and made them more vulnerable to abuse and exploitation.[22]

While, on paper, labor contracts may have appeared enticing, soon negative reports from Canal workers began to appear in the Spanish press. In 1906, the pages of *El Socialista,* the organ of the Spanish Socialist Party, published letters from workers who warned possible recruits about the situation in Panama. The high cost of living, they wrote, made it difficult to save money. They also expressed dissatisfaction with the poor quality of the food, the pitiable lodgings (initially, they were housed in tents), and deplorable sanitary conditions that resulted in high rates of disease. Spaniards also complained of poor working conditions that led to a high number of accidents and deaths, and of the abusive treatment experienced at the hands of foremen and police.[23] When complaints reached a breaking point, strikes and desertion were common

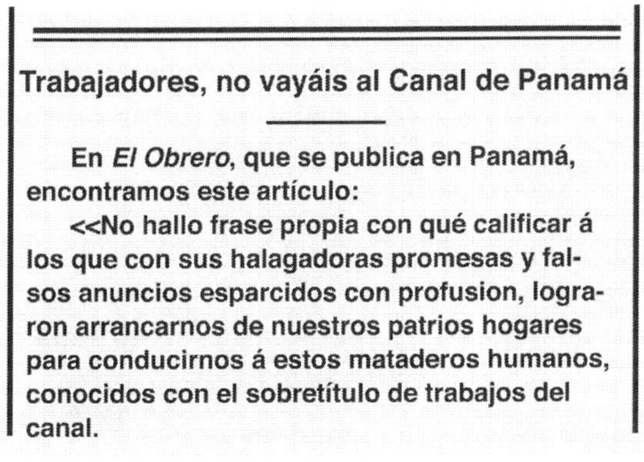

Trabajadores, no vayáis al Canal de Panamá

En *El Obrero*, que se publica en Panamá,
encontramos este artículo:
<<No hallo frase propia con qué calificar á
los que con sus halagadoras promesas y fal-
sos anuncios esparcidos con profusion, logra-
ron arrancarnos de nuestros patrios hogares
para conducirnos á estos mataderos humanos,
conocidos con el sobretítulo de trabajos del
canal.

FIGURE 8.1. Headlines
in the Spanish press
warned potential Spanish
emigrants against the
dangers of migrating to
the Panama Canal (*Las
Dominicales*, August 30,
1908).

---

responses.[24] By 1908, headlines in the Spanish press alerted: "Trabajadores, no
vayáis al Canal de Panamá" (Workers, do not go to the Panama Canal; figure
8.1 and, for warnings against going to Hawai'i, figure 8.2).[25]

A strong racial discourse permeated newspaper accounts of the Spanish
experience in Panama and Hawai'i; the recruitment of workers was often
equated with modern-day slavery. The Madrid daily *El País* compared Spanish
immigrants to African slaves when it denounced the conditions in which they
were taken from Málaga to Hawai'i in the *Heliópolis*. The unhealthy surround-
ings in these "slave ships" also underscored the weakness of the Spanish state
and economy, since foreign companies competed for most of the emigrant
traffic coming out of the peninsula.[26] Ramiro de Maeztu wrote in another
Madrid daily, *La Correspondencia de España*, about the "[Spanish] emigrants
who go to Panama and Hawaii only to be beaten by black and Japanese foremen."[27] For his part, Fabián Vidal told his readers that in Hawai'i "Yankee and
Japanese planters . . . treat Spaniards as they would treat Chinese coolies."[28]
An article titled "Yankee Barbarism. The Spaniards in Panama," compared
the Spanish emigrant experience in Panama and in Morocco, and concluded,
"the Moroccans are less barbaric than the Yankees."[29] The members of the
first Congreso Africanista, convened in Madrid in 1907, suggested that the
Spanish migration to Panama should be channeled instead to Morocco, a
new center of colonialism for Spain.[30]

The outcry over the recruitment and reported mistreatment of Spaniards
in Panama reached the halls of the Congress and the Senate, and became a
main factor in the discussion and passage of the Emigration Act approved by

MISERIA TRÁGICA

LA EMIGRACIÓN Á LAS HAWAI
DETALLES HORRIBLES
POR TELEGRAFO

Visita á bordo. — Impresión dolorosa. — El buque cloaca. — Los ranchos. — Raciones insuficientes. — Requisa: detención de Indocumentados.

Málaga 9 (8 noche)

El puerto está atestado de curiosos que comentan vivamente los abusos cometidos con los emigrantes.

FIGURE 8.2. Headlines in the Spanish press warned potential Spanish emigrants against the dangers of migrating to Hawai'i (*El Imparcial*, March 10, 1907).

the Spanish Parliament in December 1907. The law recognized the "freedom of all Spaniards to emigrate," but it also stressed the tutelary role of the state over a population seen as increasingly vulnerable to the false promises and depredations of foreign recruiters.[31] An important outcome of this legislation was the creation of the Consejo Superior de Emigración (High Council on Emigration), an institution tasked with "safeguarding the application and execution of the law."[32] This proved to be quite challenging, as the consejo lacked the resources to enforce the law, and there were often loopholes to circumvent the legislation. For example, while the Emigration Act banned emigration agencies on Spanish soil, the illegal recruiting of workers continued, with the ships leaving not from Spain but from France and the British port of Gibraltar. One of the consejo's attributions was to propose the temporary halt of migration to specific countries or areas, based on reasons of "public order, health, or exceptional risk to the emigrants."[33] Indeed, less than a year after the promulgation of the Emigration Act, the consejo did recommend a ban on the emigration of Spaniards to the Panama Canal.[34] Alfonso XIII signed the royal decree in November 1908. By then, however, the Isthmian Commission had already decided that Spanish workers were no longer profitable and had instructed LeRoy Park to stop recruiting there.[35] In the following months, the Spanish consul in Panama reported the seemingly irrational dismissal of Spanish workers in the canal, which resulted in hundreds of them leaving Panama for other countries.[36]

The consular body was a key element in the effort of the Spanish government to carry out the tutelary role described in the Emigration Act. A common criticism of the Spanish workers who denounced poor labor conditions in the Panama Canal was the "abandonment" they felt on the part of the representative of the nation. As the Emigration Act was being discussed in the Senate, an article in *El País* stated that "the reform of our most deficient consular representation . . . is precisely connected, and very closely so, to the grave problem of emigration."[37] In a heated debate in the Spanish Congress over the budget assigned to the Ministry of Foreign Affairs, deputies asked the minister about the allotment of funds to repatriate Spanish emigrants from Panama, and blamed the consul in Panama for the situation. "The honorary consul that represented Spain in Panama informed favorably on this migration," said one deputy. "Why? Because that consul was not Spanish, he was not a career professional, and he did not feel the interests of Spain and of Spaniards." "We want to save money on consuls," he continued, "but we will have to spend more money on the repatriation [of Spanish workers] all at once than we would have spent on consuls in a decade."[38]

The Emigration Act echoed some of these concerns. Article 56 stated that the government would "try" to assign Spanish citizens as consuls to the areas that received significant Spanish migration. It also indicated that the government would try to increase the consular personnel "according to the needs of the emigration flow." This was indeed the case in Panama. By 1907, the Consulate had been upgraded (it was no longer an honorary consulate), and at its head was a young career diplomat, Juan Potous, with consular experience in the United States, the Caribbean, and North Africa.[39] Lack of resources, however, plagued Potous's tenure in Panama. With a monthly budget of $33, he could barely afford the rent for the consular office. His request of an increase that would allow him to hire an assistant to help him as he traveled through the Canal Zone to attend to the demands of the thousands of Spanish workers already there was denied.[40]

A number of pressing issues faced Consul Potous as he reached Panama in 1907. Ominously, the task that he highlighted in his letter to the minister of foreign affairs, together with the investigation of complaints brought up by Spanish workers, was the disposal of the property left by those immigrants who had died building the canal. In the few weeks that he had been at his post, Potous had processed thirty-four intestates, and he anticipated that the rainy season would only increase the number, as many Europeans succumbed to the fevers. Disease and accidents were the main causes of workers' deaths in the canal. In fact, Potous believed that one of the reasons that explained this high rate of accidents was the cheapness of the life of immigrant workers, as workers' compensation legislation did not apply to the canal zone. This meant that neither injured workers nor their families, in case of their death, were entitled to any indemnity.[41]

A workmen's compensation bill, covering workers in the canal, eventually became law on May 30, 1908.[42] While an improvement, it still presented some difficulties for the Spanish workers. In his report to Madrid, Consul Potous pointed out three main problems. First, workers were entitled to compensation only if the injury took more than two weeks and less than one year to heal. Because many of the injuries suffered by Spanish workers resulted in amputations of fingers or limbs, and they could be healed within a fifteen-day period, injured workers might not receive any compensation. Potous also considered the amount of the indemnity given for total incapacity or death (a year's salary, which in the Spanish case he estimated at $584) to be too small. Finally, there were matters of procedure. The law established that those dependents entitled to compensation had to present the proper documentation within ninety days of the date of the accident, an impossible deadline to meet for many Spanish families residing in poorly communicated villages and hamlets. The law also established that the indemnity could only be paid to the dependents or their legal representatives in the United States, therefore limiting the role of the Spanish consuls in the process, and adding another obstacle to the families of the deceased immigrants. While the Spanish government could not do much about the first two points, it did pursue the procedural matter. After years of correspondence, in 1911, the Spanish minister in Washington was informed that a new act of Congress had extended to one year the time allowed for dependents to file their claims for compensation.[43]

On April 4, 1913, the Spanish government lifted the temporary ban on emigration to Panama, which had been in place since 1908. But, the decree also stated that since construction of the canal was coming to an end, workers were no longer in demand; in fact, their numbers were dwindling. So, while Spaniards were now, legally, free to go there, the law encouraged them not to go unless they had a job in hand. Beginning in 1908, however, Spanish labor had ceased to be attractive to American recruiters. The debates in the press and the Parliament, the passing of the Emigration Act in 1907, and the 1908 decree banning emigration to Panama contributed to this, but, as Consul Potous also indicated in his correspondence, the Isthmian Canal Commission had by then decided that Spanish workers were no longer profitable. Spaniards had originally been hired as a counterweight to West Indian labor. Initially, their performance was stellar, and they were credited with bringing up the level of West Indian labor as well. Within a few years, though, their results had diminished. In a report published in the monthly *Bulletin* edited by the Consejo Superior de Emigración, Potous included a letter from the head of the Isthmian Commission justifying pay cuts, demotions, and dismissals of Spanish workers who, according to their foremen, were not performing as well as it had been expected. While the consul, like the workers, described these actions as abusive breaches of contract, the Isthmian Commission claimed that they were a fair response to the diminishing quality of Spanish labor. Potous stated that as a result, hundreds of Spaniards were leaving the canal each month to work in other Latin American countries.[44]

Hundreds of Spaniards left the sugar plantations of Hawai'i as well, in this case for the sunny shores of California. Working conditions in Hawai'i were not as hard as those in the Panama Canal, and they were perhaps made more bearable because entire families had migrated together, but life still proved to be difficult for Spaniards there. One of the first hardships faced by the emigrants was the length and conditions of the trip. In 1907, the departure from the port of Málaga of the *Heliópolis*, the first steamship transporting Andalusian families to Hawai'i, produced horrifying newspaper articles describing chaotic situations. This, and the ensuing proclamation of the Emigration Act, led recruiters to dock their steamships at the British port of Gibraltar. In 1911, the death at sea of twenty-seven emigrants (twenty-five of them children) during the fifty-day journey of the *Willesden* brought the plight of the emigrants again to the fore.[45] Two years later, thirty-six migrants, many of them children, perished in another trip of the *Willesden*.[46] The Consejo Superior de Emigración did not have jurisdiction over the port of Gibraltar, but it did try to warn potential emigrants of working conditions on the sugar cane plantations in Hawai'i. A press release published in a number of Spanish newspapers called attention to long working days (twelve hours daily with only half an hour for lunch), inadequate wages ($23 monthly) given the high cost of living, poor treatment by foremen used to mistreating Asian workers with whom the Spaniards would share work on the plantations, and the difficulties resulting from the emigrants' inability to speak English.[47]

The consejo based its information on reports sent by the Spanish consul in Honolulu. As had happened in Panama, Spain's representative in Hawai'i at the turn of the twentieth century had been an honorary vice-consul, the consul of Portugal. The increase in Spanish migration to the archipelago led to the upgrading of the office to Consulate, and its staffing by a Spanish consul, Ignacio de Arana. In this case, however, the appropriation to fund the Spanish consulate in Honolulu did not materialize until 1911. This was the first assignment outside of Europe for Arana, who had been a career consul for five years. When Arana arrived in 1911, he realized that only a small portion of the Spanish colony resided in Honolulu, and he set out to visit the Spanish communities in the Ewa and Waialua plantations on the island of Oahu. In this he was following the example of the consuls of Japan and Portugal, who, he had learned, tried to tour the plantations at least once a year to address any possible problems their compatriots may have had and that needed attention.[48] Indeed, the following year, Arana expanded his visit to include plantations in Hawai'i, Kauai, Maui, and Oahu. It was then that he gathered the complaints later mentioned by the consejo in the press.

Based on his interviews with Spanish workers, Arana wrote a report to the president of the Hawaiian Sugar Planters' Association. In it, the consul suggested a number of improvements. He believed that salaries should be raised (from $24 to $30 monthly) and that workers should be allowed more time to eat their meals (in most plantations, Spaniards worked ten to twelve hours with only a half an hour lunch break at 11 a.m.). Arana also called for better access to medical treatment (doctors preferred to treat Spaniards at the hospital, where interpreters might be available to translate, most Spanish workers being unable to communicate in English), and better treatment by foremen. Used to dealing roughly with Japanese and Chinese workers, Arana stated, the foremen used the same methods with the Spaniards. This mistreatment often caused fights, and it was one of the main reasons, according to the consul, that Spaniards were leaving the plantations and migrating to California.[49]

As in Panama, by 1913, the Sugar Planters' Association was considering stopping the recruitment of Spanish workers, as they looked for immigrants in regions of Austria and Russia. It was not profitable to transport Spaniards to Hawai'i if, instead of settling down as colonists, they left the plantations to go to the mainland. In the first six months of 1913, Arana wrote, 700 Spaniards had left for California. There, he explained, they could buy land relatively cheaply, be more independent, and cultivate crops similar to the ones they grew in Spain.[50]

Conditions did not improve for Spaniards who remained in Hawai'i. In 1917, a new consul, Luis Guillén, reported to the consejo very similar circumstances to those described by Arana in his reports. Guillén stated that an average of 500 Spaniards were leaving the islands for California annually (figure 8.3), as a "silent protest, the only one legally possible against the fraud they have been victims of."[51] Many, he claimed, would have liked to return to Spain, but because they could not afford the ticket ($150 per person), they migrated to California as a springboard to work and earn enough money to return to Spain. Guillén also called attention to the Spanish ambassador in Washington about the effect that the new immigration act was having on this population. The Immigration Act of 1917 barred all illiterate emigrants over sixteen from entering the United States. Guillén reported that he knew of at least ten Spanish families in Hawai'i who could not migrate to California because their members did not know how to read or write. He suggested that the ambassador request an exception to the law for Spaniards in Hawai'i, who, Guillén wrote, "when they were taken to Hawaii were not asked about their degree of culture, but whether or not they had callouses in their hands."[52] Those who did manage to enter the United States joined the Spanish immigrant contingent in California, which the Spanish consul estimated in 1917 to be between 18,000 and 20,000.[53]

THE MIGRATION OF SPANIARDS TO THE
UNITED STATES, NEW CHALLENGES

Among the topics discussed in the debate over the Emigration Act in the Spanish Senate in 1907 was the apparent contradiction between the freedom of Spaniards to emigrate, enshrined in the first article of the law, and the power given to the state to regulate, and even halt, that emigration, as

FIGURE 8.3. The Oncina family was one of the families who left Spain for Hawaiʻi in the 1910s and moved to California a few years later. Courtesy of Christine Oncina Lerone.

described in article 15. In one such debate, Gustavo Ruiz de Grijalba, a member of the liberal Commission that had proposed the legislation, addressed a conservative senator who had argued against the law based on what he interpreted as the incompatibility of "the principle of tutelage and the principle of freedom." Ruiz de Grijalba denied that the law curbed the individual freedom to emigrate; what it did, he stated, was to "forbid deception." Another senator, Luis Palomo, seemed to find a happy medium between these two apparently opposing positions. Palomo explained that the key resided in the characteristics and outcomes of two different types of emigration: some emigrations were convenient and profitable; others were harmful and pernicious. Among the "profitable" emigrations Palomo counted the temporary migration of Spaniards to North Africa and Latin America, particularly Cuba. These emigrations resulted in high levels of returns (both economic and human). Panama (and we might add Hawaiʻi) were examples of detrimental emigration because in this "contract migration" many emigrants, as Ruiz de Grijalba and Consul Guillén would argue, had been "deceived" by recruiters; they had lacked governmental protection; and, Palomo estimated, only 10 percent had returned, the majority having failed or perished in the attempt.[54]

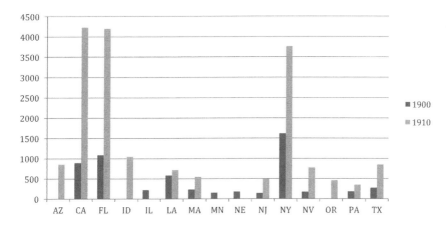

FIGURE 8.4. States with the highest population of Spaniards (1900, 1910). Bureau of the Census, *Abstract of the Twelfth Census of the United States 1900* (Washington, DC: GPO, 1904), 63; Bureau of the Census, *Thirteenth Census of the United States 1910* (Washington, DC: GPO, 1913), 205.

Voluntary migration, particularly to countries where Spaniards had already established strong communities and organizations, was seen, if not as an ideal, at least as advantageous for both the emigrants and their families as well as their communities at home. In the first quarter of the twentieth century, the United States would become increasingly attractive to potential emigrants from Spain. When the Dillingham Commission issued its report in 1911, it recorded the presence of Spaniards in all the states of the Union except North Dakota. New York, Florida, and California accounted for 55 percent of this migration, with another 23 percent distributed between Texas and the western states (figure 8.4).[55]

Spanish immigrants often populated specific labor niches: cigar making in Florida, sheepherding in Nevada, fruit picking and canning in California, mining in Arizona and West Virginia. This settlement pattern would change in the following decade, especially during World War I, when, as subjects of a neutral country, Spaniards were actively recruited to work in the war industries, thus opening the door for many Spanish immigrants to join the industrial workforce. By the 1920s and 1930s, Spanish enclaves could be found in New Jersey, Michigan, Pennsylvania, and Ohio (figure 8.5).

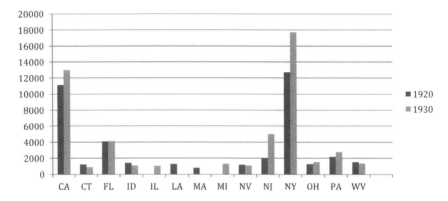

FIGURE 8.5. States with the highest population of Spaniards (1920, 1930). Bureau of the Census, *Abstract of the Fourteenth Census of the United States 1920* (Washington, DC: GPO, 1923), 308; Bureau of the Census, *Fifteenth Census of the United States 1930* (Washington, DC: GPO, 1933), 134.

These immigrant settlements, in turn, opened up opportunities for a number of supporting businesses such as boardinghouses, bars, restaurants, and stores. Some communities, such as the one in Tampa, Florida, were particularly prosperous. In 1913, Angel Cuesta, one of the most prominent Spanish cigar manufacturers in the city, wrote a letter to the Spanish minister in Washington in which he estimated that the Spanish community sent back to Spain over $250,000 annually in remittances.[56]

The arrival of these immigrants tested the limits of the already precarious consular system and illuminated how ill prepared it was to fulfill the tutelary tasks entrusted to it by the Emigration Act. For a country that had had such an extensive colonial presence in the Americas, Spain had a very limited official presence in the continent. When the Emigration Act was approved in 1907, there were no Spanish embassies in the Americas. New York housed the only Spanish Consulate General outside of Europe. In fact, the first Spanish Embassy in the continent opened in Washington in 1915, two years before the one in Buenos Aires, where a quarter of the Spanish migrants in America lived. Even then, Spain only upgraded the post, held by Juan Riaño, from Spanish minister plenipotentiary to ambassador, as a response to the United States naming an ambassador in Madrid in 1913. Because funds had not been appropriated in the budget, however,

Riaño continued to serve as minister plenipotentiary, with the credentials of ambassador, until 1915.

As a senior diplomat Juan Riaño was used to the chronic underfunding of the Spanish state, but the specific circumstances that prevailed in the United States made the task of the Spanish diplomatic service even more challenging. The sheer size of the country and the dispersion of the Spanish immigrant population resulted in far-flung consular jurisdictions where it was almost impossible for Spanish workers to travel to the consular offices or for the consuls to visit the immigrant communities. To cut costs the Spanish Ministry of Foreign Affairs had relied on a small network of honorary offices (consulates, vice-consulates, and agencies) that received little or no remuneration from the state. These offices were often held by prominent community members (lawyers, merchants) but not necessarily Spanish citizens.[57] In fact, given the nature of Spanish migration to the United States, it proved difficult in many communities to find Spaniards who could fulfill this role. In 1915, for example, the consul in San Francisco admitted to Riaño that his efforts to establish a network of honorary vice-consulates in his jurisdiction had failed. Having inquired about possible suitable candidates among members of the Spanish communities in Arizona, Idaho, Nevada, Oregon, and Utah, he could find only one fitting candidate: Reverend Bernardo Arregui, a Spanish priest serving the Basque community in Boise. This is even more remarkable if we consider the minimum qualifications the consul was seeking in the candidate. "The least we can ask," he had written to Riaño, "is [that they] be able to read, write, and count, and . . . communicate with our compatriots in our language."[58] Most Spanish immigrants could not fit the first set of specifications; many American candidates lacked the necessary fluency in Spanish.

Even when the Spanish state made an effort to upgrade honorary consulates or establish new ones, and staff them with career consuls, the low salaries and lack of resources these public officials encountered made their jobs particularly challenging. In 1912, Juan Riaño wrote a six-page letter to the minister of foreign affairs in Madrid requesting a raise in the salaries of diplomatic and consular personnel in the United States, where, he argued, the cost of living had increased 50 percent in the previous decade. Not only did the Spanish personnel receive smaller salaries than those collected by other European legations, but, Riaño explained, some consuls' salaries could not even compare with those of American manual workers. The Spanish vice-consul in New York, he claimed, earned less than a bricklayer.[59] Things had not improved a decade later. In 1922, Riaño again wrote to the minister requesting a raise. This time he sent a table with the monthly salaries of the diplomatic representatives in Washington of fourteen European and American countries, and Japan. In all cases, Spain was at the bottom. In 1923, Riaño took the opportunity to forward to the minister a newspaper article reporting on the opening of the Cuban Embassy in Washington. The salary of the new Cuban ambassador was $9,000; Riaño's was under $1,500.[60]

As Riaño explained in his reports to Madrid, these conditions inevitably affected the morale of the consular personnel. Many consuls lived alone, separated for years from their families in Spain because they could not afford to maintain their family in the United States. When they did get time off, some could not even afford the trip to visit their families in Spain. Often, they avoided interacting with other consuls, with Americans, and even with members of the Spanish colony, so as not to expose their poverty and lack of means. Riaño referred to the situation of the Spanish consular personnel in the United States as "a kind of banishment."[61]

For some, it literally was a banishment. When a young Andrés Iglesias Velayos committed an infraction as consul in Mogador (Morocco), the minister of foreign affairs, considering his inexperience, was lenient enough not to pursue a disciplinary action that could have resulted in his expulsion from the diplomatic corps. Instead, he sent him to the newly created Consulate in Galveston, Texas. Not only was Iglesias afraid of traveling by sea, but, as he wrote to his superior regarding his case, he believed that his services "would be useless there," since he did not know the language.[62] Iglesias did learn English, and he served in a variety of posts in the United States during his career. This was not the case, however, with his predecessor in Galveston, Manuel de la Escosura, who stubbornly refused to learn English and carried on his correspondence with American authorities in French.[63] In a letter to Riaño defending this extraordinary behavior, De la Escosura stated that in the European posts where he had served, there had been paid interpreters. He, of course, had no allowance for that expense in the United States. De la Escosura had been appalled at the lack of resources in the Spanish consulates in the United States since his arrival in Galveston. He described his salary as "little more than the wages earned by a regular laborer, therefore, a pauper," and found his "start-up budget" inadequate to set up a consulate where there were "no stamps . . . no furniture, no forms . . . not even a flag or shield that would indicate to our nationals the existence of a Consulate."[64]

The Spanish nationals were the main concern of Ambassador Riaño. While the consulate in Galveston attended a relatively small community, the size of the Spanish immigrant population in De la Escosura's new appointment, Philadelphia (encompassing honorary agencies in Baltimore, Clarksburg, Norfolk, and Pittsburgh) was bigger and growing.[65] The behavior of De la Escosura in Philadelphia was so outrageous that a few months after his appointment, Ambassador Riaño requested that the minister in Madrid transfer the consul as soon as possible to another post. De la Escosura's obstinacy in continuing to use French in his correspondence with American authorities, Riaño stated, "rendered his actions futile, even as his conduct itself was counterproductive." Even worse was the consul's apparent lack of concern toward the Spanish subjects whose interests he was supposed to defend. On January 31, 1921, the secretary of the Union Benéfica Española, a Spanish mutual aid society based in New York, wrote to the consul requesting his assistance for one of the society's members, Modesto Caride, who lived in Philadelphia.

Modesto Caride had suffered an accident while working at the power plant at the University of Pennsylvania. The injury resulted in the loss of his left eye, damage to his right eye, and a number of other respiratory and articulatory problems that prevented him from working again. Caride stated that the university had not paid for lost wages, or for treatment in the hospital, and it had offered no compensation for the loss of his left eye. This compensation is what he sought when he asked the aid of the Benéfica. Its secretary, after informing the consul of Caride's plight, suggested that he present a claim to the university and sue for damages. De la Escosura wrote a scathing reply to his correspondent, taking issue with his "impertinence" for telling a consul what he should or should not do, for not writing his letter as a respectful request, and for not using the proper channels (i.e., writing through the Spanish Consul General in New York). Upon receiving this letter, the secretary of the Benéfica denounced the case to Riaño. He expressed "surprise and indignation" at the consul's reply, told Riaño that Caride had not been received by De la Escosura, and asked for advice on how to proceed in the future, because, "as a private individual and as the Secretary of this association, I do not wish to be treated in the way that the Spanish Consul in Philadelphia has treated me."[66]

Riaño added this case to the list of grievances piling up against De la Escosura, qualifying the response of the consul to the Benéfica as "inadmissible." The minister of foreign affairs agreed. The letter he sent to the consul imposing a disciplinary action, censured the conduct of De la Escosura regarding the case of Modesto Caride, "whose rights you ought to have defended as soon as you became aware of the accident he suffered, regardless of the form or channel used to inform you of it." By the time the minister's letter reached De la Escosura, he was no longer consul in Philadelphia.[67] In fact, Riaño believed that he had deliberately behaved that way in order to be transferred to a better post outside of the United States.

The Spanish immigrants' ignorance or poor command of English and of American customs and law contributed to many of the situations that prompted them to appeal to the Spanish authorities for redress. Immigrants and their families often denounced American companies and lawyers for cheating them of injury and death benefits. Although the consuls and the ambassador were diligent in requesting state authorities and the State Department to carry out investigations, the more likely outcome was an appeal to the courts—a daunting and expensive endeavor for many of these immigrants.

In 1908, Manuel Patiño Sánchez requested compensation from the Florida East Coast Railway Company for the death of his son, Francisco, in Miami, where he worked building the railroad line to Key West. Two years later, when Patiño wrote to Riaño, he had not received the money or even an official acknowledgment of the death of his son.[68] The official response from the governor of Florida to the State Department, to which Riaño had written, was that this was a private matter that should be taken up by the courts. It was impossible for Patiño to sue the company.[69] Through the intercession of the Spanish vice-consul in Tampa Patiño received from the company $12, the wages his son had earned up to the day he was killed, but no further compensation.

In states such as New Mexico or West Virginia, with thousands of Spanish miners, the Workman's Compensation Laws did not allow dependents of workers who were not residents of the United States to receive any indemnities. In Pennsylvania the law provided compensation for widows and children of workers, even if they resided abroad (one-third the amount they would have received had they resided in the United States). The law, however, did not provide anything for other relatives, such as elderly parents, who made up a high proportion of the dependents among Spanish immigrants, many of whom were young single men. In 1921, Ambassador Riaño suggested to the minister of foreign affairs the drawing up of a treaty between the two countries that would put an end to what he considered an "injustice." He also informed the Consejo Superior de Emigración to let prospective emigrants know about these laws.[70]

This was not the first time that Riaño had denounced discrimination against Spanish immigrants in the United States. In 1914 he wrote to the minister of foreign affairs recommending that emigration to the United States be temporarily stopped on the basis of article 2 of the regulations of the consejo: "countries whose governments impede our consuls from carrying out the inspection functions attributed to them by the Emigration Act." Riaño supported his request with reports from the consul in New York that deplored the vulnerability of Spanish workers facing the immigration officials at Ellis Island. The consul stated, for example, that a group of Spanish immigrants who had come to the United States to work as farmhands, had been told at Ellis Island that in order to be allowed in the country they ought to go to work in the zinc-smelting plants in Pennsylvania. The immigrants were made to sign a contract and pay for the trip to Pennsylvania. The consul explained that conditions in the smelting plants (including daily wages as low as $1.85) made it difficult to find workers in the country. The officers in Ellis Island, working together with these companies, coerced defenseless immigrants into working there under the threat of deportation.[71]

Other times, the consul stated, Spanish immigrants were forbidden entry on account that they would become a public charge. This is what happened to a group of sixteen Spaniards arriving in Providence, Rhode Island, on May 4, 1914. The representative of the steamship company that had transported the immigrants to the United States wrote to the Spanish consul in Boston to inform him that the Spaniards were being held at the Immigrant station (some having been prevented from leaving ship). The letter claimed that these men were "sound of body and mind, and plentifully supplied with money."[72] In his report to Riaño the honorary vice-consul in Boston reiterated this information, calling the decision to prevent the landing of the immigrants unjust.[73] The Spaniards were eventually deported, under the claim that they were "likely to become public charges," despite the fact that, apparently, each of them had $45 to $50 in their pockets. Riaño denounced the case to the secretary of state, and informed him that he was recommending his government to discourage the emigration of Spaniards to the United States because of the arbitrary behavior of the immigration authorities. In his letter to the consejo recommending the temporary ban of emigration, Riaño acknowledged that "the limited Spanish consular service and the absence of Immigration Commissioners, as other countries have," contributed to the difficult situation faced by Spaniards, even if they did manage to enter the country.[74]

While American authorities may have overstepped their powers in some cases, the situation was aggravated by the lack of resources in the Spanish consular system that placed Spanish immigrants at a disadvantage. As the consul in New York explained in his report to Riaño, most European nations had delegates in Ellis Island available to counsel and help their arriving immigrants. The Spanish Consulate in New York could not afford to pay such agents. The resourceful consul, however, had persuaded the leaders of the newly founded Unión Benéfica Española, a Spanish mutual aid society the consul had been instrumental in creating, to take charge of that mission.[75] But new regulations imposed under war conditions prevented the Benéfica from securing the authorization to work at Ellis Island.

The Benéfica did succeed in helping Spanish immigrants already in the country. In July 1918, the president of the society, Jose Camprubí, informed Riaño that the mutual aid society now housed the offices of a Spanish Local Law Board created to help Spanish immigrants deal with the Selective Service Law. Every day, from 2 to 10 p.m., a committee of American lawyers and auxiliary staff helped Spaniards to fill out the forms required to exempt them from the draft. Camprubí explained that the cost of maintaining these offices would be at least $300 a week for a number of months, and asked the embassy for a contribution.[76] By November 1918, the board had grown from five to twelve lawyers and as many auxiliary staff costing the Benéfica $3,170.[77]

World War I stretched to the limit the already precarious Spanish consular system. The war itself had contributed to the rise of Spanish migration to the United States. The labor shortage caused by the return to Europe of migrants from belligerent countries, and later, by America's own entry into

FIGURE 8.6. Advertisement in the Spanish New York daily *La Prensa* encouraged Spanish workers to apply for jobs in the war industry during World War I. June 23, 1917.

the conflict, opened up employment opportunities for Spanish immigrants, subjects of a neutral country. New York's Spanish daily *La Prensa* published ads from labor agencies catering to Spaniards to work in a variety of industries, mines, and public works (figure 8.6). Spanish women too were encouraged to do "patriotic labor," making chocolate candy for American servicemen in Europe (figure 8.7).[78]

In 1919, *The Literary Digest* estimated that 80,000 Spaniards resided in the United States, and it stated that during the war, "30 to 40 percent of the unskilled workers in munitions plants, shipyards, mines, and other industries were Spaniards."[79] By all accounts they performed well. In August 1916, the president of the United States Zinc Company wrote to the consul in New York that "the Spaniards connected with the smelting interest in the South West in Kansas and Oklahoma, are nice clean cut crowd of men and really are better citizens than the average American who is connected with the same work."[80] The context for the expression of this laudable statement, however, was not a happy one. Two weeks earlier a mob had driven a group of 300 Spanish mine workers out of the town of Sand Springs, near Tulsa. While the specific reason for this violence does not appear in the consular correspondence, both the Spanish victims and the president of the company cited

EMPLEO SE OFRECE

MUCHACHAS Y SENORAS
Trabajo patriótico y esencial

Trabajen en fábrica de caio y rhocolte y ayuden a sus hijos, hermanos y novios, que están luchando por nosotros, a tener chocolates que necesitan urgentemente. Despachamos pedidos diariamente a Francia y necesitamos brazos.
Trabajó todo el día o parte del mismo. Buen salario para comenzar. Con rápido adelanto si Ud. nos demuestra que no tiene miedo a un trabajo liviano.

Fábrica limpia y Saludable

Donde las condiciones de trabajo son agradables. Las horas de tabajo son de 7.30 a 5.30. Sábados de 7 a 11 a.m.

Localidad conveniente

Queda apenas a pocas yardas de la Estación del Elevado de la Novena Avenida. Runkel Chocolate's 451 West 30th St., Entre la 9th Ave. y la 10th Ave., N. Y. City.

FIGURE 8.7. Advertisement in the Spanish New York daily *La Prensa* encouraged Spanish women to apply for jobs during World War I. October 23, 1918.

fear of foreigners and corrupt local politics as the culprits. By September, the State Department had responded to Riaño's request for an investigation into the matter stating that local authorities were doing everything in their power to find and prosecute the perpetrators and that the governor had been urged to guarantee the protection of the Spanish workers.

In this case, the company sided with the Spanish workers; in other states relations between American companies and Spanish immigrants were tenser. In November 1917, a committee representing over a thousand Spanish workers in the mines of the Globe-Miami district in Arizona wrote to Riaño asking for help. They explained that, following a strike, some companies refused to hire them unless they became American citizens and were approved by the Loyalty League. The writers appealed to the ambassador to defend them against this case of discrimination. They reaffirmed their own patriotism, stating that they would rather leave the United States than renounce their Spanish citizenship. Riaño could do little in this case, but he did ask the State Department to intercede with the governor of Arizona. Most of the Spanish workers were eventually rehired, but the consular correspondence shows that Spaniards in other locations such as Lorain (Ohio) and Rome (New York) faced similar threats.[81]

Spanish immigrants also confronted the hostility of their coworkers, particularly when the United States entered World War I. In 1918, the consul in New York received a letter signed by sixty-five Spaniards from Canton, Ohio. In it, they denounced the abuses suffered by Antonio Fernández at the hands of a number of American workers affronted because he had refused to buy Liberty Bonds. A police investigation, requested by Riaño, downplayed the level of violence inflicted on Fernández and highlighted instead his unpatriotic response. When asked to contribute, he had allegedly replied, "To Hell with Liberty Bonds!" The Spaniards, who in solidarity with Fernández had refused to return to work, were eventually persuaded to do so, but Fernández, who was offered a transfer to a position in another part of the plant, decided to get his pay and leave.[82] Emilio Veiga, too, left his job in South Bethlehem after he was tarred and feathered for not buying Liberty Bonds. Once again the report of the investigation requested by Riaño stated that the violent response was the consequence of Veiga's utterance: "To hell with the flag. I'm going back to Spain!"[83] Spanish workers in Lackawanna Steel Co. also claimed that two Spaniards had been tarred, and over 100 fired, after they had chosen not to contribute to the "For the Boys over there united War Work Campaign." "The Spanish community . . . would be the first one to contribute to a war tax," one worker wrote to Riaño, "but charity must be given willingly."[84] The Spanish owner of a boardinghouse in Rome, New York, writing to Riaño to denounce another case of discrimination by the police on account of his nationality, explained: "Spaniards are not well liked here because we did not become citizens during the war."[85]

While Spanish patriotism may have played a role in this decision, also at issue was the risk of being drafted in the American Army once the immigrants renounced their Spanish citizenship. Indeed, this matter took most of Riaño's time when the United States entered the war. The draft of Spanish citizens to serve in the army violated Article V of the Treaty of Friendship between the two countries. Although the Department of State often agreed with Riaño when he brought up his protests, he was less successful with the Department of War. In October 1918, a desperate Riaño wrote to the private secretary of the king, suggesting that Alfonso XIII have a conversation with the American military attaché in Madrid regarding the matter.[86] In 1918 Riaño had processed over 1,400 requests from Spaniards who had been illegally drafted in the American Army.[87]

The Spanish immigrant population was on edge. As one worker put it to Riaño: "Every day we are made to suffer as we are told that we will have to leave this country unless we enroll in the army."[88] The situation had become even more complicated in May 1918, when the United States denounced the Treaty of Friendship. This meant that the treaty would expire in May 1919, therefore leaving without validity Article V, and opening the road to the drafting of Spaniards in the American Army. This information caused a flurry of correspondence from Spanish immigrants to the ambassador. Even employers wrote to the embassy on behalf of their Spanish workers. The superintendent of a factory in Rome, New York, explained to Riaño that the Spanish workers "are very restless and are at their wits end to know whether to remain in this Country or to return to their Home Land." Repeating information received from the State Department, Riaño responded that, like all foreigners, Spaniards would only have to serve in the military if they became American citizens. Those who had taken the first papers would not be drafted, but they would lose the right to apply for citizenship in the future.[89] Having been notorious for their disregard to register in the Spanish consulates, Spaniards now turned to those offices in droves trying to secure the documents that proved their nationality. In the event, the war ended before the expiration of the treaty of friendship, but the postwar situation was to pose new challenges to Spanish immigrants.

In January 1921 an article appeared in the *Philadelphia North American*, an interview with a commissioner from the Pennsylvania Department of Labor and Industry describing the "unusual and interesting experience" of the Pennsylvania Railroad with Spanish labor. The demand for Spanish labor at the PRR came out of the high turnover they had experienced for years with "American white and negro labor." In May 1920 the company hired 1,600 Spaniards. Most of them were already living in the United States, but others came directly from Spain. By December of that year, only sixteen had been dropped from the rolls (four of them having died at work). This turnover of "almost zero," the commissioner explained, "marks a record never before made . . . in the United States by any railroad or large industrial corporation." "How was this wonderful result attained?" the commissioner asked. "The answer," he replied, "is a remarkable human-interest story of human relations."[90]

At the Pennsylvania Railroad Spaniards had their own camps and they chose their own "subforemen," who acted as mediators between workers and management. The article praised the good relations between employers and workers. Whenever the employers spent time with the Spanish workers, these would show their appreciation with Spanish food and wine and so many presents that, had the American managers taken them, they "would have needed a moderate-sized truck in which to haul them all away." Spaniards were also apparently impervious to the appeal of so-called labor agitators, having been advised by the company "not to let anyone influence them to become dissatisfied with their work." The PRR manager stated that wages were not the highest priority for the Spanish workers, but "what they want and what, in fact, they insist upon, are good living conditions and fair treatment." "Give them decent leadership," he explained, "and like most Americans, the Spaniards will take care of themselves." Americanization was an important aspect of this enterprise. The PRR "conducted an Americanization course . . . both by correspondence and by personal contact." It included "pamphlets, motion pictures, and lantern slide exhibits" and, the article reassured its readers, "it brought the heartiest response from these future citizens."[91]

Others were not so sure that Spanish immigration was good for the country and that Spaniards would make good American citizens. At the same time that the Pennsylvania Railroad was praising the virtues of Spanish workers, Congress was considering measures to drastically cut the immigration from "radical" countries. Harold Knutson, a Republican congressman from Minnesota, singled out Spain as a particular culprit. "Before the war, immigration from Spain was practically unknown," Knutson stated, as he explained that in a recent visit to Ellis Island he had found that 2,000 immigrants from Spain had arrived in one day. Knutson believed that this increase responded to Spanish government policies. "Spain is a seething mass of anarchy," he declared, "and the [Spanish] Government is gathering these anarchists up and dumping them on us."[92]

When Riaño reported Knutson's statement to the government in Madrid, the minister of foreign affairs denied the charges. Spain's "social conditions are visibly improving," he wrote to the ambassador. The country, therefore, "has no interest whatsoever in helping emigration and it will not lament that the American government establish whatever limits it wishes to immigration."[93] In fact, in November 1920, the Spanish consul in New York had already suggested to Riaño that he recommend to Madrid a temporary ban of emigration to the United States given the poor economic conditions immigrants would face. The consul repeated the suggestion a few months later, anticipating the inability of the consulate to succor and repatriate those in need.[94] In March 1921, the situation was so dire that the Spanish government budgeted the unprecedented sum of 500,000 pesetas to repatriate unemployed Spaniards from the United States. In 1923, close to 1.5 million pesetas more were budgeted to cover repatriations from Cuba and the United States.[95] That year the Spanish consul in New York estimated the Spanish immigrant population to be at 57,670.[96] The 1924 National Quota Act would drastically reduce those figures and practically put an end to Spanish migration to the United States.[97] In Spain, too, 1924 would see the passing of a new Emigration Act. It happened a few months after the military coup that began the dictatorship of General Miguel Primo de Rivera. The new regime would redefine the relationship between the state and the Spanish subjects, and between Spain and her immigrant communities in the Americas.[98]

NOTES

1. The posthumous son of Alfonso XII, Alfonso had been born king on May 17, 1886, but ruled under the regency of his mother, Queen María Cristina. The ceremony celebrating Alfonso's coming of age and his swearing of loyalty to the laws and Constitution of Spain was not a coronation, but it marked the end of the Regency and the beginning of Alfonso's rule in his own right.

2. Edwin Anderson Alderman and Armistead Churchill Gordon, *J. L. M. Curry: A Biography* (New York: The Macmillan Company, 1911), 370.

3. Curry pointed out that "after the precedence extended to the foreign representatives of 'blood royal' and to the papal nuncio, the American ambassador had the place of honor at the oath taking, in the Cortez [sic], at royal banquet, at official receptions, at the celebration of the Te Deum, at the military review, at all ceremonies and functions." "Celebration of Majority of Alfonso XIII," *Foreign Relations of the United States* (Washington, DC: Government Printing Office, 1902), 958.

4. "Treaty of Friendship and General Relations between the United States of America and Spain." The treaty was signed in Madrid, July 3, 1902, and ratified a

year later (April 14, 1903). "Treaty Between the United States and Spain: Friendship and General Relations," *Foreign Relations of the United States* (Washington, DC: Government Printing Office, 1903), 721–30.

5. On the development of the Latin immigrant community in Tampa, see Gary R. Mormino and George E. Pozzetta, *The Immigrant World of Ybor City: Italians and Their Latin Neighbors in Tampa, 1885–1985* (Chicago: University of Illinois Press, 1987). For a study of these regional *centros* in Cuba, see Elwood Warren Shomo Jr., "The Centros Regionales of Havana, Cuba, with Special Emphasis on the History and Services of the Centro Asturiano" (master's thesis, University of Miami, 1959). On Tampa's Spanish mutual aid societies, see Ana Varela-Lago, "From Patriotism to Mutualism: The Early Years of the Centro Español de Tampa, 1891–1903," *Tampa Bay History* 15, no. 2 (1993): 5–23.

6. On the modern migration of Spaniards to the United States, see R. A. Gómez, "Spanish Immigration to the United States," *Americas* 19 (July 1962): 59–78; Germán Rueda, *La emigración contemporánea de españoles a los Estados Unidos, 1820–1950: De "Dons" a "Misters"* (Madrid: Mapfre, 1993); and Ana Varela-Lago, "Conquerors, Immigrants, Exiles: The Spanish Diaspora in the United States (1848–1948)" (PhD diss., University of California San Diego, 2008). On the disaster and its consequences in Spain, see Sebastian Balfour, *The End of the Spanish Empire, 1898–1923* (Oxford: Clarendon Press, 1997).

7. W. Leon Pepperman, *Who Built the Panama Canal?* (New York: E. P. Dutton, 1915), 176.

8. In his note to the minister of foreign affairs informing on the discussion of the 1903 Hay-Herrán treaty in Colombia, the Spanish minister in Washington stated that "following the Spanish-American War Europe seems to have forgotten certain principles of justice and solidarity that before would have moved her to intervene in the Americas." He concluded his report remarking on the United States' "invading march towards the conquest of the northern American hemisphere, which more or less covertly is now and will be tomorrow the goal of its [foreign] policy." Emilio de Ojeda to minister of foreign affairs, November 7, 1903, in Agustín Alberto Martínez Rivera, "Panamá y la construcción de un canal interoceánico en las relaciones exteriores de España en el siglo XIX" (PhD diss., Universidad Complutense, Madrid, 1990), 501–2. Unless otherwise stated, all translations are by the author.

9. Pepperman, *Who Built the Panama Canal?* 176.

10. Pepperman, *Who Built the Panama Canal?* 176.

11. Julie Greene, *The Canal Builders: Making America's Empire at the Panama Canal* (New York: Penguin, 2009), 15–36. The list of "Latin" failures included not only the Spanish "disaster" of 1898, but also the French defeat in the Franco-Prussian war of 1870 and the Italian defeat in Ethiopia in 1896. On the debate between "Latins"

and "Anglo-Saxons," see Lily Litvak, *Latinos y anglosajones: Orígenes de una polémica* (Barcelona: Puvill, 1980).

12. Interestingly, Mateos followed the characterization of the young American used by French writer Jules Huret, as a man interested only in business, material progress, and the conquest of the world. J. Mateos, *A través del Istmo de Panamá* (Barcelona: Herederos de Juan Gili, 1907), 19.

13. Mateos, *A través del Istmo de Panamá*, ch. 6. This history lesson, however, did not impress the American engineer, who was portrayed as even more convinced of the superiority and greatness of America over all other nations.

14. Modesto Pérez Hernández, *Los precursores españoles del canal interoceánico* (Madrid: Perlado, Páez y Compañía, 1915), vii–viii.

15. Instituto de Reformas Sociales, *La emigración* (Madrid: Imprenta de la Sucesora de M. Minuesa de los Ríos, 1905), 112–14. On the emigration debate in Spain, see Blanca Sánchez Alonso, *Las causas de la emigración española, 1880–1930* (Madrid: Alianza Universidad, 1995), 62–93.

16. "Spaniards for Canal Work," *New York Times*, September 23, 1905, 5.

17. Cited in Louis A. Pérez, *Cuba. Between Reform and Revolution* (Oxford: Oxford University Press, 1988), 203.

18. Pepperman, *Who Built the Panama Canal?* 173–74.

19. Yolanda Marco Serra, *Los obreros españoles en la construcción del Canal de Panamá* (Panama: Portobelo, 1997). On the emigration of Galicians to the Panama Canal, see Juan Manuel Pérez, *Pro Mundi Beneficio: Los trabajadores gallegos en la construcción del canal de Panamá, 1904–1914* (A Coruña: Fundación Pedro Barrié de la Maza, 2007); and Carolina García Borrazás and Francisco Sieiro Benedetto, *Galicia en Panamá: Historia de una emigración* (Santiago de Compostela: C. García, 2011).

20. On the Spanish migration to Hawai'i, see Germán Rueda Hernánz, "Vida y desventuras de ocho mil españoles en Hawai durante las primeras décadas del siglo XX," *Revista de Historia Contemporánea* 3 (1984): 125–42; and Beverly Lozano, "The Andalucia-Hawaii-California Migration: A Study in Macrostructure and Microhistory," *Comparative Studies in Society and History* 26, no. 2 (April 1984): 305–24 (chapter 2 in this volume). Personal accounts of this migration can be found in Anne Aguilar Santucci, *Memories of Spain* (Rocklin, CA: Club Español, 1994); Manuela Rodríguez, *Memories of a Spaniard* (typescript in author's possession); Gloria López, *An American Paella* (n.p.: Autry Lopez Production Company, 2007); and Patricia Ruiz Steele, *The Girl Immigrant* (Casa Grande, AZ: Plumería Press, 2013); and *Silván Leaves* (Casa Grande, AZ: Plumería Press, 2014).

21. On the appeal of the "conqueror" narrative to Spanish immigrants in the United States, see Varela-Lago, "Conquerors, Immigrants, Exiles," ch. 3. For a discussion of the role of the "discovery" and conquest of America on modern Spanish

nationalism, see Fredrick B. Pike, *Hispanismo, 1898–1936: Spanish Conservatives and Liberals and Their Relations with Spanish America* (Notre Dame, IN: University of Notre Dame Press, 1971); and Isidro Sepúlveda, *El sueño de la Madre Patria: Hispano-americanismo y nacionalismo* (Madrid: Marcial Pons, 2005).

22. On the racial dynamics that prevailed in the Canal Zone see Greene, *The Canal Builders*, chs. 3 and 4.

23. "República de Panamá," *El Socialista*, December 21, 1906, in Marco Serra, *Los obreros españoles*, 45–46. The article had appeared originally in *Solidaridad*, a Socialist newspaper published in Vigo, a main urban center in Galicia.

24. During a strike in 1907 over 500 Spaniards tried to leave the Canal Zone, but they were forced back to the camps by American marines. Luis Navas, *El movimiento obrero en Panamá (1880–1914)* (Ciudad de Panamá: Editorial Universitaria, 1974), 150.

25. "Trabajadores, no vayáis al Canal de Panamá," *Las Dominicales*, August 30, 1908, 4. The article had originally appeared in Panama's newspaper *El Obrero*.

26. "Nuestros cónsules," *El País*, July 7, 1907, 1.

27. Ramiro de Maeztu, "Los poetas, la vida y el catalanismo," *La Correspondencia de España*, May 17, 1907, 1. Maeztu addressed the article to Azorín (José Martínez Ruiz). Both writers are considered representative members of the Generation of 1898. See Donald L. Shaw, *The Generation of 1898 in Spain* (London: Ernest Benn, 1975).

28. Fabián Vidal, "Quédate," *La Correspondencia de España*, April 10, 1914, 1.

29. "Barbarie Yanki: Los Españoles en Panamá," *El País*, November 13, 1907, 1.

30. "El Congreso Africanista," *El Liberal*, January 11, 1907, 1. *Primer Congreso Africanista* (Barcelona: Imprenta de la Casa Provincial de Caridad, 1907), 70–76.

31. Ley de Emigración, *Gaceta de Madrid*, December 22, 1907, 1085–88.

32. Article 8, Ley de Emigración, 1086; Article 18, "Reglamento Provisional para la aplicación de la Ley de Emigración de 21 de diciembre de 1907," *Gaceta de Madrid*, May 6, 1908, 638.

33. Article 15, "Ley de Emigración," *Gaceta de Madrid*, December 22, 1907, 1086.

34. The royal decree was issued on November 12, 1908. *Gaceta de Madrid*, November 13, 1908, 618. The ban was lifted on April 4, 1913, based also on a recommendation from the Consejo Superior de Emigración, *Gaceta de Madrid*, April 5, 1913, 59.

35. Chief quartermaster to LeRoy Park, October 27, 1908, National Archives, Record Group 185, Alpha Files, 1904–1960, 2-E-2/Spain.

36. "Los españoles en Panamá," *Boletín del Consejo Superior de Emigración*, 1909: 587–92.

37. Marco Serra, *Los obreros españoles*, 35–40; "Nuestros Cónsules," El País, July 7, 1907, 1.

38. "Congreso," *La Correspondencia de España*, November 15, 1907, 2.

39. Juan Potous Martínez was named consul in Panama on January 1, 1907. Archivo Histórico Nacional–Ministerio de Asuntos Exteriores (hereafter, AHN-MAE), Expediente Personal, Juan Potous Martínez, P-33.844 / PG 691.

40. Juan Potous to Ministry of Foreign Affairs, June 22, 1907, AHN-MAE, H-2005. A few months later, his request to create a Vice-Consulate received the same response. Juan Potous to Ministry of Foreign Affairs, August 30, 1907, Archivo General de la Administración–Ministerio de Asuntos Exteriores (hereafter, AGA-MAE), Caja 8088.

41. During his first year as Consul in Panama, Potous wrote repeatedly about these cases. The Spanish minister in Washington requested several times to the Department of State the establishment of Workmen's Compensation in the Canal Zone. AGA-MAE, Caja 8745; AGA-MAE, Caja 8088.

42. H.R. 21844, "An act granting to certain employees of the United States the right to receive from it compensation for injuries sustained in the course of their employment."

43. Juan Potous to Ministry of Foreign Affairs, February 20, 1909, AGA-MAE, Caja 8104.

44. "Los Españoles en Panamá," *Boletín del Consejo Superior de Emigración* (1909): 587–92.

45. The *Willesden* carried 1,306 immigrants from Spain and 545 from Portugal. Upon arrival in Honolulu, the ship was quarantined. Besides the twenty-seven deaths, the Spanish consul reported eighteen cases of smallpox and thirty-six of measles. The consul also called attention to the fact that over 150 emigrants had left illegally (being subjected to the military draft). Ignacio de Arana to Spanish minister in Washington, December 6, 1911, AGA-MAE, Caja 8101. Fabián Vidal wrote a scathing denunciation of this case, blaming the Spanish political system and Spanish politicians for this tragedy. "La tragedia del 'Willesden,'" *La Correspondencia de España*, March 9, 1912, 1.

46. Ignacio de Arana to Spanish minister in Washington, April 1, 1913, AGA-MAE, Caja 8121.

47. "La emigración: Advertencias oportunas," *La Correspondencia de España*, December 26, 1912, 4. The *Sun* reproduced this information on its pages as well, "Spanish Emigrants Warned," *Sun*, December 31, 1912, 3.

48. Ignacio de Arana to Spanish minister in Washington, October 6, 1911; October 31, 1911, AGA-MAE, Caja 8101.

49. Ignacio de Arana to Ministry of Foreign Affairs, September 25, 1912, AGA-MAE, Caja 8121.

50. Ignacio de Arana to Ministry of Foreign Affairs, July 1, 1913, AGA-MAE, Caja 8121.

51. Luis Guillén Gil, "Nuestra emigración en las Islas Hawai," *Boletín del Consejo Superior de Emigración* (1917): 168.

52. Luis Guillén to Spanish ambassador in Washington, April 27, 1917; May 19, 1917, AGA-MAE, Caja 8143. Consul Guillén estimated the illiteracy rate among Spaniards in Hawai'i at over 50 percent. Luis Guillén Gil, "Nuestra emigración en las Islas Hawai," *Boletín del Consejo Superior de Emigración* (1917): 166.

53. El Conde del Valle de Salazar, "Los Españoles en California," *Boletín del Consejo Superior de Emigración* (1917): 580.

54. *Diario de Sesiones del Senado*, October 12, 1907, 1309–1321. First quotation (p. 1311); second quotation (p. 1313).

55. US Immigration Commission, *Reports of the Immigration Commission*, vol. 20, *Statistical Review of Immigration 1820–1910* (Washington, DC: Government Printing Office, 1911). Named after senator William P. Dillingham, the commission produced a forty-one-volume report which sought to stop the immigration of Eastern and Southern Europeans, considered to be less easily assimilated than the "old stock" Europeans from Northern and Western Europe.

56. Angel Cuesta to Spanish minister in Washington, February 21, 1913, AGA-MAE, Caja 8120.

57. This was the case in Clarksburg, West Virginia, where the honorary vice-consul of Spain was the naturalized Italian lawyer Biagio Merendino (also consul of Italy). In Chicago, the honorary vice-consul (who became honorary consul in 1916) was the American lawyer Berthold Singer. AGA-MAE, Caja 8143.

58. El Conde del Valle de Salazar to Spanish ambassador in Washington, May 27, 1915, AGA-MAE, Caja 8143.

59. Spanish minister in Washington to minister of foreign affairs, September 6, 1912, AHN-MAE, H-1483.

60. Spanish ambassador to minister of foreign affairs, May 8, 1922; March 10, 1923, AHN-MAE, H-1488.

61. Spanish ambassador to minister of foreign affairs, May 8, 1922, AHN-MAE, H-1488.

62. Andrés Iglesias Velayos to Manuel González Hontoria, October 1, 1921, AHN-MAE, Expediente Personal, Andrés Iglesias Velayos, P-469/33764.

63. Spanish ambassador in Washington to minister of foreign affairs, December 20, 1920; December 26, 1920, AHN-MAE, Expediente Personal, Manuel de la Escosura y Fuertes, P-291/21865.

64. Manuel de la Escosura to minister of foreign affairs, April 28, 1920, AHN-MAE, H-1890. According to de la Escosura, this was the first time in thirteen years of diplomatic career that he had asked for a salary raise.

65. In 1923, the consul at Galveston estimated at 1,500 the number of Spaniards in his jurisdiction. In Philadelphia the estimate was around 15,000. Andrés Iglesias Velayos to Spanish ambassador in Washington, May 30, 1923; Emilio de Motta to Spanish ambassador in Washington, May 30, 1923, AGA-MAE, Caja 8227.

66. Spanish ambassador in Washington to minister of foreign affairs, February 5, 1921, AHN-MAE, Expediente Personal, Manuel de la Escosura y Fuertes, P-291/21865.

67. Minister of foreign affairs to Manuel de la Escosura, June 9, 1921, AHN-MAE, Expediente Personal, Manuel de la Escosura y Fuertes, P–291/21865. De la Escosura was sent to Manaus (Brazil).

68. Manuel Patiño Sánchez to minister of foreign affairs, April 16, 1910, AGA-MAE, Caja 8104. On the construction of the railway, which used an international labor force, see Dan Gallagher, *Florida's Great Ocean Railway: Building the Key West Extension* (Sarasota: Pineapple Press, 2003).

69. Albert W. Gilchrist (governor of Florida) to secretary of state, June 16, 1910, AGA-MAE, Caja 8104.

70. Spanish ambassador in Washington to minister of foreign affairs, April 1, 1921, AGA-MAE, Caja 8206. Spanish law offered compensation for labor accidents to "all injured workers, or their relatives, in case of death, regardless of nationality or residence." Instituto de Reformas Sociales to Ministry of Foreign Affairs, July 3, 1919, AHN-MAE, H-2444.

71. Spanish minister in Washington to minister of foreign affairs, January 1, 1914, AGA-MAE, Caja 8125.

72. James W. Elwell to Spanish consul, Boston, May 7, 1914, AGA-MAE, Caja 8125.

73. Spanish vice-consul in Boston to Spanish minister in Washington, May 16, 1914, AGA-MAE, Caja 8125.

74. Spanish minister in Washington to minister of foreign affairs, June 12, 1914, AGA-MAE, Caja 8125.

75. Spanish consul in New York to Spanish minister in Washington, March 7, 1914, AGA-MAE, Caja 8125. The Unión Benéfica Española was established on May 10, 1914.

76. Jose Camprubí to Spanish ambassador, July 17, 1918, AGA-MAE, Caja 8206.

77. Jose Camprubí to Spanish ambassador, November 8, 1918, AGA-MAE, Caja 8223.

78. "Muchachas y señoras, trabajo patriótico y esencial," *La Prensa*, October 23, 1918. See, for example, *La Prensa*, June 23, 1917, 8.

79. "Spaniards in the United States," *Literary Digest* 60, no. 2 (March 22, 1919): 40.

80. C. A. H. de Saulles to Spanish consul in New York, August 1, 1916, AGA-MAE, Caja 8139.

81. La Comisión to Spanish ambassador, November 30, 1917, AGA-MAE, Caja 8187. This box also has correspondence from Spanish workers at Rome Brass &

Copper Co., Rome, NY (1917), and at the National Tube Company in Lorain, Ohio (1919). Similar letters from California and Montana about rumors that noncitizens would not be hired can be found in AGA-MAE, Caja 8176.

82. Antonio Fernández Menéndez to Spanish ambassador, April 21, 1918, AGA-MAE, Caja 8173.

83. Spanish consul in New York to Spanish ambassador, May 6, 1918; Robert E. Lipton to Spanish ambassador, June 27, 1918, AGA-MAE, Caja 8177.

84. Agustín Fandiño Pose to Spanish ambassador, November 22, 1918, AGA-MAE, Caja 8180.

85. José Palmón Filgueiras to Spanish ambassador, July 19, 1919, AGA-MAE, Caja 8181.

86. Juan Riaño to Emilio Ma. De Torres, October 21, 1918, AGA-MAE, Caja 8187.

87. Spanish ambassador to minister of foreign affairs, January 5, 1919, AHN-MAE, H-1486.

88. José Martín to Spanish ambassador, August 25, 1918, AGA-MAE, Caja 8173.

89. M. A. Kent to Spanish ambassador, August 15, 1918, AGA-MAE, Caja 8182.

90. "Spanish Laborers Make Best Track Workmen, Says P.RR," *Philadelphia North American*, January 24, 1921. The Pennsylvania Department of Labor and Industry mailed a copy of the article to the Spanish consul in New York. Spanish consul in New York to Spanish ambassador, January 28, 1921, AGA-MAE, Caja 8206.

91. "Spanish Laborers Make Best Track Workmen, Says P.RR," *Philadelphia North American*, January 24, 1921.

92. "House Cuts to Year Bar on Immigration," *New York Times*, December 11, 1920, 1.

93. Minister of foreign affairs to Spanish ambassador, December 12, 1920, AHN-MAE, H-1487.

94. Spanish consul in New York to Spanish ambassador, November 20, 1920; May 3, 1921, AGA-MAE, Caja 8254.

95. *Gaceta de Madrid*, March 15, 1921, 883; August 5, 1923, 548.

96. Spanish consul in New York to Spanish ambassador, June 2, 1923, AGA-MAE, Caja 8227.

97. While specific figures are hard to find, the repeated calls on the pages of the Spanish publication *La Emigración Española* warning Spaniards of the dangers they faced if they tried to be smuggled through Cuba or Mexico, give an indication of their participation in an illegal and clandestine migratory traffic. See, for example, "No dejarse engañar: La emigración clandestina a Norteamérica," *La Emigración Española* 17 (1927): 822.

98. In 1924, the Madrid daily *El Sol* estimated that 5 million Spaniards, nearly a quarter of the total population of Spain, lived abroad. *El Sol*, November 15, 1924.

POSTSCRIPT

HIDDEN NO LONGER

Spanish Migration and the Spanish Presence in the United States

ANA VARELA-LAGO AND PHYLIS CANCILLA MARTINELLI

As these essays have made clear, Spaniards were very much a part of the migrations that characterized the modern period of global economic expansion, and more particularly of the mass migration of Europeans to the Americas, a veritable "exit revolution" as Aristide Zolberg has dubbed it.[1] Like other Southern Europeans, they joined this enterprise in greater numbers as the nineteenth century progressed. The legacy of Spanish imperialism in the continent made the Spanish-speaking American republics and the overseas provinces in the Spanish Caribbean particular magnets for this migration. It was through these networks that many Spaniards first reached the United States. In this book, we have examined a variety of these networks and destinations. We hope that continuing research on this area will illuminate the characteristics of the Spanish presence in other locales and contexts, and provide a fuller picture of their participation in this process.

This exodus, part of a worldwide process of proletarianization, necessarily affected the countries of origin.[2] Chapter 8, by Ana Varela-Lago on the Spanish state, shows how this migration became an intensely sensitive

DOI: 10.5876/9781607327998.c009

issue for Spain in the aftermath of the Spanish-Cuban-American war. To the dismay of politicians and opinion makers, thousands of their countrymen were recruited as laborers by American companies (Andalusians hired to work in Hawai'i and Galicians in the Panama Canal). Thousands more developed their own migratory networks. Some, like the miners studied by Phylis Cancilla Martinelli in chapter 6, started their migration within Spain, moving from the northern regions to the mines in Andalusia, before reaching mining camps in the American Southwest. Others acquired their skills not in the homeland but at the point of destination, as was the case of Asturians and Galicians employed in Cuba's cigar factories who made their way to Florida and New York. Thus, Spanish migrants could be perceived as contributing to America's global economic and imperial ascendancy. As scholars of migration further investigate the dynamics that influenced policies of emigration as well as immigration, it is important to examine how migration to the United States may have contributed to shaping the political discourse on citizenship and national identity in Spain in the context of debates on the so-called regeneration of the nation that followed the traumatic defeat of 1898. In what other ways did discourses of emigration affect these broader debates? This is an area for fertile research.

While some of these enclaves became stable communities, continuing mobility was the hallmark of this migration. Like other migrants, many Spaniards lived "transnational" lives, traveling between different locales in search of opportunities and returning to Spain when conditions allowed. Patterns of chain migration were fueled by the presence and support of relatives or neighbors from the "old country" (*paisanos*) already in the area. Thus, Spaniards engaged in what scholars define more precisely as a "glocal" system that created circuits connecting specific local communities across the globe. This glocalism was reflected also in the migrants' associational life, as the descriptions of some of the organizations and mutual aid societies mentioned in these essays illustrate. The study of these glocal networks and associations deserves attention, not only for the light they shed on the connections between homeland and diaspora communities, but also, as Brian Bunk indicates in chapter 5, for the role they played in the socialization of the second generation. His analysis of these clubs as complex arenas of encounter between genders and generations, the public and the private, control and contestation, offer a particularly promising line of research.

Another source that displays the strength of these transnational connections is the press, a crucial element, as Benedict Anderson has persuasively argued, in the development of "imagined communities."[3] Considering the relatively small size of the immigrant presence, Spaniards in the United States produced a remarkably rich and diverse collection of periodical publications, from the nineteenth century onward, in Castilian Spanish as well as Catalan and Basque.[4] While many of these journals were short lived, some enjoyed decades of success and at least one, El Diario–La Prensa of New York, has celebrated its centennial.

The history of this daily illustrates the development of the Spanish community and its interactions with the larger Hispanic community of which it was a part. Spaniard Rafael Viera began publishing the weekly La Prensa in 1913, on the emblematic date of October 12, marking Columbus's "discovery" of America. After a few difficult years, it became a daily under the ownership of José Camprubí in 1918. Camprubí embodied the connections between Spain, the Hispanic Caribbean, and the United States. The scion of a family linked to American wealth on his Puerto Rican mother's side, Camprubí was born in Puerto Rico but grew up in Barcelona, where his Spanish father worked as a civil engineer. In 1896, he returned to the United States, graduated from Harvard, and married into a prominent New York family related to the Roosevelts. In 1921, Camprubí decided to dedicate himself fully to the newspaper. By the time of his death two decades later, he had transformed La Prensa into one of the most successful Spanish newspapers in the United States, and, as Emilia Cortés Ibáñez has asserted, a "pillar of Hispanismo."[5]

The preeminence of La Prensa as the organ of the Spanish community in New York is evident in chapter 5, by Brian Bunk. But even at its height, in the 1920s, the paper faced competitors and received criticism for its support of the Spanish monarchy. These criticisms would only intensify in the 1930s, with the establishment of a republic in Spain, and the ensuing Civil War. The conservative and traditional tone prevalent in many publications that defended the discourse of Hispanismo was challenged not only by members of the broader Hispanic community, but also, as Christopher Castañeda (chapter 4), and Gary Mormino and George Pozzetta (chapter 3) have shown, by the more progressive members of the Spanish diaspora. These critics supported an alternative labor, internationalist, and particularly anarchist, press. The Spanish immigrant press still awaits detailed studies. Sadly, many publications have disappeared or are difficult to track down, but others have been recovered and made available online through digitization projects in Spain and the United States. We hope that these developments will contribute to further research on this relatively untapped source on the history of the community and its relations to the larger Hispanic community and American society as a whole.

Race and ethnicity are a necessary complement to the study of Spanish migration to the United States. Among the memories of the subjects interviewed by Thomas Hidalgo in chapter 7 are their recollections of experiencing discrimination and being the target of prejudice. Racial and ethnic hierarchies were reinforced by patterns of spatial segregation that contributed to the development of ethnic enclaves. The size and composition of these communities were, of course, also shaped by local circumstances. In some instances, as the Arizona mining camps studied by Phylis Cancilla Martinelli in chapter 6, Spaniards, as "white" Europeans, enjoyed a somewhat better position than other Spanish-speaking immigrants, such as Mexicans.

Spaniards fit uncomfortably under the labels "Hispanic" or "Latino," the ones most commonly applied to Spanish-speaking populations in the United States.[6] Some books that deal with Hispanic/Latinos refer to Spaniards and their descendants in the United States as "Iberians"; in others, they are not included at all. It was this complex situation that led one of these immigrants, writer Felipe Alfau, to coin a new term to refer to this community: Americaniards.[7] Although the debate on whether or not to include Spaniards among Latinos continues, we hope that the chapters in this book have opened the path to further study of the Spanish immigrant experience, and through it to contribute to broader conversations on transnationalism, migration/diaspora studies, ethnic/Latino(a) studies, and American/Spanish cultural studies.[8]

A number of studies have called attention to the need to study the process of immigrant assimilation and Americanization as a process of whitening.[9] The concept of race is not strange to the country that developed the notion of *limpieza de sangre* (purity of blood) in the fifteenth century and has been defined as "the first racial state."[10] But, as scholars of Borderlands and Latino/a studies note, the already complex racial dynamics at play are further complicated by the history of the Spanish presence in the Americas. In New Mexico, John Nieto-Phillips explains, Spanish-speaking *nuevomexicanos* responded to political marginalization as perceived members of "inferior" and mixed-blood populations by defining "their racial identity as Spanish, in part by resurrecting archaic notions of 'purity of blood.'"[11] In her study of Anglo-American identity, María de Guzmán argues that in the United States, "the drama of the repulsion of and attraction to figures of Spain has evolved to include Latinas/os and the Spanish language itself." She calls on scholars to explore the connections between Spanish and Latino identity, connections that remain "largely unexamined because of the lingering effects of the Black Legend against Spain in both Anglo-American and Latina/o criticism."[12]

It is hard to imagine any area left unaffected by the dizzying speed of change and the opportunities opened by digital technology in the past decades. Migration and diaspora studies are no exception. Like scholars in other fields, we have seen our research transformed by the digital revolution. Growing numbers of databases provide access to thousands of digitized records (censuses, newspapers, ship manifests, to name a few), allowing us to better document and understand the lives of Spanish immigrants and the communities they created.[13] University libraries and other institutions are also digitizing their collections and making them available online to an ever-widening public. These include, for example, oral histories, and the records of Spanish immigrant mutual aid societies.[14]

Equally important has been the use of these resources by the immigrants and their offspring. The last decade has seen the publication of memories and family histories of Spaniards in California, Florida, Hawaii, Oklahoma, and West Virginia.[15] The number of immigrant organizations' websites continues to grow, and social media (through Facebook pages and discussion forums) has made possible the creation of a flourishing virtual community of immigrants and descendants of Spanish immigrants.[16] This is a wonderful resource for scholars, but the ephemeral nature of social media also challenges us to find ways of preserving this material for future generations. The project "Traces of Spain in the United States," led by James D. Fernández and Luis Argeo, in collaboration with Spanish communities on both sides of the Atlantic, is an outstanding example of the possibilities of such enterprises. As a new wave of Spaniards migrate to the United States and develop their own physical and virtual communities, we anticipate that the opportunities for research will continue to expand, and that the story of the Spanish migration to the United States will remain no longer hidden.[17]

NOTES

1. Aristide R. Zolberg, "The Exit Revolution," in *Citizenship and Those Who Leave: The Politics of Emigration and Expatriation*, ed. Nancy L. Green and François Weil (Chicago: University of Illinois Press, 2007), 33–60.

2. Dirk Hoerder, "Migrations and Belongings," in *A World Connecting, 1870–1945*, ed. Emily S. Rosenberg (Cambridge: Belknap Press of Harvard University Press, 2012), 495–99.

3. Benedict Anderson, *Imagined Communities: Reflections on the Origin and Spread of Nationalism*, 2nd ed. (London: Verso, 1991).

4. *La Llumanera de Nova York*, published in New York from 1874 to 1881, is considered the first Catalan magazine produced in the Americas. (See chapter 1 in this volume.) The short-lived *Escualdun Gazeta* began publication in California in 1885. *California'ko Eskual Herria* was published from 1893 to 1898. Javier Díaz Noci, "Historia del periodismo en lengua vasca de los Estados Unidos: Dos semanarios de Los Angeles en el siglo XIX," *Zer: Revista de Estudios de Comunicación* 10 (May 2001), http://www.ehu.eus/ojs/index.php/Zer/issue/view/470/showToc (accessed September 3, 2018). Other sources on the Spanish press include Raymond R. MacCurdy, *A History and Bibliography of Spanish-Language Newspapers and Magazines in Louisiana, 1808–1949* (Albuquerque: University of New Mexico Press, 1951); James F. Shearer, "Periódicos españoles en los Estados Unidos," *Revista Hispánica Moderna* 20 (1954): 44–57; Rafael Chabrán and Richard Chabrán, "The Spanish-Language and Latino Press of the United States: Newspapers and Periodicals," in *Handbook of Hispanic Cultures in the United States: Literature and Art*, ed. Francisco Lomelí (Houston: Arte Público Press, 1993): 360–83; Nicolás Kanellos (with Helvetia Martell), *Hispanic Periodicals in the United States* (Houston: Arte Público Press, 2000); Nicolás Kanellos, "Recovering and Re-Constructing Early Twentieth-Century Hispanic Immigrant Print Culture in the US," *American Literary History* 19 (2007): 438–55.

5. Emilia Cortés Ibáñez, "Jose Camprubí y *La Prensa*, pilar del Hispanismo en Nueva York," *Oceánide* 5 (2013), http://oceanide.netne.net/articulos/art5-3.pdf (accessed September 3, 2018).

6. For an analysis of the problematic nature of these ethnic labels, see Suzanne Oboler, *Ethnic Labels, Latino Lives: Identity and the Politics of (Re)Presentation in the United States* (Minneapolis: University of Minnesota Press, 1995); and Clara E. Rodríguez, *Changing Race: Latinos, the Census, and the History of Ethnicity in the United States* (New York: New York University Press, 2000).

7. Felipe Alfau, *Chromos* (Elmwood Park, IL: Dalkey Archives Press, 1990), 13–14.

8. See, for example, Nancy Kang and Silvio Torres-Saillant, "'Americaniards' as Latinos: Spain in the United States today," *Latino Studies* 8 (2010): 556–68.

9. See, for example, Matthew Frye Jacobson, *Whiteness of a Different Color: European Immigrants and the Alchemy of Race* (Cambridge, MA: Harvard University Press, 1998); and David R. Roediger, *Working toward Whiteness: How America's Immigrants Became White* (New York: Basic Books, 2005).

10. Joshua Goode, *Impurity of Blood: Defining Race in Spain, 1870–1930* (Baton Rouge: Louisiana State University Press, 2009), 11.

11. John M. Nieto-Phillips, *The Language of Blood: The Making of Spanish-American Identity in New Mexico, 1880s–1930s* (Albuquerque: University of New Mexico Press, 2004), 2.

12. María de Guzmán, *Spain's Long Shadow. The Black Legend, Off-Whiteness, and Anglo-American Empire* (Minneapolis: University of Minnesota Press, 2005), xxi.

13. Among them, the Statue of Liberty-Ellis Island Foundation https://www .libertyellisfoundation.org; ancestry.com (https://www.ancestry.com); Fold3.com (https://www.fold3.com); and GenealogyBank.com (https://www.genealogybank .com/gbnk), which includes a number of Spanish immigrant newspapers. (All websites accessed September 3, 2018.)

14. The Special Collections Department at the Library of the University of South Florida, Tampa, has a rich digital collection of records of the Spanish immigrant community, including records of the two Spanish mutual aid societies (Centro Español and Centro Asturiano), and the Spanish Civil War Oral History Project, documenting the response of the Spanish community to the Spanish Civil War (1936–39). (http://www.lib.usf.edu/special-collections/florida-studies/ybor -city-west-tampa) (accessed September 3, 2018). The Basque Studies Library at the University of Nevada, Reno, and the Basque Museum and Cultural Center in Boise, Idaho, have made available dozens of oral histories of immigrants from the Basque Country (http://basque.unr.edu/oralhistory/) (accessed September 3, 2018).

15. See, for example: José R. Oural, *Oural: The Name, the Family, and the Story as I Remember* (Tampa: n.p., 2002); Gavín W. González, *Pinnick Kinnick Hill: An American Story* (Morgantown: West Virginia University Press, 2003); Gloria López, *An American Paella* (n.p.: Autry Lopez Production Company, 2007); Jack Espinosa, *Cuban Bread Crumbs* (n.p.: Xlibris, 2007); Juli Ann Nishimuta, *The Nishimutas: An Oral History of a Japanese and Spanish Family* (Lincoln, Nebraska: iUniverse, 2006); Patricia Ruiz Steele, *The Girl Immigrant* (Casa Grande, AZ: Plumería Press, 2013); and *Silván Leaves* (Casa Grande, AZ: Plumería Press, 2014). Other narratives of this type include Elisabeth Ramon Bacon, *Santander to Barre: Life in a Spanish Family in Vermont* (Randolph Center, VT: Greenhills Book, 1988); Ferdie Pacheco, *Ybor City Chronicles. A Memoir* (Gainesville: University Press of Florida, 1994); and Anne Aguilar Santucci, *Memories of Spain* (Rocklin, CA: Club Español, 1994).

16. See, for example, the Asturian-American Migration Forum (https://www .asturianus.org); Spanish Immigrants in the United States (https://tracesofspain intheus.org); and the Facebook pages of Hawaiian Spaniards (https://www .facebook.com/HawaiianSpaniard) and Spanish Immigrants in the United States (https://www.facebook.com/tracesofspaintheus) (all accessed September 3, 2018)

17. Rubén Moreno, "Los españoles 'invaden' Estados Unidos: En diez años ha crecido su presencia en un 534%," *20 minutos*, February, 19, 2003, https://www .20minutos.es/noticia/1735850/0/espanoles/crisis/emigran-eeuu-trabajo/. See, for example, the Facebook page of Españoles in USA (https://www.facebook.com /espanolesinusa). (Both accessed September 3, 2018.)

CONTRIBUTORS

BRIAN D. BUNK is a senior lecturer in the History Department at the University of Massachusetts, Amherst. He is the author of *Ghosts of Passion: Martyrdom, Gender, and the Origins of the Spanish Civil War* (2007) and coeditor of *Nation and Conflict in Modern Spain: Essays in Honor of Stanley G. Payne* (2008). His recent work centers on the history of sport, especially boxing and soccer. He has published "Boxer in New York: Spaniards, Puerto Ricans and Attempts to Construct a Hispano Race," *Journal of American Ethnic History* (2016); "A 'Suspiciously Swarthy' Boxer: Luis Firpo and the Ambiguities of the Latin Race," *Radical History Review* (2016); and "*Sardinero* and Not a Can of Sardines: Soccer and Spanish Identities in New York City during the 1920s," *Journal of Urban History* (2015). Bunk is founder and host of the monthly podcast Soccer History USA.

CHRISTOPHER J. CASTAÑEDA is professor of history at California State University, Sacramento. He began researching Spanish-speaking immigrants with a focus on business, labor, and radicalism after discovering his own family connection to these themes. Previously, he authored numerous books and articles related to business history as well as contributing to and coediting *River City and Valley Life: An Environmental History of the Sacramento Region* (2013). He is the author of "Times of Propaganda and Struggle: *El Despertar* and Brooklyn's Spanish Anarchists, 1890–1905," in *Radical Gotham: Anarchism in New York City from Schwab's Saloon to Occupy Wall Street* (2017), ed. Tom Goyens, and, with Montse Feu López, coedited *Writing Revolution: Hispanic Anarchism in the United States* (2019).

THOMAS HIDALGO is the grandson of Spaniards who immigrated to West Virginia in the 1920s to work in the coal mines. He is a graduate of West Virginia University, Springfield College (Massachusetts), and the University of Massachusetts, Amherst, where he received a doctorate in education based on his research on Spanish immigration into southern West Virginia early in the twentieth century. He previously published an article on this topic for *Goldenseal*, the magazine of West Virginia traditional life. He is currently working on a book about Spanish immigration into West Virginia. He is an education specialist for the Massachusetts Department of Elementary and Secondary Education.

BEVERLY LOZANO earned a doctoral degree in Sociology at the University of California, Davis, where she held appointments as a lecturer and a research associate. Lozano's principal research interest lies in identifying the manner in which structural forces are expressed, understood, and often misunderstood, at the level of individuals whose work is shaped by those factors. In addition to the article on migration reprinted here, Lozano has published research on the so-called informal sector, including home-based self-employment and independent contracting. Among her publications are "Informal Sector Workers: Walking out the System's Front Door?" *International Journal of Urban and Regional Research* (1983) and *The Invisible Work Force: Transforming American Business with Outside and Home-Based Workers* (1989).

PHYLIS CANCILLA MARTINELLI is professor emerita at St. Mary's College, where she taught in the Sociology and Collegiate Seminar for twenty-five years. A native of San Francisco, and the granddaughter of Italian immigrants, she earned a PhD in sociology from Arizona State University. Her

extensive publications on the topic of ethnic identity include Edward
Murguia and Phylis Cancilla Martinelli, eds., "A Special Issue on Latino/
Hispanic Ethnic Identity," *Latino Studies Journal* (1991); "Transformation of
an Ethnic Community: Phoenix's Italians, 1880–1980," in *Phoenix in the 20th
Century* (1993), ed. G. Wesley Johnson; Martha E. Bernal and Phylis Cancilla
Martinelli, eds. *Mexican American Ethnic Identity* (1993, 2005); *Undermining
Race, Ethnic Identities in Arizona Copper Camps, 1880–1920* (2009); and "From
Acceptance to 'Not Quite White' in Bisbee Arizona, a White Man's Town,"
in *Italian-Americans: Bridges to Italy, Bonds to America* (2010), ed. Luciano J.
Iorizzo and Ernest E. Rossi, eds.

GARY R. MORMINO is the Frank E. Duckwall professor emeritus in history
at the University of South Florida, St. Petersburg. He holds a PhD from the
University of North Carolina. His first book, *Immigrants on the Hill: Italian-
Americans in St. Louis, 1882–1892* (1986), received the Howard Marraro Prize
for the best work in Italian history. In 1987, he collaborated with George
Pozzetta in the publication of *The Immigrant World of Ybor City*. In 2005,
Mormino wrote *Land of Sunshine, State of Dreams: A Social History of Modern
Florida*, which was adapted for the PBS documentary *The Florida Dream*. In
2015, he was the recipient of the Florida Humanities Council's Lifetime
Achievement in Writing.

GEORGE E. POZZETTA, the son and grandson of Italian immigrants,
received his PhD from the University of North Carolina, Chapel Hill,
where he enrolled after serving as a captain in Vietnam. He taught at the
University of Florida from 1972 until his death in 1994. He was a prolific
scholar, writing scores of articles on Italian immigrants, among myriad top-
ics. He edited and coedited several books, most notably, *Pane e Lavoro: The
Italian American Working Class* (1980); *Shades of the Sunbelt: Essays on Ethnicity,
Race, and the Urban South* (1988); and *The Italian Diaspora: Migration across the
Globe* (1992). In 1987, Pozzetta and Gary Mormino coauthored *The Immigrant
World of Ybor City: Italians and Their Latin Neighbors in Tampa, 1885–1985.*

ANA VARELA-LAGO is a senior lecturer in the History Department at
Northern Arizona University. She received her PhD from the University of
California, San Diego, with a dissertation titled "Conquerors, Immigrants,
Exiles: The Spanish Diaspora in the United States 1848–1948." Her research

focuses on transnational spaces, and the interplay of migration, imperialism, nationalism, and class and ethnic identity. Her most recent publication is "From Migrants to Exiles: the Spanish Civil War and the Spanish Immigrant Communities in the United States," in *Camino Real* (2015). She is currently working on a study of the Spanish press in New York during the Cuban war of independence (1895–1898), and a study of Spanish cigar makers in Tampa at the turn of the twentieth century.

INDEX